Cooking with
CRAIG CLAIBORNE
and
PIERRE FRANEY

Other Books by Craig Claiborne

The New York Times Cook Book
The New York Times Menu Cook Book
Craig Claiborne's Kitchen Primer
Cooking with Herbs and Spices
Classic French Cooking (with Pierre Franey)
The New York Times International Cook Book
The Chinese Cookbook (with Virginia Lee)
Craig Claiborne's Favorites Volume One
Craig Claiborne's Favorites Volume Two
Craig Claiborne's Favorites Volume Three
Craig Claiborne's Favorites Volume Four
Veal Cookery (with Pierre Franey)
Craig Claiborne's The New New York Times Cookbook (with Pierre Franey)
Craig Claiborne's Gourmet Diet (with Pierre Franey)
A Feast Made for Laughter

Other Books by Pierre Franey

The New York Times 60-Minute Gourmet
The New York Times More 60-Minute Gourmet
Pierre Franey's Kitchen (with Richard Flaste)

Cooking with CRAIG CLAIBORNE *and* PIERRE FRANEY

❧

Craig Claiborne and Pierre Franey

Published by TIMES BOOKS,
The New York Times Book Co., Inc.
Three Park Avenue, New York, N.Y. 10016

Published simultaneously in Canada by
Fitzhenry & Whiteside, Ltd., Toronto

Library of Congress Cataloging in Publication Data

Claiborne, Craig.
Cooking with Craig Claiborne and Pierre Franey.

Includes index.
1. Cookery, International. I. Franey, Pierre.
II. Title.
TX725.A1C558 1983 641.5 83-45038
ISBN 0-8129-1078-8

Recipes selected and edited by Joan Whitman

Coordinating Editor: Rosalyn T. Badalamenti

Designed by Susan Windheim

Manufactured in the United States of America

83 84 85 86 87 5 4 3 2 1

CONTENTS

INTRODUCTION

It has been my conviction for a period of long standing that, where food and appetite are concerned, nothing better reflects the taste of a nation than the recipes that appear in the daily journals. And I know this is true of this book.

We have come an astonishingly long way since I first joined the food staff of *The New York Times* twenty-five years ago. Back in those days, some of the staple dishes of today's homes were wholly unknown to the general public and these would include, of all things, quiche lorraine, saltimbocca, bouillabaisse, guacamole, ratatouille and pesto sauce, made with fresh basil and pine nuts. Only a small handful of home cooks had ever heard of basil and pine nuts and today the markets are full of such items. A couple of decades ago, when I mentioned zucchini, it was absolutely essential that I further identify it as that "green Italian squash." Today it has become as familiar as the common Irish potato.

Within the past few years there has been great discussion of changes in the American palate. We hear of nouvelle cuisine on every hand and occasion and its influence is certainly discernible on the American table as it is now provided with the good things of life from the native kitchen. It is reflected to a great degree in the foods that Pierre Franey and I offer to readers of *The New York Times.* It is certainly reflected in a far briefer cooking time for such foods as fish and vegetables. And it is reflected in interesting salads with seemingly odd but wonderful flavor combinations. It is a far healthier kind of enjoyment and that is what we have emphasized.

You will find in this book the nouvelle cuisine recipes of such distinguished European chefs as Roger Vergé of the Moulin de Mougins above Cannes; Eckart Witzigmann of the Aubergine in Munich; Alain Senderens of L'Archestrate in Paris, and Gerard Boyer of Chez Boyer in Reims.

There was a great temptation to label this book a diet cookbook for it does, indeed, reflect lighter foods and an enormous economy in the use of salt, which the medical profession assures us is injurious to the health. Since I had a bout with high blood pressure several years ago, the use of salt has been abandoned in the preparation of foods in my kitchen for the enlightenment and enjoyment of readers of *The New York Times.* Although we only occasionally make mention of the fact, foods prepared by us for our readers have been tailored for taste while ignoring the saltshaker. This can be seen in a more discriminate use of herbs and spices. Since I have altered my diet for the better, the listing of salt in recipes is very often "Salt to taste, if desired."

You will find in this book an abundance of stuffed foods because all of my life I have had a passion for them, whether it be a dumpling, a pastry, a vegetable or a pasta like canneloni and shells. And stuffed foods are at their best made with a variety of flavors—things like finely chopped onion and garlic and parsley and herbs. And spices like chili and curry powders. They may also provide an uncommon contrast in texture, and such a contrast is, in my book, an exceptional "salt substitute."

The recipes in this book are not wholly without butter and cream and yet in the preparation of foods we have also cut down the amount of these ingredients to a more reasonable degree. And where we did not find them essential we have eliminated them. It would be a total falsehood to claim that this is a diet book, and yet it reflects a good deal of my own life-style of the past few years and that of many other health-conscious Americans.

There are two other things that have delighted me by way of trends where the American appetite is concerned. One is our more adventurous ways with pasta; the other is our keener appreciation of the American regional heritage.

Years ago when I first started writing a food column it was unthinkable to use the generic term "pasta." It was necessary to speak of "macaroni products." Today it is a rare cook indeed who is not immediately conversant with the word "pasta" and to know that it refers to such hitherto little known cuts as fettucine, vermicelli, spaghettini, linguine, rigatoni, ziti and on and on. The pasta recipes included here have come from diverse sources, including professional chefs and personal friends, as well as those of our own devising. You will find such dishes as orechiette (ear-shaped pasta) with Gorgonzola, an incredible blend of flavors; pasta with field mushrooms; buccatini with kidneys and fresh mushrooms; spaghetti with smoked salmon and cream, and a host of cold pasta salads.

As far as American cooking is concerned, we find that the current nationwide interest on that score embraces two things: a renaissance or renewed interest in dishes that are inherently a part of this nation's cultural heritage, foods like gumbos and jambalayas, plus new creations that reflect American products and inspirations. You will find here recipes derived from Paul Prudhomme of K. Paul's Louisiana Kitchen in New Orleans, and

Alice Waters of Chez Panisse in Berkeley, California. They are, to our way of thinking, two of this nation's most talented chefs and prized possessions. Both are native born and that is a rarity where professional restaurant chefs and owners are concerned.

Over the years, Pierre Franey and I have been asked many times about the evolution of our recipes, how we manage to create new and innovative dishes month after month and without repetition. To choose but one example, if we spot a basket of snow-white, well-puffed mushrooms in our local market, note is made somewhere in the back of our minds. Pierre telephones me at 8:45 sharp and mention is made of the mushrooms. Let us, we agree, prepare an article on that subject.

"Buy a pound of veal, Parmesan cheese, a couple of pounds of spinach, a jar of pine nuts, and so on," the conversation continues. I sit at my typewriter for an hour or so after that, pursuing another column that might have been explored the day before in my kitchen. Pierre arrives around 10:30, his arms loaded with those groceries in bags, which are promptly unloaded.

I move to my IBM machine situated on the center island in the kitchen and he dons an apron and moves to the cook stove. At that point, neither he nor I knows precisely what will come off those burners. It depends more or less on instant inspiration. But before the day is over we will have prepared, to choose a few random notions, a mushroom meat loaf, mushroom caps stuffed with veal, mushroom caps stuffed with spinach and pine nuts, mushrooms stuffed with mushrooms. As he cooks, I duplicate his actions in words.

The next morning, it is back to the typewriter to write about the availability of mushrooms, how they are harvested, a bit of mushroom lore, the techniques of cooking mushrooms and so on.

We often are, and have been for many years, paid visits by some of the greatest chefs from Paris to Bangkok and beyond. After our days in the kitchen with them, it is back to the typewriter.

And eventually that is what you will read in the morning edition. And those recipes, of course, are what are represented in this book.

Cooking with

CRAIG CLAIBORNE

and

PIERRE FRANEY

❧ APPETIZERS ❧

THERE was a food column called "Receipts" in *The New York Times* more than a century ago. One of our favorites from that period is for potted salmon. The recipe, which ran on January 4, 1880, reads: "Take your salmon out of the can, and pick out bones, but mostly they are so soft as to do no harm. Just you pound that smooth in a mortar. Take that pounded fish and put it in a jar, which jar place in a pipkin with hot water. Bring up the water to a boil; when your fish is hot, say for a two-pound can, stir in a quarter of a pound of good butter and a teaspoonful of essence of anchovy; or you may take three anchovies and bruise them up fine and mix them in. It must be hot, so put in a saltspoonful of cayenne pepper and a shred of mace; chop your mace fine. Now you want a teaspoonful of tarragon vinegar and a half dozen whole black peppers. Keep stirring the fish until it cools, and let it stay in the jar. If you want it to keep good over a week, melt a little beef suet and when the fish is cold pour that over it—Bob the Sea Cook."

Here is our updated version of potted salmon.

❧

Potted Salmon

- 4 7¾-ounce cans salmon, or 2 pounds cooked salmon
- ¼ pound butter
- 2 teaspoons anchovy paste, or use chopped anchovy fillets
- ¼ teaspoon ground mace or grated nutmeg
- ¼ teaspoon cayenne pepper
- 1 tablespoon tarragon vinegar
- Freshly ground black pepper to taste

1. If using canned salmon, drain it well. Flake the salmon and remove and discard the skin and bones. Put the salmon into the container of a food processor or blender and process as fine as possible.

2. Add the butter, anchovy paste, mace, cayenne, vinegar and pepper. Continue blending until all the ingredients are thoroughly combined and smooth. Spoon into a crock or mold. Serve with buttered toast or crackers.

YIELD: 12 or more servings.

Note: This spread will keep well in the refrigerator for more than a week provided you pour enough melted butter over the top to completely cover the surface.

Headcheese Vinaigrette

- 1 pound headcheese, homemade or purchased
- 6 tablespoons finely chopped onion
- 1 teaspoon finely chopped garlic
- ¼ cup finely chopped parsley
- 2 tablespoons prepared mustard, preferably imported Dijon or Düsseldorf
- 2 tablespoons red wine vinegar
- 6 tablespoons olive oil
- Salt and freshly ground black pepper to taste

1. Cut the headcheese into bite-sized morsels and place in a mixing bowl.

2. Add the remaining ingredients and toss.

YIELD: 4 or more servings.

Julia Harrison Adams's Pimiento Cheese Spread

- ½ pound yellow mild Cheddar or longhorn cheese
- ½ pound white, aged, sharp Cheddar cheese, preferably Vermont or New York
- 1 7-ounce can pimientos
- 1 cup chopped scallions, including green part
- ½ cup mayonnaise, preferably homemade (see recipe page 415)
- 2 teaspoons lemon juice
- 1 teaspoon finely minced garlic
- 2 tablespoons Worcestershire sauce
- 6 drops Tabasco sauce
- ½ teaspoon freshly ground black pepper

1. Use a meat grinder, if possible, to grate the cheese, using the cutter with large holes. Otherwise, use the coarse side of a cheese grater. Put the cheese in a mixing bowl and add half the juice from the canned pimientos. Dice the drained pimientos and add them along with the scallions.

2. Combine the mayonnaise, lemon juice and garlic and add to the cheese mixture. Add the Worcestershire, Tabasco and pepper and blend well.

3. Serve at room temperature as a spread for crisp crackers and raw vegetables or use as a sandwich spread. Unused pimiento cheese may be tightly sealed and kept for several days in the refrigerator.

YIELD: 8 to 12 servings.

One of our favorite lines about cheese comes from Robert Louis Stevenson, who wrote in *Treasure Island,* "Many's the long night I've dreamed of cheese—toasted mostly." We second that, and would add deep-fried, as in this breaded Brie appetizer.

Brie Pané et Frit

DEEP-FRIED BREADED BRIE CHEESE

- 1 pound Brie cheese
- 1 egg
- 2 tablespoons water
- ½ cup flour
- 2 cups fine fresh bread crumbs
- Corn, peanut or vegetable oil for deep frying

1. Do not peel off the skin of the cheese. Cut the cheese into 34 pieces (triangles, rectangles, etc.) of more or less equal size and shape.

2. Beat the egg with the water and pour it into a flat dish.

3. Put the flour in a second dish and the bread crumbs in a third.

4. Dip each piece of Brie in flour to coat it thoroughly and shake off any excess. Dip each piece in the egg mixture and then in the crumbs to coat well. Chill.

5. Heat 2 inches of oil in a skillet, wok or electric deep-fat cooker. The exact temperature for deep frying, if you use a thermometer, is 360 degrees. Add several pieces of the Brie at a time, stirring almost constantly, and cook 10 to 15 seconds, or until the pieces are neatly browned and the cheese is melted within. Serve hot.

YIELD: 34 pieces.

Crostini

TOAST WITH LIVER SPREAD

- ¼ cup olive oil
- ¾ cup finely chopped onion
- 1 clove garlic, finely chopped
- 3 small fresh sage leaves, or ½ teaspoon dried sage
- ¾ pound chicken livers, picked over and cut in half
- Salt and freshly ground black pepper to taste
- 4 anchovy fillets
- 2 ounces thinly sliced prosciutto
- 12 to 16 hot, freshly made toast points or rounds
- Olive oil for brushing toast

1. Heat the ¼ cup oil in a wide saucepan and add the onion and garlic. Cook briefly until wilted and add the sage and chicken livers. Sprinkle with salt and pepper. Cook over high heat, turning the pieces. Do not overcook. The livers should remain a trifle pink in the center.

2. Scrape the mixture into the container of a food processor or the bowl of an electric mixer. Add the anchovy fillets and prosciutto and chop coarsely but thoroughly. The texture should not be too fine. Let cool briefly.

3. Brush the pieces of toast with oil and smear the chicken liver mixture on top. Serve warm.

YIELD: 12 or more crostini.

Amuse-gueule au Fromage

DEEP-FRIED CHEESE APPETIZERS

- 12 ounces cream cheese
- ½ teaspoon finely minced garlic
- 1 egg yolk
- 1 cup loosely packed grated Gruyère or Swiss cheese
- Freshly ground black pepper to taste
- ¼ cup finely chopped parsley
- 1 tablespoon finely grated onion
- 1 teaspoon Worcestershire sauce
- ¾ cup flour
- 1 egg
- 2 tablespoons water
- 2 cups fine fresh bread crumbs
- Corn, peanut or vegetable oil for deep frying

1. Combine the cream cheese, garlic, egg yolk, Gruyère, pepper, parsley, onion and Worcestershire sauce in a mixing bowl. Blend well.

2. Add ¼ cup of the flour and continue blending until smooth.

3. Divide the mixture into 24 equal portions and roll each portion into a round ball. Chill thoroughly.

4. Beat the egg with the water and pour the mixture into a flat dish.

5. Put the bread crumbs in a second dish and the remaining flour in a third.

6. Dip each ball in flour to coat thoroughly and shake off any excess. Dip each piece in the egg mixture and then in the crumbs to coat well.

7. Heat 2 inches of oil in a skillet, wok or electric deep-fat cooker. The exact temperature for deep frying, if you use a thermometer, is 360 degrees. Add several of the cheese balls at a time, stirring almost constantly. Cook 20 to 30 seconds, or until the pieces are neatly browned and the cheese mixture piping hot throughout. Serve hot.

YIELD: 24 pieces.

Dolmades

GRAPE LEAVES STUFFED WITH LAMB

- 36 or more grape leaves bottled in brine
- ⅓ cup rice
- ½ pound ground lean lamb, or equal portions of lamb and veal
- 3 tablespoons butter
- ¾ cup finely chopped onion
- ½ teaspoon finely minced garlic
- 3 tablespoons finely minced fresh dill
- 2 teaspoons chopped fresh mint, or ¼ teaspoon dried
- Salt to taste, if desired
- Freshly ground black pepper to taste
- 2 cups fresh or canned chicken broth
- Avgolemono sauce (see following recipe)

1. Drain the grape leaves and separate them. Put them in a mixing bowl and pour boiling water over them. Let stand until ready to use.

2. Put the rice in a saucepan of boiling water and simmer for 8 minutes. Drain well.

3. Put the lamb in a mixing bowl and add the rice.

4. Melt 2 tablespoons of the butter in a saucepan and add the onion and garlic. Cook, stirring, until the onion is wilted. Add this mixture to the lamb and rice.

5. Add the dill, mint, salt and pepper and blend well.

6. Drain the leaves and, if necessary, pat dry and cut off the stems.

7. Place the leaves, a few at a time, shiny side down, on a flat surface. Spoon about a tablespoon of the lamb mixture near the stem end. Fold the stem end over to partly enclose the meat. Fold the sides over into a neat, compact package. If the leaves are particularly small, it may be necessary to overlap two or three leaves to be stuffed.

8. Arrange the stuffed leaves in a single layer, placing them close together in rows, in a large skillet in which they fit snugly. Dot with the remaining butter and pour the broth over all.

9. Cover tightly and cook for 45 minutes to 1 hour.

10. Serve hot with avgolemono sauce spooned over each serving.

YIELD: 6 servings.

AVGOLEMONO SAUCE

- 2 tablespoons butter
- 2 tablespoons cornstarch
- 1¾ cups chicken broth
- 2 eggs
- 3 tablespoons lemon juice
- Salt to taste, if desired
- Freshly ground black pepper to taste

1. Melt the butter in a saucepan and add the cornstarch, stirring with a wire whisk. When blended and smooth, add the chicken broth, stirring rapidly with the whisk. When blended and smooth, cook for about 1 minute. Remove from the heat.

2. Beat the eggs and the lemon juice in a mixing bowl.

3. While beating vigorously with the whisk, add the egg mixture, salt and pepper to the sauce. Return to the heat and continue beating. Bring just to the boil and remove from the heat. Do not cook further or the eggs will curdle.

YIELD: About 2 cups.

Even after decades of working with virtually all aspects of food preparation, we continue to be awed by the miracles that occur when various foods are submitted to oven heat. One of the most remarkable of all is the easily made and delectable cream puff, which has thousands of uses both as a savory dish and as a dessert. We particularly like cream puffs as stuffed appetizers. The cream puffs are baked briefly until puffed and golden, and then filled with any of a number of tasty fillings.

We propose three that are easily made: curried shrimp, mushrooms in port wine and a delectable, sinfully rich and irresistible chicken hash. These puffs are perfectly suitable for cocktail parties or for a first course at a seated affair.

Profiteroles aux Crevettes à l'Indienne

CREAM PUFFS WITH CURRIED SHRIMP FILLING

- ¾ pound fresh shrimp, shelled and deveined
- 1 tablespoon butter
- 3 tablespoons finely chopped onion
- 1 tablespoon curry powder
- 1 cup heavy cream
- 3 tablespoons finely chopped chutney
- Salt, if desired
- Freshly ground black pepper to taste
- 24 cream puffs (see following recipe)

1. Cut the shrimp into ½-inch or slightly smaller pieces. There should be about 1¼ cups. Set aside.

2. Melt the butter in a saucepan and add the onion. Cook, stirring, until wilted. Add the curry powder and stir to blend.

3. Add the cream and chutney and cook down to about ½ cup. Add the salt, pepper and shrimp, and cook, stirring, for 1 or 2 minutes, or until the shrimp lose their raw look throughout.

4. Slice off the tops of all the cream puffs. Spoon an equal portion of the mixture into the bottom of each cream puff. Replace the tops and serve.

YIELD: 24 filled cream puffs.

PROFITEROLES

Cream Puffs

- 8 tablespoons butter plus additional butter for greasing the pan
- 1 cup flour plus additional flour for flouring the pan
- 1 cup water
- Salt, if desired
- 4 large eggs

1. Preheat the oven to 425 degrees.

2. Lightly, but thoroughly, butter a jelly roll pan. Sprinkle the pan with flour and shake it around until the pan is well coated. Shake and tap out any excess flour.

3. Put the water in a saucepan and add the 8 tablespoons of butter and salt to taste. Bring to the boil and add the flour all at once, stirring vigorously and thoroughly in a circular motion until a ball is formed and the mixture pulls away from the sides of the saucepan.

4. Add 1 egg, beating thoroughly and rapidly with the spoon until it is well blended with the mixture. Add another egg, beat and so on. When all the eggs are added, fit a pastry bag with a round-tipped, No. 6 pastry tube. Spoon the mixture into the bag. Holding the pastry bag straight up with the tip close to the floured surface of the jelly roll pan, squeeze the bag to make mounds of pastry at intervals all over the pan. There should be about 24 mounds.

5. The mounds may have pointed tips on top. To flatten these, wet a clean tea towel and squeeze it well. Open it up, fold it over in thirds. Hold it stretched directly over the mounds, quickly patting down just enough to rid the mounds of the pointed tips. Do not squash the mounds.

6. Place the pan in the oven and bake for 30 minutes, or until the cream puffs are golden brown and cooked throughout. Remove and let cool.

YIELD: 24 cream puffs.

Profiteroles à la Reine

CREAM PUFFS WITH TARRAGON-FLAVORED CHICKEN HASH

- 2 tablespoons butter
- 2 tablespoons flour
- ½ cup fresh or canned chicken broth
- ½ cup heavy cream
- Salt, if desired
- Freshly ground black pepper to taste
- Pinch of grated nutmeg
- Pinch of cayenne pepper
- 2 teaspoons chopped fresh tarragon, or 1 teaspoon dried
- 1½ cups leftover chicken cut into cubes
- 24 cream puffs (see preceding recipe)

1. Melt the butter in a saucepan and add the flour, stirring with a wire whisk. When blended, add the broth, stirring rapidly with the whisk. When thickened and smooth, stir in the cream.

2. Add the salt, pepper, nutmeg, cayenne and tarragon. Let simmer, stirring, for about 2 minutes.

3. Stir in the chicken and bring to the boil.

4. Slice off the tops of all the cream puffs. Spoon an equal portion of the mixture into the bottom of each cream puff. Replace the tops and serve.

YIELD: 24 filled cream puffs.

Profiteroles aux Champignons

CREAM PUFFS WITH MUSHROOMS IN PORT WINE FILLING

- 2 tablespoons butter
- 1 tablespoon finely chopped shallots
- ¾ pound mushrooms, cut into ¼-inch cubes, about 3 cups
- 2 tablespoons lemon juice
- Salt, if desired
- Freshly ground black pepper to taste
- ¼ cup port wine
- 1 cup heavy cream
- 24 cream puffs (see recipe page 9)

1. Melt the butter in a skillet and add the shallots. Cook briefly, stirring.
2. Add the mushrooms, lemon juice, salt and pepper. Cook, stirring, until the liquid evaporates. Add the wine and cook until it is almost wholly evaporated.
3. Add the cream and cook down about 10 minutes, or until the mixture is reduced to 2 cups.
4. Slice off the tops of all the cream puffs. Spoon an equal portion of the mixture into the bottom of each cream puff. Replace the tops and serve.

YIELD: 24 filled cream puffs.

On a visit to China, I never did get to taste the highly praised dem sum, those varied Chinese appetizers, at the Pan Hsi restaurant. My guide took me for suckling pig instead. But recently, a group of chefs from that restaurant came to the United States for a series of banquets and I invited them to come into my kitchen to demonstrate the making of dumplings, all marvelously inventive. The rabbit dumplings, particularly, are enchanting to behold and they are easy to make.

Beehive Dumplings

- 4 salted duck eggs, available in Oriental groceries and supermarkets
- ¾ cup plus 1 tablespoon wheat starch, available in Oriental groceries and supermarkets
- ½ cup plus 2 tablespoons rapidly boiling water
- Beehive stuffing (see following recipe)
- Oil for deep frying

1. Crack the eggs and separate the whites from the yolks. Put the yolks in a small mixing bowl. (The whites may be discarded or saved for another purpose.) Set the bowl in a steamer and place it over boiling water. Cover and let steam for 30 minutes. Remove from the heat and let cool.

2. Put the wheat starch in a small mixing bowl.

3. Add the ½ cup plus 2 tablespoons boiling water, stirring rapidly with chopsticks. Turn the dough out onto a flat surface and knead for about 30 seconds. The dough must be quite thick and a trifle—but only a trifle—sticky.

4. Put the cooked yolks through a sieve. Combine the yolks with the dough, kneading rapidly but thoroughly for about 30 seconds. Roll the dough into a long sausage shape. Bring up the ends to the center. Press down and knead. Again, roll the dough into a sausage shape, bring up the ends, knead and so on for about 1 minute.

5. Now shape the dough again into a long sausage shape about 1 inch thick. Cut the dough into 16 pieces.

6. Using the fingers, shape each piece into a slightly curved cup. Fill the cups with about 1 teaspoon of the beehive stuffing. Bring the edges together and seal with the fingers to make a football shape with pointed ends.

7. Heat the oil for deep frying. Add the dumplings and cook until crisp and golden all over, about 5 minutes.

YIELD: 16 dumplings.

BEEHIVE STUFFING

- ¾ cup finely diced lean pork
- 4 tablespoons cornstarch
- ⅓ cup finely chopped peeled and deveined shrimp, about 7 ounces
- 2 cups peanut, vegetable or corn oil
- ½ cup finely chopped black Chinese mushrooms that have been soaked in warm water, drained and squeezed to extract most of their liquid
- 1 tablespoon shaoxing wine or dry sherry
- 1 teaspoon light soy sauce
- 1 teaspoon sugar
- 1 teaspoon salt
- 5 tablespoons chicken broth

1. Combine the pork, 1 tablespoon of the cornstarch and the shrimp and blend well.

2. Heat the oil in a wok and, when it is quite hot, add the shrimp mixture, stirring. Cook, stirring, for about 15 seconds, or until the mixture loses its raw color. Pour and scrape the mixture into a strainer.

3. Return about 2 tablespoons of the oil to the wok. Return the drained shrimp mixture to the wok. Add the mushrooms and cook for about 10 seconds. Add the wine, soy sauce, sugar and salt, stirring.

4. Blend the remaining 3 tablespoons cornstarch and broth and add it gradually, stirring. Add 1 tablespoon oil and stir. Remove from the heat.

YIELD: Enough stuffing for 16 or more dumplings.

Note: This mixture can be used as a stuffing for beehive dumplings or it may be served with rice. The amount indicated here will be in excess of that used in the recipe for beehive dumplings. Leftover stuffing may be reheated and served.

Rabbit-shaped Dem Sum

THE DOUGH

- ¾ cup plus 1 tablespoon wheat starch, available in Oriental groceries and supermarkets
- ½ cup plus 2 tablespoons rapidly boiling water

THE FILLING

- ¾ cup finely chopped unsalted pork fat
- ¾ cup finely chopped peeled and deveined shrimp
- ⅓ cup finely diced water chestnuts
- ½ teaspoon sugar
- ¼ teaspoon salt
- ⅛ teaspoon freshly ground white pepper
- ¼ teaspoon sesame oil
- 20 very small pieces cooked ham

1. Put the wheat starch in a small mixing bowl.

2. Add the boiling water, stirring rapidly with chopsticks. Turn the dough out onto a flat surface and knead briefly. The dough must be quite thick and a trifle—but only a trifle—sticky. Set aside briefly.

3. To make the filling, put the pork fat in a sieve and place the sieve in a pan of boiling water. Let stand for about 10 seconds. Drain well. Run under cold water to chill. Drain thoroughly on paper toweling.

4. In a bowl, combine the shrimp, water chestnuts, sugar, salt, pepper, sesame oil and the pork fat. Blend well with the fingers.

5. Using the palms of the hands, roll the dough out into a long sausage shape about 1 inch thick. Cut the dough into 1-inch lengths. This should produce about 20 pieces.

6. Place each piece on a small, flat surface and roll it into a ball. Using a large, smooth cleaver, flatten each piece into a circle as perfectly as possible. If the circle of dough tears, it may be gathered up and rolled again.

7. Fill each circle with about 1 teaspoon of filling. Gather up the edges of the dough. Twirl the dough around with the fingers of the left hand while pressing the top of the dough with the fingers of the right hand. There will be excess dough at the point where the dough is sealed. Twirl this excess dough out into a thin, smooth pencil shape with a pointed end about 1 inch long.

8. Using a pair of scissors, cut through the "pencil" lengthwise. Bend the split ends back over the dumpling to resemble a pair of rabbit ears.

9. Press the dumpling slightly inward at the base of the ears. This will fashion an indentation for the eyes and at the same time will fashion the rabbit's nose so that it protrudes slightly.

10. Add one tiny cube of cooked ham on either side of the nose to make a pink-eyed rabbit.

11. Arrange the dumplings in a bamboo or metal steamer. Cover. Place the steamer over boiling water and steam for 8 minutes.

YIELD: 20 dumplings.

Phoenix Rolls

- ⅓ cup finely chopped peeled and deveined shrimp, about 7 ounces
- 1 cup finely diced lean raw pork
- 2 eggs
- Salt to taste
- 1 teaspoon shaoxing wine or dry sherry
- 1½ tablespoons cornstarch
- 1 teaspoon peanut, vegetable or corn oil
- ¼ teaspoon sesame oil
- 2 tablespoons finely chopped black Chinese mushrooms that have been soaked in warm water, drained and squeezed to extract most of their liquid
- 2 tablespoons finely chopped cooked ham
- 2 hard-boiled eggs, peeled and each cut into three wedges
- ½ cup wheat starch, available in Oriental groceries and supermarkets
- Oil for deep frying

1. Combine the shrimp, pork, 1 egg and salt in a mixing bowl. Blend well with the hands, stirring and beating vigorously for about 2 minutes.

2. Add the wine and cornstarch and blend well. Add 1 teaspoon of the oil and the sesame oil and blend well.

3. Add the chopped mushrooms and ham and blend well.

4. Put half the mixture on a flat surface. Flatten it with the hands into a rectangle measuring about 4½ by 7 inches. Arrange 3 egg wedges lengthwise near the bottom of the rectangle, ends touching.

5. Using a knife, lift up one side of the rectangle and fold it over the eggs. Roll the mixture over itself to form a thick sausage shape, sealing the ends with the fingers.

6. Repeat with the remaining mixture and egg wedges.

7. Place the rolls in a bamboo or metal steamer. Cover and place the steamer over boiling water and steam for 20 minutes.

8. Remove from the heat and let cool.

9. When thoroughly cool, coat the rolls all over with the remaining egg, which has been well beaten.

10. Coat the rolls all over with wheat starch.

11. Heat the oil for deep frying. Add the rolls and cook until golden brown all over, about 5 minutes.

12. Drain and let cool. Serve cut into ¼-inch-thick slices.

YIELD: About 50 dumplings.

Shrimp in Bamboo Shape

¼ pound fresh shrimp, about 24
1¼ teaspoons salt
½ teaspoon sesame oil
1 cup cornstarch
3 eggs
3 cups peanut, vegetable or corn oil

1. Peel and devein the shrimp, but leave the last tail segment intact. Rinse the shrimp and pat dry.

2. Give each shrimp a slight gash crosswise at the top.

3. Sprinkle the shrimp with 1 teaspoon of the salt and the ½ teaspoon of sesame oil and rub them with the mixture.

4. Dip the shrimp, one at a time, into the cornstarch. Arrange on a platter.

5. Put ½ cup of the leftover cornstarch in a bowl. Add the eggs and remaining ¼ teaspoon salt. Mix well with the fingers.

6. Heat the oil in a wok until it is hot and almost but not quite smoking. Dip the shrimp into the egg-cornstarch mixture. Lift them one at a time and slide them into the hot oil. Cook, turning the shrimp, until golden brown, about 2 minutes. Cook a few at a time, draining and setting aside after browning.

7. Return the shrimp to the hot fat and deep-fry a second time, for about 1 minute longer.

YIELD: 24 shrimp.

Some years ago when we added hazelnuts to a basic cheesecake and printed the recipe, our readers responded appreciatively. Lora Brody, who has a catering business in and around Wellesley, Massachusetts, wrote to tell us that when she found herself with a surplus of cream cheese from her regular recipe cheesecakes, as well as some leftover smoked salmon and blue cheese, she concocted a smoked salmon and onion cheesecake and one made with blue cheese and bacon. She was both amused and delighted with the results, sending the recipes on to us. We have tried them and they are not only commendable but wildly rich and tasty. Not quite enough for a main course, and too rich for a first course, they are delicious as an accompaniment to cocktails.

Smoked Salmon and Onion Cheesecake

- Basic cheesecake mixture (see following recipe)
- 3 tablespoons butter plus butter for greasing the pan
- ⅓ cup fine bread crumbs
- ¼ cup plus 3 tablespoons freshly grated Parmesan cheese
- ½ cup chopped onion
- ½ cup chopped green pepper
- ⅓ pound Nova Scotia salmon
- ½ cup grated Gruyère cheese
- Salt and freshly ground black pepper to taste

1. Prepare the basic cheesecake mixture and set aside.

2. Butter the inside of a metal cheesecake pan 8 inches wide and 3 inches deep. Sprinkle the inside with the bread crumbs combined with ¼ cup Parmesan cheese. Shake the crumbs around the bottom and sides until coated. Shake out the excess crumbs.

3. Sauté the onion and green pepper in 3 tablespoons butter.

4. Cut the salmon into small dice.

5. Preheat the oven to 300 degrees.

6. Fold the salmon, Gruyère cheese, remaining 3 tablespoons Parmesan cheese and sautéed onion and green pepper into the basic cheesecake mixture. Add salt and pepper to taste.

7. Pour the batter into the prepared pan and shake gently to level the mixture.

8. Set the pan in a slightly larger pan and pour boiling water into the larger pan to a depth of 2 inches. Do not let the edges of the pans touch. Bake for 1 hour and 40 minutes. At the end of that time, turn off the oven heat and let the cake sit in the oven 1 hour longer.

9. Lift the cake out of its water bath and place it on a rack to cool for at least 2 hours before unmolding.

10. Place a round cake plate over the cake and carefully turn both upside down to unmold. Cut into wedges.

YIELD: 12 to 20 servings.

BASIC CHEESECAKE MIXTURE

- 3½ 8-ounce packages cream cheese at room temperature
- 4 large eggs
- ⅓ cup heavy cream

Place the cream cheese, eggs and heavy cream in the bowl of an electric mixer. Beat the ingredients until thoroughly blended and quite smooth.

YIELD: Enough for 1 8-inch cheesecake.

Blue Cheese Cheesecake

- Basic cheesecake mixture (see preceding recipe)
- Butter
- ⅓ cup fine bread crumbs
- ¼ cup grated Parmesan cheese
- ½ pound bacon
- 1 medium-sized onion, finely chopped
- ½ pound blue cheese, crumbled
- Salt and freshly ground black pepper to taste
- 2 or 3 drops Tabasco sauce

1. Prepare the basic cheesecake mixture and set aside.

2. Butter the inside of a metal cheesecake pan 8 inches wide and 3 inches deep. Sprinkle the inside with the combined bread crumbs and Parmesan cheese. Shake the crumbs around the bottom and sides until coated. Shake out the excess crumbs.

3. Sauté the bacon until very crisp. Chop finely and set aside.

4. Sauté the onion in 1 tablespoon of the bacon fat until it is wilted.

5. Preheat the oven to 300 degrees.

6. Add the bacon, onion, crumbled blue cheese, salt, pepper and Tabasco sauce to the basic mixture. Blend together thoroughly.

7. Pour the batter into the prepared pan and shake gently to level the mixture.

8. Set the pan in a slightly larger pan and pour boiling water into the larger pan to a depth of 2 inches. Do not let the edges of the pans touch. Bake for 1 hour and 40 minutes. At the end of that time, turn off the oven heat and let the cake sit in the oven 1 hour longer.

9. Lift the cake out of its water bath and place it on a rack to cool for at least 2 hours before unmolding.

10. Place a round cake plate over the cake and carefully turn both upside down to unmold. Cut into wedges.

YIELD: 12 to 20 servings.

Blessed, indeed, is the house that finds itself the recipient of fresh black caviar. No matter how small the amount, it can be served in festive ways. Paul Steindler, a chef and longtime friend, contributes a caviar parfait (served in tall parfait glasses), made with scrambled eggs to stretch the sturgeon roe. There is also a recipe for bite-sized potato halves topped with sour cream and caviar, from James Nassikas, proprietor of the elegant Stanford Court Hotel in San Francisco. Mr. Nassikas has his chef, Marcel Dragon, prepare this simple but marvelous fare on request for special occasions. The potatoes are split in half, the pulp scooped out, the potato shells deep-fried. The crisp shells are then refilled with potato, dabbed with sour cream and served with a spoonful of caviar on top. For those less fortunate, we offer a relatively inexpensive red caviar pie.

Caviar Parfait

- 4 eggs
- 6 tablespoons butter
- ¼ cup heavy cream
- Salt to taste
- 8 tablespoons red caviar (salmon roe)
- 8 tablespoons sour cream
- ¼ cup plain yogurt
- 8 teaspoons minced chives
- 8 tablespoons fresh black caviar

1. Beat the eggs in a mixing bowl.

2. Melt half the butter in a skillet and, when it is hot and bubbling but not brown, add the eggs, stirring with a rubber or plastic spatula over gentle heat. Cook until the eggs start to set, then add the cream, stirring to blend. When the eggs are almost ready, stir in the remaining butter. Add salt to taste and remove from the heat.

3. Spoon equal portions of the eggs into eight warmed parfait glasses. Add a layer of red caviar to each glass. Blend the sour cream and yogurt and apportion it. Sprinkle with chives and add a final layer of black caviar.

YIELD: 8 servings.

Caviar and Potatoes Marcel Dragon

12 to 14 small, red potatoes, 1 pound or less
4 to 5 cups rock salt
Oil for deep frying
½ cup sour cream, approximately
1 14-ounce tin fresh caviar or less

1. Preheat the oven to 450 degrees.

2. Wash and dry the potatoes. Arrange them on a bed of rock salt and place in the oven. Bake for 30 to 35 minutes, or until tender.

3. Remove the potatoes and slice them in half.

4. Scoop out the center pulp with a melon-ball cutter or small spoon; reserve both the pulp and skins. Mash the pulp slightly and keep it warm.

5. Heat the oil for deep frying to 375 degrees. Drop the potato shells into the oil and cook quickly until they are golden brown and crisp. Drain well.

6. Fill the shells with the mashed potato. Top with a spoonful or so of sour cream. Then add a teaspoon or more of caviar to the top. Serve on a bed of hot rock salt, if desired.

YIELD: 24 to 28 pieces.

Eggs with Caviar Paul Steindler

12 eggs at room temperature
2 scallions, green part and all
Crushed ice
Salt
¾ cup sour cream
½ to 1 pound fresh caviar
Lemon halves for garnish
Parsley for garnish

1. Place the eggs in a saucepan and add cold water to cover. Bring to the boil and simmer for about 6 minutes. (When the eggs are cooked this briefly, the whites should remain firm and the center of the yolk a bit runny. But if the eggs do become firm throughout, it does not matter.) Drain the eggs and run under cold water until chilled.

2. Using a heavy knife with a serrated blade, crack around the top of each egg in a neat circle. Remove and discard the tops.

3. Spoon out the inside of each egg into a mixing bowl. Using a fork, mash the whites and yolks together coarsely. Set the hollowed-out egg-shells aside.

4. Trim the scallions and chop them. Add them to the eggs and blend.

5. Make layers of crushed ice in a bordered dish and sprinkle each layer with salt. Make indentations over the surface to hold the eggshells.

6. Using a spoon, fill each reserved eggshell about one-third full with the egg and scallion mixture. Serve the remaining egg and scallion mixture separately as refills. Arrange the eggs over the ice.

7. Using a pastry bag, pipe equal amounts of sour cream into the shells. Add a rounded heaping spoonful of caviar to each shell. Serve the remaining sour cream and caviar separately as refills.

8. Garnish the dish with lemon halves and small, tight clusters of parsley.

YIELD: 6 servings.

Red Caviar Pie

- 6 large hard-boiled eggs, peeled
- 8 tablespoons butter at room temperature
- ½ cup finely chopped onion
- Tabasco sauce to taste
- ½ cup sour cream
- 4 ounces red caviar (salmon roe)
- Buttered toast wedges

1. Put half the eggs through a sieve. Chop the remainder on a flat surface until fine and blend the two together. Add the butter, onion and Tabasco. Blend well and shape into a flat round cake. Chill until set.

2. Make a built-up rim of sour cream around the upper rim of the pie. Make a shallower, flat layer of sour cream in the center. Spoon the red caviar over the flat layer. Cut the pie into wedges and serve with buttered toast.

YIELD: 6 to 8 servings.

Margaret Sichel's Herring Salad

- ¾ pound pickled beets (see following recipe)
- 4 sour pickles, about ¾ pound, ends trimmed
- 8 matjes herring fillets, about 1¼ pounds
- 2 sour apples, about 1 pound, peeled, quartered and cored
- 4 hard-boiled eggs, peeled
- ¾ cup drained imported lingonberries
- ½ cup sour cream
- Freshly ground pepper to taste

1. Drain the chilled beets and cut them into ¼-inch cubes. Place them in a mixing bowl. Cut the pickles into ¼-inch cubes and add them to the bowl.

2. Cut the herring lengthwise into ½-inch-wide strips. Cut the strips into ½-inch-long pieces or slightly smaller. Add these to the bowl.

3. Cut the apples into ¼-inch cubes and add them to the bowl.

4. Chop the eggs and add them. Add the lingonberries, sour cream and pepper. Blend well, cover and chill. Serve with thin slices of rye bread or pumpernickel. Leftover herring salad keeps well, covered tightly, in the refrigerator.

YIELD: 16 servings.

PICKLED BEETS

- ¾ pound beets, tops trimmed but with 1 inch of stem intact
- Salt to taste, if desired
- ¼ cup red wine vinegar
- 2 tablespoons sugar
- 2 whole cloves

1. Put the beets in a saucepan and add water to cover and salt to taste. Bring to the boil and cook for 25 to 45 minutes, or until tender. Cooking time will depend on the age and size of the beets. Drain the beets.

2. Bring the vinegar, sugar and cloves to the boil in a small saucepan. Simmer for 5 minutes.

3. Peel the beets and cut them into ½-inch-thick slices. Pour the vinegar mixture over the beets and let stand until cool. Chill.

YIELD: 4 servings as a salad.

Marianne Lipsky's Mustard Herring

- 24 herring fillets in wine sauce
- ¾ cup Gulden's spicy brown mustard
- 4 tablespoons prepared mustard, preferably imported Dijon
- 6 tablespoons white vinegar
- 6 tablespoons sugar
- Salt to taste, if desired
- Freshly ground black pepper to taste
- 1 cup corn, peanut or vegetable oil
- 1 cup chopped fresh dill

1. Drain the herring and cut each fillet into 1-inch pieces. Put the pieces in a mixing bowl.

2. Put the two mustards, vinegar, sugar, salt and pepper in another mixing bowl. Start beating with a wire whisk while adding the oil in a thin stream. When all the oil has been added, stir in the dill. Pour the sauce over the herring pieces and blend. Refrigerate for 24 hours. This will keep for 2 weeks refrigerated. Serve, preferably, from an earthenware crock.

YIELD: 24 or more servings.

If we had to name the single best convenience food imported from France, it would be the snails that come packaged in tins. The reason is that snails, long considered a great delicacy, require hours, if not days, of tedious preparation; they must be washed several times, purged in a blend of salt, vinegar and flour, cooked, and so on.

We have often printed recipes for escargots à la bourguignonne, the traditional preparation, in which snails are served in the shell with garlic butter. Recently, however, we have prepared snails in other ways that are equally compelling.

Curiously, packagers rarely include the proper instructions for cooking the snails in a court bouillon once they are removed from the can and drained. This gives a fresh taste to the snails and makes them more tender.

Escargots aux Fines Herbes

SNAILS IN A WHITE BUTTER SAUCE WITH HERBS

- 36 drained snails cooked in court bouillon (see following recipe)
- 2 heads Boston lettuce
- 6 tablespoons butter
- ¼ cup finely chopped shallots
- ½ cup dry white wine
- 2 tablespoons white vinegar
- ½ teaspoon anchovy paste
- ½ teaspoon finely chopped fresh tarragon, or ¼ teaspoon dried

1 tablespoon finely chopped chives
1 tablespoon finely chopped fresh basil, or 1 teaspoon dried
¼ cup peeled, seeded and diced tomatoes
12 toast rectangles

1. Prepare the snails and set them aside.

2. Remove the core from the lettuce. Wash the leaves well and drain them well. Stack the leaves and cut them into very thin shreds. There should be about 8 cups loosely packed. Set aside.

3. Melt 2 tablespoons of the butter in a skillet and add the lettuce. Cook, stirring, until it is wilted.

4. Combine the shallots, wine and vinegar in a saucepan. Bring to the boil. Cook over high heat until most of the liquid has evaporated.

5. Cut the remaining 4 tablespoons of butter into cubes.

6. Stir the shallots with a wire whisk and cook over low heat while adding the butter, two or three cubes at a time. Continue stirring vigorously until all the butter had been added. Add the anchovy paste, tarragon, chives and basil.

7. Heat the tomatoes for about 5 seconds in a hot skillet, stirring. Add them to the butter sauce.

8. Reheat the lettuce. Spoon an equal portion on top of each toast rectangle. Arrange three snails neatly on the lettuce and spoon the sauce over each serving.

YIELD: 6 servings.

ESCARGOTS AU COURT BOUILLON

A Basic Preparation for Snails

24 to 36 drained canned snails
½ cup coarsely chopped carrot
½ cup coarsely chopped onion
⅓ cup coarsely chopped celery
4 sprigs fresh parsley, tied into a bundle
½ cup dry white wine
1 cup water
5 whole black peppercorns
1 clove garlic, peeled

Combine all the ingredients in a saucepan or skillet. Bring to the boil and simmer for 10 minutes. Let cool and drain.

YIELD: 24 to 36 snails ready for use in other recipes.

Snails Florentine

- 36 drained snails cooked in court bouillon (see preceding recipe)
- 6 tablespoons butter
- 3 tablespoons finely chopped shallots
- ½ teaspoon finely minced garlic
- 1 cup loosely packed watercress leaves
- 4 cups loosely packed spinach leaves
- 1 cup loosely packed parsley leaves
- ¼ teaspoon Tabasco sauce
- 1 teaspoon anchovy paste
- 2 teaspoons Pernod or Ricard

1. Prepare the snails and set them aside.

2. Preheat the oven to 400 degrees.

3. Melt the butter in a saucepan and add the shallots and garlic. Cook, stirring, until they are wilted. Add the watercress, spinach and parsley and cook, stirring, until the leaves wilt, about 30 seconds.

4. Put the mixture into the container of a food processor or electric blender. Blend to a fine purée. There should be 1 cup or slightly less. Spoon and scrape the mixture into a mixing bowl and add the Tabasco sauce, anchovy paste and Pernod. Blend well.

5. Fill each of 36 shells (natural, ceramic or otherwise) with 1 cooked snail. Spoon enough of the spinach mixture into the shells to fill them. Arrange the filled shells on baking dishes or snail dishes.

6. Place in the oven and bake for 10 minutes. Serve piping hot.

YIELD: 6 servings.

Champignons Farcis aux Escargots et Noix

MUSHROOMS STUFFED WITH SNAILS AND PECANS

- 24 drained snails cooked in court bouillon (see recipe page 23)
- 24 mushrooms, about 1 pound
- 6 tablespoons butter
- 2 tablespoons finely chopped shallots
- 1 teaspoon finely minced garlic
- ¼ cup finely chopped pecans
- ½ cup finely chopped parsley
- Salt, if desired
- Freshly ground black pepper to taste
- 2 tablespoons Cognac

1. Prepare the snails and set them aside.

2. Preheat the oven to 400 degrees.

3. Remove the stems from the mushrooms. The stems may be set aside for another recipe.

4. Melt 2 tablespoons of the butter in a large saucepan. Add the mushrooms, stemmed side up, and cook for about 2 minutes, or until lightly browned. Turn the mushrooms and cook for about 1 minute longer.

5. Arrange the mushrooms close together, stemmed side up, in a baking dish.

6. Place one snail in each mushroom cavity.

7. Combine the remaining 4 tablespoons of butter, the shallots, garlic, pecans, parsley, salt and pepper in the container of a food processor or electric blender. Process until well blended.

8. Spoon an equal portion of the butter on top of each snail. Place the mushrooms in the oven and bake for 10 minutes.

9. Sprinkle with Cognac and serve.

YIELD: 4 to 6 servings.

A number of years ago, when I was a student at a hotel school in Switzerland, a favorite diversion was an occasional visit with a friend to a restaurant in Lausanne called Aux Trois Tonneaux. A short while ago that same friend forwarded a recipe from Aux Trois Tonneaux: It was for stuffed mushrooms with snail butter. It is unusual and good.

Mushrooms with Snail Butter Aux Trois Tonneaux

THE STUFFED MUSHROOMS

- 24 large, fresh mushrooms, about 1 pound
- ½ cup dry white wine
- Juice of 1 lemon
- Salt and freshly ground black pepper to taste
- 2 tablespoons butter
- 1 tablespoon olive oil
- 2 tablespoons finely chopped shallots
- 1½ tablespoons flour
- ¾ cup milk
- ½ cup bread crumbs
- ⅛ teaspoon grated nutmeg
- 1 tablespoon finely chopped parsley

THE SNAIL BUTTER

- 3 tablespoons butter
- 1 tablespoon finely chopped garlic
- 1 tablespoon finely chopped parsley

1. Wash and drain the mushrooms well. Remove and reserve the stems from the mushrooms.

2. Put the caps in a skillet and add the wine, half of the lemon juice, salt and pepper. Bring to the boil. Cover and cook, stirring occasionally, for about 5 minutes. Remove from the heat and drain the caps. Discard the liquid.

3. Chop the mushroom stems. There should be about 1¼ cups.

4. Heat 1 tablespoon of the butter and the oil in a saucepan and add the shallots, chopped mushroom stems, remaining lemon juice and salt and pepper to taste. Cook until wilted and the moisture has evaporated.

5. Melt the remaining tablespoon of butter in a small saucepan and add the flour, stirring to blend. When blended, add the milk, stirring rapidly with a wire whisk. Add the chopped mushroom mixture, bread crumbs, nutmeg and salt and pepper to taste. Stir in the parsley. Let cool slightly.

6. Spoon equal portions of the mixture into the mushroom caps and mound it up, smoothing it over with a spatula. Continue until all the caps are filled and all the filling is used. Arrange the filled caps in a baking dish.

7. Preheat the oven to 400 degrees.

8. Bake the filled caps for about 5 minutes, or until piping hot throughout.

9. To make the snail butter, heat the butter with the garlic and parsley. When it is bubbling, pour the mixture over the mushrooms and serve hot.

YIELD: 4 to 8 servings.

Champignons Farcis aux Palourdes

MUSHROOMS STUFFED WITH CLAMS

- 18 cherrystone or 24 littleneck clams
- 24 large mushrooms, about 1 pound
- 1 tablespoon butter
- 2 tablespoons finely chopped shallots
- ½ cup dry white wine
- ¾ cup heavy cream
- ½ cup clam juice from opened clams
- 1 teaspoon arrowroot or cornstarch
- 1 egg yolk
- 2 tablespoons finely chopped chives
- 1 teaspoon finely chopped fresh tarragon
- 2 tablespoons finely chopped fresh basil
- 1 tablespoon Pernod or Ricard

1. Open the clams but reserve both the clams and the liquid. Discard the shells. There should be about ½ cup liquid. Chop the clams.

2. Remove the stems from the mushrooms. The stems may be set aside for another recipe.

3. Melt the butter in a large saucepan. Add the mushrooms, stemmed side up, and cook for about 2 minutes, or until lightly browned. Turn the mushrooms and cook for about 1 minute longer.

4. Meanwhile, combine the shallots and wine in a saucepan. Cook until the wine is almost completely reduced.

5. Add the cream and all but 1 tablespoon of the clam juice and bring to the boil. Cook down over moderately high heat until slightly reduced.

6. Blend the arrowroot and remaining tablespoon of clam juice. Stir this into the simmering sauce. Beat the egg yolk and add about 2 tablespoons of the sauce. Add the clams and the yolk mixture to the simmering sauce, stirring. Remove immediately from the heat.

7. Add the chives, tarragon, basil and Pernod.

8. Arrange the hot mushroom caps, stemmed side up, on a serving dish. Spoon equal portions of the filling inside each cap. Serve hot.

YIELD: 4 to 6 servings.

Note: The sauce in this recipe is also delectable served over and tossed with 1 pound of cooked pasta, such as linguine.

❧

Mushrooms with Mushroom and Ham Stuffing

24 large, fresh mushrooms, about 1 pound
Juice of 1 lemon
Salt and freshly ground black pepper to taste
1 tablespoon peanut, vegetable or corn oil
3 tablespoons butter
½ cup finely chopped onion
½ cup finely chopped cooked ham
¼ cup plus 1 tablespoon fresh bread crumbs
1 egg yolk
3 tablespoons finely chopped parsley

1. Preheat the oven to 400 degrees.

2. Wash and drain the mushrooms well. Remove and reserve the stems from the mushroom caps.

3. Sprinkle the caps with half of the lemon juice, salt and pepper to taste and the oil. Arrange the mushrooms, stemmed side down, in a baking dish. Bake for about 5 minutes. Remove and set aside.

4. Chop the mushroom stems. There should be about 1¼ cups. Set aside.

5. Melt 2 tablespoons of the butter in a saucepan and add the onion. Cook, stirring, until wilted.

6. Add the chopped mushroom stems and remaining lemon juice. Cook, stirring occasionally, for about 5 minutes, or until most of the moisture has evaporated.

7. Add the ham and stir. Cook briefly and remove from the heat. Add ¼ cup bread crumbs and the egg yolk and stir to blend. Add the parsley.

8. Spoon equal portions of the mixture into the caps and mound it up, smoothing it over with a spatula. Continue until all the caps are filled and all the filling is used. Arrange the mushrooms stuffed side up in a baking dish.

9. Melt the remaining tablespoon of butter and brush the tops of the stuffed mushroom caps with it. Sprinkle with the remaining bread crumbs.

10. Bake for 10 minutes, or until piping hot throughout.

YIELD: 4 to 8 servings.

Mushrooms Stuffed with Chopped Liver

- 24 large, fresh mushrooms, about 1 pound
- 2 tablespoons butter
- 1 cup finely chopped onion
- Juice of 1 lemon
- Salt and freshly ground black pepper to taste
- 1 tablespoon peanut, vegetable or corn oil
- ¼ pound bacon, cut into very small pieces
- 1 pound chicken livers
- 1 teaspoon chopped fresh sage
- 1 tablespoon fresh bread crumbs
- ¼ cup port wine, optional

1. Preheat the oven to 400 degrees.

2. Wash and drain the mushrooms well. Remove the stems from the mushroom caps and chop the stems. There should be about 1¼ cups.

3. Melt the butter in a saucepan and add half the onion. Cook until wilted and add the chopped stems and half the lemon juice. Add salt and pepper to taste. Cook until most of the moisture has evaporated.

4. Sprinkle the caps with salt and pepper to taste and the remaining lemon juice and the oil. Stir to blend. Place the caps, cavity side down, on a baking dish. Bake for 5 minutes and remove from the oven.

5. Cook the bacon in a skillet until it is crisp and gives up most of its fat. Add the remaining onion and cook until wilted.

6. Pick over the livers to remove any tough connecting membranes. Add the livers to the onion. Cook, stirring, until the livers have lost their red color throughout. Add salt and pepper to taste. Add the sage and stir.

7. Pour and scrape the liver mixture into the container of a food processor or blender. Purée until fine. Scrape this mixture into the chopped mushroom mixture and stir to blend. Add salt and pepper to taste.

8. Spoon equal portions of the mixture into the caps and mound it up, smoothing it over with a spatula. Continue until all the caps are filled and all the filling is used.

9. Arrange the filled caps in a lightly buttered baking dish. Sprinkle with bread crumbs. Bake for about 10 minutes, or until piping hot throughout. If desired, remove from the oven and pour the wine over, then return to the oven for 1 or 2 minutes longer.

YIELD: 4 to 8 servings.

There is definitely a hierarchy among greens—who could contemplate okra or cabbage in sophisticated realms—and if I should rank them, artichokes would certainly be at the top of the list. Although I like them whole, either hot or cold, one of my favorite ways to serve them is pared of their leaves. The neatly turned heart at the bottom of the artichoke makes a fancy and flavorful cup for any number of stuffings.

Fonds d'Artichauts Niçoise

ARTICHOKE BOTTOMS WITH TOMATOES AND MUSHROOMS

- 8 large artichoke bottoms prepared for stuffing (see instructions)
- 2 tablespoons olive oil
- ½ pound mushrooms sliced thin, about 3 cups
- Salt to taste, if desired
- Freshly ground black pepper to taste
- 1 tablespoon finely chopped garlic
- 2 cups chopped imported canned tomatoes with liquid
- ⅛ teaspoon hot red pepper flakes
- 2 tablespoons finely chopped parsley
- ½ cup freshly grated Parmesan cheese

1. Prepare the artichoke bottoms and set aside.

2. Preheat the oven to 425 degrees.

3. Heat the oil in skillet and add the mushrooms. Cook, stirring, until they give up their liquid. Cook until the liquid has evaporated and they start to brown. Add the salt, pepper and garlic and cook briefly.

4. Add the tomatoes and cook down, stirring often, for about 8 minutes. Add the pepper flakes and parsley.

5. Spoon equal portions of the mixture into the artichoke shells. Arrange in a baking dish. Sprinkle with equal amounts of cheese. Bake for 5 minutes.

YIELD: 8 servings.

Fonds d'Artichauts et Huîtres Florentine

ARTICHOKE BOTTOMS WITH OYSTERS AND SPINACH

- 8 large artichoke bottoms prepared for stuffing (see instructions)
- 2 tablespoons butter
- 1 cup finely chopped scallions
- 2 pounds fresh spinach, or 2 10-ounce packages, cleaned and stems removed
- Salt to taste, if desired
- Freshly ground black pepper to taste
- ½ cup heavy cream
- 8 oysters
- ¼ cup freshly grated Gruyère or Parmesan cheese

1. Prepare the artichoke bottoms and arrange them stemmed side down in a baking dish.

2. Preheat the oven to 450 degrees.

3. Melt the butter in a saucepan and add the scallions. Cook, stirring, briefly. Add the spinach and cook, stirring, until wilted. Add the salt and pepper.

4. Divide the spinach mixture in half. Use half to stuff the artichoke shells, an equal portion in each.

5. Return the remaining spinach mixture to the stove and add the cream. Bring to the boil and cook for 2 minutes. Add the oysters and cook briefly, just until edges curl, 30 or 40 seconds. Do not overcook. Arrange 1 oyster on top of each spinach-filled artichoke bottom. Spoon the spinach in cream over all.

6. Sprinkle each portion with cheese. Bake for 8 minutes.

YIELD: 8 servings.

HOW TO PREPARE ARTICHOKE BOTTOMS

Cut off the stems of the artichokes, using a sharp knife to produce a neat, flat base. Rub any cut surfaces with lemon to prevent discoloration. Trim all around the sides and base until the base is smooth and white, with the green exterior pared away.

Place the artichoke on its side on a flat surface. Slice off the top, leaving a base about 1½ inches deep. Using a paring knife, trim around the sides and bottom to remove the green exterior that remains. Don't remove the fuzzy choke yet; it comes out easily when the artichokes are cooked.

They are now ready to be cooked in a blanc légume, or vegetable whitener, a blend of water and flour. Use enough to barely cover the artichoke bottoms. For each 6 cups of water use ¼ cup of flour.

Place a sieve over the saucepan in which the artichokes will be cooked. Add the flour. Pour cold water over the flour, rubbing to dissolve it. Add salt to taste. Add the artichoke bottoms and bring to the boil. Cover the pot closely and cook for about 25 minutes, or until the bottoms are tender. Remove the pot from the heat.

If the artichokes are not to be used immediately, let them rest in the cooking liquid. Before using, drain the artichoke bottoms and pull or scrape out the chokes.

Clams are best—whether eaten raw on the half shell or cooked—when they are opened with a clam knife just shortly before they are to be eaten or cooked. And they can be opened more easily if they are well chilled. Put them in the freezer for a few minutes to ensure this, but take care that they do not freeze.

Stuffed Clams

- 18 to 24 cherrystone clams
- ¼ pound butter at room temperature
- 3 tablespoons finely chopped shallots
- 1 teaspoon finely minced garlic
- ¼ cup finely chopped parsley
- 1 tablespoon chopped fresh basil, or half the amount dried
- 1 cup bread crumbs
- 8 tablespoons freshly grated Parmesan cheese
- 2 tablespoons dry white wine
- ¼ cup finely chopped prosciutto or other ham
- ⅛ to ¼ teaspoon hot red pepper flakes
- Salt and freshly ground black pepper to taste
- 2 tablespoons olive oil

1. Preheat the oven to 425 degrees.

2. Open and remove the clams. There should be about 1 cup. Reserve 24 shells for stuffing.

3. Process the clams briefly in a food processor. Do not overprocess or the clams will become liquid.

4. In a saucepan, combine the clams with the butter, shallots, garlic, parsley, basil, bread crumbs, 6 tablespoons of the cheese, wine, prosciutto, pepper flakes and salt and pepper. Cook, stirring, until well blended. Stuff the reserved clam shells with the mixture, smoothing over the tops.

5. Sprinkle the remaining 2 tablespoons of cheese over the tops. Arrange the clams in a shallow baking dish. Sprinkle with the olive oil.

6. Bake for 15 minutes. Run the clams under the broiler briefly for a final glaze.

YIELD: 8 servings.

Palourdes Farcies Creole

STUFFED CLAMS CREOLE

- 18 cherrystone clams
- 1½ cups coarsely chopped sweet green and/or red pepper
- ⅔ cup coarsely chopped celery
- ⅔ cup coarsely chopped onion
- 1 clove garlic, coarsely chopped
- 8 tablespoons butter
- 1 teaspoon curry powder
- ¾ cup plus 2 tablespoons fresh bread crumbs
- 1 egg, lightly beaten
- ½ cup finely chopped parsley
- Freshly ground black pepper to taste
- ¼ teaspoon Tabasco sauce

1. Preheat the oven to 400 degrees.

2. Open the clams; there should be about 1 cup of them. Coarsely chop them and set them aside. Reserve 20 shells for stuffing.

3. Put the sweet pepper, celery, onion and garlic in the container of a food processor. Process until finely chopped. There should be about 1½ cups.

4. Melt the butter in a saucepan and add the vegetables. Sprinkle with curry powder. Cook, stirring, for about 5 minutes. Remove from the heat and stir in the chopped clams, ¾ cup of the bread crumbs, egg, parsley, pepper and Tabasco sauce. Blend well.

5. Stuff the 20 clam shells, rounding the mixture over. Sprinkle with the remaining 2 tablespoons of bread crumbs. Bake for 10 minutes and serve.

YIELD: 4 to 6 servings.

A *tasca,* Penelope Casas explained to us as she prepared an awesomely good Spanish dinner, is a small bar, a gathering place for Spaniards who like to sip sherry or beer and exchange gossip. While they do this, they eat tapas, small foods resembling appetizers that come in a thousand varieties. This mussel dish is just one of those tapas. The following version of stuffed mussels is a Turkish delight, mussels in the shell stuffed with rice.

Mejillones Rellenos Gayango

DEEP-FRIED STUFFED MUSSELS

- 18 medium-sized fresh mussels
- ¾ cup water
- 1 lemon slice
- 1 tablespoon olive oil
- ¼ cup finely minced onion
- 2 tablespoons finely minced prosciutto or other ham
- 1 clove garlic, finely minced
- 1 teaspoon tomato sauce
- 1 teaspoon finely minced parsley
- Salt and freshly ground black pepper to taste
- 2 cups white mussel sauce (see following recipe)
- 1 tablespoon freshly grated Parmesan cheese
- 1 cup fresh bread crumbs
- 2 eggs
- Oil for deep frying

1. Rinse and scrub the mussels well. Place them in a pan with the water and lemon slice. Cover. Let steam briefly. Remove the mussels as they open, discarding any that do not open. They must not overcook. Reserve ½ cup of the mussel broth for use in the white mussel sauce.
2. Remove the mussels from the shells. Save half the shells for stuffing.
3. Chop the mussels coarsely.
4. Heat the oil in a small skillet. Add the onion and cook, stirring, until it is wilted. Add the ham and garlic and cook for about 1 minute, stirring.
5. Add the tomato sauce, chopped mussels, parsley and salt and pepper. Cook for 5 minutes. Half fill the reserved mussel shells with this mixture, smoothing it over with a spatula.
6. Using a small spoon, cover the filled mussels with the white sauce, smoothing it over to the edges of each mussel. Arrange the mussels in one layer on a baking sheet and refrigerate for 1 hour.
7. Blend the cheese and bread crumbs.
8. Beat the eggs. Dip the mussels, filled side down, first in the beaten eggs, then in the cheese mixture to coat them well.

9. Heat the oil. It must be at least 1 inch deep. Add the mussels, stuffed side down, and cook until well browned.

YIELD: 18 mussels.

Note: You may keep these mussels warm for half an hour or less in a 200-degree oven.

SALSA BLANCA DE MEJILLONES

White Mussel Sauce

- 3 tablespoons butter
- 4 tablespoons flour
- ½ cup broth from steamed mussels
- ½ cup milk
- Salt and freshly ground black pepper to taste

1. Melt the butter in a saucepan and add the flour, stirring with a wire whisk.

2. When blended, add the mussel broth and milk, stirring constantly with the whisk. When blended and smooth, add the salt and pepper. This sauce should be quite thick. Remove from the heat and stir occasionally until needed.

YIELD: About 1¼ cups.

Midye Dolmasi

MUSSELS STUFFED WITH RICE AND CURRANTS

- ½ cup rice
- ¼ cup olive oil
- ½ cup finely chopped onion
- ¼ cup pine nuts
- 2 tablespoons dried black currants
- ½ cup drained canned imported tomatoes
- ½ teaspoon ground allspice
- ½ teaspoon sugar
- 1¾ cups fish stock, beef broth or water
- ¼ cup finely chopped parsley
- Salt, if desired
- Freshly ground black pepper to taste
- 30 to 40 well-scrubbed, debearded mussels, depending on size
- Lemon wedges for garnish
- Parsley sprigs for garnish

1. Do not cook the rice. Put it in a bowl and add the hottest water possible from the faucet. Set aside until the water reaches room temperature. Drain the rice.

2. Heat the oil in a saucepan and add the onion. Cook briefly, stirring, until the onion is wilted. Add the pine nuts and currants and cook for 30 seconds, stirring. Add the tomatoes, rice, allspice and sugar and stir.

3. Add ¾ cup of the broth, the chopped parsley, salt and pepper to taste. Bring to the simmer and cover closely. Simmer for 15 minutes. Remove from the heat.

4. Using a sharp knife, open the mussels one at a time, leaving them hinged at one side.

5. Using a spoon, fill each mussel half with two or three teaspoons of the filling. Close each mussel and tie each one tightly with string. Arrange the mussels in close layers in a small kettle and add the remaining 1 cup of stock. Bring to the boil and cover closely. Simmer for 30 minutes.

6. Remove from the heat and let stand, covered, until cool. Drain. Cut away the strings from the mussels. Serve at room temperature garnished with lemon wedges and parsley sprigs.

YIELD: 30 to 40 stuffed mussels.

It has been said that today's nouvelle cuisine stems from the fact that within the last few decades French chefs have traveled beyond France and have broadened their culinary scope. Roger Vergé's principal influence has been North Africa and Kenya, where he worked in various jobs when he was in his twenties and thirties. He displayed that influence in my kitchen by preparing one of the most interesting oyster dishes I have ever eaten. It is an appetizer made with oysters on the half shell, briefly heated and served with an orange butter and orange sections. It is an extraordinary and appealing combination of flavors.

Les Huîtres Chaudes au Beurre d'Orange

OYSTERS WITH ORANGE BUTTER

- 24 unshucked oysters
- 2 oranges
- 6 tablespoons butter
- 1 teaspoon lemon juice
- Freshly ground black pepper to taste

1. Preheat the broiler to high.

2. Shuck the oysters but save half the shells and all their liquor.

3. Arrange the oyster shells on a flat dish and put them under the broiler until dry. Remove and set aside.

4. Put the oyster liquor in a saucepan and add the oysters. Bring just to the boil and strain, reserving the oysters and liquid. Put one oyster in each shell.

5. Grate the rind of 1 orange and reserve. Peel that orange and the remaining one. Cut between the membranes of each orange to remove each section neatly, saving any juice that drips from the oranges as they are sectioned.

6. Arrange 1 orange section on top of or next to each oyster.

7. Pour the reserved oyster liquor into a saucepan and cook down to 2 tablespoons. Add half of the grated orange rind. Discard the rest. Add the orange drippings.

8. Heat the liquor and swirl in the butter. Add the lemon juice.

9. Sprinkle the oysters with pepper. Heat as briefly as possible under the broiler. Spoon an equal amount of the sauce over each portion and serve.

YIELD: 4 to 6 servings.

Marinated Seafood Cocktail, Mexican Style

- 24 littleneck clams
- ½ pound shrimp, peeled and deveined
- Salt to taste, if desired
- 1 bay leaf
- 1 dried hot red pepper
- 20 small mussels, well scrubbed
- 3 tablespoons dry white wine
- ½ cup cubed ripe tomatoes
- ½ cup finely chopped onion
- 1 tablespoon finely minced garlic
- 1½ cups cubed avocado
- ¼ cup fresh lime juice
- 1 cup tomato juice
- 2 teaspoons crushed coriander seeds
- ¼ teaspoon hot red pepper flakes
- 2 teaspoons chopped fresh coriander leaves or parsley, optional

1. Open and save the clams and their liquid. There should be about 1 cup of liquid.

2. Place the shrimp in a saucepan and add water to cover, salt, bay leaf and hot red pepper. Bring to the boil. Remove from the heat and let cool. Drain and cut into cubes. Set aside.

3. Put the mussels in a saucepan with the wine. Cover closely and bring

to the boil. Cook 4 or 5 minutes, or until the mussels open. Drain. Remove the mussels from the shells. Remove and discard the rubber band-like strand that surrounds each mussel.

4. Put the clams and their liquid in a mixing bowl. Add the shrimp, mussels, tomatoes, onion, garlic, avocado, lime juice, tomato juice, coriander seeds, pepper flakes and coriander leaves. Cover and refrigerate for several hours, or until ready to serve.

YIELD: 8 or more servings.

If the summer hath his joys, to borrow a phrase from the poet Thomas Campion, it also hath its dishes. Not the least of these is a category of foods, basically related to one another, that includes the escabeches of Spain and Latin America, the soused dishes of England and certain marinated dishes of France and Italy. All are served cold and all have a combination of ingredients in common: a discreet amount of vinegar judiciously blended with herbs and spices and, often, with slices of lemon, lime and onion and garlic.

❧

Soused Mackerel

- 6 fresh boneless mackerel fillets with skin left on, ½ to ¾ pound each
- 4 bay leaves
- 1 cup tarragon vinegar
- 1 cup water
- 1½ cups finely chopped onion
- 6 whole cloves
- 6 whole allspice
- 1 teaspoon whole black peppercorns
- ½ teaspoon dried thyme
- ¼ teaspoon grated nutmeg or ground mace
- Salt to taste, if desired
- 1 teaspoon sugar
- 2 tablespoons finely chopped parsley

1. Preheat the oven to 350 degrees.

2. Arrange the fillets close together in one layer in a baking dish. Cover with the bay leaves.

3. Combine the vinegar, water, onion, cloves, allspice, peppercorns, thyme, nutmeg, salt, sugar and parsley in a bowl. Blend well and pour over the fillets.

4. Bake for 30 minutes.

5. Remove from the oven and let stand at room temperature until cool. Cover closely and refrigerate overnight.

YIELD: 6 to 8 servings.

Soused Shrimp

- 1½ pounds shrimp, about 42
- ½ cup dry white wine
- ½ cup apple cider vinegar
- ½ cup water
- ⅓ cup thinly sliced carrot rounds
- 2 tablespoons lime juice
- 1 cup coarsely chopped onion
- 1 teaspoon whole black peppercorns
- 2 teaspoons sugar
- 6 whole allspice
- 6 whole cloves
- 2 hot dried red peppers
- 1 teaspoon powdered mustard
- ⅛ teaspoon cayenne pepper
- Salt to taste, if desired
- 2 bay leaves
- 2 sprigs fresh parsley
- 14 thin seeded lemon slices

1. Peel and devein the shrimp. Put them in a bowl.

2. Combine all the remaining ingredients except the lemon slices in a saucepan and bring to the boil. Simmer for 5 minutes. Add the lemon slices.

3. Pour the boiling marinade over the shrimp. Let stand until cool. Cover closely and refrigerate overnight or longer.

YIELD: 6 to 8 servings.

Whiting in Escabeche

- 4 boneless whiting fillets with skin left on, about 2 pounds (see Note)
- ½ cup flour
- Salt to taste, if desired
- Freshly ground black pepper to taste
- ⅓ cup plus ¼ cup olive oil
- 1 cup finely chopped onion
- 6 whole cloves garlic, unpeeled
- ⅓ cup carrots cut into very small cubes
- ¼ cup coarsely chopped parsley
- 2 bay leaves
- ½ teaspoon dried thyme
- 2 small dried hot red peppers
- ⅔ cup red wine vinegar

1. Cut each fillet in half crosswise.

2. Blend the flour with salt and pepper. Dip the fish pieces into the seasoned flour.

3. Heat ⅓ cup of the oil in a skillet and cook as many fish fillets as will fit into the skillet. Cook for 1 or 2 minutes on one side until golden brown. Turn the pieces and cook for 1 or 2 minutes on the second side. Transfer the fish as it is cooked to a platter. Repeat cooking the remaining fish. Transfer these pieces to the platter as a second layer.

4. To the skillet add the remaining ¼ cup of oil. Add the onion, garlic, carrots, parsley, bay leaves, thyme and hot red peppers. Cook, stirring, until onion is wilted. Add the vinegar and bring to the boil. Add salt and pepper to taste. Pour the mixture over the cooked fish. Let stand at room temperature until cool.

5. Cover closely and refrigerate for 24 hours.

YIELD: 6 to 12 servings.

Note: You may substitute red snapper, striped bass, fluke or other fish for the whiting.

Marinated Mackerel

4 pounds fresh boneless mackerel fillets with skin left on
4 cups water
1 cup dry white wine
1¼ cups white vinegar
3 tablespoons lemon juice
2 dried hot red peppers
2 teaspoons coriander seeds
4 whole cloves
12 whole allspice
1 large onion, about ½ pound, coarsely chopped
1 carrot, scraped, trimmed and thinly sliced
Salt to taste, if desired
1 tablespoon whole black peppercorns
2 sprigs fresh parsley

1. Cut the mackerel crosswise into 3-inch widths. Put the pieces in a bowl.

2. Combine the remaining ingredients in a saucepan or kettle and bring to the boil. Simmer for 10 minutes. Pour this marinade over the mackerel and let stand at room temperature until cool.

3. Cover closely and refrigerate for 24 hours. This keeps well for 2 or 3 weeks and improves with aging.

YIELD: 16 servings.

Pâté de Légumes

VEGETABLE PÂTÉ

- 9 beets, about 1¼ pounds
- 1 pound carrots, trimmed, scraped and cut into rounds, about 2½ cups
- 2 pounds spinach in bulk, or 2 10-ounce packages, cleaned and stems removed
- 1½ pounds lean veal, cut into cubes
- 1 egg
- 1½ cups heavy cream
- Salt to taste, if desired
- Freshly ground black pepper to taste
- ⅛ teaspoon grated nutmeg
- Corn, peanut or vegetable oil for greasing the pan
- Herb mayonnaise (see recipe page 415)

1. Cut off and discard the stems from the beets. Put the beets in a saucepan. Add water to cover and bring to the boil. Let simmer for about 35 minutes, or until tender. Drain.

2. Meanwhile, drop the carrots into a saucepan of boiling water. Cook for about 5 minutes. Drain. Put the carrots into the container of a food processor or electric blender and blend thoroughly. There should be about 1½ cups. Spoon and scrape the mixture into a bowl.

3. Drop the spinach into a kettle of boiling water and stir down. Let cook for about 1 minute. Drain well. When cool enough to handle, squeeze to extract most of the liquid. Put the spinach into the container of a food processor or electric blender and process until smooth. There should be about 1½ cups. Spoon and scrape this into a bowl.

4. Put the veal into the container of a food processor or electric blender and blend well. Add the egg and blend. Gradually add the cream while blending. Season with salt, pepper and nutmeg.

5. Add one third of the veal mixture to the spinach and blend thoroughly. Add another third to the carrots and blend well. Set both mixtures aside.

6. Slice the beets and put the slices into the container of a food processor or electric blender. Blend thoroughly. Spoon and scrape the mixture into a mixing bowl. Add the remaining veal mixture and blend well.

7. Preheat the oven to 400 degrees.

8. Using oil, lightly grease the inside of a loaf pan that measures 9 by 5 by 2¾ inches. The goal in filling the pan is to achieve a checkered pattern with each purée. Spoon half the spinach mixture carefully to cover half the bottom of the pan lengthwise, smoothing over the top. Spoon half the carrot mixture next to it, smoothing over the top. Top the spinach mixture with

half of the beet mixture, smoothing over the top. Top the carrot mixture with the remaining spinach mixture, smoothing over the top. Top the beet mixture with the remaining carrot mixture, smoothing over the top. Top the middle spinach mixture with the remaining beet mixture, smoothing over the top.

9. Cover the loaf pan closely with aluminum foil. Place the loaf pan in a larger pan of water and bring it to the boil on top of the stove.

10. Place the pans in the oven and bake for 1 hour and 15 minutes. Remove and let cool. Chill thoroughly before unmolding and slicing. Serve with herb mayonnaise.

YIELD: 12 or more servings.

Pâté de Saumon

SALMON PÂTÉ

- 1½ pounds skinless salmon, totally free of bones and cut into 2-inch cubes
- 1 egg
- 2 cups heavy cream
- Salt to taste, if desired
- Freshly ground black pepper to taste
- ⅛ teaspoon cayenne pepper
- ⅓ cup finely chopped chives, optional
- ½ pound shrimp, peeled and deveined
- ½ pound bay or sea scallops
- 2 tablespoons finely chopped shallots
- 1½ teaspoons butter
- 4 skinless, boneless fillets of sole, about ¾ pound
- Herb mayonnaise (see recipe page 415), optional

1. Preheat the oven to 400 degrees.

2. Put the cubed salmon into the container of a food processor or electric blender. Blend and add the egg. Continue blending while gradually adding the cream, salt, pepper and cayenne. Spoon and scrape the mixture into a mixing bowl. Add the chives, if used, and mix well.

3. Cut the shrimp into ½-inch cubes. If bay scallops are used, leave them whole. If sea scallops are used, cut them into ½-inch cubes.

4. Put the scallops, shrimp and shallots in a dry skillet and cook briefly, stirring, until the seafood gives up its liquid. Add the mixture to the salmon mixture and blend.

5. Butter the inside of a loaf pan that measures 9 by 5 by 2¾ inches.

6. Split each fillet of sole in half lengthwise.

7. Make a layer of salmon mixture on the bottom of the loaf pan, using one fifth of the mixture. Top, lengthwise, with two sole fillet halves, placed parallel over the salmon layer. Continue making layers of salmon and sole fillet halves, ending with the salmon mixture. Smooth it over.

8. Cover the loaf pan closely with aluminum foil. Place the loaf pan in a larger pan of water and bring it to the boil on top of the stove.

9. Place the pans in the oven and bake for 1 hour and 15 minutes. Remove from the oven and let cool. Chill thoroughly before unmolding and slicing. Serve, if desired, with herb mayonnaise.

YIELD: 12 or more servings.

Gâteau de Viande

CHICKEN AND VEAL PÂTÉ

- 1 pound skinless, boneless chicken breast, cut into 1-inch cubes
- ¾ pound chicken livers
- 1 tablespoon butter plus butter for greasing the pan
- 1½ cups finely chopped onion
- 1 teaspoon finely minced garlic
- ¼ teaspoon finely minced fresh or dried thyme
- 1¼ cups finely diced, sweet green or red pepper
- ½ pound spinach, trimmed and cleaned, about 6 cups loosely packed
- 1 cup plus 2 tablespoons fine fresh bread crumbs
- 1½ pounds ground veal
- 1 egg, lightly beaten
- ⅛ teaspoon grated nutmeg
- Salt to taste, if desired
- Freshly ground black pepper to taste

1. Put the chicken breast into the container of a food processor and blend it to a coarse grind. Or put it through the medium blade of a meat grinder. Set aside.

2. Put the chicken livers into the container of a food processor or electric blender and process to a fine purée. Set aside.

3. Melt the 1 tablespoon of butter in a heavy skillet and add the onion, garlic, thyme and diced pepper. Cook, stirring often, until the mixture is wilted.

4. Chop the spinach coarsely and add it. Cook, stirring, until it is wilted. Spoon and scrape the mixture into a mixing bowl. Let cool briefly.

5. Add the liver purée, chicken, 1 cup of the bread crumbs, veal, egg and nutmeg. Add salt and pepper to taste. Blend thoroughly.

6. Preheat the oven to 400 degrees.

7. Lightly butter a 9- by 5- by 2¾-inch loaf pan. Spoon in the mixture, smooth over the top,and sprinkle with the remaining bread crumbs.

8. Cover the loaf pan closely with aluminum foil. Place the loaf pan in a larger pan and pour an inch or so of water around it. Bring the water to the boil on top of the stove. Place the pans in the oven and bake for 1 hour and 15 minutes. Remove from the oven and let cool. Chill thoroughly before unmolding.

YIELD: 10 or more servings.

Terrine de Ris de Veau avec Épinards

SWEETBREAD PÂTÉ WITH SPINACH

- 2 pounds sweetbreads
- Salt
- 2 pounds fresh spinach in bulk, or 2 10-ounce plastic bags of spinach
- 1½ pounds lean veal
- 1½ pounds lean pork
- 1 pound unsalted pork fat
- ½ cup thinly sliced shallots
- 1 teaspoon freshly ground black pepper
- ½ teaspoon ground coriander
- ½ teaspoon grated nutmeg
- ¼ teaspoon ground allspice
- ⅛ teaspoon ground cinnamon
- ⅛ teaspoon cayenne pepper
- 2 eggs
- ½ cup heavy cream
- 1 tablespoon Cognac
- ¼ pound caul fat, or ½ pound unsalted fatback thinly sliced

1. Pick over the sweetbreads to remove all outer membranes, bloody tissues and connecting tissues. Soak the sweetbreads overnight in cool water to cover.

2. Drain and put the sweetbreads in a saucepan. Add cold water to cover and salt to taste. Bring to the boil. Simmer for about 5 minutes. Drain. Chill under cold running water. Drain well. Arrange the sweetbreads on a rack and weight them down with a heavy skillet. Chill overnight.

3. Pick over the spinach to remove any tough stems or blemished leaves. Rinse the spinach well to remove all traces of sand. Bring enough water to the boil to cover the spinach when it is added. Add the spinach. Cook for 1 minute, stirring often. Drain. Let cool. Squeeze the spinach between the palms to extract most of the excess moisture. Chop the spinach. There should be 1½ to 2 cups. Set aside.

4. Cut the veal and pork into 1-inch cubes. Cut one quarter of the sweetbreads into 1-inch cubes.

5. Combine the veal, pork and cubed sweetbreads in the container of a food processor. Process well. Spoon and scrape the mixture into a large mixing bowl.

6. Cut the pork fat into cubes and add it to the container of the food processor. Add the shallots, pepper, coriander, nutmeg, allspice, cinnamon, cayenne, eggs and 1 tablespoon salt. Start processing while gradually pouring the cream through the funnel of the processor.

7. Spoon and scrape this mixture into the bowl with the pork and veal mixture. Add the Cognac and spinach and blend well with the hands.

8. Select a 12-cup earthenware terrine with a cover. Line the terrine with caul fat or thin, slightly overlapping slices of fatback. Let the caul fat or fatback slices extend over the rim of the terrine.

9. Cut the remaining sweetbreads in half lengthwise. Add a layer of the pork and veal mixture to the terrine. Arrange about one third of the sweetbreads in the center. Add a second layer of the pork and veal mixture. Add more sweetbreads. Continue making layers, ending with the pork and veal mixture.

10. With the fingers slightly moistened with water, make a smooth rounded mound of the pork and veal mixture. Bring up the overlapping edges of the caul fat or fatback slices to cover the top of the meat. Put the cover on the terrine.

11. Preheat the oven to 375 degrees.

12. Set the terrine in a larger pan of water. Bring the water to the boil on top of the stove. Place the pan holding the terrine in the oven and bake for 1 hour.

13. Reduce the oven temperature to 350 degrees. Bake for 1 hour longer.

14. Remove from the oven and take the terrine out of the pan of water. Uncover the terrine and lay a sheet of aluminum foil over it. Set a weight on top to improve its texture. Set the terrine on a rack to cool.

YIELD: 16 or more servings.

SOUPS

Yogurt and Barley Soup

- 1 quart plain yogurt
- 7 cups water
- ⅓ cup barley
- 2 tablespoons butter
- ½ cup finely chopped onion
- 6 eggs
- 2 tablespoons flour
- Salt and freshly ground white pepper to taste
- 2 tablespoons finely chopped chives
- 1 tablespoon finely chopped fresh mint
- 1 tablespoon finely chopped fresh coriander

1. Place a sieve in a mixing bowl. Line the sieve with cheesecloth that has been soaked in cold water and wrung out. Add the yogurt and let it drain for 1 hour.

2. Meanwhile, combine 3 cups of the water and the barley in a saucepan and bring to the boil. Cover closely and let simmer for 1 hour, or until the barley is tender. Drain.

3. In a mixing bowl, combine the remaining 4 cups of water and the drained yogurt. Blend well.

4. Melt the butter in a saucepan. Add the onion and cook, stirring, until it is wilted. Do not let the onion brown.

5. In a large casserole, combine the eggs and flour, stirring rapidly with a wire whisk until the mixture is smooth. The flour should not be lumpy.

6. Add the yogurt mixture and cook over very low heat for about 5 minutes, stirring rapidly with the whisk. Let simmer gently but do not boil. When the soup has thickened slightly, remove it from the heat. Add the barley and onion and stir. Add salt and pepper to taste and the chives, mint and coriander. Serve very hot or well chilled.

YIELD: 10 to 12 servings.

On a recent trip through Scotland, the soups were unfaltering in their excellence. Not the customary hearty fare, such as Scotch broth, hotchpotch or Kilmeny kail (which is made with rabbit and green vegetables), but the untraditional specialties of the house. Especially remembered and subsequently recreated in our kitchen are a splendid cream of chicken soup with bits of diced veal kidneys throughout, an uncommonly good curried cream of rice soup with diced raw apples giving it a special fillip, and most of all, perhaps, a cheese soup. To tell the truth, I have never been all that keen on cheese soups, but the one at the Ardsheal House, Kentallen of Appin, Argyll, was exceptional. The American owners of the inn, Robert and Jane Taylor, were willing to reveal their "secret." The soup is made with a blend of Cheddar and Stilton cheeses, and it is perfectly suited as the preface to a winter supper.

Cream of Chicken with Kidney Soup

- 4 tablespoons butter
- ½ cup finely chopped onion
- ½ teaspoon finely minced garlic
- 6 cups rich chicken broth (see recipe page 418)
- ½ pound skinless, boneless chicken breast
- 1 pound veal kidney
- 1 cup milk
- 5 tablespoons arrowroot or cornstarch
- 5 tablespoons water
- ¾ cup heavy cream
- Salt, if desired
- Freshly ground black pepper to taste

1. Melt 2 tablespoons of the butter in a large saucepan and add the onion and garlic. Cook, stirring, until the onion wilts.

2. Add the broth and bring to the boil.

3. Trim the veins and membranes from the chicken breast and add it to the broth. Simmer for 10 minutes. Remove the chicken and set aside. Reserve the broth.

4. Meanwhile, cut the kidney in half. Cut away the white center core. Trim the kidney well and slice it into pieces. Cut each piece into ¼-inch cubes. There should be about ⅔ cup.

5. Put the kidney pieces in a small saucepan and add cold water to cover. Bring to the boil and simmer for 30 seconds. Drain immediately.

6. Add the milk to the reserved broth and cook for 15 minutes longer. Blend the arrowroot with the water and stir it into the simmering soup. Cook until thickened.

7. Cut the chicken into very small, ¼-inch cubes.

8. Put the soup through a fine sieve, preferably the sort known in French kitchens as a chinois.

9. Reheat the soup and add the cream, chicken and kidney. Add salt and pepper to taste.

10. Just before serving, add the remaining 2 tablespoons of butter and stir until melted.

YIELD: 6 to 8 servings.

Curried Cream of Rice Soup with Apples

- 4 tablespoons butter
- 1½ cups finely chopped onion
- 1 cup finely chopped celery
- 1 teaspoon finely minced garlic
- 6 tablespoons curry powder
- 1 pound ripe tomatoes, cored and cubed, about 3 cups, or use imported canned tomatoes
- 1 bay leaf
- 2 sprigs fresh thyme, or ½ teaspoon dried
- 1 cup long-grain rice
- 7 cups rich chicken broth (see recipe page 418)
- ½ cup heavy cream
- Salt, if desired
- Freshly ground black pepper to taste
- 1½ cups peeled and cored apple cut into ¼-inch cubes

1. Melt the butter in a large saucepan and add the onion, celery and garlic. Cook, stirring, until the vegetables are wilted. Add the curry powder and cook, stirring, for about 1 minute.

2. Add the tomatoes, bay leaf, thyme and rice and stir. Bring to the boil and add the chicken broth. Return to the boil and simmer for 30 minutes, or until the rice is quite tender. Remove the bay leaf and thyme sprigs.

3. Pour the soup into the container of a food processor or blender and blend until smooth.

4. Return the soup to a saucepan and bring to the boil. Add the cream, salt and pepper and apple cubes. Serve piping hot.

YIELD: 10 or more servings.

Ardsheal House Cheese Soup

- 2 tablespoons butter
- ¾ cup finely chopped onion
- 1 teaspoon finely minced garlic
- ½ pound Stilton cheese, crumbled
- ½ pound Cheddar cheese, crumbled
- ⅓ cup flour
- 3 cups rich chicken broth (see recipe page 418)
- 1 cup heavy cream
- ⅓ cup dry white wine
- Salt, if desired
- Freshly ground black pepper to taste
- 1 bay leaf

1. Melt the butter in a saucepan and add the onion and garlic. Cook, stirring, until the vegetables are wilted.

2. Add the cheeses and sprinkle with flour, stirring. Cook, stirring, for about 2 minutes, then remove from the heat.

3. Gradually add the chicken broth, cream and wine. Add salt and pepper to taste and the bay leaf. Bring to the boil slowly. Simmer for 5 to 10 minutes. Remove the bay leaf. If desired, thin with a little milk. This soup may be reheated and thinned if desired.

YIELD: 8 servings.

Chicken and Tomato Broth with Sour Cream and Herbs

- 3 cups rich chicken broth (see recipe page 418)
- 3 cups tomato juice
- Tabasco sauce to taste
- Salt and freshly ground black pepper to taste
- Juice of ½ lemon or more to taste
- ½ cup chopped fresh parsley (see Note)
- ½ cup chopped scallions
- ¼ cup chopped, canned (or fresh) mild green chilies, optional
- Other chopped herbs if desired (see Note)
- 1 cup sour cream

1. Combine the chicken broth and tomato juice in a saucepan and bring to the boil. Add the Tabasco, salt and pepper and lemon juice. Bring to a simmer without boiling.

2. Spoon equal amounts of parsley, scallions, green chilies and other

herbs, if desired, into the bottom of each of 6 to 8 soup bowls. Pour equal portions of the soup into each bowl.

3. Beat the sour cream with salt to taste and spoon equal portions of the sour cream on top of each serving. Serve immediately.

YIELD: 6 to 8 servings.

Note: Chopped Chinese parsley, which is really fresh coriander, is excellent in this dish. Other herbs that might be added include dill and a touch of celery leaf.

The gazpacho that most Americans know, a zesty blend of tomatoes, chopped peppers, cucumbers, garlic and oil, hails from Seville. What few people in this country are aware of are the gazpachos of other regions that contain neither a speck nor a smidgen of tomatoes. These are the white gazpachos. The palate-beguiling version here was served to me in the home of Dr. Luis Casas, a Spanish physician, and his American-born wife, Penelope. Penny has subsequently written what I consider the finest and most comprehensive book on Spanish food ever published in English.

❧

Gazpacho Extremeño

WHITE GAZPACHO, ESTREMADURA STYLE

- 1 egg
- 4 slices day-old bread
- 7 tablespoons olive oil
- 2 cloves garlic, peeled and cut in half
- 1 green pepper, seeded and cut into thin strips
- 2 small or 1 large very fresh cucumber, peeled and cut into cubes
- Salt and freshly ground black pepper to taste
- ¼ teaspoon sugar
- 2 tablespoons red wine vinegar
- 2 tablespoons white tarragon vinegar
- 3 cups chilled vegetable broth (see following recipe)
- ½ cup cold water
- Finely chopped cucumber and green pepper and toasted bread croutons for garnish

1. Break the egg into the container of a food processor or electric blender. Beat until light colored.

2. Soak the bread in cold water. Squeeze to extract most of the moisture.

3. With the motor of the food processor running, add the oil to the egg, pouring it in in a thin stream. Add the bread, garlic, green pepper, cucumber, salt, pepper, sugar and the vinegars. Blend until no large pieces remain.

4. Beat in 1 cup of the broth. Hold a sieve over a bowl and pour in the soup. Strain, forcing the solid pieces through the sieve with the back of a wooden spoon. Discard the solids that will not pass through.

5. Stir in the remaining broth and the water. Add more seasonings as desired.

6. Cover and refrigerate overnight. Serve very cold, garnished with finely chopped cucumber and green pepper and toasted bread croutons.

YIELD: 6 servings.

CALDO DE LEGUMBRES

Vegetable Broth

2 tablespoons olive oil
1 onion, finely chopped
3 parsnips, scraped and cut into 1-inch lengths
3 carrots, scraped and cut into 1-inch lengths
3 small white turnips, scraped and quartered
2 celery stalks, cut into 1-inch lengths
Salt and freshly ground black pepper to taste
2 sprigs fresh parsley
¼ teaspoon dried thyme
1 bay leaf
Pinch of cayenne pepper
3 cups water

1. Heat the oil in a large saucepan. Add the onion and cook, stirring occasionally, until the onion is wilted.

2. Add the parsnips, carrots, turnips, celery, salt, pepper, parsley, thyme, bay leaf and cayenne. Stir.

3. Add the water. Cover and simmer for 1 hour. Strain and chill thoroughly.

YIELD: About 3 cups.

Avgolemono Soup with Orzo

8 cups rich chicken broth (see recipe page 418)
½ cup orzo
Salt
3 eggs
½ cup lemon juice

1. Bring the chicken broth to the boiling point. Add the orzo and cook until the orzo is tender, about 15 minutes. Add salt to taste.

2. Beat the eggs until frothy. Add the lemon juice to the beaten eggs and continue beating until the mixture thickens and is tripled or quadrupled in volume.

3. Continue beating while slowly adding 2 cups of hot chicken broth to the egg mixture. Return this mixture to the simmering chicken broth. Turn off the heat and serve immediately. Do not let the soup continue to cook after the egg mixture is added or it is apt to curdle.

YIELD: 8 servings.

Soupe aux Poireaux avec du Cari

CURRIED LEEK AND POTATO SOUP

- 4 to 8 trimmed leeks, about 1¼ pounds
- 1 small onion
- 5 medium-sized potatoes, about 1¼ pounds
- 2 tablespoons butter
- 2 tablespoons curry powder
- 4 cups water
- 3 cups rich chicken broth (see recipe page 418)
- ½ cup heavy cream
- Salt and freshly ground black pepper to taste

1. Split the leeks in half lengthwise and rinse thoroughly between the leaves to remove all traces of sand and dirt. Drain well. Cut the leeks into ½-inch cubes. There should be about 6 cups. Set aside.

2. Split the onion in half. Cut the onion halves crosswise into very thin slices. There should be about ½ cup.

3. Peel the potatoes. Split them in half. Cut the potato halves crosswise into very thin slices. There should be about 3 cups.

4. Melt the butter in a kettle and add the onion slices. Cook, stirring, until they are wilted.

5. Add the leeks and cook for about 5 minutes, stirring often. Add the curry powder and stir. Add the potatoes, water and broth and bring to the boil. Simmer for 30 minutes.

6. Pour the mixture into the container of a food processor and blend until smooth.

7. Return the mixture to the kettle. Add the cream and salt and pepper. Reheat and serve.

YIELD: 8 or more servings.

Curried Tomato Soup

- 3 pounds tomatoes, cored but not peeled
- 4 tablespoons butter
- ½ pound onions, diced, about 1¾ cups
- 1 small clove garlic, finely minced
- 2 to 3 tablespoons curry powder
- 3 cups rich chicken broth (see recipe page 418)
- 1 bay leaf
- 1 small dried hot red pepper, optional
- Salt
- ½ cup sour cream

1. Cut the tomatoes into eighths. There should be about 6 cups.

2. Melt the butter and add the onions and garlic. Cook, stirring, until the onion is wilted. Sprinkle with the curry powder and stir. Cook for about 5 minutes without browning. Add the tomatoes, broth, bay leaf and red pepper.

3. Bring to the boil and simmer, uncovered, for 20 to 30 minutes. Remove the bay leaf and hot pepper.

4. Pour half or less of the mixture into the container of a food processor. (If an electric blender is used, it will be necessary to blend even smaller portions at a time.) Process or blend thoroughly. Continue processing until all the soup is blended and smooth. As it is processed pour it into a large bowl. Add salt to taste.

5. Stir in the sour cream. Serve hot or very cold.

YIELD: 12 or more servings.

Although we have had a fair amount of success tracking down the origins of recipes and their names, we have had some difficulty with the curried cream soup dubbed Senegalese. Although the name derives from Senegal, the former French West African territory, we have been unable to find it in any French reference work. We suspect that it may even be an American creation. Whatever its origins, the soup is a delight, whether served hot or cold. The two versions that follow, each created in our kitchen in East Hampton, differ substantially in preparation and end results. Crème Senegalese I has a tomato and banana base that adds a sweet subtlety lacking in the second. But they have one thing in common: When well chilled, they are excellent, refreshing soups for hot summer days. Serve with hot, buttered garlic bread or toast and a tossed green salad.

Crème Senegalese I

CURRIED CREAM OF CHICKEN SOUP

- 2 tablespoons butter
- ½ cup chopped onion
- 1 tablespoon curry powder
- 1 cup chopped leeks
- 1 clove garlic, finely minced
- ½ cup diced bananas
- 1½ cups peeled, cored and diced apples
- 1 cup peeled, chopped tomatoes
- 1 cup peeled, cubed potatoes
- Salt and freshly ground black pepper to taste
- 4 drops Tabasco sauce, or more to taste
- 3½ cups rich chicken broth (see recipe page 418)
- 1 cup heavy cream
- ½ cup finely diced, cooked chicken breast

1. Melt the butter in a heavy casserole and add the onion. Cook, stirring, for about 1 minute. Add the curry powder and stir to coat the onion.

2. Add the leeks, garlic, bananas, apples, tomatoes, potatoes, salt and pepper and Tabasco. Stir well.

3. Add the chicken broth and simmer for 20 minutes.

4. Pour half of the mixture at a time into the container of a food processor or blender and blend well. When the soup is well blended, pour it into a bowl and chill thoroughly. When ready to serve, add the heavy cream and chicken and mix well. Serve thoroughly chilled.

YIELD: 4 to 8 servings.

Crème Senegalese II

CURRIED CREAM OF CHICKEN SOUP

- 6 leeks
- 1 pound potatoes
- 1 tart green apple
- 4 tablespoons butter
- ¾ cup finely chopped onion
- ½ teaspoon chopped garlic
- 2 tablespoons curry powder, more or less to taste
- 6 cups rich chicken broth (see recipe page 418)
- Salt and freshly ground black pepper to taste
- 1 cup heavy cream
- Tabasco sauce to taste
- ½ cup finely diced, cooked chicken breast

1. Trim off and discard the ends of the leeks. Split the leeks lengthwise and rinse them well to remove any sand. Chop the leeks. There should be about 4 cups.

2. Peel the potatoes and drop them into cold water. Slice them thinly, then cut the slices into ½-inch cubes. Let the pieces stand in cold water to cover.

3. Peel and core the apple and cut it into ½-inch cubes.

4. Melt the butter in a soup kettle and add the leeks, apple, onion and garlic. Cook until the leeks are limp. Sprinkle with the curry powder and cook, stirring, for about 5 minutes.

5. Drain the potatoes well and add them. Cook, stirring, for about 3 minutes and add the chicken broth. Simmer for 45 minutes. Add salt and pepper to taste.

6. Put the soup through a food mill, then blend it, one third at a time, in a food processor or blender. When the soup is well blended, pour it into a bowl and chill thoroughly. When ready to serve, add the heavy cream and Tabasco sauce and mix well. Add the chicken and serve thoroughly chilled.

YIELD: 8 to 12 servings.

Potage à la Bretonne

A CREAMED BRITTANY SOUP WITH LEEKS

- 1 pound dry white beans, such as Great Northern, California or Michigan pea beans
- 12 cups water
- Salt
- 1 cup chopped fresh or canned tomatoes
- ½ pound onions, thinly sliced, about 2 cups
- 2 cloves garlic, finely chopped
- 1 bay leaf
- 2 leeks, cleaned and finely chopped, about 1 cup
- 2 sprigs fresh thyme, or ½ teaspoon dried
- ½ cup heavy cream
- 4 tablespoons butter
- Freshly ground black pepper to taste

1. Place the beans in a bowl and add cold water to cover to a depth of 1 inch above the top of the beans. Soak overnight.

2. Drain the beans and put them in a kettle. Add the 12 cups of water, salt to taste, tomatoes, onions, garlic, bay leaf, leeks and thyme. Bring to the boil and simmer for about 1¼ hours, or until the beans are tender.

3. Put the bean mixture through a food mill or purée it in the container of a food processor.

4. Return the puréed mixture to a kettle and cook for 15 minutes. Add the cream and bring to the boil. Swirl in the butter and add salt and pepper to taste.

YIELD: 10 or more servings.

Cream of Carrot Soup with Dill

- 2 pounds carrots, trimmed and scraped
- 4 tablespoons butter
- ½ pound onions, finely chopped, about 1¾ cups
- 4 cups rich chicken broth (see recipe page 418)
- Salt
- 1 cup heavy cream
- 1 cup milk
- 2 tablespoons finely chopped fresh dill
- ¼ teaspoon cayenne pepper

1. Cut the carrots into ¼-inch rounds. There should be about 6 cups.

2. Melt the butter in a kettle and add the onion. Cook briefly, stirring, to wilt. Add the carrots, broth and salt to taste. Bring to the boil and simmer for 20 minutes.

3. Pour half or less of the mixture into the container of a food processor. (If a blender is used, it will be necessary to blend even smaller portions at a time.) Process or blend thoroughly. Continue processing until all the soup is blended and smooth. As it is processed, pour it into a large bowl.

4. Add the cream, milk, dill and salt to taste. Add the cayenne pepper (use less if desired). Serve hot or very cold.

YIELD: 12 servings.

Cream of Celery Soup

- 3 cups milk
- 1 cup rice
- 10 celery stalks, trimmed and cut into cubes
- 5 cups rich chicken broth (see recipe page 418)
- Salt
- ½ teaspoon ground mace or grated nutmeg
- ¼ teaspoon cayenne pepper

1. Combine the milk and rice in a saucepan and cook until the rice is quite tender and soft, about 30 minutes. Pour this into the container of a food processor or blender and blend thoroughly. Pour the mixture into a saucepan.

2. Blend the celery in a food processor or blender until coarse-fine. There should be about 2 cups.

3. Add the celery to the milk and rice mixture. Add the chicken broth, salt to taste, the mace and cayenne pepper. Simmer for about 10 minutes and serve.

YIELD: About 8 servings.

Although most people don't think of food in sociological terms, there are commonly held notions about certain foods that reflect social attitudes. Dried peas and beans, for example, are widely viewed as the food of the poor and, therefore, unsophisticated—which is nonsense.

Beans have an infinite variety and, properly cooked, their appeal can be out of the ordinary. A well-made black bean soup, properly garnished, is a delight, as are many others offered here that make for hearty winter feasting.

Black Bean Soup

- 1 pound black beans (frijoles negros), such as black turtle beans
- 2 tablespoons olive oil
- ¼ pound lean salt pork, cut into small cubes
- 2 cups finely chopped onion
- 1 tablespoon finely minced garlic
- 1½ cups finely diced green pepper
- 8 cups beef broth or water
- 1 bay leaf
- 1 teaspoon dried oregano
- 1½ pounds smoked pork hocks
- Salt and freshly ground black pepper to taste
- 1 or 2 hot dried red peppers
- 2 tablespoons wine vinegar
- ¼ cup dry sherry, optional
- *Garnishes:* Rice, chopped onion or scallion, lime slices, chopped pork hock or ham

1. Put the beans in a large bowl and add cold water to cover to about 2 inches above the top of the beans. Soak overnight.

2. Heat the oil in a kettle and add the salt pork. Cook, stirring often, until it is rendered of fat. Add the onion, garlic and green pepper. Cook until the vegetables are wilted.

3. Drain the beans and add them to the kettle. Add the beef broth (it must not be too salty).

4. Add the bay leaf and oregano, pork hocks, salt and pepper and red pepper. Bring to the boil and simmer for about 2 hours, or until the beans are quite soft.

5. Remove the pork hocks. If desired, remove the meat from the hocks and chop it finely to use as a final garnish. Or discard the hocks.

6. Pour and scrape half the bean mixture into the container of a food processor or blender. Blend to a fine purée. Return this to the soup and stir to blend. Add the vinegar and sherry. Heat thoroughly.

7. Serve, if desired, with cooked rice as a garnish to be spooned into the soup; chopped onion or scallion; lime slices to float on top of the soup, and chopped pork hock or ham.

YIELD: About 12 servings.

Ribollita means twice-cooked (actually, twice-boiled), and is a kind of minestrone. It was served to us, well chilled, on a scorching hot day at the distinguished Sabatini restaurant in Milan. One rarely thinks of bean soup as something to serve cold, but this one is delicious. And our version is cooked only once.

La Ribollita

A TUSCAN BEAN SOUP

- 2 tablespoons olive oil
- 1 cup finely chopped onion
- ½ cup finely chopped celery
- 1 clove garlic, finely minced
- 3 cups chopped leeks
- ½ pound zucchini, trimmed, unpeeled and cut into ½-inch cubes, about 2 cups
- ½ cup finely diced carrot
- ½ pound cabbage, coarsely chopped
- 2 cups chopped fresh or canned tomatoes
- 1 teaspoon finely chopped fresh rosemary
- 1 dried hot red pepper
- Salt
- 1 pound dried white pea beans, Navy beans or Michigan beans (use the no-soaking variety)
- 4 cups beef broth
- 6 cups water
- Freshly grated Parmesan cheese
- Dry toast, 1 or 2 pieces per serving, made from crusty French or Italian loaves
- 1 whole clove garlic, peeled
- Olive oil

1. Heat the 2 tablespoons of olive oil in a kettle and add the onion, celery and minced garlic. Cook briefly, stirring, and add the leeks, zucchini, carrot, cabbage, tomatoes, rosemary, red pepper and salt.

2. Cook for about 5 minutes and add the beans, broth and water. Bring to the boil. Cover and simmer for 1½ hours.

3. Purée half the soup at a time and then combine the two mixtures. The soup may be served hot at this point with grated Parmesan cheese on the side.

4. To serve the soup cold, let it cool, then refrigerate it. Prepare the dry toast and, when it is crisp, rub the toast on both sides with the whole clove of garlic. Brush liberally with olive oil. Serve the toast in the soup with a trace more olive oil poured over. Serve with grated Parmesan cheese.

YIELD: 12 or more servings.

Lamb and White Bean Soup

- 1 pound dried Great Northern beans
- 2 tablespoons butter
- 1 cup coarsely chopped onion
- 1 clove garlic, finely minced
- 2 lamb shanks, about 1 pound each
- 10 cups water
- 1½ cups peeled and diced tomatoes
- 1 bay leaf
- 6 sprigs fresh parsley tied in a bundle
- 3 sprigs fresh thyme tied in a bundle, or ½ teaspoon dried
- 2 whole cloves
- 20 whole black peppercorns
- Salt, if desired
- ¼ cup finely chopped parsley

1. Soak the beans or not according to package directions.

2. Melt the butter in a kettle and add the onion, garlic and lamb shanks. Cook, stirring the onion and turning the shanks, for about 5 minutes.

3. Drain the beans and add them to the kettle. Add the water, tomatoes, bay leaf, parsley sprigs, thyme, cloves, peppercorns and salt to taste. Bring to the boil and simmer for 2 hours.

4. Remove the lamb shanks, bay leaf and parsley and thyme sprigs.

5. Remove the skin from the shanks. Remove the meat from the bones and shred it or cut it into small bite-sized pieces. Return the meat to the soup. Reheat and serve sprinkled with chopped parsley.

YIELD: 8 or more servings.

Potage Musard

A PURÉE OF FLAGEOLETS SOUP

- 1 pound dried flageolets
- 12 cups water
- Salt
- 1 carrot, scraped but left whole
- 1 onion stuck with 2 whole cloves
- 1 bay leaf
- 2 cloves garlic, finely minced
- 2 sprigs fresh thyme, or ½ teaspoon dried
- ½ cup milk
- ½ cup heavy cream
- 4 tablespoons butter
- Freshly ground black pepper to taste
- Bread croutons

1. Put the beans in a bowl and add cold water to cover to a depth of 1 inch above the top of the beans. Soak overnight.

2. Drain the beans and put them in a kettle. Add the water, salt to taste, carrot, onion, bay leaf, garlic and thyme. Bring to the boil and simmer for about 1¼ hours, or until the beans are tender.

3. Remove and reserve 1 cup of the beans to be used as garnish.

4. Put the remaining bean mixture through a food mill or purée in a food processor. Return the puréed mixture to the kettle and add the milk, cream and reserved flageolets. Bring to the boil and swirl in the butter. Add salt and pepper to taste. Serve hot with croutons on each serving.

YIELD: 10 or more servings.

Avocado Soup

- 4 tablespoons butter
- 2 cups finely chopped onion
- 1 teaspoon finely minced garlic
- ¼ cup flour
- 4 cups rich chicken broth (see recipe page 418)
- 2 avocados
- 2 tablespoons lime juice
- 1 cup sour cream
- Salt and freshly ground black pepper to taste

1. Melt the butter in a saucepan and add the onion and garlic. Cook, stirring, until the onion is wilted.

2. Add the flour and stir. Add the broth, stirring rapidly with a wire whisk until thickened and smooth. Cook over low heat for 15 minutes.

3. Pour the mixture into the container of a food processor and blend thoroughly. Return the mixture to the saucepan.

4. Peel the avocados. Cut them in half and discard the pits. Cut the halves into cubes and toss with lime juice to prevent discoloration. There should be about 3 cups. Put the cubes into the container of a food processor and process to a fine purée. There should be about 1½ cups.

5. Stir the purée into the soup. Add the sour cream and stir to blend. Add salt and pepper to taste. Reheat gently without boiling and serve.

YIELD: 6 to 8 servings.

Soups are by far the most difficult of foods to cook well without salt. But we recently created an onion soup in which we used fish stock as a base rather than the more traditional and salty beef broth and the results were impressive. The flavor and body were produced by simply puréeing it in a food processor rather than leaving the solids in their original cooked form. And onions have an intrinsic sweetness that makes them naturally assertive.

Onion Soup with Fish Stock

- 4 pounds fish bones, preferably with head on but gills removed
- 8 cups water
- 1 cup coarsely chopped onion
- ½ cup coarsely chopped celery
- 2 bay leaves
- 10 sprigs fresh parsley
- 6 sprigs fresh thyme, or 1 teaspoon dried
- 1 clove garlic
- 12 whole black peppercorns
- 4 to 5 onions, about 2½ pounds
- 4 tablespoons butter
- 1 teaspoon finely minced garlic
- ½ teaspoon dried thyme
- ¼ cup flour
- 1 cup dry white wine
- 1 hot dried red pepper
- Freshly grated Parmesan cheese, optional

1. Combine the fish bones, water, chopped onion, celery, 1 bay leaf, parsley sprigs, thyme sprigs, clove of garlic and peppercorns in a kettle. Bring to the boil and let simmer for 20 minutes. Strain. There should be about 8 cups. Discard the solids. Set the stock aside.

2. Peel the onions and cut them into quarters. Cut the quarters crosswise into thin slices. There should be about 8 cups.

3. Melt the butter in a heavy Dutch oven or casserole and add the onions. Cook until the onions are wilted. Add the minced garlic, remaining bay leaf and the ½ teaspoon dried thyme and continue cooking, stirring often, for about 15 minutes, or until the onions are nicely caramelized without browning.

4. Sprinkle the onions with the flour, stirring to distribute it evenly. Add the wine, stirring, and the reserved fish stock. Bring to the boil and add the hot pepper. Simmer for 20 minutes.

5. Remove the hot pepper or leave it in, depending on the hotness desired. Remove the bay leaf. Put the soup through a food mill or purée it in the container of a food processor.

6. Return the soup to the saucepan and bring to the boil. Serve, if desired, with grated Parmesan cheese sprinkled over.

YIELD: 8 to 10 servings.

Soupe aux Champignons

MUSHROOM SOUP

- 4 tablespoons butter
- 1 cup coarsely chopped onion
- 1 cup finely chopped celery, optional
- 1¼ pounds mushrooms, thinly sliced, about 7 cups
- Juice of 1 lemon
- ¼ cup flour
- 6 cups rich chicken broth (see recipe page 418)
- Freshly ground black pepper to taste
- ¼ cup dry sherry

1. Melt half of the butter in a large saucepan and add the onion and celery. Cook, stirring often, for about 2 minutes. Add the mushrooms and lemon juice and stir. Cover and cook over low heat for about 15 minutes.

2. Sprinkle the mushroom mixture with the flour and stir to coat evenly. Add the broth and stir. Simmer, uncovered, for about 10 minutes.

3. Pour and scrape the mixture into the container of a food processor. Process to a fine purée. Return the mixture to a saucepan and bring to the boil. Swirl in the remaining 2 tablespoons of butter and add a generous grinding of pepper. Add the sherry and serve hot.

YIELD: 4 to 6 servings.

Spinach Soup

- 1 pound fresh spinach in bulk, or 1 10-ounce plastic bag of fresh spinach
- 2 tablespoons butter
- ½ cup finely chopped onion
- 2 tablespoons flour
- 1½ cups rich chicken broth (see recipe page 418)
- 1½ cups water
- 1 cup sour cream
- Salt and freshly ground black pepper to taste
- Pinch of ground nutmeg
- Tabasco sauce to taste

1. Pick over the spinach to remove any tough stems or blemished leaves. Rinse the spinach well to remove all traces of sand. Drain thoroughly.

2. Melt the butter in a kettle and add the onion. Cook, stirring, just until the onion is wilted and sprinkle with flour. Add the broth and water, stirring, and bring to the boil. Simmer for about 10 minutes.

3. Add the spinach and cook, stirring, for about 1 minute. Remove from the heat.

4. Put the mixture into the container of a food processor or blender and purée. Pour the mixture into a mixing bowl. Let cool, then chill. Stir in the remaining ingredients and serve cold in soup bowls or cups.

YIELD: 4 to 6 servings.

Margretha's Zucchini Soup

THE SOUP

- 3 tablespoons butter
- 2 cups thinly sliced yellow onions
- 2 tablespoons water
- 1 pound zucchini or yellow squash, scrubbed, trimmed and thinly sliced, about 4 cups
- 1 cup thinly sliced green pepper
- 1 clove garlic, finely chopped
- Salt and freshly ground black pepper to taste
- ⅓ cup finely chopped parsley
- ⅓ cup finely shredded basil
- 1 tablespoon chopped fresh tarragon
- ½ cup sour cream
- 2 cups buttermilk
- 1 tablespoon lemon juice
- ½ teaspoon sugar
- ¼ teaspoon Worcestershire sauce
- 2 teaspoons finely chopped fresh dill

THE GARNISH

1 hard-boiled egg
1 teaspoon finely chopped parsley
1 teaspoon finely chopped chives

1. Melt the butter in a kettle and add the onions. Cook, stirring, until the onions are soft, about 10 minutes. Take care that the onions do not brown.

2. Add the water, zucchini, pepper, garlic, salt and pepper. Cover and cook over high heat for 3 to 5 minutes, stirring occasionally. Reduce the heat to medium and cook, covered, for about 5 minutes. Uncover and let part of the liquid evaporate.

3. Remove from the heat. Stir in the parsley, basil and tarragon.

4. Blend the mixture in a food processor. There should be about 2 cups. Pour into a bowl and let cool.

5. Put the sour cream in another mixing bowl and add 2 cups of the purée. Add the buttermilk, lemon juice, sugar, Worcestershire sauce, dill and salt to taste. Chill thoroughly.

6. When ready to serve, put the egg through a coarse sieve or chop it finely. Add 1 teaspoon each of parsley and chives. Blend. Spoon a little of the garnish over each serving of soup.

YIELD: 8 to 12 servings.

Queue de Boeuf en Hochepot

OXTAIL SOUP

2 well-trimmed oxtails, about 1½ pounds each, and each cut into 8 crosswise sections
12 cups water
6 whole black peppercorns
1 bay leaf
½ teaspoon dried thyme
6 sprigs fresh parsley
Salt and freshly ground black pepper to taste
2 small carrots, trimmed and scraped
3 turnips, peeled
12 small white onions, peeled, about 1 cup
4 cups coarsely chopped cabbage, about ½ pound
1 cup celery, trimmed, split in half and cut into 1½-inch lengths
2 cups trimmed, rinsed leeks cut into 1-inch lengths

1. Put the oxtails in a kettle and add cold water to cover. Bring to the boil and simmer for about 1 minute. Drain. Run the oxtails under cold water until chilled.

2. Return the oxtails to a clean kettle and add the water, peppercorns, bay leaf, thyme, parsley and salt and pepper. Bring to the boil and simmer over low heat for 2½ hours.

3. Cut the carrots into 1½-inch lengths. Cut each piece lengthwise into quarters. There should be about 1½ cups.

4. Cut the turnips into pieces of a size to match that of the carrots. There should be about 1½ cups.

5. Add all of the vegetables to the kettle and cook for about 1 hour longer.

YIELD: 6 to 8 servings.

We have always believed that the seasons are as much a state of mind as they are a state of weather. We can see a robin in the snow, and suddenly it feels a bit like spring. And that means asparagus and shad are on the way.

Similarly, there is nothing by way of food that speaks to us more of summer than a piping hot bowl of fish soup. We live at the eastern end of Long Island close by the good things of the sea, creeks and bays—clams, mussels, striped bass, tilefish, bluefish and oysters. And there is no way we would rather celebrate a summer's day than by filling our kettle with a mixture of these things and sitting down with a crusty loaf of homemade French bread and a well-chilled bottle of dry white wine.

Soupe de Poisson Bourgeoise

FISH SOUP, COUNTRY STYLE

- 1 pound skinless, boneless, white-fleshed, nonoily fish, such as striped bass or tilefish
- ¼ cup olive oil
- 1 cup coarsely chopped onion
- 2 cups chopped leeks
- 1 large clove garlic, sliced
- ¾ cup coarsely chopped celery
- ¾ cup thinly sliced carrot
- 1 teaspoon loosely packed saffron stems, optional
- 4 sprigs fresh parsley
- 1 bay leaf
- 2 sprigs fresh thyme, or ½ teaspoon dried
- 1 cup chopped tomatoes, preferably fresh
- ¾ cup tomato paste
- 1 cup dry white wine
- 1 teaspoon fennel seeds
- Salt and freshly ground black pepper to taste
- 1 teaspoon hot red pepper flakes
- 6 cups fish stock (see recipe page 419)
- 1 tablespoon Pernod or Ricard
- ¼ cup finely chopped parsley

1. Cut the fish into 1-inch cubes and set aside.

2. Heat the oil in a heavy casserole and add the onion, leeks and garlic. Cook, stirring, for about 1 minute. Add the celery, carrot and saffron. Stir and cook for about 1 minute. Add the parsley sprigs, bay leaf and thyme.

3. Add the tomatoes and tomato paste. Blend well and cook for about 1 minute. Add the wine, fennel seeds, salt and pepper and pepper flakes.

4. Bring to the boil and add the fish and fish stock. Simmer for about 20 minutes.

5. Remove and discard the bay leaf and parsley sprigs.

6. Ladle the soup, 3 or 4 cups at a time, into the container of a blender or food processor. Blend. After each portion of the mixture has been processed, pour it into a casserole or large saucepan. Continue until all the soup is blended.

7. Reheat the soup. Stir in the Pernod and the chopped parsley and serve.

YIELD: 8 or more servings.

Fish Soup Valenciana

- ⅔ cup olive oil
- 2 green peppers, cored, seeded and chopped, about 2 cups
- 2½ cups finely chopped onion
- ½ cup chopped leeks, optional
- 1 teaspoon chopped fresh thyme, or ½ teaspoon dried
- 2 bay leaves
- 1½ tablespoons finely chopped garlic
- 1 teaspoon chopped stem saffron, or to taste, optional
- 1 can (2 pounds, 3 ounces) Italian peeled tomatoes
- Salt and freshly ground black pepper to taste
- 3 live lobsters, about 2 pounds each
- 30 shrimp, shelled and deveined
- 30 clams, well rinsed and drained
- 2 pounds boneless, skinless striped bass (or use the equivalent of any white, nonoily, fresh ocean fish), cut into 1½-inch cubes
- 10 cups fish stock (see recipe page 419)
- ½ pound pasta, such as spaghettini, capellini or vermicelli, broken into 3- or 4-inch lengths
- 30 mussels, well scrubbed
- Tabasco sauce to taste, optional
- 3 tablespoons Pernod or Ricard, optional

1. Heat the oil in a large, deep kettle and add the chopped green peppers, onion and leeks. Cook, stirring, for about 5 minutes. Add the thyme, bay leaves, garlic and saffron and cook, stirring, for about 5 minutes.

2. Add the tomatoes and salt and pepper and cover. Cook for about 20 minutes, stirring occasionally.

3. Meanwhile, prepare the lobsters. Plunge a knife into the midsection where the tail and main body meet to kill them instantly. Sever the tail from the body and cut the tail section into 3 or 4 crosswise pieces. Pull off and discard the tough sac near the eyes of the lobsters. Cut the body in half lengthwise, then cut each half in two. Do not remove the coral and liver, but leave them intact.

4. Add the lobster pieces to the kettle and stir. Add the shrimp, clams and fish. Add the stock and salt and pepper to taste. Cover and cook for 20 minutes.

5. Carefully remove the pieces of fish, shrimp and the tail pieces of the lobster to a large bowl. Cover with foil to keep warm.

6. Add the pasta to the kettle and cook for about 5 minutes. Add the mussels and cook, uncovered, over high heat for 15 to 20 minutes, or until the pasta has the desired degree of doneness. (Note that pasta cooked in a tomato sauce requires longer cooking to become tender than it does in boiling water.) Return the fish and seafood to the kettle and heat thoroughly. Taste for seasoning and add more salt and pepper if necessary. If you wish, add a touch of Tabasco sauce and the Pernod.

YIELD: 8 to 10 servings.

Soupe de Poisson avec Calmar

FISH SOUP WITH SQUID

- ½ pound squid, cleaned
- ¾ pound skinless, boneless monkfish
- 1 pound skinless, boneless codfish
- ¼ cup olive oil
- 2 tablespoons finely minced garlic
- 1¾ cups finely chopped onion
- 1½ cups finely diced, cleaned leeks, both white and green part
- 2 cups cubed ripe tomatoes, or use imported canned tomatoes, drained
- Salt to taste, if desired
- Freshly ground black pepper to taste
- ½ teaspoon saffron threads
- 3 tablespoons tomato paste
- ½ cup dry white wine
- 1 bay leaf
- ½ teaspoon dried thyme
- 1 teaspoon fennel seeds, crushed
- 4 cups water or unsalted fish stock (see recipe page 419)
- ½ cup finely chopped parsley
- 2 hot dried red peppers

1. Cut the body of the squid into ½-inch circles. Cut the flat portions of the squid into 1½-inch squares. Cut the tentacles into bite-sized portions. There should be about 3 cups.

2. Cut the fish into 1½-inch squares. There should be about 1½ cups monkfish, 2 to 2½ cups cod.

3. Heat the oil in a casserole or Dutch oven and add the garlic and onion. Cook, stirring, until the onion is wilted. Add the leeks and tomatoes. Bring to the boil, stirring. Add salt and pepper.

4. Add the saffron, tomato paste, wine, bay leaf, thyme and fennel seeds. Stir and bring to the boil.

5. Add the squid and monkfish and water. Add half the parsley and the red peppers. Bring to the boil and let boil for 10 minutes. The fish should boil rather than simmer. Add the cod and reduce the heat. Let the soup simmer for about 2 minutes, no longer. Serve with remaining parsley sprinkled over each serving.

YIELD: 4 or more servings.

One of our all-time favorite fish soups is called bourride. Unlike the famed bouillabaisse of Marseilles and environs, it does not contain shellfish. Another distinctive feature is its use of aïoli, a Mediterranean specialty and a sort of garlic mayonnaise. Part of this aïoli is stirred into the soup, the remainder is served on the side to be added at will.

Bourride

A FISH STEW

- 2 tablespoons olive oil
- ¾ cup finely chopped onion
- 1 cup finely chopped celery
- 1 cup finely chopped leeks
- 1 clove garlic, finely minced
- 1 teaspoon loosely packed saffron threads
- 1 bay leaf
- 1 cup dry white wine
- ¾ pound small potatoes, peeled and cut into ¼-inch rounds (there should be about 2 cups)
- 4 cups fish stock (see recipe page 419)
- Salt and freshly ground black pepper to taste
- ⅛ teaspoon cayenne pepper
- 2 cups aïoli (see following recipe)
- 2 pounds white-fleshed fish fillets from nonoily fish
- 1 loaf French bread
- 1 whole clove garlic, peeled

1. Heat the oil in a kettle and add the onion. Cook, stirring, until the onion is wilted. Add the celery, leeks, minced garlic, saffron, bay leaf, wine, potatoes, fish stock, salt and pepper and cayenne. Bring to the boil and simmer for 30 minutes.

2. While the soup cooks, prepare the aïoli.

3. Cut the fish fillets into 2-inch cubes and arrange them in one layer in a large casserole.

4. Put the soup through a food mill, pressing to purée the vegetables. Pour the soup over the fish and cover. Bring to the boil and simmer for about 3 minutes.

5. Meanwhile, rub the outside of the French bread with the whole clove of garlic. Cut the bread into 12 or 14 very thin slices, ¼ inch or less thick. Arrange the slices in a baking dish and place under the broiler. Brown on both sides.

6. When the fish is done, use a slotted spoon and transfer the pieces to a heated round or oval serving dish.

7. Spoon half the prepared aïoli into a serving dish. Spoon the remaining aïoli into a saucepan. While stirring the aïoli vigorously with a wire whisk, add the hot soup. Heat thoroughly, but do not boil or the soup will curdle.

8. Arrange the toast over the fish and pour the hot soup over all. Serve the soup with the remaining aïoli on the side.

YIELD: 8 servings.

AÏOLI

A Garlic Mayonnaise

- 3 egg yolks
- Salt and freshly ground black pepper to taste
- 1 tablespoon prepared mustard, preferably imported Dijon or Düsseldorf
- 1 tablespoon finely minced garlic, or more according to taste
- 1 tablespoon white wine vinegar
- 2 cups olive oil
- Tabasco sauce, optional

1. Put the yolks in a mixing bowl and add the salt and pepper, mustard, garlic and vinegar.

2. Start beating with a wire whisk or an electric beater and gradually add the oil. When the mixture starts to thicken, the oil may be added in ever increasing quantities. Continue beating until all the oil is used. Add Tabasco sauce to taste. If a thinner mayonnaise is desired, beat in a teaspoon of cold water.

YIELD: About 2 cups.

Lobster is one of the most prized ingredients of nouvelle cuisine, and plays a prominent role in this pot au feu of seafood. The recipe is our adaptation of a dish prepared by Maurice Cazalis of the Henri IV restaurant in Chartres, one of the practitioners of the new cuisine. Although the consommé and soup are time consuming, the dish is well worth the effort.

Pot au Feu de Fruits de Mer

SEAFOOD SOUP

- 2 live lobsters, about 2½ pounds each
- 8 cups lobster consommé (see following recipe)
- 6 very small white onions
- 1 cup water
- 1 large carrot
- 2 small white turnips
- 6 littleneck or cherrystone clams
- ½ pound skinless, boneless fish fillets, preferably monkfish, striped bass or red snapper, cut into 1½-inch cubes
- 12 mussels, well scrubbed
- 18 medium-sized shrimp, about ¾ pound, shelled and deveined
- 1 cup leeks cut into very fine 2-inch shreds
- 6 thin slices French bread
- 1 or 2 tablespoons olive oil
- ½ cup sauce rouille (see following recipe)

1. To prepare the soup, you will have to prepare a clear lobster consommé made from the carcass of the lobsters. You will use the tails and claws of the lobsters in the finished dish. Begin by removing the claws and tails of the lobsters and refrigerate them while you prepare the consommé, which requires about 3 hours.
2. Peel the onions.
3. Put 1 cup of consommé and 1 cup of water into a small casserole or kettle and add the onions. Cover and cook for about 5 minutes.
4. Meanwhile, trim and peel the carrot and cut it into 1½-inch lengths. Cut each piece lengthwise into quarters. Shape the pieces into long ovals or batons. You will need 12 pieces.
5. Pare the turnips; cut each piece lengthwise into 6 pieces. Trim each piece into long oval or baton shapes.
6. Add the carrots, turnips, clams, fish and lobster tails and claws to the casserole and, at the boil, cook for 5 minutes.
7. Add the mussels. Cook for 2 minutes.
8. Remove the lobster tails and claws from the casserole and set aside.

Add the shrimp to the casserole and cook for 2 minutes. Remove the casserole from the heat.

9. Remove the clams and mussels. Remove the meat from the clams and mussels. Discard the shells.

10. Meanwhile, put the remaining 7 cups of consommé into another kettle or casserole and bring to the boil. Add the leek shreds. Return to the boil and add the clam and mussel meat.

11. Transfer the onions, carrots, turnips, fish, shrimp and the liquid in which they cooked into the casserole with the leeks.

12. Remove the meat from the lobster tails and claws. Cut each tail and claw crosswise into three pieces. Add them to the casserole with the other seafood.

13. Brush each bread slice with equal amounts of olive oil. Run under the broiler until browned on both sides.

14. Ladle equal portions of soup and seafood into 6 hot soup bowls. Top each serving with a piece of toast. Serve the sauce rouille on the side, to be ladled onto the toast.

YIELD: 6 servings.

CONSOMMÉ DE HOMARD

Lobster Consommé

- 2 lobster carcasses (see recipe for pot au feu, step 1)
- 8 cups water
- 4 cups chicken broth
- 1 cup dry white wine
- 1 bay leaf
- 3 sprigs fresh thyme, or ½ teaspoon dried
- 12 whole black peppercorns
- 4 egg whites
- 6 sprigs fresh parsley with stems, coarsely chopped
- ¼ cup coarsely chopped carrot
- ¼ cup coarsely chopped celery
- 1 cup coarsely chopped tomatoes
- 1 cup coarsely chopped leeks
- ½ cup coarsely chopped onion
- ¼ teaspoon cayenne pepper
- ½ cup tomato paste
- Salt to taste

1. Put the lobster carcasses in a large saucepan or small kettle. Add the water, broth, wine, bay leaf, thyme and peppercorns.

2. Bring to the boil and simmer for about 2 hours. Strain and set aside to cool.

3. Put the egg whites, parsley, carrot, celery, tomatoes, leeks, onion, cayenne pepper and tomato paste in a kettle. Beat until the whites are frothy. Add the cooled liquid and salt to taste. Bring slowly to the boil, stirring gently and often.

4. When the mixture comes to a full rolling boil, reduce the heat and simmer for about 15 minutes.

5. Line a sieve with a clean cotton cloth or a double thickness of cheesecloth wrung out in cold water. Strain the consommé through it. Discard solids.

YIELD: 8 cups.

SAUCE ROUILLE

A Spicy Mayonnaise

- 1 egg yolk
- 1 teaspoon finely chopped garlic
- ½ teaspoon red wine vinegar
- ¼ teaspoon paprika
- Salt and freshly ground black pepper to taste
- ¼ cup olive oil

1. Put the egg yolk, garlic, vinegar, paprika and salt and pepper in a bowl.

2. Stir rapidly with a wire whisk while gradually adding the oil. Beat until thickened like mayonnaise.

YIELD: About ½ cup.

Brodetto alla Triestina

TRIESTE-STYLE FISH STEW

- 1½ pounds cleaned, whole sea bass, without the head, tail and fins
- 2 pounds cleaned, whole striped bass, without the head, tail and fins
- ¾ pound cleaned, ready-to-cook squid
- 2 8-ounce lobster tails in the shell
- ½ cup olive oil
- 2 cups finely chopped onion
- ½ cup red wine vinegar
- 4 cups fish stock (see recipe page 419)
- 2 cups marinara sauce (see recipe page 410)
- Salt, if desired
- Freshly ground black pepper to taste
- 6 medium-sized shrimp, shelled and deveined
- 12 littleneck clams
- 14 mussels, scrubbed
- Polenta (see recipe page 384)

1. Put the sea bass on a flat surface and cut it crosswise into 1½-inch pieces. Repeat with the striped bass. Set both fish aside.

2. Cut the cleaned squid into 1-inch lengths. Set aside.

3. Cut each lobster tail crosswise into 3 or 4 pieces.

4. Heat the oil in a very large casserole with a heavy bottom and, when it is hot and almost smoking, add the onion. Cook, stirring constantly, until the onion is golden brown, about 10 minutes. Take care not to burn the onion.

5. Arrange the pieces of sea bass, striped bass and lobster tails in the casserole. Cook over high heat for about 3 minutes, turning the pieces occasionally. Add the vinegar and stir. Cover and cook for about 1 minute.

6. Add the fish stock and bring to the simmer. Cover and cook for about 5 minutes.

7. Add the marinara sauce and cover. Cook for 3 minutes.

8. Add the squid, salt and pepper to taste and partly cover. Cook for 8 minutes.

9. Add the shrimp, clams and mussels and cook for 5 minutes longer, or just until the mussels and clams open. Serve with portions of polenta.

YIELD: 6 to 8 servings.

Bisque de Homard

LOBSTER BISQUE

3 lobster carcasses (see recipe for poached lobster page 295)
2 tablespoons olive oil
2 tablespoons butter
1 cup coarsely chopped onion
¼ cup thinly sliced shallots
¾ cup coarsely chopped carrot
1 cup coarsely chopped celery with a few leaves included
1 bay leaf
1 teaspoon finely chopped garlic
½ teaspoon dried thyme
12 whole black peppercorns
1 dried hot red pepper
⅓ cup flour
6 tablespoons Cognac
2 cups dry white wine
3 cups chopped ripe tomatoes, or use 1 28-ounce can tomatoes with tomato paste
4 cups water
4 sprigs fresh parsley
½ cup rice
Salt and freshly ground black pepper to taste
1½ cups heavy cream

1. Chop and cut the carcasses (including the body, claw and tail portions) into 1- or 2-inch pieces. Set these aside along with any bits and pieces of lobster flesh that are leftover or that may cling to the shells.

2. Heat the oil and butter in a kettle and add the onion, shallots, carrot, celery, bay leaf, garlic, thyme and peppercorns. Cook, stirring often, until the vegetables are wilted.

3. Add the lobster carcasses and the hot red pepper. Sprinkle with the flour and stir to distribute it evenly.

4. Add 4 tablespoons of the Cognac, the wine, tomatoes, water and parsley. Bring to the boil and add the rice. Cover and simmer for 20 minutes.

5. Put the mixture, solids and all, through a food mill (not a food processor). Press well to extract as much liquid as possible from the solids. It will probably be necessary to do this in several stages. Discard the solids after they have been pressed.

6. Pour the liquid bisque into the container of a food processor or blender. Process until as smooth as possible. Pour the mixture into a large saucepan or kettle. Add salt and pepper to taste and the cream. Bring to the boil and add the remaining Cognac. Serve.

YIELD: 8 cups.

One of the great gustatorial glories of the East Coast is that extraordinary bivalve known as the quahog, the American Indian name for clam. There are three kinds of quahogs: littlenecks, which are three to four years old; cherrystones, next in size and five years old, and chowder clams, the oldest and largest. A superb clam and spinach soup that uses cherrystones was created by Steve Busby, a pitcher for the Kansas City Royals, and Sheridan Blackman, a fine cook from Shawnee Mission, Kansas, for a March of Dimes benefit that we judged.

Spinach and Clam Soup

- 36 cherrystone clams
- ½ pound fresh spinach
- ¼ pound salt pork, cut into ½-inch cubes
- 1 cup finely chopped onion
- 1 clove garlic, finely minced
- 4 anchovy fillets, chopped
- 8 tablespoons butter
- 2 tablespoons flour
- 4 cups rich chicken broth (see recipe page 418)
- 1 cup heavy cream
- Salt and freshly ground black pepper to taste

1. Wash the clams well. Put them in a kettle and add 2 cups water. Cover closely and bring to the boil. Cook until the clams open. Drain, reserving the clam broth if desired (see Note). Let the clams stand until cool enough to handle.

2. Meanwhile, bring enough water to the boil to cover the spinach when added. Add the spinach and cook for about 30 seconds. Drain. When cool enough to handle, press the spinach between the hands to extract most of the moisture. Chop the spinach coarsely and set aside.

3. Heat the salt pork in a small skillet until it is rendered of fat. Scoop out and discard the pork solids. Pour off all but 1 tablespoon of the fat. Add the onion and garlic and cook until the onion is wilted. Add the chopped anchovies and stir. Heat briefly and set aside.

4. Melt the butter in a casserole and add the flour, stirring with a wire whisk. Cook, stirring, over low heat for about 2 minutes. Do not brown. Add the chicken broth gradually, stirring constantly with the wire whisk. Stir in the onion and anchovy mixture.

5. Chop the clams finely. This may be done in a food processor but do not overprocess. Add the clams to the soup. Add the spinach, cream and salt and pepper. Bring to the simmer and serve piping hot.

YIELD: 6 to 8 servings.

Note: Two cups of the clam broth may be substituted for 2 cups of chicken broth if a stronger clam flavor is desired in the soup. You may also combine equal parts of leftover clam broth with chicken broth, heat and sprinkle with chopped chives and chopped parsley. This makes an excellent clear chicken and clam soup.

Stuffed Squid Soup, Thai Style

- 8 to 10 squid, about 1½ pounds
- ¼ pound unsalted pork fat, cut into ½-inch cubes
- 2 teaspoons small dried shrimp (see Note)
- ¼ pound skinless, boneless chicken thigh
- 4 teaspoons finely chopped shallots
- 2 teaspoons finely chopped ginger
- ½ teaspoon freshly ground dried coriander seeds
- 1 teaspoon water
- 4 teaspoons fish sauce (see Note)
- 6 cups rich chicken broth (see recipe page 418)
- Fresh coriander leaves for garnish

1. Clean the squid well, removing the interior cartilage and soft matter. Pull off the skin with the fingers while washing the squid under cold running water. Set the squid aside.

2. Put the pork fat in the freezer until it is almost but not quite frozen.

3. Put the dried shrimp in a mortar and grind thoroughly with a pestle. Set aside.

4. Put the chicken meat into the container of a food processor and process until coarse-fine. Add the partly frozen pork fat and continue processing until finely chopped.

5. Spoon the chicken and pork fat mixture into a bowl. Add the ground shrimp, shallots, ginger, coriander seeds, water and fish sauce. Blend well.

6. Stuff each squid with equal portions of the mixture. Secure the openings with toothpicks.

7. Put the broth in a large saucepan or kettle and bring it to the boil. Add the stuffed squid to the broth and simmer for 20 minutes.

8. Remove the squid and let them cool. Remove the toothpicks and cut the squid crosswise into rings about ¼ inch thick. Reheat the broth, add the stuffed squid rings. Top each serving with fresh coriander leaves.

YIELD: 8 or more servings.

Note: Dried shrimp and fish sauce, called nuoc mam or nam pla, are available in Oriental groceries and supermarkets.

Thai Shrimp Soup

- 1¼ pounds raw, unshelled shrimp, about 40
- 10 cups water
- 1 medium-sized onion, unpeeled and cut in half
- Salt to taste
- 5 lime leaves, soaked overnight in cold water (see Note)
- 2 tablespoons dried lemon grass, soaked overnight in cold water (see Note)
- ½ pound mushrooms, preferably very small button mushrooms
- 2 tablespoons shrimp paste with bean oil (see Note)
- 2 tablespoons Thai chili in oil (see Note)
- ¼ teaspoon monosodium glutamate, optional
- 6 tablespoons lemon juice
- 5 tablespoons fish sauce (see Note)
- 6 sprigs or more fresh coriander leaves

1. Peel the shrimp but leave the last tail segment intact. Save the shells. Set the shrimp aside.

2. Combine the shells, water and onion in a saucepan. Bring to the boil and cook, uncovered, for about 15 minutes. Strain the liquid. Discard the solids.

3. Pour the strained liquid into a kettle. Add salt to taste.

4. Add the drained lime leaves and drained lemon grass. Simmer for 15 minutes.

5. If small mushrooms are used, leave them whole. Otherwise, slice or quarter them and add them to the kettle.

6. Blend the shrimp paste, chili in oil, monosodium glutamate and lemon juice in a small bowl. Add it to the soup. Add the fish sauce and shrimp. Bring to the boil and simmer for about 2 minutes.

7. Add the fresh coriander leaves and simmer about 1 minute longer. Serve hot.

YIELD: 6 to 8 servings.

Note: All the foreign ingredients necessary for this soup can be found in Oriental groceries and supermarkets. Fish sauce, which is essence of anchovy, is called nuoc mam or nam pla.

EGGS AND LUNCHEON DISHES

THERE are some foods for which we have an unabashed enthusiasm, and one of them is stuffed eggs.

The stuffed eggs of our childhood were, more often than not, deviled, which is to say flavored with mustard, Worcestershire sauce and a dash or two of Tabasco, perhaps.

We still have a fancy for those deviled eggs, but our taste overall is a bit more sophisticated now. We recently created several luncheon dishes based on eggs stuffed with a mushroom filling, topped with a sauce of one sort or another and then baked. The flavors included a dandy provençale sauce made with tomatoes and mushrooms, plus, of course, a touch of garlic; a chicken in cream sauce with a bit of nutmeg, and cubed shrimp in a light curry sauce containing a little yogurt.

We might note that the basic recipe for eggs stuffed with mushrooms is delicious served cold and unsauced.

Les Oeufs Farcis aux Champignons

MUSHROOM-STUFFED EGGS

- ¼ pound mushrooms
- 2 tablespoons butter
- 2 tablespoons finely chopped onion
- 2 tablespoons finely chopped shallots
- Juice of ½ lemon
- 2 tablespoons heavy cream
- 8 hard-boiled eggs, peeled and split in half
- 2 tablespoons prepared mustard, preferably imported Dijon or Düsseldorf
- 3 tablespoons finely chopped parsley
- Salt to taste, if desired
- Freshly ground black pepper to taste

1. Slice the mushrooms and chop them as finely as possible. This may be done in a food processor after slicing.

2. Melt the butter in a small skillet and add the onion and shallots. Cook, stirring, until they are wilted. Add the mushrooms and lemon juice. Cook, stirring, for about 1 minute.

3. Add the cream and continue cooking for about 2 minutes. There should be about ½ cup of the mushroom mixture.

4. Put the egg yolks through a fine sieve into a mixing bowl. Set the whites aside.

5. Add the mushroom mixture, mustard, parsley, salt and pepper to the sieved egg yolks. Blend well. Stuff each egg half with an equal portion of the stuffing and set aside.

6. Serve the stuffed eggs hot, topped with a sauce and baked according to the following recipes. Or serve them cold, each simply garnished with a rolled anchovy fillet, half a stuffed olive or a small morsel of sardine.

YIELD: 16 stuffed egg halves.

Les Oeufs Farcis Sauce Provençale

BAKED STUFFED EGGS WITH TOMATO SAUCE

- 16 mushroom-stuffed, hard-boiled egg halves (see preceding recipe)
- 3 tablespoons butter
- ½ cup finely chopped onion
- ½ teaspoon finely minced garlic
- 1 tablespoon cornstarch or arrowroot
- ¼ pound mushrooms, thinly sliced, about 1½ cups
- 1 cup imported canned tomatoes
- ½ cup fresh or canned chicken broth
- Salt to taste, if desired
- Freshly ground black pepper to taste
- 2 tablespoons finely chopped parsley
- ½ bay leaf
- 2 sprigs fresh thyme, or ½ teaspoon dried

1. Prepare the stuffed eggs.

2. Preheat the oven to 400 degrees.

3. Use 1 tablespoon of the butter to grease 4 individual ramekins, each large enough to hold 4 stuffed egg halves. Arrange 4 stuffed egg halves, stuffed side up, in each ramekin. Set aside.

4. Melt the remaining 2 tablespoons of butter in a saucepan and add the onion and garlic. Cook, stirring, until they are wilted. Sprinkle with cornstarch and stir to blend. Add the mushrooms and cook until they are wilted.

5. Add the tomatoes and broth, stirring. Bring to the boil and add the salt, pepper, parsley, bay leaf and thyme. Simmer for about 10 minutes.

6. Place the ramekins in the oven and bake the stuffed eggs for 5 minutes.

7. Spoon equal portions of the sauce over the stuffed eggs and serve hot.

YIELD: 4 servings.

Les Oeufs Farcis aux Crevettes à l'Indienne

BAKED STUFFED EGGS IN CURRIED SHRIMP SAUCE

- 16 mushroom-stuffed, hard-boiled egg halves (see recipe page 77)
- 4 tablespoons butter
- ¼ cup finely chopped onion
- 2 tablespoons curry powder
- 2 tablespoons flour
- 1 cup fish stock, or use bottled clam juice
- Salt to taste, if desired
- Freshly ground black pepper to taste
- ¼ cup heavy cream
- ½ cup plain yogurt
- ¼ cup chopped chutney
- ¾ pound fresh raw shrimp, peeled and deveined

1. Prepare the stuffed eggs.

2. Preheat the oven to 400 degrees.

3. Use 1 tablespoon of the butter to grease 4 individual ramekins, each large enough to hold 4 stuffed egg halves. Arrange 4 stuffed egg halves, stuffed side up, in each ramekin. Set aside.

4. Melt 2 tablespoons of the butter in a saucepan and add the onion. Cook, stirring, until the onion is wilted. Sprinkle with curry powder and flour and stir with a wire whisk. Add the stock, stirring rapidly with the whisk. When blended and smooth, add the salt, pepper, cream, yogurt and chutney. Bring to the boil.

5. Cut the shrimp into ½-inch cubes.

6. Melt the remaining 1 tablespoon of butter in a small saucepan and add the shrimp pieces. Cook, stirring, for about 1 minute, or until the shrimp pieces lose their raw look.

7. Add the shrimp to the curry sauce.

8. Place the ramekins in the oven and bake the stuffed eggs for 5 minutes.

9. Spoon equal portions of the hot shrimp sauce over the stuffed eggs and serve.

YIELD: 4 servings.

Les Oeufs Farcis à la Reine

BAKED STUFFED EGGS WITH CHICKEN CREAM SAUCE

- 16 mushroom-stuffed, hard-boiled egg halves (see recipe page 77)
- 3 tablespoons butter
- 3 tablespoons flour
- 1¼ cups fresh or canned chicken broth
- Salt to taste, if desired
- Freshly ground black pepper to taste
- ⅛ teaspoon grated nutmeg
- ½ cup heavy cream
- Pinch of cayenne pepper
- 1 teaspoon finely chopped parsley
- 1 teaspoon finely chopped chives, optional
- Juice of ½ lemon
- 1½ cups skinless, boneless breast of chicken cut into ½-inch cubes

1. Prepare the stuffed eggs.

2. Preheat the oven to 400 degrees.

3. Use 1 tablespoon of the butter to grease 4 individual ramekins, each large enough to hold 4 stuffed egg halves. Arrange 4 stuffed egg halves, stuffed side up, in each ramekin. Set aside.

4. Melt the remaining 2 tablespoons of butter in a saucepan and add the flour, stirring with a wire whisk. Add the broth, stirring rapidly with the whisk. When the mixture is blended and smooth, add the salt, pepper and nutmeg. Stir in the cream, cayenne pepper, parsley, chives and lemon juice. Add the chicken and bring to the boil.

5. Place the ramekins in the oven and bake the stuffed eggs for 5 minutes.

6. Spoon equal portions of the sauce over the stuffed eggs and serve hot.

YIELD: 4 servings.

Note: If desired, sprinkle each serving with a little grated Parmesan cheese and heat briefly under the broiler.

Eggs with Sauce Soubise

- 8 eggs
- 2 onions, about ¾ pound
- 2 tablespoons butter
- 3 tablespoons flour
- 1 cup milk
- ⅛ teaspoon grated nutmeg
- ¼ cup heavy cream
- 2 tablespoons finely chopped parsley

1. Put the eggs in a saucepan and add cold water to cover. Bring to the boil and simmer for about 12 minutes, or until hard cooked.

2. Meanwhile, peel the onions and chop them finely.

3. Melt the butter in a heavy saucepan and add the onions. Cook over low heat, stirring often, for about 2 minutes. Cover closely and cook for about 10 minutes, or until tender without browning. The onions should take on no color whatever. Sprinkle with flour and stir to distribute it evenly. Add the milk, stirring rapidly. Add the nutmeg. Simmer for about 15 minutes.

4. Put the sauce through a fine sieve or pureé it in a food processor. There should be about 2 cups. Return the sauce to the saucepan. Add the cream and bring to the boil.

5. Peel the eggs and put them through an egg slicer, cutting them crosswise. Put the eggs in a small casserole and spoon the sauce over all.

6. Serve hot on toast points or with rice. Serve sprinkled with finely chopped parsley.

YIELD: 4 to 6 servings.

❧

Eggs in Sherry Cream Sauce

- 4 large eggs
- ½ pound lean bacon
- ¼ pound mushrooms
- 4 tablespoons butter
- 6 tablespoons flour
- 2½ cups milk
- Salt and freshly ground black pepper to taste
- ¼ teaspoon grated nutmeg
- ⅛ teaspoon cayenne pepper
- ½ cup grated Swiss or Gruyère cheese
- 2 tablespoons dry sherry
- ½ cup chopped parsley

1. Put the eggs in a saucepan and add cold water to cover. Bring to the boil and simmer for 12 minutes. Drain the eggs and run them under cold water.

2. Crack the eggs and peel them. Cut the eggs in half and chop them on a flat surface. Put the chopped eggs in a mixing bowl and cover. Set aside.

3. Cook the bacon until browned and quite crisp. Drain on paper toweling. Let cool. Chop the bacon finely. There should be about ½ cup. Set aside.

4. Rinse the mushrooms and pat them dry. Slice them thinly and then chop them finely.

5. Melt the butter in a saucepan and add the mushrooms. Cook, stirring, until the mushrooms give up their liquid. Continue cooking until the liquid has evaporated.

6. Sprinkle the mushrooms with the flour and stir. Add the milk and cook, stirring with a wire whisk, until it becomes thick and smooth. Continue cooking for 5 minutes, stirring often.

7. Add the salt and pepper, nutmeg and cayenne. Remove from the heat and stir in the cheese. Add the sherry.

8. When ready to serve, fold in the chopped eggs. Spoon the mixture into an oval platter, then sprinkle with the chopped bacon and chopped parsley. Serve hot or lukewarm.

YIELD: 4 to 6 servings.

A properly prepared omelet is a joy to the eye and an absolute pleasure to the palate. It is infinite in the number of flavors with which it can be made, ranging from all manner of vegetables to jams or jellies. We are of the school that much prefers the savory omelet to the sweet.

Omelette Nature

BASIC OMELET

- 3 eggs, well beaten
- Salt, if desired
- Freshly ground black pepper to taste
- 1½ teaspoons butter

1. Combine the eggs, salt and pepper in a mixing bowl.

2. Place an 8- or 9-inch well-cured metal or Teflon omelet pan on the stove and heat well. Add the butter and, when melted, add the egg mixture and start cooking, shaking the skillet and simultaneously stirring rapidly with a fork, holding the tines parallel to the bottom of the skillet. Try not to scrape the surface.

3. Cook to the desired degree of doneness. Ideally, in the minds of most fine cooks, the omelet must remain runny in the center, yet firm on the bottom. Remember that the omelet will continue to cook until the moment it is turned out of the pan and that it cooks quickly.

4. When the omelet is properly done, lift the handle of the skillet with the left hand. Knock the omelet pan on the surface of the stove so that the

omelet jumps to the bottom curve of the pan. Use the fork and quickly fold the omelet from the top down. Let the omelet stand as briefly as possible over high heat until it browns on the bottom. Turn it out neatly onto a hot serving plate, seam side down.

YIELD: 1 serving.

OMELETTE FOURRÉE

Filled Omelet

Prepare the omelet exactly as for the omelette nature. But in step 4, when the omelet is ready to be folded, add a spoonful or so of any desired filling and then fold. Turn out as indicated.

Classically, if one wants to garnish a filled omelet, one makes a slight gash on the top of the omelet once it is turned out. Spoon into the gash a bit of the filling used for the interior of the omelet.

CREVETTES AU PAPRIKA ET À LA CRÈME AIGRE

Shrimp in Paprika and Sour Cream Sauce

- ½ pound raw shrimp in the shell
- 1 tablespoon butter
- 2 tablespoons finely chopped shallots
- 2 tablespoons dry sherry
- Salt, if desired
- Freshly ground black pepper to taste
- 1 tablespoon paprika, preferably mild Hungarian
- ½ cup sour cream
- 1 tablespoon finely chopped fresh dill

1. Peel and devein the shrimp. Cut them into ½-inch cubes.

2. Melt the butter in a small skillet and add the shallots. Cook briefly and add the wine. Cook until the wine has almost evaporated. Add the shrimp, salt, pepper and paprika. Cook, stirring, for about 1 minute.

3. Add the sour cream and cook just until the cream is piping hot without boiling. Stir in the dill. Use as a filling for omelets.

YIELD: 4 servings.

FOIES DE VOLAILLE AU MADÈRE

Chicken Livers in Madeira Wine Sauce

- ½ pound chicken livers
- 4 tablespoons corn oil
- Salt, if desired
- Freshly ground black pepper to taste
- 2 tablespoons butter
- 2 tablespoons finely chopped shallots
- ¼ cup Madeira wine

1. Pick over the livers. Cut away and discard any connective tissue. Cut the livers in half.

2. Heat the oil in a skillet and add the livers, salt and pepper. Cook for about 1 minute and drain well. Pour off all fat from the skillet and wipe it out well with paper toweling. Transfer the livers to a very small saucepan.

3. Melt 1 tablespoon of the butter in the skillet and add the shallots. Cook, stirring, until they are wilted. Add the Madeira and cook until the wine is reduced by half. Pour this over the livers. Heat the livers in the sauce and swirl in the remaining tablespoon of butter. Use as a filling for omelets.

YIELD: 4 servings.

SAUCE PROVENÇALE

- 2 tablespoons olive oil
- 1 cup thinly sliced, halved onions
- 1 cup thinly sliced cored and seeded green pepper
- 1 tablespoon finely minced garlic
- 1 cup drained imported canned tomatoes
- ¼ teaspoon dried thyme
- 1 bay leaf
- Salt, if desired
- Freshly ground black pepper to taste

1. Heat the oil in a small skillet and add the onions, green pepper and garlic. Cook, stirring often, for about 2 minutes.

2. Add the tomatoes, thyme, bay leaf, salt and pepper. Cook, stirring, for about 1 minute. Cover closely and cook for about 5 minutes longer. Uncover and cook until the tomato sauce is thickened, 1 minute or less. Use as a filling for omelets.

YIELD: 4 servings.

Omelette Joinville

TOMATO, NOODLE AND SPINACH OMELET

- 3 tablespoons butter
- 1 cup peeled and chopped tomatoes
- Salt, if desired
- Freshly ground black pepper to taste
- ¾ cup fine noodles
- ½ pound spinach
- ½ cup water
- 6 eggs
- ¼ cup finely chopped parsley

1. Melt 1 tablespoon of the butter in a small saucepan and add the tomatoes. Add the salt and pepper. Simmer for about 15 minutes.

2. Meanwhile, drop the noodles into boiling salted water and simmer until tender. Drain and set aside.

3. Pick over the spinach. Remove and discard any tough stems. Rinse thoroughly. Combine the spinach and ½ cup water in a large saucepan and bring to the boil. Stir the spinach until it wilts. Cover and cook for about 1 minute. Drain well and let cool. Press the spinach between the hands to extract most of the moisture. Chop the spinach coarsely and set it aside.

4. Beat the eggs in a mixing bowl and add salt and pepper to taste. Add the parsley.

5. Melt the remaining 2 tablespoons of butter in an omelet pan or Teflon skillet and add the spinach and noodles. Pour the eggs over and cook the omelet, shaking the skillet while stirring with a fork. When the omelet is done on the bottom and sufficiently cooked inside, spoon the tomatoes onto the center. Fold the omelet over and turn it out onto a hot oval platter.

YIELD: 2 servings.

Omelette Savoyarde

CHEESE AND POTATO OMELET

- 2 medium-sized potatoes, about ¼ pound
- 4 tablespoons peanut, vegetable or corn oil
- Salt, if desired
- Freshly ground black pepper to taste
- 6 eggs
- ¾ cup finely diced Gruyère or Swiss cheese
- 2 tablespoons chopped chives, optional
- 2 tablespoons butter

1. Peel the potatoes and cut them into very thin slices.

2. Heat the oil in a skillet and add the potatoes. Add salt and pepper. Cook, shaking the skillet and redistributing the potatoes so that they cook on all sides, for about 10 minutes, or until golden brown on the bottom and top. Drain well.

3. Beat the eggs in a mixing bowl and add salt and pepper to taste, the cheese, potatoes and chives.

4. Melt the butter in an omelet pan or Teflon skillet and add the egg mixture, stirring. Cook until the omelet is done on the bottom. Invert the omelet onto a hot round platter and cut into wedges to serve.

YIELD: 2 to 4 servings.

Crêpes are, without question, one of the finest creations of Western cuisine, admirable on many counts. Primary among these is the contrast between their texture and flavor and whatever they are allied with—sweet crêpes with the likes of a Grand Marnier sauce or savory crêpes to be filled with countless foods in cream and other sauces. There are many ways to fold crêpes. They may be folded in quarters to make a fan shape. They may be rolled cigar shape with the filling in the center. And they may be folded into a lily shape, with the top open slightly and the bottom pointed.

Basic Crêpes

1 egg
½ cup flour
Salt to taste, if desired
½ cup plus 2 tablespoons milk
2 tablespoons butter

1. Put the egg, flour and salt into a mixing bowl and start beating and blending with a wire whisk. Add the milk, stirring.

2. Melt 1 tablespoon of the butter in a 7- or 8-inch Teflon pan. When it is melted, pour the butter into the crêpe batter.

3. Line a mixing bowl with a sieve and pour the batter into the sieve. Strain the batter, pushing any solids through with a rubber spatula.

4. Melt the remaining tablespoon of butter and use this to brush the pan each time, or as necessary, before making a crêpe.

5. Brush the pan lightly and place it on the stove. When the pan is hot but not burning, add 2 tablespoons of the batter (it is preferable if you use a small ladle with a 2-tablespoon capacity), and swirl it around neatly to

completely cover the bottom of the pan. Cook over moderately high heat for 30 to 40 seconds, or until lightly browned on the bottom. Turn the crêpe and cook the second side for about 15 seconds. Turn the crêpe out onto a sheet of wax paper.

6. Continue making crêpes, brushing the pan lightly as necessary to prevent sticking, until all the batter is used. As the crêpes are made, turn them out, edges slightly overlapping, onto the wax paper.

YIELD: 8 or 9 crêpes.

Crêpes Homard Newburg

CRÊPES FILLED WITH LOBSTER NEWBURG

- ½ pound cooked lobster meat
- 3 tablespoons butter
- 2 tablespoons finely chopped shallots
- 1 tablespoon paprika
- 1 tablespoon flour
- 1 cup milk
- ½ cup heavy cream
- Salt to taste, if desired
- Freshly ground black pepper to taste
- 1 tablespoon Madeira
- 1 egg yolk
- Pinch of cayenne pepper
- 8 crêpes (see preceding recipe)

1. Cut the lobster into bite-sized cubes. There should be about 1½ cups.

2. Melt 2 tablespoons of the butter in a saucepan and add the shallots and paprika. Cook briefly, stirring. Sprinkle with flour, stirring with a wire whisk.

3. Add the milk, stirring rapidly with the whisk. Add the cream and any liquid that has accumulated around the lobster. Add salt and pepper to taste. Add the Madeira and egg yolk, stirring rapidly with the whisk. Stir in the cayenne pepper.

4. Melt the remaining tablespoon of butter and add the cubed lobster, shaking the skillet and stirring just until the lobster pieces are heated through.

5. Put the sauce through a strainer.

6. Pour half of the sauce over the lobster pieces and stir to blend.

7. Use equal, small portions of the lobster in the sauce to fill each of 8 crêpes. About 2 tablespoons of filling will suffice for each crêpe.

8. Fold the crêpe over. Spoon the remaining sauce without the lobster meat over the filled crêpes.

YIELD: 4 servings.

Crêpes à l'Indienne

CRÊPES FILLED WITH CURRIED SHRIMP

- 1 pound raw shrimp in the shell
- 3 tablespoons butter
- ¼ cup finely chopped onion
- 1 teaspoon finely minced garlic
- 2 tablespoons flour
- 2 tablespoons curry powder
- ⅓ cup milk
- 1 cup plain yogurt
- Salt to taste, if desired
- Freshly ground black pepper to taste
- 8 crêpes (see recipe page 86)
- 2 tablespoons finely chopped fresh coriander leaves, optional

1. Shell and devein the shrimp. Cut the shrimp into bite-sized pieces. There should be about 1½ cups.

2. Melt 1 tablespoon of the butter in a saucepan and add the onion and garlic. Cook, stirring, until the onion is wilted. Add the flour and curry powder and stir.

3. Add the milk, stirring rapidly with the whisk. Add the yogurt, salt and pepper and bring to the boil, stirring with the whisk.

4. Melt 1 tablespoon of butter in a skillet and add the shrimp. Cook, stirring, for about 1 minute or less, just until the shrimp lose their raw look throughout. Pour and scrape the sauce over the shrimp. Stir to blend.

5. Lay out 2 crêpes on each of four plates. Spoon equal portions of the shrimp curry on each crêpe, leaving enough left over to be spooned on top as garnish. Roll the crêpes.

6. Melt the remaining 1 tablespoon of butter and brush the tops of the crêpes with butter. Spoon the reserved curried shrimp on top. Sprinkle with chopped coriander and serve.

YIELD: 4 servings.

Crêpes de Volaille à l'Estragon

TARRAGON CHICKEN CRÊPES

- 2 cups cooked skinless, boneless chicken cut into bite-sized cubes
- 2 tablespoons butter
- 3 tablespoons flour
- 1¾ cups chicken broth
- ¾ cup heavy cream
- Salt to taste, if desired
- Freshly ground black pepper to taste
- ⅛ teaspoon cayenne pepper

⅛ teaspoon grated nutmeg
1 tablespoon finely chopped fresh tarragon, or ½ teaspoon dried
8 crêpes (see recipe page 86)
3 tablespoons finely chopped parsley

1. Put the chicken in a saucepan and set aside.

2. Melt the butter in a saucepan and add the flour, stirring with a wire whisk. When blended and smooth, add the broth, stirring rapidly with the whisk. Add the cream, salt, pepper, cayenne pepper, nutmeg and tarragon.

3. Add half the sauce to the chicken and stir to blend and heat through.

4. Use equal portions of the chicken filling to fill each of 8 crêpes. Fold the crêpes as desired.

5. Spoon the remaining cream sauce over each serving and sprinkle with chopped parsley.

YIELD: 4 servings.

There are many excellent dishes that can be attributed to the kitchens of Russia. Some of the best known, of course, are borscht, blini, beef stroganoff and chicken Kiev. But one of our favorites is a baked filled pastry known as a pirog. It is prepared with an outer crust of brioche and stuffed with fillings ranging from salmon and dill to meat and mushrooms to mushrooms and eggs.

In Russia, pirogi are usually served at lunch with a cup of consommé. It is our feeling, however, that a well-made pirog makes an elegant main dish for lunch or a light supper.

HOW TO FILL AND BAKE A PIROG

Prepare the brioche pastry the day before as indicated in the recipe. Put the dough in the refrigerator and let stand until it is to be rolled out.

Lightly flour a flat surface, preferably cold marble. Roll the dough into a rectangle, measuring about 16 inches by 24 inches. Add the filling, placing it dead center. Do not let the filling get closer than 4 inches from the edge of the rectangle.

Fold one long side of the pastry over the filling.

Blend 1 egg yolk with 2 teaspoons of water.

Brush the top and exposed parts of the dough (including the inside portion of the unfolded portion of dough) with the egg wash. Fold over the second fold of dough to completely and compactly enclose the filling. Cut off about 2 or 3 inches of the bottom and top ends of the dough to use for decoration. Neatly and carefully fold over the bottom and top of the dough to compactly enclose the ends of the filling.

Turn the filled pastry over onto a baking sheet. Brush the top with more egg wash.

Roll out the cut-off pieces of dough and cut them into strips about ¼ inch wide. Place these strips of dough crosswise at parallel intervals over the dough as decoration. Cut a hole about ½ inch in diameter in the direct center of the pastry top.

Set the dough in a warm place for about 30 minutes.

Meanwhile, preheat the oven to 375 degrees.

Place in the oven and bake for 20 minutes. Reduce the oven temperature to 325 degrees and continue baking for 25 minutes longer.

Let stand for at least 15 minutes before slicing. Serve, if desired, with melted butter to be spooned on top of the slices.

YIELD: 6 to 8 servings.

BRIOCHE DOUGH

¾ cup milk
¼ teaspoon sugar
3 packages granular yeast
4 to 4½ cups flour
12 egg yolks
8 tablespoons butter at room temperature plus butter for greasing the bowl

1. Put the milk in a saucepan and heat it gradually to lukewarm. Remove from the heat. If the milk has become too hot, let it cool to lukewarm.

2. Sprinkle the milk with sugar and yeast and stir to dissolve. Cover with a towel. Let stand for about 5 minutes and place the mixture in a warm place (the natural warmth of a turned-off oven is good for this) for about 5 minutes. It should ferment during the period and increase in volume.

3. Place 4 cups of the flour in the bowl of an electric mixer fitted with a dough hook, or use a mixing bowl and wooden spoon. Make a well in the center and pour in the yeast mixture, egg yolks and 8 tablespoons of the butter. With the dough hook or wooden spoon, gradually work in the flour until well blended. Then beat vigorously until the dough is quite smooth and can be shaped into a ball.

4. Turn the dough out onto a lightly floured board and knead it until it is smooth and satiny, 10 to 15 minutes. As you work the dough, continue to add flour to the kneading surface as necessary to prevent sticking, but take care not to add an excess or the finished product will be tough.

5. Lightly butter a clean mixing bowl and add the ball of dough. Cover with a clean towel and let stand in a warm place for about 1 hour, or until doubled in bulk. Punch the dough down. Turn it out once more onto a lightly floured board. Knead it for about 1 minute and return it to a clean bowl. Cover closely with plastic wrap and refrigerate overnight.

6. The next morning, punch the dough down again and continue to refrigerate, covered, until ready to use.

YIELD: Enough for 1 large pirog.

SALMON FILLING FOR PIROGI

- 4 cups skinless, boned salmon, preferably poached (see recipe page 119), or use canned salmon
- 8 tablespoons butter
- ¼ cup finely chopped shallots
- ½ pound mushrooms, sliced, about 3 cups
- Salt to taste, if desired
- Freshly ground black pepper to taste
- ¼ cup dry white wine
- ¼ cup stock from the poached salmon
- ½ cup finely chopped fresh dill
- 4 hard-boiled eggs, peeled and chopped, about 2 cups
- 4 cups cooked rice
- ¼ cup lemon juice

1. Put the salmon in a large mixing bowl.

2. Melt half of the butter in a saucepan and add the shallots. Cook until the shallots are wilted and add the mushrooms and salt and pepper. Cook, stirring, until mushrooms give up their liquid.

3. Add the wine and stock and bring to the boil. Cook the liquid down by about half. Add half the dill.

4. To the salmon, add the chopped eggs, rice and mushroom mixture with its liquid. Melt the remaining butter and add it. Add the remaining dill and lemon juice. Blend well.

YIELD: About 10 cups.

MEAT AND MUSHROOM FILLING FOR PIROGI

- 1¾ pounds lean ground sirloin
- 6 tablespoons butter
- ½ cup finely chopped onion
- 1 tablespoon finely minced garlic
- ¾ pound mushrooms, thinly sliced, about 5 cups
- Salt to taste, if desired
- Freshly ground black pepper to taste
- 2 tablespoons flour
- ¼ cup chicken broth
- ⅓ cup lemon juice
- 4 hard-boiled eggs, peeled and chopped, about 2 cups
- 4 cups cooked rice
- ½ cup finely chopped fresh dill

1. Put the meat in a mixing bowl and set aside.

2. Melt the butter in a fairly deep skillet and add the onion and garlic. Cook, stirring, until the onion is wilted. Add the mushrooms and cook until the mushrooms give up their liquid. Sprinkle with salt and pepper. Sprinkle with flour and stir to distribute it evenly.

3. Add the meat and stir, chopping down with the side of a heavy metal spoon to break up any lumps. Add the broth and continue cooking, stirring, until the meat loses its raw look. Add the lemon juice, a generous grinding of black pepper, the chopped eggs, rice and dill. Blend well.

YIELD: About 10 cups.

Piroshki, in our minds best made with a rich, sour cream pastry, are really miniature versions of pirogi. They are usually served with a soup, such as a rich clear beef broth, borscht, cabbage or sauerkraut soup.

Beef Piroshki

- Sour cream pastry (see following recipe)
- 2 tablespoons butter
- 3 cups finely chopped onion
- 1 pound ground beef
- Salt, if desired
- Freshly ground black pepper to taste
- 3 hard-boiled eggs, peeled and finely chopped, about 1 cup
- ¼ cup finely chopped fresh dill
- 1 egg, lightly beaten
- 3 tablespoons water

1. Prepare the pastry and chill it.

2. Preheat the oven to 400 degrees.

3. Melt the butter in a skillet and add the onion. Cook, stirring, until the onion is wilted.

4. Add the beef and, using a heavy metal kitchen spoon, stir and chop down to break up any lumps in the meat. Cook until the meat loses its raw look. Add salt and pepper.

5. Add the chopped egg and dill. Stir to blend. There should be about 4 cups. Remove to a mixing bowl and let cool.

6. Roll out the pastry as thinly as possible (less than ⅛ inch thick). Using a cookie cutter, cut the dough into rounds. We used a 4-inch cookie cutter to produce 30 rounds. The dough will shrink after cutting. You may roll out the circles or rounds to make them larger or you may stretch them carefully by hand. Beat the egg with the water. Brush the top of each pastry with the egg mixture.

7. Use about 2 tablespoons of the filling for each circle of dough. Shape the filling into an oval and place it on half of the circle of dough. Fold the other half of the circle of dough over to enclose the filling. Press the edges of the dough with the fingers or the tines of a fork to seal. Brush the tops with egg mixture to seal.

8. Arrange the filled pieces on a lightly greased baking sheet and bake for 25 minutes.

YIELD: 30 piroshki.

SOUR CREAM PASTRY

3½ cups flour
Salt, if desired
1 teaspoon baking powder
½ cup butter, chilled and cut into small pieces
2 eggs
1 cup sour cream

1. Put 3¼ cups of the flour, salt to taste, the baking powder, butter, eggs and sour cream into the container of a food processor. Process until thoroughly blended.

2. If a food processor is not used, put the flour, salt to taste and baking powder in a mixing bowl. Add the butter and cut it in with two knives or a pastry blender until the mixture looks like coarse cornmeal. Using a fork, add the eggs and thoroughly blend.

3. Scrape the mixture out onto a lightly floured board and knead as briefly as possible, using as little flour as possible to make a smooth and workable dough.

4. Shape the dough into a flat cake and wrap it in plastic wrap. Chill until ready to use.

YIELD: 2 pounds of dough.

Mushroom Piroshki

- Sour cream pastry (see preceding recipe)
- 2 tablespoons butter
- 2 cups finely chopped onion
- ¾ pound mushrooms, finely chopped, about 3½ cups
- Salt, if desired
- Freshly ground black pepper to taste
- ¼ cup sour cream
- 2 tablespoons finely chopped fresh dill
- 1 hard-boiled egg, peeled and finely chopped, about ⅓ cup
- 1 cup cooked rice
- 1 egg, lightly beaten
- 3 tablespoons water

1. Prepare the pastry and chill it.

2. Preheat the oven to 400 degrees.

3. Melt the butter in a skillet and add the onion. Cook, stirring, until the onion is wilted.

4. Add the mushrooms and cook, stirring often, until they give up their liquid. Cook until most but not all of the liquid evaporates. Add salt and pepper and stir.

5. Add the sour cream, dill, chopped egg and rice. Blend well. There should be about 4 cups. Remove to a mixing bowl and let cool.

6. Roll out the pastry as thinly as possible (less than ⅛ inch thick). Using a cookie cutter, cut the dough into rounds. We used a 4-inch cookie cutter to produce 30 rounds. The dough will shrink after cutting. You may roll out the circles or rounds to make them larger or you may stretch them carefully by hand. Beat the egg with the water. Brush the top of each pastry round with the egg mixture.

7. Use 2 tablespoons of the filling for each circle of dough. Shape the filling into an oval and place it on half of the circle of dough. Fold the other half of the circle of dough over to enclose the filling. Press the edges of the dough with the fingers or the tines of a fork to seal. Brush the tops with egg mixture to seal.

8. Arrange the filled pieces on a lightly greased baking sheet, and bake for 25 minutes.

YIELD: 30 piroshki.

We have written often about the virtues of ratatouille, not the least of which is that it improves on standing. When we found ourselves with an impressive amount of yesterday's ratatouille, it occurred to us that the mélange of eggplant, tomatoes, zucchini and so on would make a fine filling for a vegetable pie. We used the ratatouille in layers with sliced Fontina and Parmesan cheeses, and the result was of such goodness it occurred to us that the pie could well be an end in itself. That is to say, why wait for leftovers?

At approximately the same time we had a serendipitous visit from a young woman named Alison Boteler, a student at C. W. Post College on Long Island. Miss Boteler is a fine cook who also has a talk show on the college's radio station, WCWP. She brought with her another uncommonly tasty vegetable pie, this one made with spinach and mayonnaise. It turned out to be a marvelous cold creation for a summer lunch.

Tarte Côte d'Azur

A RATATOUILLE PIE

- 1 eggplant, about 1¾ pounds
- 2 small zucchini, about 1¼ pounds, trimmed
- 1 large onion, peeled
- 2 green peppers, cored and seeded
- 1 pound ripe tomatoes, cored and peeled
- ¼ cup olive oil
- 2 tablespoons finely chopped garlic
- 1 teaspoon finely chopped fresh thyme, or ½ teaspoon dried
- 1 bay leaf
- Salt and freshly ground black pepper to taste
- 1 cup coarsely chopped parsley
- ½ cup pitted black olives
- 1 recipe for pie pastry (see following recipe)
- 2 cups grated Fontina cheese, preferably imported
- ¾ cup freshly grated Parmesan cheese
- 1 egg yolk
- 2 teaspoons water

1. Preheat the oven to 425 degrees.
2. Peel the eggplant and cut it into 1½-inch cubes. There should be about 4½ cups.
3. Cut each zucchini in half. Cut each half crosswise into ¾-inch pieces.
4. Cut the onion into ½-inch cubes.
5. Cut the green peppers into 1½-inch cubes.
6. Cut the tomatoes into 2-inch cubes. There should be about 2½ cups.

7. Heat the oil in a casserole and add the eggplant. Cook, stirring occasionally, for about 5 minutes. Add the onion, zucchini and green pepper. Stir to blend the ingredients.

8. Add the garlic, thyme, bay leaf and salt and pepper. Cook for about 4 minutes, stirring.

9. Add the tomatoes and parsley and stir. Cook for about 5 minutes longer.

10. Place the casserole in the oven and bake for 30 minutes. Stir in the olives and bake for 10 minutes longer.

11. Let the ratatouille stand until thoroughly cold.

12. When ready to bake the pie, reheat the oven to 425 degrees.

13. Line a 10-inch pie plate with half of the pastry, letting 1 inch of the pastry hang over the side. Add about one third of the ratatouille mixture, a layer of Fontina and a layer of Parmesan cheese and so on. Continue making layers until all of the ratatouille mixture and cheese are used.

14. Brush the overlapping rim of the pastry with a little of the egg blended with the water. Cover with a second layer of pastry. Seal by pressing the edges together. Flute, if desired, or use the tines of a fork to make a pattern all around.

15. Use a small biscuit cutter to make a hole in the center of the top pastry. This will allow the steam to escape. Brush the top all over with the egg yolk mixture.

16. Bake the pie for 30 minutes. Reduce the oven temperature to 375 degrees and bake for 15 to 20 minutes longer, or until golden brown on top.

YIELD: 6 servings.

PIE PASTRY

1¾ cups flour
½ teaspoon salt
12 tablespoons butter
2 tablespoons chilled, solid white shortening
2 to 3 tablespoons ice water

1. Put the flour and salt into the container of a food processor.

2. Cut the butter into small pieces and add it. Add the shortening in small bits.

3. Activate the machine off and on until the mixture resembles coarse cornmeal. Start processing while gradually dribbling in the water. Add just enough water so that the dough can be gathered into a mass. Do not overblend.

4. Turn the dough out onto a lightly floured board and shape into a ball. Pat the dough into a large flat round biscuit shape.

5. Dust the dough on both sides with flour. Wrap in plastic wrap and chill for 1 hour. Roll out on a lightly floured board.

YIELD: Pastry for a 2-crust pie.

Tarte aux Épinards

A SPINACH PIE

- 1¼ pounds fresh, unblemished spinach leaves
- 1 recipe for pie pastry (see preceding recipe)
- 1 egg yolk
- 2 tablespoons water
- ¾ to 1 cup homemade mayonnaise (see recipe page 415)
- 2 teaspoons prepared mustard, preferably imported Dijon or Düsseldorf
- ½ cup finely chopped scallions, green part and all
- Salt and freshly ground black pepper to taste
- ⅓ pound Swiss cheese, grated, or crumbled feta cheese, optional
- 1 hard-boiled egg, peeled and chopped, optional

1. Preheat the oven to 400 degrees.

2. Pick over the spinach to remove any tough stems. Bring enough water to the boil to cover the spinach when it is added. Add the spinach and cook, stirring down, until spinach is wilted. Do not overcook.

3. Drain the spinach. Run under cold water to chill. Gather the spinach into a ball and squeeze to extract as much excess liquid as possible.

4. Line a 10-inch quiche tin with slightly more than half of the pastry rolled into a circle. Prick the bottom with the tines of a fork. Line the pastry with wax paper and scatter dried beans or peas to prevent the pie from buckling as it bakes.

5. Roll out the remaining pastry into a circle. If desired, cut the pastry into fancy shapes. In any event, brush the pastry lightly with a blend of egg yolk and water. Arrange the pastry ring or cutouts on a baking sheet.

6. Place the pie tin and the baking sheet in the oven. Bake the pie shell for 8 minutes and remove it from the oven. Remove the wax paper and beans. Brush the bottom of the pie shell lightly with egg yolk blended with water. Return the pie shell to the oven and continue baking 8 to 10 minutes until golden brown. Remove from the oven and let cool.

7. Meanwhile, continue baking the pastry ring or cutouts for a total of 8 to 10 minutes, or until golden brown. Remove from the oven and let stand until thoroughly cool.

8. Coarsely chop the spinach and put it in a mixing bowl. Add enough mayonnaise to bind the spinach, the mustard, scallions, salt and pepper, cheese and chopped egg. Blend well. Chill.

9. Spoon the spinach mixture into the pie shell. Cover with the pastry ring or with the cutouts. Serve as a light luncheon course.

YIELD: 6 servings.

Tarte aux Poireaux

LEEK TART

Pastry for a 9- or 10-inch pie (see recipe page 96)
4 to 8 trimmed leeks, about 1 pound
3 eggs
1 egg yolk
1 cup heavy cream
2 tablespoons butter
Salt and freshly ground black pepper to taste

1. Preheat the oven to 400 degrees.

2. Line a pie or quiche pan with the pastry. Cover it with wax paper and add dried beans to weight down the bottom.

3. Bake the pastry for 10 minutes. Remove the wax paper and beans. Bake for 5 minutes longer.

4. Meanwhile, trim the leeks. Split them in half and rinse thoroughly between the leaves to remove all trace of sand and dirt. Drain well.

5. Finely chop the leeks crosswise. There should be about 5 cups. Set aside.

6. Combine the eggs, egg yolk and ½ cup of the cream. Set aside.

7. Melt the butter in a skillet and add the leeks. Sprinkle with salt and pepper and cook, stirring often, for about 5 minutes.

8. Add the remaining ½ cup of cream and simmer for about 5 minutes. Remove from the heat. Add the cooked leeks to the egg and cream mixture and blend well.

9. Pour the custard mixture into the baked pie shell.

10. Reduce the oven temperature to 350 degrees; bake the tart for 40 minutes. Serve hot, lukewarm or at room temperature.

YIELD: 8 servings.

The American fondness for pizza, the great Neapolitan specialty that invaded these shores after the Second World War, is one we share. More recently, we have become enthusiastic about a stuffed version of pizza, another Italian specialty called calzoni.

Although we've admired many variations of the dish, we encountered the finest and most inspired we have ever eaten during a visit to Chez Panisse, an excellent restaurant in Berkeley, California. It is run by Alice Waters, one of the finest cooks in this country. Her version of the dish was pizza dough filled with goat cheese and chopped prosciutto, seasoned to perfection and baked until crisp and golden on the outside. We cannot claim to have entirely duplicated her calzoni, but we have made an earnest effort and are particularly proud of the result.

Calzoni

A CHEESE-FILLED YEAST PASTRY

- Pizza dough made with 4 cups of flour (see following recipe)
- ½ pound goat cheese
- ¼ pound mozzarella cheese, cut into small cubes
- ¼ cup ricotta cheese
- ½ cup prosciutto cut into small cubes, about 2 ounces
- ¼ cup grated Parmesan cheese
- ¼ teaspoon chopped fresh rosemary
- 4 fresh basil leaves, chopped, about 1 tablespoon, or ½ teaspoon dried
- 2 tablespoons finely chopped parsley
- Freshly ground black pepper to taste
- 2 eggs, lightly beaten
- 1 tablespoon water

1. Prepare the pizza dough and divide it into 4 portions. Shape into balls. Keep covered with a cloth.

2. Preheat the oven to 400 degrees.

3. Combine the goat cheese, mozzarella, ricotta, prosciutto, Parmesan, rosemary, basil, parsley, pepper and 1 egg in a mixing bowl. Blend well.

4. Roll out each ball of pizza dough on a lightly floured surface into a circle 8½ to 9 inches in diameter.

5. Spoon an equal portion of the filling onto one half of each circle, leaving a margin for sealing. Beat the remaining egg with the water. Rub a small amount of the egg mixture around the margin. Fold over the unfilled half and press around the margin with the fingers or a fork to seal.

6. As the calzoni are filled and sealed, arrange them on a baking sheet. Cut a 1-inch slit in the top of each to allow steam to escape. Brush the calzoni all over with the egg mixture.

7. Bake the calzoni for 30 minutes.

YIELD: 4 servings.

PIZZA DOUGH

- 1½ envelopes dry yeast
- 1½ cups lukewarm water
- 2 tablespoons olive oil
- 4 cups flour
- Pinch of salt, if desired

1. Put the yeast, water and oil into the container of a food processor.

2. Add the flour and salt and process until the mixture becomes a soft but firm and kneadable mixture.

3. If a food processor is not used, soak the yeast in the water and oil. Put the flour and salt into a mixing bowl. Add the yeast liquid and blend by hand.

4. Turn the dough out onto a lightly floured board and knead briefly. Shape into a ball. Place the ball in a mixing bowl and cover. Let stand until doubled in bulk, 45 minutes to 1 hour. It is now ready to be used for calzoni or pizza.

YIELD: Enough dough for 4 large calzoni or 2 pizzas.

Pizza con Tutti

PIZZA WITH EVERYTHING

- Pizza dough made with 4 cups of flour (see preceding recipe)
- ¼ cup olive oil plus oil for greasing a pizza pan
- 2 cups marinara sauce (see recipe page 411)
- 1 cup thinly sliced mushrooms
- 1 cup thinly sliced sausages, such as Italian sausages or salami or Polish sausages
- 2 cups coarsely grated mozzarella cheese
- ¼ cup freshly grated Parmesan cheese
- Hot red pepper flakes

1. There are two recommended ways of cooking pizza at home. It may be prepared and cooked in a 14-inch pizza pan, or it may be baked on a baking stone. If it is to be baked in a pizza pan, preheat the oven to 475 degrees; if it is to be baked on a stone, preheat the oven to 500 degrees and put the stone in the oven.

2. Divide the dough in half. Flatten each half with the hands into a circle. Start punching it all around with the back of a clenched fist to shape it into a larger circle 12 or 13 inches in diameter. Keep the surface floured lightly but enough so that the dough does not stick.

3. If pizza pans are used, rub the surface of each with 1 tablespoon of oil. If a baking stone is used, you will place the pizza circle on the wooden paddle. You should bake 1 pizza first and continue to make the second after the first is baked.

4. Arrange 1 circle of dough on each pan or on the wooden paddle. Add half of the marinara sauce to the center of each circle of pastry and smooth it almost, but not quite, to the edge. Scatter half of the mushrooms, half of the sausage slices, half of the mozzarella and half of the Parmesan over the sauce. Sprinkle each pizza with 2 tablespoons of olive oil.

5. If a pizza pan is used, place it in the oven for 14 minutes, or until the pizza is well done. If the baking stone is used, slide the pizza off onto the stone and bake for 14 minutes, or until the pizza is well done. Repeat with the second pizza. Serve with red pepper flakes on the side.

YIELD: 2 14-inch pizzas.

Pissaladière

A PROVENÇALE PIZZA

- 1½ cups flour
- 7 tablespoons plus 1 teaspoon olive oil
- 2½ teaspoons granular yeast
- ½ cup lukewarm water
- 2 or 3 large onions
- 2 teaspoons finely chopped garlic
- ½ teaspoon dried thyme
- 2 whole cloves
- 1 bay leaf
- 12 flat anchovy fillets
- 12 pitted imported black olives, preferably oil-cured

1. Put the flour, 4 tablespoons olive oil and the yeast into the container of a food processor and blend. Gradually add the water and continue processing until the dough can be gathered into a ball. Rub the outside of the

dough with 1 teaspoon oil. Put the ball of dough into a mixing bowl and cover. Let stand for 30 minutes in a warm but not hot place.

2. Meanwhile, peel the onions and cut them in half. Slice each onion half thinly. There should be about 10 cups.

3. Heat 1 tablespoon of the oil in a large, heavy Dutch oven or casserole and add the sliced onions, garlic, thyme, cloves and bay leaf. Cook, stirring often, for 20 to 30 minutes, or until the onions are nicely browned or light amber colored.

4. Pat the dough into a flat shape. Rub 1 tablespoon of oil all over the surface of a round 14-inch pizza pan. Place the dough in the center of the pan and pat it out with the fingers and knuckles all the way to the rim. Build up the rim slightly with the fingers. Cover and let stand in a warm place for 30 minutes.

5. Preheat the oven to 450 degrees.

6. Spoon the onion mixture in the center of the dough-lined tin. Spread it out to the rim. Arrange the anchovy fillets in a crossed pattern over the onions. Dot with the olives. Spoon the remaining tablespoon of oil over the onions.

7. Put the pissaladière in the oven and bake for 30 minutes.

YIELD: 4 to 8 servings.

Empanaditas Fritas

MEAT-FILLED TURNOVERS

- Pastry for deep-fried turnovers (see following recipe)
- 3 tablespoons olive oil
- ½ cup finely chopped onion
- 2 teaspoons finely chopped garlic
- ¾ cup finely chopped green pepper
- ¾ pound ground top sirloin
- 1 teaspoon ground cumin
- ½ teaspoon hot red pepper flakes
- Salt to taste, if desired
- Freshly ground black pepper to taste
- ¾ cup peeled, seeded and chopped tomatoes
- 12 stuffed olives, finely chopped, about ¼ cup
- ¼ cup raisins or currants
- ⅓ cup pine nuts
- 2 hard-boiled eggs, peeled and chopped
- 2 tablespoons finely chopped parsley
- 2 tablespoons finely chopped fresh coriander leaves, optional
- Corn, peanut or vegetable oil for deep frying

1. Prepare the pastry and let stand, covered, while preparing the filling.

2. Heat the olive oil in a skillet and add the onion, garlic and green pepper. Cook, stirring, until wilted. Add the beef and cook, stirring and chopping down with the sides of a metal spoon to break up any lumps. Cook until the meat has lost its raw look.

3. Add the cumin, pepper flakes, salt, pepper, tomatoes, olives and raisins. Cook, stirring, until most of the liquid has evaporated.

4. Add the pine nuts, eggs, parsley and coriander. Blend well. Let cool. The chilling may be hastened if the filling is spooned onto a platter and placed briefly in the freezer. Stir occasionally. By all means do not freeze.

5. Roll out the pastry on a lightly floured board to a thickness of ⅛ inch or less.

6. Use a cutter 6 inches in diameter, such as the rim of an emptied can of tomatoes or coffee, and cut out circles.

7. Gather together the scraps of dough and form a ball quickly. Roll this dough out to the same thickness and cut it into 6-inch circles.

8. Fill one half of each circle of dough with about 2 tablespoons of filling, leaving a slight margin for sealing when the dough is folded. Moisten all around the edges of the circle of dough. Fold the unfilled half of dough over to enclose the filling. Press around the edges with the tines of a fork to seal well.

9. Heat the oil to 360 degrees. Add the empanaditas, four to six at a time without crowding. Cook, turning the empanaditas in the hot fat until nicely browned and cooked through, for about 8 minutes. Drain well on paper toweling. Serve hot.

YIELD: 20 empanaditas.

PASTRY FOR DEEP-FRIED TURNOVERS

4 cups flour
Salt to taste, if desired
¼ cup lard
¼ cup olive oil
1⅓ cups water

1. Put the flour and salt into the container of a food processor.

2. Heat the lard, oil and water in a saucepan just until the lard is melted.

3. Start processing while gradually adding the lard mixture.

4. Remove the dough and shape it into a ball. Set it on a lightly floured board and cover with a cloth. Let stand for about 15 minutes before rolling out.

YIELD: Enough pastry for 20 6-inch circles of dough.

Natchitoches Meat Pies

Pastry for deep-fried turnovers (see preceding recipe)
3 tablespoons bacon fat or corn oil
¾ cup finely chopped onion
1½ teaspoons finely minced garlic
½ pound ground lean beef
¾ pound ground lean pork
1 cup finely chopped scallions
⅓ cup finely chopped parsley
Salt to taste, if desired
Freshly ground black pepper to taste
2 teaspoons finely chopped hot red or green pepper, or use Tabasco sauce or cayenne pepper to taste
Corn, peanut or vegetable oil for deep frying

1. Prepare the pastry and let stand, covered, while preparing the filling.

2. Heat the fat or oil in a skillet or saucepan and add the onion and garlic. Cook, stirring, until wilted. Add the beef and pork and cook, stirring and chopping down with the sides of a metal spoon to break up any lumps. Cook until the meat loses its raw look. Add the scallions, parsley, salt, pepper and chopped pepper. Let cool.

3. Roll out one quarter of the dough at a time on a lightly floured board to the thickness of ⅛ inch or less.

4. With a cutter 6 inches in diameter, cut out circles.

5. Gather the scraps of dough and form a ball quickly. Roll out this dough to the same thickness, and cut it into 6-inch circles.

6. Continue rolling and cutting circles until all the dough has been used.

7. Fill one half of each circle of dough with about 3 tablespoons of the filling, leaving a margin for sealing when the dough is folded. Moisten all around the edges of the circle of dough. Fold the unfilled half of dough over to enclose the filling. Press around the edges with the tines of a fork to seal well.

8. Heat the oil to 360 degrees. Add the meat pies, 4 to 6 at a time without crowding. Cook, turning the pies in the hot fat until nicely browned and cooked through, for about 8 minutes. Drain well on paper toweling. Serve hot.

YIELD: About 20 meat pies.

Note: If you wish to freeze the meat pies, it is best if you deep-fry them as indicated in the recipe. Drain and let stand at room temperature until cool. Wrap each individually in foil and freeze. To reheat, preheat the oven to 350 degrees. Bake them without defrosting on a baking sheet for about 25 minutes.

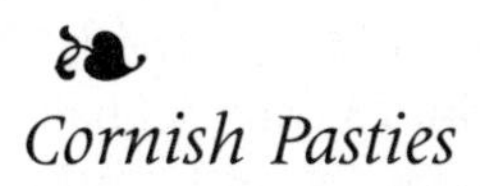

Cornish Pasties

- Pastry for baked turnovers (see following recipe)
- ¾ pound steak, cut into ¼-inch pieces, about 1½ cups
- 1 cup potatoes cut into small cubes, less than ¼ inch
- ½ cup turnips, preferably rutabagas, peeled and cut into small cubes, less than ¼ inch
- ½ cup finely chopped onion
- Salt to taste, if desired
- Freshly ground black pepper to taste
- 1 egg, lightly beaten

1. Prepare the pastry and let stand, covered, while preparing the filling.

2. Preheat the oven to 400 degrees.

3. Combine the steak, potatoes, turnips, onion, salt and pepper in a mixing bowl. Blend well.

4. Roll out the pastry to a ⅛-inch thickness or less. Using the rim of a 7½- or 8-inch mixing bowl, cut out the pastry into three uniform circles. Gather the excess pastry from around the circles and form a ball. Roll it out a second time into a circle. Cut it into a fourth 7½- or 8-inch circle.

5. Spoon generous and equal portions of the meat mixture (about ¾ cup) into the center of each circle of dough. Carefully bring up the edges and press to seal, making each turnover into a boat-shaped oval with slightly pointed ends.

6. As the turnovers are shaped, arrange them, sealed side up, on a baking sheet. Brush the tops lightly with beaten egg. Place the baking sheet in the oven and bake for 20 minutes.

7. Reduce the oven temperature to 350 degrees. Continue baking for 40 minutes longer.

YIELD: 4 pasties.

PASTRY FOR BAKED TURNOVERS

- 2 cups flour
- ¼ cup olive oil
- 2 tablespoons butter
- Salt to taste, if desired
- 1 egg yolk
- 6 to 7 tablespoons ice water

1. Put the flour into the container of a food processor. Add the oil, butter, salt and egg yolk.

2. Start processing while gradually adding the water. Add only enough water so that the pastry can be handled and gathered into a compact ball. Wrap tightly in plastic wrap and chill in the refrigerator for an hour or longer.

YIELD: Enough for 4 large Cornish pasties.

There are few vegetables that have more virtues than potatoes. They are delectable served hot or cold, but the flavor of a potato depends to a great extent on the flavors and textures of the foods with which it is combined. Put it in league with a garlic-tinged sauce, a chopping of parsley, chives or scallions, or a purée of leeks or other vegetables, and there is a flavor explosion of the most refined and delectable sort.

We thought of this recently in creating a series of luncheon or supper dishes with baked potatoes as a base. From childhood we have found stuffed baked potatoes, with a topping of cheese, irresistible. Why not, we wondered, blend them with an assortment of savory ingredients such as shrimp, ground pork with rosemary, or oysters and those Creole vegetables, onions, green pepper and celery? The results were all to the good.

Pommes de Terre aux Crevettes

BAKED POTATOES WITH SHRIMP

- 4 large Idaho baking potatoes, about ½ pound each
- ½ pound raw shrimp in the shell
- 3 tablespoons butter
- 1 cup coarsely diced mushrooms
- 2 tablespoons dry sherry
- ¼ cup heavy cream
- Salt, if desired
- Freshly ground black pepper to taste
- A few drops of Tabasco sauce
- 1 tablespoon freshly grated Parmesan cheese

1. Preheat the oven to 400 degrees.

2. Arrange the potatoes on a baking sheet and place them in the oven. Bake for about 1 hour, or until done.

3. Meanwhile, shell and devein the shrimp. Cut the shrimp into small cubes.

4. Melt 1 tablespoon of the butter in a saucepan and add the shrimp and mushrooms. Cook, stirring, for about 1 minute. Add the wine and stir. Remove from the heat.

5. When the potatoes are done, slice off the top of each, about half an

inch from the top. Carefully scoop out the center of each potato to make a boat for stuffing. Put the scraped out potato pulp into a saucepan or bowl and mash well and uniformly. Add this to the shrimp mixture. Add the cream and 1 tablespoon of the butter and cook briefly, stirring. Add salt and pepper and a few drops of Tabasco. Blend.

6. Fill the potato boats with the mixture, piling it up and smoothing it over.

7. Arrange the potatoes, stuffed side up, in a baking dish. Sprinkle with cheese. Melt the remaining tablespoon of butter and pour it over the potatoes. Bake for 15 minutes.

YIELD: 4 servings.

Pommes de Terre Charcutière

BAKED POTATOES STUFFED WITH PORK

- 4 large Idaho baking potatoes, about ½ pound each
- 5 tablespoons butter
- ¼ cup finely chopped onion
- ¼ cup finely chopped celery
- ⅓ pound very lean ground pork
- 2 teaspoons crumbled leaf sage, or ½ teaspoon ground
- Salt, if desired
- Freshly ground black pepper to taste
- ⅓ cup milk
- 3 tablespoons finely chopped parsley
- ½ teaspoon paprika

1. Preheat the oven to 400 degrees.

2. Arrange the potatoes on a baking sheet and place in the oven. Bake for about 1 hour, or until done.

3. Meanwhile, melt 1 tablespoon of the butter in a saucepan and add the onion and celery. Cook, stirring, until the vegetables are wilted. Add the pork, sage, salt and pepper and cook, stirring down with the side of a heavy metal spoon to break up any lumps, until the meat loses its raw look.

4. When the potatoes are done, slice off the top of each, about half an inch from the top. Carefully scoop out the center of each potato to make a boat for stuffing. Put the scraped out potato pulp into the saucepan and mash well and uniformly with the meat mixture. Add the milk, 3 tablespoons of the butter, salt and pepper to taste and parsley and blend thoroughly.

5. Fill the potato boats with the mixture, piling it up and smoothing it over.

6. Arrange the potatoes, stuffed side up, in a baking dish. Melt the remaining tablespoon of butter and brush the tops of each potato with it. Hold a sieve over the top of each potato and sprinkle the paprika through the sieve onto the tops of the potatoes.

7. Return the potatoes to the oven and bake for 15 minutes.

YIELD: 4 servings.

Pommes de Terre aux Huîtres

BAKED POTATOES WITH OYSTERS

- 4 large Idaho baking potatoes, about ½ pound each
- 4 tablespoons butter
- ¼ cup finely chopped onion
- ¼ cup finely chopped green pepper
- ¼ cup finely chopped celery
- ¼ cup heavy cream
- Salt, if desired
- Freshly ground black pepper to taste
- ⅛ teaspoon grated nutmeg
- ¼ cup finely chopped scallions
- ½ pint shucked oysters
- 1 tablespoon fine fresh bread crumbs

1. Preheat the oven to 400 degrees.

2. Arrange the potatoes on a baking sheet and place in the oven. Bake for about 1 hour, or until done.

3. Meanwhile, melt 1 tablespoon of the butter in a saucepan and add the onion, green pepper and celery. Cook, stirring, until the vegetables are wilted but still crisp.

4. When the potatoes are done, slice off the top of each, about half an inch from the top. Carefully scoop out the center of each potato to make a boat for the stuffing. Put the scraped out potato pulp into the saucepan and mash well and uniformly with the green pepper mixture. Add the cream, 2 tablespoons of the butter, salt and pepper to taste, nutmeg and scallions. Blend well.

5. Cut each oyster in half if they are large and add them to the potato mixture. Cook, stirring, over moderate heat for about 2 minutes.

6. Fill the potato boats with the mixture, piling it up and smoothing it over.

7. Sprinkle the top of each potato with bread crumbs. Arrange the potatoes, stuffed side up, in a baking dish. Melt the remaining tablespoon of butter and pour it over the crumbs. Bake for 15 minutes.

YIELD: 4 servings.

I would be hard put to argue the merits or demerits of the numerous and variously styled deep-fat fryers that are now—to use a word guardedly—saturating the market. It remains a heartening fact, however, that Americans are learning that more can come out of a fryer than Southern fried chicken, fish and chips, and tempura (although I suspect it is these foods that have spurred an interest in, and sales of, the appliances).

But however good the equipment and the raw ingredients, the success of deep frying depends on the temperature of the oil and on the batter. A good fritter batter is one of the simplest things to make and its uses are countless. This batter-fried chicken is delectable when served with lemon wedges and a delicate, French-style tomato sauce. It is excellent as a luncheon or supper dish.

Friture de Volaille

BATTER-FRIED CHICKEN PIECES

- 2 large, whole, skinless, boneless chicken breasts, about 1¼ pounds
- Salt and freshly ground black pepper to taste
- ¼ cup peanut, vegetable or corn oil
- ¼ cup lemon juice
- 4 tablespoons finely chopped parsley
- Fritter batter (see following recipe)
- Oil for deep frying
- Lemon wedges for garnish
- Tomato sauce, French style (see recipe page 408)

1. Place the chicken breasts on a flat surface. Split each whole breast in half. Slice the meat on the bias into about 18 pieces.

2. Put the pieces of chicken in a bowl and add salt and pepper, ¼ cup oil, lemon juice and parsley. Let stand for 20 minutes.

3. Remove the chicken pieces from the marinade, one piece at a time, and add them to a small bowl containing the fritter batter. Manipulate the pieces in the batter so that they are well coated.

4. Heat the oil for deep frying and, when it is quite hot, or 365 degrees, add the batter-coated chicken pieces, one at a time. Do not crowd them in the oil. Cook, turning the pieces occasionally, for about 2 minutes, or until each piece starts to float. Remove with a slotted spoon and drain on paper toweling.

5. Add the remaining chicken pieces to the oil and cook until done. When drained, sprinkle with salt to taste. Garnish with lemon wedges and serve with tomato sauce.

YIELD: 4 servings.

FRITTER BATTER

- 1½ cups flour
- 3 tablespoons peanut, vegetable or corn oil
- 1 teaspoon salt
- 2 large eggs
- ½ cup water

Sift the flour into a mixing bowl. Add the oil and salt. Add the eggs and stir with a wire whisk. Add the water gradually, beating with the whisk.

YIELD: About 2 cups.

SALADS

Salade de Betterave et Thon

BEET AND TUNA SALAD

- 10 medium-sized beets, about 2 pounds
- 18 small, red-skinned potatoes, about 2 pounds
- Salt to taste, if desired
- 1½ cups finely chopped onion
- 2 7-ounce cans solid white tuna packed in oil, drained and flaked
- 1 2-ounce can flat anchovies, drained and chopped
- 2 tablespoons prepared mustard, preferably imported Dijon or Düsseldorf
- ¼ cup red wine vinegar
- 9 tablespoons corn, peanut or vegetable oil
- Freshly ground black pepper to taste
- ⅓ cup finely chopped parsley
- 2 tablespoons finely chopped fresh dill

1. Put the beets in one kettle and the potatoes in a second. Add cold water to cover and salt to taste to each kettle. Bring to the boil. Cook the potatoes for about 25 minutes and the beets for 25 to 45 minutes, or until each vegetable is tender. Drain and let cool.

2. Peel both the beets and potatoes.

3. Slice the beets and potatoes into a large mixing bowl. There should be about 5 cups of potatoes and 4 cups of beets. Add the onion, tuna and anchovies.

4. Put the mustard in a mixing bowl and add the vinegar, stirring with a wire whisk. Gradually add the oil, stirring vigorously with the whisk. Season to taste with the pepper.

5. Pour the sauce over the salad. Add the parsley and dill and toss to blend.

YIELD: 8 to 12 servings.

Topinambours et Crevettes Vinaigrette

JERUSALEM ARTICHOKES OR SUN CHOKES AND SHRIMP VINAIGRETTE

1 pound Jerusalem artichokes or sun chokes, about 8 to 10
Salt to taste, if desired
1 tablespoon prepared mustard, preferably imported Dijon
2 tablespoons red wine vinegar
½ cup olive oil
Freshly ground black pepper to taste
1½ pounds shrimp, cooked, shelled and deveined
½ cup finely chopped red onion
1 teaspoon finely minced garlic
¼ teaspoon hot red pepper flakes
¼ cup finely chopped parsley

1. Using a small regular or swivel-bladed paring knife, peel the artichokes. If the artichokes are very large, cut them in half. Ideally, the artichokes or pieces of artichokes should be of uniform size or the size of the smallest whole artichoke.

2. Put the artichokes in a saucepan. Add cold water to cover and salt to taste. Bring to the boil and simmer for 10 to 15 minutes, or until tender but still a little crisp. Drain well.

3. While the artichokes are still warm cut them into ¼-inch-thick slices. Put them in a bowl.

4. Put the mustard and vinegar in a small bowl. Start beating with a wire whisk while gradually adding the oil. Beat in salt and pepper to taste.

5. Add the shrimp, onion, garlic, pepper flakes and parsley to the artichokes. Pour the sauce over all and stir to blend. Serve warm.

YIELD: 4 to 6 servings.

Shrimp with Tarragon and Anchovy Mayonnaise

1½ pounds raw shrimp, about 36
12 whole allspice
1 dried hot red pepper
Salt
1 cup freshly made mayonnaise (see recipe page 415)
2 teaspoons fresh lemon juice, or more to taste
6 anchovies, finely chopped
1 tablespoon chopped fresh tarragon, or 1 teaspoon dried

1. Place the shrimp in a saucepan and add cold water to cover. Add the allspice, hot red pepper and salt to taste. Bring to the boil and simmer for 1 minute. Remove the shrimp from the heat and let cool. Drain, shell and devein the shrimp.

2. Combine the mayonnaise with the lemon juice, chopped anchovies and tarragon. Cut the shrimp in half and add them. Chill and serve cold.

YIELD: 6 or more servings.

At a glorious picnic on the grass at Tanglewood (actually on an 8- by 10-foot Persian rug set on the lawn with overstuffed pillows to sit on), we were served this unusual chilled shrimp by Marianne Lipsky, who, with her husband Karl, owns a thriving country store in nearby Great Barrington. They explained that the recipe had come from one of their favorite restaurants, the Chesa Grischuna in Klosters, Switzerland.

Chesa Grischuna Shrimp

- 4 cups shredded iceberg lettuce
- 3 pounds cooked shrimp, shelled, deveined and chilled
- 1½ cups mayonnaise, preferably freshly made (see recipe page 415)
- ½ cup freshly grated horseradish
- ¾ cup tomato ketchup
- 1 tart green apple, preferably a Granny Smith
- ½ cup heavy cream
- Salt to taste
- Freshly ground pepper, preferably Tellicherry, to taste
- 1 teaspoon Worcestershire sauce
- ½ teaspoon Tabasco sauce
- 3 tablespoons dry sherry

1. Arrange the lettuce in a crystal bowl and put the shrimp on top and set aside.

2. Put the mayonnaise in a bowl and add the horseradish and ketchup.

3. Core and peel the apple. Cut it into very thin slices. Stack the slices and cut into very thin strips. Cut the strips into the finest possible dice to make 1 cup. Add this to the mayonnaise.

4. Whip the cream until stiff and fold it in. Add salt, pepper, Worcestershire sauce, Tabasco and sherry. Blend well.

5. Spoon the sauce over the shrimp and serve cold.

YIELD: 15 to 20 servings.

Shrimp with Oranges and Rosemary Vinaigrette

- 1 cup chopped celery
- Salt
- 3 oranges, peeled and sliced
- 1½ pounds cooked shrimp
- 1 bunch watercress, rinsed and drained well
- 2 tablespoons red wine vinegar
- 6 tablespoons olive oil
- ½ teaspoon paprika
- Salt and freshly ground black pepper to taste
- ½ teaspoon chopped garlic
- 1 teaspoon chopped fresh rosemary leaves, or ½ teaspoon dried

1. Put the celery into a saucepan and add cold water to cover and salt to taste. Bring to the boil and simmer for about30 seconds. Drain and set aside to let cool.

2. Arrange alternating, overlapping slices of oranges and shrimp on a bed of watercress. Sprinkle with the chopped celery.

3. Blend the vinegar with oil, paprika, salt and pepper to taste, garlic and rosemary. Pour the sauce over the salad and serve at room temperature.

YIELD: 4 servings.

Shrimp and Fruit with Curried Yogurt Mayonnaise

- 3½ cups cooked, shelled, deveined shrimp
- ¾ cup orange sections cut into bite-sized pieces
- 2 cups peeled, seeded papaya or mango cut into bite-sized cubes
- ½ cup white seedless grapes
- ½ cup banana cut into ½-inch cubes
- 1⅔ cups curried yogurt mayonnaise (see recipe page 417)
- Juice of ½ lemon
- 6 cantaloupe halves, seeded
- 6 mint sprigs for garnish

1. Cut the shrimp into bite-sized cubes. There should be about 2½ cups. Put the cubes in a bowl.

2. Add the orange sections, papaya, grapes, banana, ½ cup of the mayonnaise and the lemon juice. Toss to blend.

3. Pile equal portions of the fruit salad into the cantaloupe halves. Spoon a little additional mayonnaise on top of each serving. Garnish each with a mint sprig. Serve the remaining mayonnaise on the side.

YIELD: 6 servings.

One of the best tasting and most interesting types of pasta is called orzo, which is most closely identified with Greek cooking. The word for the pasta in Greek is *kritharaki,* and both it and orzo mean barley, which refers to the shape of the grain, although orzo, like most pasta, is made from wheat flour. Orzo also has more or less the same shape and size as pine nuts or long grains of rice.

Leon Lianides, proprietor of the well-known Coach House Restaurant in Manhattan and our favorite authority on Greek cooking, uses the pasta in a seafood salad that is his own invention.

Seafood and Orzo Salad

- 1 live 2½-pound lobster
- ½ pound large shrimp
- Salt
- ½ cup orzo
- 2 cups freshly made mayonnaise (see recipe page 415)
- 2 teaspoons powdered mustard
- 1 teaspoon finely chopped fresh dill
- 1 teaspoon chopped fresh chives
- Juice of 1 lemon
- 2 tablespoons finely chopped parsley
- Freshly ground black pepper to taste
- 4 large ripe tomatoes

1. Bring enough water to the boil to cover the lobster and shrimp when added. Add salt to taste. Add the lobster and shrimp and cook for 10 minutes.

2. Remove the lobster and shrimp and run under cold water to chill.

3. Strain the cooking liquid and return it to the boil. Add the orzo and cook for 10 minutes, or until tender. Drain. Chill.

4. Remove the meat from the lobster, and shell and devein the shrimp. Cut the lobster meat and shrimp into small, bite-sized pieces.

5. Combine the mayonnaise, mustard, dill, chives, lemon juice and half the parsley in a bowl. Add salt and pepper to taste. Blend well.

6. Fold in the lobster, shrimp and orzo. Cover and refrigerate until ready to serve.

7. Remove the cores from the tomatoes. Cut the tomatoes partly into quarters, but do not cut them all the way to the bottom. Open up each tomato and fill with the orzo mixture. Serve sprinkled with the remaining finely chopped parsley.

YIELD: 4 servings.

Salade d'Asperges et Homard

ASPARAGUS AND LOBSTER SALAD

- 2 to 4 live 1-pound lobsters, preferably female
- Salt to taste
- 16 asparagus spears, ends trimmed
- 2 tablespoons imported mustard with green peppercorns
- 1 tablespoon raspberry or other berry vinegar
- ¼ cup virgin olive oil
- 2 tablespoons walnut oil
- Freshly ground black pepper to taste
- 3 cups shredded Boston lettuce leaves
- 8 raw mushrooms, sliced
- 4 sprigs fresh coriander

1. Bring enough water to the boil to cover the lobsters when they are added. Add salt to taste. Add the lobsters. When the water returns to a full rolling boil, remove the kettle from the heat. Let stand for 15 minutes.

2. Drain the lobsters. Cut off the tails and claws. Crack the tails and claws and remove the meat. Cut the tail meat in half lengthwise. Leave the claw meat whole. Discard the shells.

3. Bring enough water to the boil in a skillet to cover the asparagus spears when they are added. Add salt to taste. Add the asparagus spears and simmer for about 2 minutes, or until crisp-tender. Drain. Run under cold water and drain again.

4. Put the mustard in a small bowl and add the vinegar, stirring with a wire whisk. Gradually add the oils, salt and pepper to taste, beating vigorously with the wire whisk.

5. Arrange a bed of lettuce in the center of four dinner plates. Arrange the lobster pieces on the lettuce. Garnish with asparagus spears and overlapping slices of raw mushrooms. Spoon the sauce over all.

6. Garnish with sprigs of fresh coriander and serve at room temperature.

YIELD: 4 servings.

Crab and Yogurt Mayonnaise Salad

- 1 pound lump crabmeat, or use 2 cups cooked shrimp or lobster cut into bite-sized pieces
- 2 cups yogurt and watercress mayonnaise (see recipe page 416)
- 8 to 10 Boston lettuce leaves
- 3 radishes, cut into thin slices for garnish
- 12 cucumber slices
- 1 hard-boiled egg

1. Handle the crabmeat as little as possible to avoid breaking up the large, firm lumps. Remove any pieces of shell or cartilage, however. Put the crabmeat in a bowl and add ½ cup of the yogurt and watercress mayonnaise. Stir gently to blend.

2. Arrange the lettuce leaves in a circular pattern on a serving dish, stem sides toward the center. Pile the crab salad in the center.

3. Garnish around the sides of the crabmeat with slices of radish and cucumber, arranging them symmetrically.

4. Put the egg through a sieve. Sprinkle it over the crabmeat. Serve with the remaining yogurt and watercress mayonnaise on the side.

YIELD: 4 servings.

Coquilles St. Jacques à la Mayonnaise

SCALLOPS WITH MAYONNAISE SAUCE

- ¼ cup water
- ¼ cup dry white wine
- 1 bay leaf
- 1 sprig fresh thyme, or ¼ teaspoon dried
- 2 sprigs fresh parsley
- Salt and freshly ground black pepper to taste
- 2 cups (1pint) fresh bay scallops
- 1 egg yolk
- 2 teaspoons prepared mustard, preferably imported Dijon or Düsseldorf
- ⅛ teaspoon Tabasco sauce
- ¼ teaspoon Worcestershire sauce
- 1 tablespoon finely chopped shallots
- 1 cup peanut, vegetable or corn oil
- 2 cups Boston lettuce cut into fine shreds (chiffonade)
- 2 hard-boiled eggs, each cut in half, for garnish
- 4 tomato wedges for garnish
- 1 tablespoon finely chopped parsley for garnish

1. In a saucepan combine the water, wine, bay leaf, thyme, parsley sprigs, salt and pepper. Bring to the boil and add the scallops. When the cooking liquid returns to the boil, let simmer, stirring occasionally so that the scallops cook evenly. Cook for about 1 minute and drain, taking care to reserve 2 tablespoons of the cooking liquid. Set the scallops aside until cool.

2. Combine the egg yolk, mustard, Tabasco sauce, Worcestershire sauce and shallots in a mixing bowl. Add salt and pepper to taste.

3. Start beating with a wire whisk while gradually adding the oil. Continue beating until all the oil is added. Beat in the 2 tablespoons of reserved cooking liquid.

4. Arrange the lettuce shreds over the bottom of a serving dish. Spoon the scallops in the center. Spoon the mayonnaise over all. Garnish with the egg halves and tomato wedges. Serve sprinkled with chopped parsley.

YIELD: 4 to 6 servings.

Salade de Filets de Poisson aux Capres

WARM FISH SALAD WITH CAPERS

- 1 head Belgian endive
- 1 bunch watercress
- 8 heart of lettuce leaves
- 1 cup finely shredded heart of lettuce
- 4 small skinless, boneless fillets of fish, such as flounder, sea bass or sole, about ¾ pound
- 2 tablespoons milk
- Salt to taste, if desired
- Freshly ground black pepper to taste
- ½ cup flour
- ¼ cup corn, peanut or vegetable oil
- ⅓ cup olive oil
- ⅓ cup drained capers
- ¼ cup raspberry or red wine vinegar

1. Make neat, symmetrical, generous arrangements of endive leaves, watercress and lettuce leaves on four large dinner plates. Arrange equal portions of shredded lettuce in the center of each arrangement.

2. Cut each fish fillet lengthwise down the center. Cut each fillet half crosswise in two.

3. Put the milk in a small dish and add the fish pieces and salt and pepper to taste. Stir to coat each piece of fish evenly.

4. Put the flour in a flat dish and dredge the pieces of fish in the flour, turning to coat evenly.

5. Heat the corn oil over high heat and add a few pieces of fish at a time. Do not crowd them in the skillet. Cook for about 45 seconds on one side until golden brown. Turn quickly and cook until golden on the second side, about 30 seconds.

6. Arrange 4 fish pieces close together on each of the salad arrangements.

7. Heat the olive oil in a skillet and, when it is quite hot, add the capers. Cook over high heat for 30 seconds, no longer. Add the vinegar, swirl it around and pour an equal portion of the caper mixture over each serving of fish.

YIELD: 4 servings.

Salade de Saumon Printanière

SALMON SALAD WITH VEGETABLES

- 1 cup fresh peas
- Salt
- 1 cup carrots scraped and cut into ¼-inch cubes
- ½ cup diced celery
- 1 cup turnips peeled and cut into ¼-inch cubes
- 1 cup freshly made mayonnaise (see recipe page 415)
- ¼ teaspoon Tabasco sauce
- ½ cup thinly sliced onion
- ½ teaspoon Worcestershire sauce
- ¼ cup finely chopped fresh dill
- Freshly ground black pepper to taste
- 1 large ripe tomato, cored, seeded and cut into eighths
- 4 cups poached salmon cut or broken into large bite-sized pieces (see following recipe)

1. Drop the peas into cold water with salt to taste. Bring to the boil and simmer for 1 to 2 minutes, or until barely tender. Do not overcook. Drain and set aside.

2. Bring enough water to the boil to cover the carrots, celery and turnips when added. Add salt to taste. Add the carrots and simmer for about 3 minutes.

3. Add the celery and turnips and simmer for 1 or 2 minutes longer. Drain. Run under cold water to chill. Drain well on a clean towel.

4. Put the peas, turnips, celery and carrots in a large mixing bowl.

5. Add the mayonnaise, Tabasco sauce, onion, Worcestershire sauce and dill. Add salt and pepper to taste and toss.

6. Put the vegetables in mayonnaise in a serving dish. Surround it with the tomato wedges and pile the salmon on top.

YIELD: 6 servings.

SAUMON POCHÉ

Poached Salmon

- 2¼ pounds salmon with skin and bones
- Salt and freshly ground black pepper to taste
- 6 sprigs fresh parsley
- 1 small onion, peeled and quartered
- ¼ cup white vinegar
- ½ cup sliced carrot
- 1 bay leaf
- 2 sprigs fresh thyme, or ½ teaspoon dried

1. Put the salmon in a kettle and add water to cover to about 1 inch above the fish. Add the remaining ingredients.

2. Bring to the boil and simmer for 20 minutes. Remove from the heat. Let stand until ready to use.

3. Remove the salmon. Remove the skin and bones. Use the salmon in salads.

YIELD: 4 cups flaked salmon.

There are many people who find an octopus preparation a bit bizarre. We can assure them that this one is not. It is delectable. And octopus, fresh or frozen, is widely available in communities with a large Greek population. Squid is also a delectable foundation for a salad as is conch, or scungilli, one of my personal favorites.

Octopus Salad à la Grecque

- 1 3-pound octopus
- 2 tablespoons white wine vinegar
- 1 teaspoon finely minced garlic
- ½ cup coarsely chopped onion, preferably red
- ¼ cup lemon juice
- 3 tablespoons red wine vinegar
- 6 tablespoons olive oil
- Salt to taste, if desired
- A generous grinding of black pepper
- ¼ cup finely chopped parsley

1. Cut away and discard the "beak" and "mouth" of the octopus. Remove and discard the viscera and the ink sac.

2. Bring enough water to the boil to cover the octopus when it is added.

3. Drop the octopus into the water and cook for 5 seconds. Remove the octopus but leave the water boiling. Drop the octopus into a basin of cold water and let stand for 1 minute.

4. Return the octopus to the boiling water for 5 seconds. Remove it a second time, leaving the water boiling. Chill briefly in cold water.

5. Add the white wine vinegar to the boiling water. Add the octopus a third time, cover closely and cook for 1 hour. Drain and let cool.

6. It is not essential to clean away the skin and suckers (suction cups) of the octopus, for they are edible. It is better, however, for appearance's sake. If you want to remove the skin and tentacles, it is easier if you cut off the tentacles before cleaning.

7. Cut the tentacles and meaty center portion of the octopus into bite-sized pieces and place in a bowl. There should be about 4 cups.

8. Add the remaining ingredients and blend well. Cover and refrigerate for several hours before serving.

YIELD: 6 to 8 servings.

Salade de Calmar

SQUID SALAD

- 2 pounds squid, cleaned
- ¼ cup dry white wine
- Salt to taste, if desired
- Freshly ground black pepper to taste
- 2 cloves garlic, peeled and left whole
- 1 hot red pepper, or ¼ teaspoon hot red pepper flakes
- 1 bay leaf
- 4 sprigs fresh parsley
- 2 teaspoons finely minced garlic
- 3 tablespoons finely chopped parsley
- 2 tablespoons lemon juice
- 1 tablespoon red wine vinegar
- ¼ cup olive oil
- ½ cup finely chopped red onion

1. Cut the bodies of the squid into rings about ½ inch wide. Cut the tentacles into bite-sized pieces. There should be about 3½ cups.

2. Put the squid in a saucepan or small kettle and add the wine, water to cover, salt, pepper, garlic cloves, red pepper, bay leaf and parsley sprigs. Bring to the boil. Cover and cook for about 1 minute, or just until squid pieces firm up. Drain and chill.

3. Put the squid in a mixing bowl and add the remaining ingredients. Toss and serve chilled.

YIELD: 4 or more servings.

Note: Freshly cooked shelled shrimp are also excellent in a salad with squid. Simply substitute a portion of shrimp for any given quantity of the squid.

Scungilli (Conch) Salad

- 3 cups cooked, cleaned, sliced conch (see method for cooking page 363)
- 1 tablespoon finely chopped garlic
- 4 to 6 tablespoons lemon juice
- 3 tablespoons olive oil
- ½ teaspoon hot red pepper flakes
- ½ teaspoon crushed dried oregano
- ¼ cup finely chopped parsley
- Salt to taste

1. Put the sliced conch in a bowl and add the garlic. Toss. Add the lemon juice and toss. Add the remaining ingredients. Toss well.

2. Taste and add more lemon juice, oil, salt and so on if desired.

YIELD: 4 to 6 servings.

Note: This salad may be covered closely and will keep for 3 or 4 days in the refrigerator.

Chicken Salad with Grapes

- 2 firm, ripe but not too sweet apples
- 2 cups white seedless grapes
- 2 teaspoons curry powder
- 2 tablespoons chicken broth
- 1 egg yolk
- 2 teaspoons prepared mustard, preferably imported Dijon or Düsseldorf
- 2 tablespoons lemon juice
- Salt and freshly ground black pepper to taste
- 1½ cups peanut, vegetable or corn oil
- Tabasco sauce
- ¼ teaspoon Worcestershire sauce
- 4 cups cooked, skinless, boneless chicken breast cut into neat, bite-sized pieces
- ¾ cup walnuts
- 1 cup finely diced heart of celery
- Boston lettuce leaves
- 1 sprig basil or parsley for garnish

1. Core and peel the apples. Cut them into quarters. Cut each quarter crosswise into thin slices. There should be about 2 cups.

2. If the grapes are large, cut each in half lengthwise. Set aside.

3. Combine the curry powder and broth in a small saucepan. Bring to the boil, stirring. Set aside. Let cool.

4. Put the egg yolk in a mixing bowl and add the mustard, lemon juice and salt and pepper. Start beating with a wire whisk while gradually adding the oil. Add the Tabasco sauce to taste and Worcestershire sauce. Beat in the curry mixture.

5. Combine the chicken, apples, grapes, walnuts and celery in a mixing bowl. Add the curried mayonnaise and fold it in.

6. Arrange the lettuce leaves on a serving dish and pile the salad in the center. Garnish with a sprig of fresh basil or parsley.

YIELD: 8 to 10 servings.

Leslie Newman's Lotos Salad for a Crowd

- 2 unskinned, unboned whole chicken breasts, about 1¾ pounds
- 1¼ pounds fresh bean sprouts
- 2 cucumbers, peeled
- 2 sweet red or green peppers, cored, seeded and cut into thin strips, about 2 cups
- 2 cups shredded roast pork (purchased or homemade)
- 2 pounds fresh Chinese egg noodles
- 1 tablespoon corn, peanut or vegetable oil
- 1½ teaspoons sesame oil
- 3⅓ cups rich sesame sauce (see following recipe)
- ½ cup chopped fresh coriander leaves

1. Bring enough water to the boil to cover the chicken breasts when added. Cut the breasts in half and add them to the water. When the water returns to the boil, cover and simmer for 6 minutes. Remove from the heat and let stand for 15 minutes.

2. Remove the chicken pieces and plunge them into a basin of water with ice cubes. Let stand for 15 minutes. Remove the chicken and pat dry.

3. You may use the bean sprouts as they are purchased. It is more refined, however, if you pull off the curlicues and seed portions of each. There should be 4 cups plucked sprouts. Put the sprouts in a mixing bowl.

4. Cut the cucumbers lengthwise into strips. Cut the strips into spaghetti-like shreds. There should be about 4 cups. Add them to the mixing bowl.

5. Cut the peppers into thin strips and shred the pork. Add them to the mixing bowl.

6. Remove and discard the skin and bones of the chicken breasts. Shred the meat. There should be about 3 cups. Add this to the bowl.

7. Drop the noodles into a large quantity of boiling water. Cook for 4 minutes. Drain well and rinse under cold water until chilled. Drain once more. Cut into shreds of manageable length and put the noodles into a second bowl. Add the corn oil and sesame oil. Chill.

8. Combine the noodles and the pork, chicken and vegetable mixture. Add the sesame sauce and toss. Add the coriander and blend. Serve immediately.

YIELD: 20 to 25 servings.

Note: The chicken may be poached and chilled, then stored tightly wrapped in the refrigerator overnight. You may also prepare the remaining ingredients and store them tightly covered in the refrigerator. Blend the foods when ready to serve.

RICH SESAME SAUCE

- ¼ cup sesame paste (tahini), available in Oriental and Greek markets and specialty food shops
- ½ cup crunchy peanut butter
- ½ cup freshly brewed tea or water
- 2 tablespoons chili oil
- 2 tablespoons sugar
- ¾ cup light soy sauce
- ½ cup sesame oil
- 2 tablespoons finely minced garlic
- ¼ cup red wine vinegar
- 2 tablespoons Chinese black rice vinegar, available in Oriental groceries and supermarkets
- 6 tablespoons corn, peanut or vegetable oil
- 1½ tablespoons ground roasted Sichuan peppercorns (see Note)
- Freshly ground black pepper to taste
- 1 cup finely chopped scallions, green and white parts combined

1. Combine the sesame paste and peanut butter in a mixing bowl. Start beating with a wire whisk while gradually adding the tea. Stir until smooth.

2. Add all the remaining ingredients except the chopped scallions. Cover and refrigerate. This sauce may be made as far in advance as 24 hours. Stir in the scallions just before serving. This can also be used as a cold sauce on cold noodles or poached chicken.

YIELD: About 3⅓ cups, sufficient for 20 to 25 servings.

Note: Place the peppercorns in a heavy skillet and cook over moderately low heat for about 3 minutes, or until dark brown and aromatic. Grind to a powder using a coffee or spice grinder, or blender.

Foie de Canard Vinaigrette

DUCK LIVER SALAD WITH HOT VINAIGRETTE SAUCE

- 4 to 8 duck livers, about 1 pound
- 4 tablespoons butter
- Salt and freshly ground black pepper to taste
- 3 tablespoons hazelnut oil
- 3 tablespoons finely chopped shallots
- 3 tablespoons red wine vinegar
- Hearts of chicory leaves

1. Cut the duck livers in half.

2. Melt the butter in a heavy skillet and, when it is very hot, add the livers. Sprinkle with salt and pepper.

3. Cook over high heat, stirring and turning the livers gently in the sizzling butter, for about 3 minutes. Remove the livers to a hot dish.

4. To the skillet add the oil and shallots. Cook briefly, stirring. Add the vinegar and let it boil up.

5. Arrange a small bed of chicory leaves over each of 4 serving plates. Arrange the livers on top. Spoon the pan sauce over all.

YIELD: 4 servings.

When the word "salad" is bandied about, the image that springs to mind is a simple concoction of one or more varieties of greens tossed together in a bowl. The fact is that some of the most interesting salads in the modern vein are fairly substantial, salads that can easily serve as a main course any season of the year. These salads also are great for party giving because they stand nobly as a buffet item.

One of the most interesting that we have sampled in many a day is an exotic creation, the concept of Daniel Fuchs, the chef of the well-publicized Maxwell's Plum restaurant in Manhattan. This salad is made with mango, macadamia nuts, sweet peppers, lychee nuts and roast duck.

Another is Leslie Newman's many flavor duck salad, which she serves as part of an elaborate Chinese buffet on New Year's Eve.

❧

Daniel Fuchs's Duck and String Bean Salad

- 1 4-to-5-pound roast duck (see recipe page 183)
- 1 pound string beans
- 2 unblemished sweet red peppers
- 2 ripe tomatoes
- 14 lychee nuts
- 1 mango, peeled and seeded
- ½ cup macadamia nuts
- 3 tablespoons lemon juice
- ½ to ¾ cup walnut oil (or use Chinese or Japanese sesame oil)
- Salt and freshly ground black pepper to taste
- 2 tablespoons chopped fresh coriander

1. Cut the meat from the duck, discarding the skin and bones. Cut the meat into neat, bite-sized portions. There should be about 2 cups. Set aside.

2. Trim off the ends of the beans. Cut the beans into 2-inch lengths and drop them into a saucepan of boiling water. When the water returns to the boil, let simmer for 4 minutes. Drain. Run the beans briefly under cold running water. Drain thoroughly. Set aside.

3. Core and seed the peppers. Cut the peppers into thin lengthwise shreds. Drop the shreds into boiling water. When the water returns to the boil, drain. Run briefly under cold water. Drain thoroughly. Set aside.

4. Remove the cores from the tomatoes. Cut the tomatoes in half and remove the seeds. Cut the tomato halves into thin strips. Set aside.

5. Cut the lychee nuts into quarters. Cut the mango flesh into thin strips. There should be about 2 cups.

6. Combine the duck meat, beans, peppers, tomatoes, nuts, mango and remaining ingredients in a mixing bowl and blend well. Serve at room temperature.

YIELD: 8 or more servings.

Many Flavor Duck Salad

- 3 5- to 6-pound ducks, red-cooked (see recipe page 185)
- ½ cup pine nuts
- ½ teaspoon plus ¾ cup corn, peanut or vegetable oil
- 3 sweet red or green peppers, cored, seeded and cut into 1-inch pieces
- 12 cups shredded Shandong (white-ribbed Chinese cabbage)
- 1½ cups minced scallions, green and white parts combined
- 1½ tablespoons minced fresh ginger
- 1 tablespoon ground roasted Sichuan peppercorns (see Note page 124)
- Freshly ground black pepper to taste
- 3 fresh hot chili peppers, seeded and finely chopped
- 9 tablespoons dark soy sauce
- 4½ tablespoons hoisin sauce
- 3 tablespoons honey
- 2 tablespoons finely minced garlic
- 2 teaspoons bottled chili paste with garlic

1. Cut the ducks into quarters and pull the bones from the meat. Cut away and discard the skin and any fat. The ducks may be prepared to this point a day or longer in advance. If they are not to be used immediately, wrap the pieces in foil or plastic wrap and refrigerate or freeze. Cut the meat when it is at room temperature or defrosted into 1-inch-wide shreds.

2. Meanwhile, preheat the oven to 325 degrees. Put the pine nuts in an ovenproof skillet and toss them in ½ teaspoon of the corn oil. Place in the oven and bake for 10 to 15 minutes, or until golden brown. Cool.

3. Put the nuts in a large mixing bowl and add the duck, peppers and cabbage.

4. Put the remaining ¾ cup of corn oil in a saucepan and add the chopped scallions, ginger, ground Sichuan pepper, pepper and chili peppers.

5. Combine the dark soy sauce, hoisin sauce, honey, garlic and chili paste with garlic in a small bowl.

6. Bring the corn oil mixture to the simmer and cook for 1 minute, no longer. Add the soy sauce mixture and stir. Remove from the heat. Pour this simmering liquid over the salad. Toss, blending well, and serve immediately.

YIELD: 25 servings.

Salade de Pigeonneau

SQUAB SALAD

- 4 squabs, ¾ to 1 pound each, cleaned weight, split for broiling
- Salt to taste, if desired
- Freshly ground black pepper to taste
- 2 tablespoons plus ½ cup corn, peanut or vegetable oil
- 16 whole unblemished salad leaves, preferably Boston or romaine lettuce
- 16 whole unblemished Belgian endive leaves
- 4 cherry tomatoes, cored and cut into quarters
- 1 cup neatly sliced Belgian endive leaves
- 1 tablespoon prepared mustard, preferably imported Dijon or Düsseldorf
- 1 egg yolk
- ¼ cup red wine vinegar
- 1 tablespoon cold water
- 1 tablespoon finely chopped shallots

1. Preheat the broiler to high.

2. Sprinkle the squabs all over with salt and pepper. Arrange them skin side down in a baking dish. Brush on both sides with 2 tablespoons of the oil.

3. On 4 large plates, make a symmetrical pattern of Boston lettuce leaves, endive leaves and tomato quarters. Add sliced endive to the center of each arrangement.

4. Put the mustard, egg yolk, vinegar, salt and pepper in a mixing bowl. Start beating with a wire whisk. Gradually add the remaining ½ cup of oil. Beat in the water. Stir in the shallots. Set aside.

5. Place the baking dish in the oven so that the squabs are about 6 inches from the source of heat. Broil for 5 minutes and turn. Continue broiling for about 10 minutes longer, or until the squabs are still slightly rare.

6. While the squabs are still hot or warm, cut away the breasts and carve them into thin slices. Cut the meat away from the thighs and legs. Discard the carcasses. Arrange the meat as it is cut away and sliced over the lettuce. Spoon the sauce over and serve.

YIELD: 4 servings.

Anything Mayonnaise Salad

- 3 cups cubed or shredded cooked foods such as meat, poultry, fish or seafood
- 1 cup carrot cut into ¼-inch or smaller cubes
- 1 cup zucchini or other squash cut into ¼-inch cubes
- ¾ cup celery cut into ¼-inch cubes
- 1½ tablespoons finely chopped shallots
- 1 clove garlic, finely minced
- Salt and freshly ground black pepper to taste
- 1 tablespoon finely chopped parsley
- 1½ cups mayonnaise, preferably homemade (see recipe page 415)
- Lettuce leaves for garnish
- Tomato wedges for garnish
- Hard-boiled egg wedges for garnish

1. If a cooked solid such as chicken, veal, lamb, pork or beef is used, cut it into small, bite-sized cubes. If shrimp are used, leave them whole. If crabmeat is used, leave it in lumps or shred it. There should be about 3 cups.

2. Bring about 3 cups of water to the boil. Add the carrots and cook for about 5 minutes. Add the zucchini and cook both vegetables a minute longer. Add the celery and cook for 1 more minute. Do not overcook. The vegetables must remain a bit firm. Drain well. Let cool.

3. Put the vegetables and meat in a mixing bowl and add the shallots, garlic, salt and pepper and parsley. Add the mayonnaise and blend.

4. Arrange a border of lettuce leaves around a serving dish. Spoon the salad in the center of the dish. Garnish with tomato and egg wedges.

YIELD: 6 servings.

Next to the New World itself, corn was, to my mind, the greatest discovery brought about by Christopher Columbus. It not only offers sustenance in the form of breads, puddings, tortillas and the like, but it is, when properly cooked, quite simply one of the most irresistible foods known. It also gives dimension to a summery ham-and-cheese salad, the inspiration for which came, oddly enough, from a small food shop on an island in the French West Indies.

❧

Salade Printanière

CORN SALAD WITH HAM AND CHEESE

- 1 slice cooked ham, about ½ inch thick
- 1 slice Gruyère or Swiss cheese, about ¼ inch thick
- 4 to 6 hearts of celery stalks
- 24 small pimiento-stuffed green olives
- 2 cups peeled, seeded and diced ripe tomatoes
- 1 cup cooked corn cut from the cob
- ¾ cup finely chopped parsley
- 1 cup coarsely chopped onion
- ¾ cup mustard vinaigrette (see recipe page 413)

1. Cut the ham into strips ½ inch wide. Cut the strips into ½-inch cubes. There should be about 2 cups.
2. Cut the cheese into ¼-inch strips. Cut the strips into ¼-inch cubes. There should be about 1 cup.
3. Finely dice the celery. There should be about 1½ cups.
4. Cut the olives in half crosswise.
5. In a large salad bowl, combine all the ingredients and toss well with the vinaigrette.

YIELD: 6 or more servings.

Early in the sixteenth century when the Spanish first arrived in Mexico, they must have been pleasantly surprised by what the Aztecs called *ahuacatl.* The Spanish almost immediately dubbed the butter-rich, pear-shaped fruit *aguacate,* which later came to be known in English as avocado. It was not until after the Second World War that avocados came to be widely known and used in Europe. They are one of the finest of all foods for summer dining. As a base for salads (an unpeeled avocado half is itself a serving cup), they are almost without peer. They team well with almost all fish and seafood, particularly crab, lobster and shrimp. An avocado mousse flavored with Mexican tastes such as chilies and fresh coriander is a delight.

Avocado Mousse with Chilies

- 4 ripe, firm, unblemished avocados, about 3 pounds combined weight
- 8 tablespoons lime juice
- ¼ cup water
- 2 tablespoons (envelopes) unflavored granular gelatin
- 1½ cups freshly made mayonnaise (see recipe page 415)
- 1 4-ounce can chopped green chilies, drained, about ⅓ cup
- 1 8-ounce package cream cheese
- 1 to 4 canned jalapeño peppers, drained and chopped
- ¼ cup finely chopped fresh coriander
- Salt and freshly ground black pepper to taste
- 1 teaspoon peanut, vegetable or corn oil

1. Peel the avocados. Cut them in half and discard the pits. Quickly cut the halves into 1-inch cubes and add 1 tablespoon of the lime juice. Toss to prevent discoloration. There should be about 6 cups.

2. Blend the water with the gelatin in a saucepan. Heat gently, stirring, until the gelatin dissolves.

3. Put the mayonnaise in a mixing bowl and add the gelatin mixture and chopped chilies. Blend well.

4. Combine the cubed avocado, the remaining lime juice and cream cheese in the container of a food processor. Blend thoroughly. Add the chopped peppers, coriander and salt and pepper to taste. Blend well.

5. Brush the inside of a 6-cup ring mold with the oil.

6. Spoon the avocado mixture into the prepared mold. Cover the mousse with a ring of wax paper. Refrigerate overnight.

7. To unmold, surround the mold with hot towels to loosen the mousse. Unmold onto a round serving dish. Serve with mayonnaise, if desired.

YIELD: 8 or more servings.

❧

Salade de Laitue Sucrée Marocaine

LETTUCE SALAD

1 head crisp, curly-leaf lettuce
Freshly ground black pepper
5 tablespoons sugar
5 tablespoons white vinegar

1. Remove the core from the lettuce. Rinse the leaves and pat them dry. Stack the leaves and cut them into very thin strips. There should be about 4 cups loosely packed.

2. Put the leaves in a salad bowl and add a generous amount of freshly ground pepper. Add the sugar, a tablespoon at a time, tossing the greens after each addition.

3. Sprinkle with the vinegar and toss. Do not add salt. Serve at room temperature.

YIELD: 4 to 6 servings.

❧

Chez Panisse's Baked Goat Cheese with Lettuce Salad

8 rounds of very soft, mild goat cheese, about half an inch thick (see Note)
1 cup olive oil, preferably virgin oil
Freshly ground black pepper to taste
Salt, if desired
8 sprigs fresh thyme, or any desired herbs such as oregano, rosemary, sage or finely minced garlic
1 cup fresh bread crumbs
8 cups loosely packed assorted salad and herb greens such as chervil, arugula, mâche or field salad or chicory
1 tablespoon red wine vinegar

1. Arrange the goat cheese rounds on a shallow dish.

2. Pour ¾ cup of the olive oil over all. Sprinkle with pepper and salt. Turn the rounds in the oil. Arrange or sprinkle the fresh herbs over all.

3. Dip the rounds all over in the bread crumbs, patting to make the crumbs adhere. Arrange the rounds on a baking dish. Refrigerate for 15 minutes or longer.

4. When ready to cook, preheat the oven to 450 degrees.

5. Strain the herbs from the oil and reserve the oil.

6. Place the baking dish in the oven and bake for 10 to 12 minutes.

7. Meanwhile, put the salad and herb greens in a salad bowl. Blend the vinegar, the reserved oil and the remaining ¼ cup oil, salt and pepper. Pour the dressing over the greens and toss well.

8. Transfer the greens to a flat serving dish. Arrange the cheese rounds around and serve immediately.

YIELD: 4 to 8 servings.

Note: Alice Waters of Chez Panisse uses fresh Sonoma, California, goat cheese. Ask your cheese merchant for any soft, fresh, mild goat cheese. Montrachet cheese would work well for this.

❧

Asparagus with Thai Dressing

- 1½ pounds asparagus spears
- ½ clove garlic
- 1 tablespoon fish sauce (see Note)
- 1 tablespoon lime juice
- 3 tablespoons peanut, vegetable or corn oil
- ¼ teaspoon hot red pepper flakes
- ½ teaspoon freshly ground black pepper
- ½ cup loosely packed fresh mint leaves
- ½ cup loosely packed, coarsely chopped fresh coriander leaves
- ½ cup loosely packed onion rings
- Lettuce leaves for garnish

1. Cut off and discard any tough ends of the asparagus spears. Cut the spears on the bias into 1-inch lengths. Put the asparagus pieces into the top of a vegetable steamer. Steam them, closely covered, for 4 minutes or less, or until crisp-tender.

2. Put the garlic in a mortar and grind to a paste with a pestle. Add the fish essence, lime juice, oil, hot pepper flakes and black pepper and blend well.

3. In a mixing bowl, combine the mint, coriander leaves and onion rings. Add the asparagus. Spoon the sauce over all. Toss well.

4. Arrange a ring of lettuce leaves around the border of a round plate or serving dish. Spoon the asparagus salad in the center.

YIELD: 4 to 6 servings.

Note: Fish sauce, called nuoc mam or nam pla, is available in bottles in Oriental groceries and supermarkets.

Carrot Salad

- 1 pound fresh carrots, about 12
- 1 large clove garlic, peeled but left whole
- Salt
- ¼ cup lemon juice
- ⅛ teaspoon ground cinnamon
- ½ teaspoon ground cumin
- ½ teaspoon paprika
- ⅛ teaspoon cayenne pepper
- ¼ cup olive oil
- Chopped parsley for garnish

1. Trim and scrape the carrots and put them in a kettle.

2. Add water to cover, and the garlic and salt to taste. Bring to the boil and cook for 10 minutes. Drain. Cut the carrots into ½-inch cubes. There should be about 2½ cups.

3. Combine the lemon juice, salt to taste, cinnamon, cumin, paprika and cayenne in a mixing bowl and blend. Add the carrot cubes and half the oil. Stir to blend and set aside.

4. Spoon into a serving dish and sprinkle the remaining oil over the top. Sprinkle with chopped parsley and serve.

YIELD: About 6 servings.

Cucumber Salad

- 2 fresh, firm cucumbers, about ¾ pound
- ¼ cup sugar
- Salt to taste
- 5 tablespoons white vinegar
- 5 tablespoons water
- 1 tablespoon very thinly sliced shallots
- 1 tablespoon finely shredded seeded hot fresh red pepper
- ¼ cup chopped fresh coriander

1. Peel the cucumbers. Quarter the cucumbers lengthwise and slice thinly. There should be about 2 cups.

2. Combine the sugar, salt, vinegar, water and shallots in a saucepan. Bring to the boil and stir until sugar dissolves. Remove from the heat and reserve.

3. Combine the cucumbers and shredded hot red peppers in a bowl. Pour the sugar syrup over all and stir. Sprinkle with coriander. Cover and refrigerate for 2 to 3 hours.

YIELD: 4 to 6 sevings.

Mushroom and Avocado Salad

- ¼ cup olive oil
- 2 tablespoons red wine or tarragon vinegar
- 2 teaspoons prepared mustard, preferably imported Dijon or Düsseldorf
- Salt and freshly ground black pepper to taste
- 2 tablespoons finely chopped parsley
- ½ teaspoon finely minced garlic
- ½ pound mushrooms, thinly sliced, about 2½ cups
- 1 firm but ripe unblemished avocado

1. Blend the oil, vinegar, mustard, salt, pepper, parsley and garlic thoroughly with a wire whisk.

2. Pour the sauce over the mushrooms and toss until well blended.

3. Peel the avocado and cut it in half. Remove and discard the pit. Cut the avocado into 1-inch cubes. Add the cubes to the mushroom mixture and toss gently to blend. Serve at room temperature.

YIELD: 4 to 6 servings.

Celery and Mushrooms à la Grecque

- 8 celery stalks, approximately
- ½ pound small mushrooms
- 4 very small white onions
- ½ sweet red or green pepper
- 2 tablespoons olive oil
- ¼ cup lemon juice
- ¼ cup white wine vinegar
- 2 teaspoons coriander seeds
- 2 whole cloves
- Salt
- ½ teaspoon whole black peppercorns
- 1 bay leaf
- ¼ teaspoon dried thyme

1. Trim off the ends of the celery stalks. Scrape the stalks as necessary. Cut each stalk crosswise into 1½-inch lengths. There should be about 2½ cups. Set aside.

2. Rinse and drain the mushrooms. Set aside.

3. Peel the onions and cut them into quarters. There should be about ¾ cup.

4. Cut the pepper into match-like strips about 1 inch long.

5. Pour the olive oil into a saucepan and add the lemon juice, vinegar, coriander seeds, cloves, salt to taste, peppercorns, bay leaf and thyme. Add the celery, mushrooms, onions and pepper. Cover closely and cook, shaking the pan occasionally, about 10 minutes.

6. Pour the mixture into a mixing bowl and let cool. Chill. Serve cold or at room temperature.

YIELD: 4 or more servings.

Mushroom and Pepper Salad

- 1 large sweet red pepper, about ½ pound
- 1 large sweet green pepper, about ½ pound
- ¾ cup celery cut crosswise into ¼-inch pieces
- 2 large unblemished endives
- ¼ pound mushrooms, thinly sliced, about 2 cups
- ¼ cup chopped scallions
- 2 tablespoons lemon juice
- 1 tablespoon red wine vinegar
- 3 tablespoons olive oil
- ¼ teaspoon sugar

1. Cut away the core of each pepper.

2. Bring enough water to the boil in a saucepan to cover the peppers when added. Add the peppers and cook for 2 minutes, no longer. Remove the peppers but leave the water in the saucepan.

3. Using a paring knife, pull off the skin of the red pepper. The green pepper will not skin properly.

4. Cut the peppers lengthwise into quarters. Remove any veins and seeds. Cut the quartered peppers into ¼-inch crosswise strips.

5. Add the celery to the boiling water and simmer for about 30 seconds. Drain.

6. Trim off the base of the endives. Cut the endives crosswise into ¼-inch pieces.

7. Combine the peppers, mushrooms, celery, endives and scallions in a salad bowl.

8. Put the lemon juice and vinegar in a small mixing bowl and gradually beat in the oil and sugar. Beat well with a wire whisk. Pour the sauce over the mushroom mixture. Toss and serve.

YIELD: 4 servings.

Sweet Peppers, Moroccan Style

- 3 or 4 large sweet green or red peppers, preferably a combination of both, about 1 pound
- ½ teaspoon ground cumin
- 1 tablespoon lemon juice
- 2 tablespoons olive oil
- ¼ teaspoon finely chopped garlic
- ⅛ teaspoon cayenne pepper
- ¼ teaspoon paprika
- 2 tablespoons chopped parsley
- Salt and freshly ground black pepper to taste

1. Preheat the broiler or use a charcoal grill. Put the peppers under the broiler or on the grill and cook, turning often, until the skin is shriveled and partly blackened. Remove. Put the peppers in a paper bag and let stand until cool enough to handle. Peel off the skins.

2. Split the peppers in half. Remove and discard the stems and seeds. Place the halves on a flat surface. Cut into strips or cut them into fairly large, bite-sized pieces. There should be about 1½ cups.

3. Put the pieces in a mixing bowl and add all the remaining ingredients. Toss to blend. Serve at room temperature.

YIELD: About 4 servings.

String Bean and Pepper Salad with Cumin Vinaigrette

- 1 pound string beans
- 1 sweet red or green pepper
- ½ cup finely chopped onion
- 1 teaspoon prepared mustard, preferably imported Dijon
- 1 tablespoon red wine vinegar
- Salt and freshly ground black pepper to taste
- ⅓ cup olive oil
- ¼ teaspoon ground cumin
- ¼ cup finely chopped parsley

1. Trim or break off the ends of the beans. Remove the strings if any.

2. Bring enough water to the boil to cover the beans when they are added. Add the beans. When the water returns to the boil, cook until the beans are tender, about 10 minutes. Drain well. Put them in a mixing bowl.

3. Put the pepper under the broiler and turn frequently until the skin is charred on all sides. Remove and put in a paper bag until cool enough to

handle. Pull off the skin, cut the pepper in half and remove the seeds. Put each half of the roasted pepper on a flat surface. Cut it into very thin strips about ¼ inch wide. There should be about ½ cup. Add them to the beans. Add the chopped onion.

4. Put the mustard, vinegar and salt and pepper in a small mixing bowl. Start stirring with a wire whisk while gradually adding the oil. Add the cumin.

5. Stir and add the sauce to the bean mixture. Sprinkle with parsley and toss. Serve at room temperature.

YIELD: 4 to 6 servings.

Potato Salad with Walnuts and Anchovy Mayonnaise

- 2 pounds Idaho, Long Island or Maine potatoes
- Salt
- 1 cup broken walnut meats
- ¾ cup anchovy mayonnaise (see recipe page 416)
- ¼ cup chopped dill or parsley

1. Put the potatoes in a kettle and add water to cover and salt to taste. Bring to the boil and simmer for 20 minutes, or until tender. Drain.

2. When the potatoes are still hot but cool enough to handle, peel them. Cut into ¼-inch-thick slices. There should be about 6 cups. Put the slices in a bowl.

3. Add the walnuts, mayonnaise and chopped dill. Toss and serve while still warm.

YIELD: 8 or more servings.

Salade de Pommes de Terre au Vin Blanc

POTATO SALAD WITH WHITE WINE

- 16 new red, waxy potatoes, about 2 pounds
- Salt to taste, if desired
- ⅓ cup finely chopped white onion
- 2 tablespoons finely chopped shallots
- 2 tablespoons dry white wine
- ½ teaspoon finely minced garlic
- 6 tablespoons red wine vinegar
- 6 tablespoons corn, peanut or vegetable oil
- ½ cup finely chopped parsley

1. Rinse and drain the potatoes. Put them in a saucepan with water to cover and salt to taste. Bring to the boil and simmer for about 20 minutes, or until tender.

2. Drain the potatoes. When they are cool enough to handle, cut them, unpeeled, into ¼-inch-thick slices. There should be about 5 cups. Put the potatoes in a mixing bowl.

3. While the potatoes are still warm, add the remaining ingredients. Toss gently to blend. Serve, if desired, with garlic sausages (see following recipe).

YIELD: 6 to 8 servings.

SAUCISSONS À L'AIL

Garlic sausages

- 2 uncooked garlic sausages (cotechini), about 1 pound each
- 2 bay leaves
- ½ teaspoon dried thyme

1. Put the sausages in a kettle and add cold water to cover.

2. Add the bay leaves and thyme and bring to the boil. Let simmer for 30 minutes. Serve sliced, hot or cold.

YIELD: 6 to 8 servings.

❧

Creamy Coleslaw

- 1 head cabbage, 2 pounds
- 2 small carrots, trimmed and scraped
- 1 egg yolk
- 1 teaspoon prepared mustard, preferably imported Dijon or Düsseldorf
- 2 tablespoons white vinegar
- Salt and freshly ground black pepper to taste
- 1 cup peanut, vegetable or corn oil
- 1 teaspoon poppy seeds or caraway seeds
- ½ teaspoon celery seeds, optional
- 1 teaspoon sugar
- ⅛ teaspoon Tabasco sauce
- 2 tablespoons finely minced onion

1. Remove the core from the cabbage. Cut the cabbage into 2-inch cubes. Put the cubed cabbage, one batch at a time, in the container of a food

processor. Process until finely chopped. As the cabbage is chopped put it into a mixing bowl. There should be about 8 cups.

2. Cut the carrots into ½-inch rounds. Put the rounds into the container of the food processor. Process until finely chopped.

3. Put the egg yolk, mustard, vinegar, salt and pepper into a mixing bowl. Start beating with a wire whisk while adding the oil gradually until the mixture thickens like a mayonnaise.

4. Add the poppy seeds, celery seeds, sugar, Tabasco sauce and onion. Stir. Add the cabbage and carrot and blend thoroughly. Chill.

YIELD: 12 servings.

Salade Arabe Traditionnelle

MOROCCAN TOMATO SALAD

- 1 small green pepper, cored, seeded and deveined
- 1½ cups cored, peeled and seeded tomatoes cut into ½-inch cubes
- 1 tablespoon finely chopped parsley
- 1 tablespoon finely chopped onion
- ¼ teaspoon finely minced garlic
- ½ teaspoon finely minced fresh coriander
- Salt to taste, if desired
- ¼ teaspoon cayenne pepper
- ½ teaspoon ground cumin
- 1 tablespoon white vinegar
- 2 tablespoons peanut oil

1. Cut the pepper into strips about ½ inch wide. Cut the strips crosswise into thin slices. There should be about ⅓ cup.

2. Put the pepper in a bowl and add the remaining ingredients. Blend. Chill.

YIELD: 4 to 6 servings.

Lentil and Scallion Salad

- 2 small smoked pork hocks, or ½ pound piece of smoked pork
- 6 cups water, approximately
- 1 pound lentils, picked over and rinsed
- Salt to taste
- ¼ cup chopped scallions
- 4 to 6 tablespoons olive oil
- 2 to 3 tablespoons wine vinegar
- Freshly ground black pepper to taste
- ¼ to 1 teaspoon powdered mustard

1. Put the pork hocks in a large saucepan and add the water. Bring to the boil and cover. Simmer for 1½ hours.

2. Remove the pork from the saucepan and skim off any fat. Add the lentils and salt. Bring to the boil and simmer, covered, for about 25 minutes, or until tender. It may be necessary to add more water to the saucepan. The lentils, as they cook, should be almost but not quite covered with the boiling liquid. When the lentils are tender, drain them. They must not be cooked to a mushy stage.

3. Drain the lentils and let cool.

4. Cut the meat off the pork hocks and add it to the lentils. Add the remaining ingredients with salt to taste. Blend well and let stand to develop flavor for several hours.

YIELD: 6 or more servings.

Tabbouleh

- ¾ cup fine bulgur (see Note)
- 1 cup diced, seeded tomatoes
- 1 cup finely chopped parsley
- ½ cup chopped scallions
- 1 tablespoon chopped fresh mint
- ½ cup fresh lemon juice
- ½ cup olive oil
- Salt and freshly ground black pepper to taste
- Romaine lettuce leaves for garnish

1. Put the bulgur in a sieve and let cold water run over it. Transfer the bulgur to a mixing bowl and add cold water to cover to a depth of about 1 inch above the top of the wheat. Let soak for about 15 minutes.

2. Line a sieve with cheesecloth and drain the cracked wheat. Bring up the edges of the cheesecloth and squeeze to extract most of the moisture.

3. Put the bulgur in a mixing bowl and add all the remaining ingredients except the lettuce leaves. Toss to blend thoroughly.

4. Arrange the lettuce leaves around a salad bowl. Spoon in the salad and serve.

YIELD: 8 or more servings.

Note: Bulgur, which is very fine cracked wheat, is available at specialty food shops.

POULTRY

Roast Chicken with Rosemary and Garlic

- 1 3½-pound chicken with giblets
- Salt and freshly ground black pepper to taste
- 2 sprigs fresh rosemary
- 2 cloves garlic, unpeeled
- 2 tablespoons butter
- 1 onion (about ¼ pound), peeled
- ¾ cup water

1. Preheat the oven to 425 degrees.
2. Sprinkle the chicken inside and out with salt and pepper. Stuff it with the rosemary and garlic. Truss the chicken.
3. Place the chicken in a shallow, not too large roasting pan and rub the chicken with the butter. Put the chicken on its side. Scatter the onion, neck, liver, gizzard and heart around the chicken.
4. Place chicken in the oven and roast for about 15 minutes, basting occasionally. Turn the chicken on the opposite side; continue roasting, basting often.
5. Roast for 15 minutes and turn the chicken onto its back. Continue roasting and basting for 15 minutes.
6. Pour off the fat from the roasting pan. Add the water and return the chicken to the oven. Roast for 10 minutes longer, basting often. Remove from the oven and let the chicken stand for 10 minutes before carving. Serve with the pan liquid.

YIELD: 2 to 4 servings.

Most Americans probably believe that pecans are as universal as grapes, but this is not true. They are just as American as apple pie. The pecan tree is a North American member of the walnut family and its name comes from the Algonquian *pakan.* Pecans are said to have first flourished in this country in Oklahoma; from there they were introduced to Texas. And they have a venerable and deserved popularity in many American foods, from the main course, as in this poultry stuffing, to desserts such as pecan pie.

Roast Chicken with Sausage and Pecan Stuffing

- 1 3½-pound roasting chicken, with giblets
- 4 tablespoons butter
- ½ pound bulk sausage
- 1 cup finely chopped onion
- 1 tablespoon loosely packed leaf sage
- ¼ cup finely chopped parsley
- 1 cup fine fresh bread crumbs
- 1 egg, lightly beaten
- Salt and freshly ground black pepper to taste
- 1 cup toasted pecans
- 1 onion, peeled and quartered
- ¼ cup water

1. Preheat the oven to 400 degrees.

2. Remove the gizzard, heart and liver from the chicken. Cut away and discard the tough outer membrane of the gizzard. Chop the soft, fleshy part of the gizzard, the heart and liver.

3. Melt 2 tablespoons of the butter in a saucepan and add the sausage, breaking it up with the flat side of a metal spoon. Add the liver mixture and chopped onion. Cook, stirring, for about 3 minutes and add the sage.

4. Cook for about 3 minutes, stirring, or until the sausage is cooked. Add the parsley, bread crumbs, egg, salt and pepper and the pecans. Blend well and let cool.

5. Sprinkle the chicken inside and out with salt and pepper. Stuff the chicken with the pecan mixture and truss. Rub all over with the remaining 2 tablespoons of butter. Place the chicken on its side in a shallow baking dish and scatter the quartered onion around it.

6. Roast the chicken for 20 minutes. Turn the chicken to the other side and continue roasting, basting often, for about 20 minutes.

7. Turn the chicken on its back and continue roasting, basting often, for about 20 minutes.

8. Ten minutes before the chicken is done, add the water and continue baking.

9. Remove from the oven and let the chicken stand for 10 minutes before carving. Serve with the pan juices.

YIELD: 4 or more servings.

Poulet Zaza

CHICKEN WITH CHAMPAGNE SAUCE

- 1 3½-pound chicken, cut into serving pieces
- Salt to taste, if desired
- Freshly ground black pepper to taste
- ¼ cup flour
- 2 carrots, trimmed and scraped, about ¼ pound
- ¼ pound string beans
- 2 celery stalks
- 3 tablespoons butter
- 2 tablespoons peanut oil
- ¼ cup finely chopped shallots
- 2 cups brut champagne
- ½ cup chicken broth
- 1 cup heavy cream
- 4 egg yolks
- 3 tablespoons water

1. Sprinkle the chicken pieces with salt and pepper. Dredge the pieces in flour and shake off any excess.

2. Cut each carrot into 2-inch lengths. Cut each length into ⅛-inch-thick slices. Stack the slices and cut them into ⅛-inch-thick slivers (julienne). There should be about 1½ cups. Set aside.

3. Cut the string beans and celery into 2-inch lengths. Cut each length into julienne slivers. There should be about a cup of string beans and slightly less than a cup of celery. Set aside.

4. Heat the butter and oil in a heavy skillet large enough to accommodate the chicken in one layer. When the fat is quite hot, add the chicken pieces, skin side down, and cook about 3 minutes over moderately low heat. Turn and cook the second side about 2 minutes. Remove the pieces to a serving dish. Pour off all but 1 tablespoon of the fat. Add the shallots and cook briefly, stirring.

5. Return the chicken pieces to the skillet and add the champagne. Add the chicken broth and bring to the boil. Partly cover and simmer 15 minutes.

6. Have ready a basin of ice water to chill the vegetables after they are cooked.

7. Meanwhile, bring a large quantity of water to a boil. Put the carrots in a sieve and add them in the sieve to the boiling water. Let cook about 2½ minutes. Remove them in the sieve and add them to the ice water. Drain.

8. Repeat with the celery, letting it cook about 1½ minutes. Chill and drain.

9. Repeat with the green beans, letting them cook about 2 minutes. Chill and drain.

10. Remove the chicken pieces to a warm serving dish. Cover closely with foil.

11. Cook the sauce down over high heat until reduced to about ¾ cup. Add the cream and bring to a simmer.

12. Combine the egg yolks and water in a heavy saucepan. Place the pan on a heatproof pad such as a double metal Flame Tamer and heat the yolk mixture until tripled in volume and thickened like a foamy, rich custard, or sabayon. Do not overcook or the yolks will scramble. The cooking without boiling should take about 10 minutes. Remove from the heat and beat in the cream sauce.

13. Add the vegetables to the cream sauce. Pour the sauce over the chicken and serve.

YIELD: 4 servings.

Chicken Cacciatore

- 1 3-pound chicken, cut into serving pieces
- ⅓ cup plus 1 tablespoon olive oil
- 3 tablespoons finely chopped onion
- ¼ cup flour
- ¼ cup butter
- 2 teaspoons finely minced garlic
- Salt, if desired
- Freshly ground black pepper to taste
- ¼ cup dry white wine
- 1¾ cups rich chicken broth (see recipe page 418)
- 1 cup marinara sauce (see recipe page 410)

1. Carefully remove the bones from the chicken pieces or have this done by the butcher. Cut each breast half in two, crosswise.

2. Heat 1 tablespoon of oil and cook the onion, stirring, until lightly brown. Set aside.

3. Heat the remaining ⅓ cup of oil in a heavy skillet or casserole.

4. Dredge the pieces of chicken lightly in flour and shake off any excess. Add the pieces, skin side down, to the skillet and cook until golden on one side, about 3 minutes. Turn the pieces and cook on the second side, about 3 minutes.

5. Pour off the fat from the skillet and add the butter and garlic to the chicken. Add the onion, salt and pepper. Stir to blend. Add the wine and cook for about 1 minute.

6. Add the chicken broth and marinara sauce. Bring to the boil and cover closely. Let cook, covered, over high heat for about 15 minutes, or until tender. Serve with portions of polenta, if desired.

YIELD: 4 servings.

Poulet au Romarin

CHICKEN SAUTÉ WITH ROSEMARY

- 2 2½-pound chickens, cut into serving pieces
- Salt and freshly ground black pepper to taste
- 4 tablespoons butter
- 2 teaspoons finely chopped fresh rosemary leaves, or 1 teaspoon dried
- 2 tablespoons finely chopped shallots
- ¼ cup dry white wine
- 1 cup chicken broth

1. Sprinkle the chicken pieces with salt and pepper.

2. Melt 3 tablespoons of the butter in one or two heavy skillets and, when it is melted, add the chicken pieces skin side down. Cook for 15 minutes, or until golden brown on one side.

3. Turn the pieces and add the chopped rosemary. Cook for 10 to 15 minutes longer, turning the pieces occasionally. Add the shallots and cook briefly.

4. Remove the chicken pieces and arrange them neatly on a serving dish, piling them up as necessary. Keep warm.

5. Meanwhile, pour off the fat from the skillet and add the wine. Cook, stirring to dissolve the brown particles that cling to the bottom and sides of the skillet. When the wine is almost reduced, add the chicken broth and stir to blend well. Continue to cook, and, when the sauce is reduced to about ¾ cup, swirl in the remaining 1 tablespoon of butter. Pour the sauce over the chicken and serve immediately.

YIELD: 6 to 8 servings.

Chicken Sauté with Vinegar

- 2 3½-pound chickens, cut into serving pieces
- Salt and freshly ground black pepper to taste
- 4 tablespoons butter
- ⅓ cup finely chopped shallots
- 3 tablespoons red wine vinegar
- 2 cups seeded, chopped fresh tomatoes
- 1 tablespoon chopped fresh tarragon, optional

1. Sprinkle the chicken pieces with salt and pepper.

2. Melt the butter in a heavy skillet and add the chicken pieces. Brown for about 12 minutes on one side; turn and brown for about 10 minutes on the other.

3. Sprinkle the shallots between the pieces of chicken and add the vinegar and cook until most of the vinegar evaporates. Add the tomatoes, cover and cook for about 20 minutes.

4. Remove the chicken pieces to a serving platter. Reduce the tomato sauce briefly. Sprinkle it with the chopped tarragon and pour it over the chicken. Serve hot with rice.

YIELD: 6 or more servings.

Chicken with Mushrooms and Tiger Lily Stems

- ⅓ cup dried tree ears
- 100 tiger lily stems
- 10 dried black Chinese mushrooms
- 1 2½-pound chicken
- 1 tablespoon dark soy sauce
- ¼ cup peanut, vegetable or corn oil
- 4 tablespoons shaoxing wine or dry sherry
- 1½ cups water
- 2 tablespoons light soy sauce
- 1 tablespoon sugar
- Salt to taste
- ½ cup thinly sliced bamboo shoots
- 2 scallions, trimmed and cut into 4-inch lengths
- 12 fresh coriander leaves

1. Put the tree ears, tiger lily stems and mushrooms in separate mixing bowls. Pour boiling water over each and let stand for at least 30 minutes.

2. Brush the chicken all over with the dark soy sauce.

3. Heat the oil in a wok.

4. Place the chicken on one side in the hot oil. Cook, turning to brown well on all sides, for about 5 minutes.

5. Transfer the chicken to a casserole, breast side up, and add the wine and water. Spoon the light soy sauce over the chicken.

6. Add the sugar and salt to the sauce surrounding the chicken. Cover closely and cook over low heat for about 25 minutes.

7. Drain the tiger lily stems. Tie each stem into a knot. Scatter the tiger lily stems around the chicken. Cover and continue cooking for 10 minutes.

8. Drain the tree ears. There should be about 2 cups. Squeeze to extract the excess water from the tree ears. Scatter the tree ears around the chicken. Drain the mushrooms and squeeze to extract the excess water.

Add the mushrooms and bamboo shoots. Cover and continue cooking for about 10 minutes.

9. Transfer the chicken to a serving dish. Spoon the tree ear mixture over and around it. Garnish the top with the scallions and fresh coriander leaves.

YIELD: 8 or more servings.

It is ruefully true that in many American households paprika is considered nothing more than an element of color to enliven a cheese sauce. And it's no wonder, for the innocuous powder that stores often pass off as paprika has little more character than chalk. In its finer forms, however, paprika is a distinctive and much prized spice. There are three types—sweet, mild and hot—each with a pronounced flavor. The best is imported from Hungary and, logically enough, is called Hungarian or rose paprika. It is available in the gourmet sections of most high-quality supermarkets and in fine specialty food shops, as well as in Hungarian grocery stores. We include our version of chicken paprikash, as well as one from a reader who took us to task for our use of butter and garlic.

Chicken Paprikash

- 1 3-pound chicken, cut into serving pieces
- Salt and freshly ground black pepper to taste
- 2 tablespoons butter
- 1 cup thinly sliced onions
- 1 tablespoon finely minced garlic
- 1 tablespoon sweet paprika
- ½ cup fresh or canned chicken broth
- 1 cup sour cream
- 1 tablespoon flour

1. Sprinkle the chicken with salt and pepper.

2. Melt the butter in a heavy skillet and add the chicken pieces, skin side down. Cook over moderately high heat for about 5 minutes and turn the pieces. Continue cooking for about 5 minutes until brown on the second side.

3. Sprinkle the onions and garlic around the chicken pieces. Sprinkle with paprika and stir. Add the chicken broth and cover. Simmer for 10 minutes or longer, or until chicken is cooked.

4. Remove the chicken to a warm serving dish.

5. Blend the sour cream and flour and stir it into the sauce. Cook, stirring, for about 1 minute. Pour the sauce over the chicken.

YIELD: 4 servings.

Sara Mann's Chicken Paprikash

- 2 3-pound chickens, cut into serving pieces
- Salt and freshly ground black pepper to taste
- 2 to 4 tablespoons chicken fat
- 3 to 4 large onions, finely chopped, about 4 cups
- 2 to 3 tablespoons sweet paprika
- 1 cup sour cream

1. Sprinkle the chicken with salt and pepper and set aside.

2. Melt the chicken fat in a casserole and add the onions. Cook, stirring often, until wilted. Cook, without browning, until most of the liquid from the onions evaporates.

3. Add the chicken pieces and stir briefly. Cover and cook gently over very low heat until the chicken gives up some of its liquid, about 10 minutes.

4. Sprinkle the chicken with paprika. Cover and cook for about 1 hour until chicken is tender.

5. Remove from the heat. Pour the liquid from the chicken into a bowl. Skim off the fat and stir in the sour cream. Pour the sauce over the chicken in the casserole. Heat gently but do not boil.

YIELD: 8 servings.

Poulet Sauté Méditerranée

CHICKEN SAUTÉ WITH OLIVES

- 1 3-pound chicken, cut into serving pieces
- Salt and freshly ground black pepper to taste
- 4 tablespoons butter
- ¼ pound mushrooms
- ¼ cup finely chopped shallots
- ½ teaspoon finely minced garlic
- 1 cup dry white wine
- ¼ cup tomato purée
- ½ cup fresh or canned chicken broth
- 18 small, pitted green olives or small, unpitted, imported black olives (see Note)
- Chopped parsley for garnish

1. Sprinkle the chicken pieces with salt and pepper.

2. Melt the butter in a heavy skillet with a tight-fitting lid.

3. When the butter is hot, add the chicken pieces skin side down and cook, uncovered, turning occasionally, to brown well on all sides, about 10 minutes.

4. If the mushrooms are large, cut them into quarters. If they are very small button mushrooms, leave them whole. Rinse the mushrooms and drain.

5. After the chicken has browned for 10 minutes, remove it.

6. Add the mushrooms, shallots and garlic to the skillet and cook, stirring, for about 2 minutes. Add the wine and tomato purée and cook for 3 minutes. Add the chicken broth, stirring to dissolve the brown particles that cling to the bottom and sides of the pan.

7. Return the chicken to the skillet and cover. Cook for 15 minutes. Uncover, add the olives and cover again. Simmer for 15 minutes longer. Sprinkle with parsley and serve.

YIELD: 4 servings.

Note: Do not use California black olives for this dish. They are too bland and flavorless. If the imported black olives are not available, use all green olives.

If you like spicy foods, as I do, your palate will be enchanted with this devilishly hot dish of chicken with garlic, salami and hot red pepper flakes, called arrabbiato, which means enraged.

Chicken Arrabbiato

CHICKEN WITH HOT CHILI SAUCE

- 1 ounce, or slightly less, dried imported mushrooms, preferably Italian
- 1 3-pound chicken, cut into serving pieces
- Salt and freshly ground black pepper to taste
- 2 cups imported canned tomatoes
- 3 tablespoons olive oil
- 8 thin slices of hard salami, cut into very fine, match-like strips
- 1 teaspoon finely chopped garlic
- ½ cup dry white wine
- 1 teaspoon hot red pepper flakes
- Chopped parsley for garnish

1. Put the mushrooms in a mixing bowl and add warm water to cover. Let stand for an hour or so to soften.

2. Sprinkle the chicken pieces with salt and pepper.

3. Put the tomatoes in a saucepan and cook down, stirring often, until reduced to 1 cup.

4. Meanwhile, heat the oil in a large, heavy skillet and, when it is quite hot, add the chicken, skin side down. Cook for 8 to 10 minutes on each side, turning often. Add the strips of salami. Cook to heat through, stirring.

5. Remove the chicken pieces and salami strips to a platter and keep warm.

6. Pour off the fat from the skillet and add the garlic. Cook briefly and add the wine. Cook to reduce by half and add the cooked down tomatoes.

7. Drain the mushrooms but reserve ½ cup of the soaking liquid. Squeeze the mushrooms and add them and the reserved soaking liquid to the sauce. Add the red pepper flakes and salt and pepper to taste. Return the chicken to the sauce and reheat. Serve sprinkled with chopped parsley.

YIELD: 4 servings.

Poularde en Cocotte à la Bonne Femme

CHICKEN IN CASSEROLE WITH MUSHROOMS

- 4 medium-sized potatoes, about 1¼ pounds
- 6 ounces very lean salt pork
- 16 very small white onions
- 1 4½-pound chicken, cut into serving pieces
- Salt and freshly ground black pepper to taste
- 3 tablespoons butter
- 3 tablespoons vegetable, peanut or corn oil
- ½ pound mushrooms, rinsed in cold water and drained well
- 3 sprigs fresh parsley
- 2 sprigs fresh thyme, or ½ teaspoon dried
- 1 bay leaf
- ½ cup dry white wine
- ½ cup water
- Chopped parsley for garnish

1. Peel the potatoes and cut each crosswise in half. Cut each half crosswise into three wedges. Drop the wedges into cold water and let stand.

2. Cut the salt pork into ½-inch slices. Cut each slice crosswise into batonnets about ½ inch wide. There should be about 1 cup. Put them in a saucepan and cover with cold water. Bring to the boil and drain.

3. Peel the onions and put them in a saucepan with cold water. Bring to the boil, simmer 1 minute, drain and set aside.

4. Put the potatoes into a saucepan and cover with cold water. Bring to the boil, simmer 1 minute, drain and set aside.

5. Sprinkle the chicken with salt and pepper to taste.

6. Heat 1 tablespoon butter and the oil in a casserole large enough to hold the meaty pieces of chicken. Set the bony pieces (neck, back and so forth) aside. Add the meaty pieces of chicken to the casserole and brown well, about 5 minutes. Turn the pieces and cook until browned on the other side, about 5 minutes. As the pieces are browned on both sides, transfer them to a bowl. Add the bony parts to the casserole and brown; transfer them to the bowl.

7. Add the mushrooms to the casserole and cook, stirring often, until mushrooms are browned all over. Remove them with a slotted spoon to another bowl.

8. Add the batonnets of salt pork, onions and potatoes to the fat left in the casserole. Cook until the batonnets are crisp.

9. With a slotted spoon transfer the solids to the bowl.

10. Pour off the fat from the casserole.

11. Add the remaining 2 tablespoons of butter to the casserole and return the chicken.

12. Tie the parsley, thyme and bay leaf together with string. Add this to the casserole. Cover loosely; cook for about 10 minutes. Add the wine and water. Cover and cook over very low heat for about 30 minutes.

13. Add the vegetable combination to the chicken and cover. Continue cooking for about 10 minutes. Serve with a sprinkling of finely chopped parsley.

YIELD: 6 to 8 servings.

Poulet Persillade

CHICKEN WITH PARSLEY COATING

1 2½-pound chicken, cut into serving pieces
Salt to taste, if desired
Freshly ground black pepper to taste
2 tablespoons corn, peanut or vegetable oil
1 cup fine fresh bread crumbs
3 tablespoons finely chopped shallots
½ teaspoon finely minced garlic
4 tablespoons finely chopped parsley
2 tablespoons butter

1. Preheat the oven to 450 degrees.

2. Sprinkle the chicken pieces with salt and pepper. Add the oil to a skillet in which the chicken pieces will fit in one layer. Put the chicken pieces in the skillet and rub all over in the oil. Arrange the chicken pieces skin side down in the skillet.

3. Combine the bread crumbs, shallots, garlic and 3 tablespoons of the parsley.

4. Put the skillet on the stove and, when the chicken starts to sizzle, put the skillet in the oven and bake for 20 minutes. Sprinkle with half of the bread crumb and parsley mixture. Return the chicken to the oven and continue baking for 5 minutes longer.

5. Turn the chicken pieces in the skillet. Sprinkle with the remaining bread crumb and parsley mixture. Return the dish to the oven and bake for 15 minutes longer.

6. Melt the butter in a skillet and heat, swirling it around, until it is hazelnut brown. Do not burn. Pour this over the chicken. Sprinkle the chicken with the remaining 1 tablespoon of parsley.

YIELD: 4 servings.

❧

Poulet au Calvados

CHICKEN WITH CALVADOS AND CREAM SAUCE

- 1 3½-pound chicken, cut into serving pieces
- Salt and freshly ground black pepper to taste
- 2 tablespoons butter
- ¼ cup finely chopped shallots
- 2 tablespoons flour
- ¼ cup plus 2 teaspoons Calvados or applejack
- 1 cup water
- 2 sprigs fresh thyme, or ½ teaspoon dried
- 1 bay leaf
- 4 sprigs fresh parsley
- ½ cup heavy cream

1. Sprinkle the chicken with salt and pepper.

2. Melt the butter in a heavy casserole and add the shallots and the chicken pieces skin side down. Cook for about 8 minutes, turn the chicken pieces and cook for about 8 minutes longer.

3. Sprinkle with flour and stir to coat the pieces evenly. Add the ¼ cup of Calvados and stir. Add the water, thyme, bay leaf and parsley sprigs. Stir.

Bring to the boil and cover. Cook for about 15 minutes, or until chicken is tender.

4. Transfer the chicken pieces to another casserole. Remove and discard the thyme, bay leaf and parsley from the cooking liquid. Skim off the surface fat. Add the cream and bring to the boil. Add the remaining 2 teaspoons of Calvados and pour the sauce over the chicken. Bring to the boil. Serve with rice.

YIELD: 4 servings.

Since I first visited North Africa, notably Casablanca, nearly forty years ago and sampled couscous and pastilla, that incredible pigeon pie, I have felt that the cuisine of Morocco is among the most creative, subtle and sophisticated on earth. So I was delighted when Suzy Larochette, owner of the distinguished Maison Arabe in Marrakesh, visited my East Hampton kitchen and prepared one of the best and most interesting menus I've sampled in a good long while. Miss Larochette said that all the spices she had found in my pantry, with one exception, were on a par with those found in Morocco. The exception was our ground ginger, which she said was not as pungent as that she used in her own kitchen. Oddly, fresh ginger is rarely, if ever, used in the kitchens of North Africa. This chicken dish, in my opinion, did not suffer from the inferior spice.

Poulet aux Gingembre et Herbes

CHICKEN WITH GINGER AND HERBS

- 1 teaspoon whole black peppercorns
- 1 teaspoon loosely packed saffron stems
- ½ teaspoon salt, optional
- 3 teaspoons ground ginger
- 2½ cups water
- 8 tablespoons butter
- 2 2½-pound chickens, cut into serving pieces
- ½ cup finely minced onion
- ¾ cup cored, peeled, seeded and diced tomatoes

1. Grind together the peppercorns, saffron, salt and ginger, preferably in a mortar with a pestle.

2. In a kettle, combine the water, butter and spice mixture. Bring to the boil and add the chicken pieces, including the backs. Cover. Cook, stirring the pieces occasionally, for about 30 minutes.

3. Remove the chicken pieces to a warm serving dish. Cover closely with foil. Let the sauce continue cooking. Add the onion and let boil over high heat for about 15 minutes. Add the tomatoes and continue cooking over high heat for about 10 minutes, or until reduced to 2 cups. The sauce will thicken. Pour the sauce over the chicken and serve.

YIELD: 4 to 6 servings.

It amuses us that so many people have an ample supply of dry vermouth in their wine and spirits cabinet while they suffer a shortage of dry white wine. That is our supposition, at least, from the frequency with which we are asked whether one can substitute dry white vermouth for white Burgundy, Loire Valley, Rhine wine and so on. And the answer, of course, is almost always yes. The only exception would be in the preparation of a great, classic dish au vin blanc. In that case, we would certainly buy a very good white wine.

There is obviously a difference in using the apéritif known as dry vermouth and using a white wine. A dry white vermouth is designed to stimulate the appetite and is composed of, among other things, white wine plus a bit of sugar, herbs and plants and, at times, the bark of trees. When cooking with it, or substituting it for white wine, one will naturally produce a sauce that is a touch sweeter and more aromatic, as in this fricassee.

Fricassée de Volaille au Vermouth

CHICKEN FRICASSEE WITH WHITE VERMOUTH SAUCE

- 1 3½-pound chicken, cut into serving pieces
- Salt, if desired
- Freshly ground black pepper to taste
- 2 tablespoons butter
- ½ cup coarsely chopped onion
- 1 clove garlic, finely chopped
- 2 tablespoons flour
- ¾ cup dry white vermouth
- 1¼ cups chicken broth
- 1 bay leaf
- 2 sprigs fresh thyme, or ½ teaspoon dried
- 1 cup carrot cut into fine, julienne strips, about 2 inches long
- 1½ cups loosely packed leeks cut into fine, julienne strips, about 3 inches long
- ½ cup heavy cream

1. Sprinkle the chicken with salt and pepper.

2. Melt the butter in a skillet and add the chicken pieces skin side down. Cook over moderate heat for about 1 minute without browning.

3. Scatter the onion over all and cook for 30 seconds. Add the garlic and stir it around. Cook the chicken for about 4 minutes, turning the pieces often in the butter.

4. Sprinkle the flour over all, turning the pieces so that they are evenly coated. Add the vermouth, chicken broth, bay leaf and thyme. Cover and cook over moderate heat for about 20 minutes.

5. Meanwhile, bring two pans of water to the boil for the carrots and leeks. Drop the carrots into one pan, the leeks into the other. Let the carrots simmer for about 1 minute and drain. Let the leeks simmer for about 4 minutes and drain.

6. When the chicken has cooked for a total of 30 minutes (start to finish), add the carrots, leeks and cream. Let simmer for about 2 minutes.

YIELD: 4 to 6 servings.

❧

Chicken Fricassee for a Crowd

- 6 chickens, about 3½ pounds each, cut into serving pieces
- Salt to taste, if desired
- Freshly ground black pepper to taste
- ¼ cup butter
- 2 cups finely chopped onions
- 1 tablespoon finely minced garlic
- 2 whole cloves
- ⅛ teaspoon grated nutmeg
- 2 bay leaves
- ⅛ teaspoon cayenne pepper
- ½ cup flour
- 1 cup dry white wine
- 3 cups rich chicken broth (see recipe page 418)
- 6 tablespoons imported mustard, preferably of an extra-strong variety
- 1¼ pounds mushrooms, quartered if large or left whole if small
- 1 cup heavy cream
- 2 tablespoons lemon juice

1. Select one or two large, heavy casseroles or Dutch ovens of sufficient size to contain the chicken and the sauce. One casserole with a capacity of about 14 quarts (3½ gallons) is ideal. Or use two casseroles, each with approximately half that capacity.

2. Sprinkle the chicken with salt and pepper.

3. Melt the butter in one casserole or half the butter in each of two casseroles. Add the chicken pieces to the one casserole or half of the chicken to each of the two casseroles.

4. Add the onions, garlic, cloves, nutmeg, bay leaves and cayenne pepper.

5. Cook, stirring the chicken occasionally, without browning, for about 5 minutes, or until the chicken loses its raw look.

6. Sprinkle with flour and stir to coat the pieces evenly. Add the wine and stir. Add the chicken broth, stirring.

7. Dilute half of the mustard with a little of the cooking liquid and add it. Add the mushrooms and stir.

8. Cook, uncovered, for about 20 minutes, stirring occasionally. Skim the fat from the surface as it cooks.

9. Add the cream and continue cooking, uncovered, about 5 minutes longer.

10. Dilute the remaining mustard with a little of the hot sauce and add it. Add the lemon juice. Skim off any remaining fat, and serve with rice.

YIELD: 25 servings.

Paul Prudhomme's Chicken Gumbo

- 2½ cups peanut, vegetable or corn oil
- 2½ cups flour
- 2 cups finely chopped green pepper
- 2 cups finely chopped onion
- 2 cups finely chopped celery
- 1 5- to 6-pound chicken, cut into serving pieces
- 10 cups fresh or canned chicken broth
- ½ teaspoon ground cumin
- ¾ teaspoon cayenne pepper
- 1 teaspoon freshly ground white pepper
- Salt to taste
- 2 bay leaves

1. Heat a large, heavy skillet and add a cup of the oil. When it starts to smoke, add a cup and a half of the flour and cook, stirring, until the roux becomes quite dark, a rusty caramel color. Do not burn or it will become bitter. Add the green pepper, onion and celery. Cook, stirring, over low heat for about 10 minutes.

2. Meanwhile, dredge the chicken pieces in the remaining flour. Heat the remaining oil in a skillet and brown the chicken pieces on both sides.

3. Add the broth to the celery and pepper mixture, stirring constantly. This sauce will be quite thin. As the chicken is browned on both sides transfer it to the sauce.

4. Continue cooking for about 30 minutes. Add the cumin, cayenne pepper, white pepper, salt and bay leaves. Cook 10 minutes longer.

YIELD: 10 servings.

Gaylord's Tandoori Chicken

- 2 2½ pound chickens
- 2 cups plain yogurt
- ½ teaspoon ground cumin
- ½ teaspoon freshly ground black pepper
- ¼ teaspoon grated nutmeg
- ¼ teaspoon ground cloves
- ½ teaspoon ground coriander
- 1 teaspoon grated fresh ginger, or ½ teaspoon ground
- 1 clove garlic, finely minced
- ⅛ to ¼ teaspoon cayenne pepper
- Salt to taste
- ½ teaspoon ground cardamom
- ½ cup chopped white onion
- 2 tablespoons milk
- ½ teaspoon loosely packed saffron stems, or ⅛ teaspoon powdered saffron

1. Cut off and discard the small wing tips of each chicken. Using the fingers, pull off and discard the skin of the chickens.

2. Using a sharp knife, make brief gashes across the grain on both sides of the chicken breasts and legs.

3. In the container of a food processor, combine the yogurt, cumin, black pepper, nutmeg, cloves, coriander, ginger, garlic, cayenne pepper, salt, cardamom and onion. Process to a fine liquid.

4. Pour the mixture into a mixing bowl and add the chickens. Turn the chickens to coat all over. Cover and refrigerate for at least 24 hours.

5. Remove the chickens from the yogurt mixture at least 1 hour before cooking. Discard the marinade.

6. Preheat the oven to 500 degrees. Heat a charcoal grill.

7. Heat the milk in a small saucepan and add the saffron. Remove from the heat and let stand for 10 minutes.

8. Spoon the saffron mixture evenly over the chickens.

9. Line a baking sheet with heavy-duty aluminum foil. Place the chickens on it breast side up.

10. Place the chickens in the oven and bake for 20 minutes.

11. Cut the chickens into serving pieces. Put them on the grill and cook briefly on both sides.

YIELD: 4 to 8 servings.

Note: These chickens can be cooked entirely on a charcoal grill. To grill them, split the chickens as for broiling. After marinating, place on the grill breast side down. Grill on one side. Turn and continue grilling on the second side until the chickens are thoroughly cooked.

One of the greatest delicacies native to America is wild rice, which is actually produced from a water grass, not from a grain like regular rice. Wild rice was first harvested by American Indians hundreds of years ago, mostly from water that is several feet deep along the banks of the Great Lakes.

Although, in recent years, planters have learned to cultivate the wild variety by planting it in spots where the rice has never grown before, it remains one of the great luxury ingredients of the American kitchen; it costs in the vicinity of $10 to $12 a pound. The fortunate thing is that a little wild rice, properly utilized, can be stretched to serve many people. One of the best ways to do this is in casseroles, and one of the best of these is made with chicken and mushrooms.

Timbale de Volaille et Riz Sauvage

CHICKEN AND WILD RICE CASSEROLE

- 1½ cups raw wild rice
- 3 cups boneless chicken cut into cubes (see following recipe for poached chicken)
- 5 tablespoons butter
- 5 tablespoons flour
- 3½ cups rich chicken broth (see recipe page 418)
- ¾ pound thinly sliced mushrooms (about 4 cups)
- Juice of ½ lemon
- 2 tablespoons finely chopped shallots
- 1½ cups heavy cream
- ⅛ teaspoon grated nutmeg
- Salt and freshly ground black pepper to taste

1. Rinse and drain the wild rice until the water runs clear. Put the rice in a saucepan or casserole and add 4½ cups of water and salt to taste. Bring to the boil and cover. Simmer for 45 minutes to 1 hour, or until the rice grains are puffed open. If the grains are not puffed after an hour, remove the pan from the heat and let stand until the grains open. Drain well.

2. Cook and prepare the cubed chicken. Set aside.

3. Preheat the oven to 400 degrees.

4. Melt 4 tablespoons of the butter in a saucepan and add the flour, stirring with a wire whisk. When blended, add the broth, stirring rapidly with the whisk. Simmer for 15 minutes.

5. Meanwhile, melt the remaining 1 tablespoon of butter in a heavy saucepan and add the mushrooms and lemon juice. Cook, stirring often,

until the mushrooms give up their liquid. Add the shallots and continue cooking until most of the liquid has evaporated.

6. Add the mushrooms to the sauce. Add the cream, nutmeg and salt and pepper to taste. Continue cooking for about 15 minutes.

7. Combine the sauce, rice and chicken in a casserole and blend. Cover loosely and bake for 45 minutes.

YIELD: 10 to 12 servings.

POULET POCHÉ

Poached Chicken

- 1 3½-pound chicken
- 8 cups water
- ½ cup coarsely chopped carrot
- ½ cup coarsely chopped celery
- ½ bay leaf
- ½ teaspoon dried thyme
- 12 whole black peppercorns, crushed
- Salt to taste
- 1 clove garlic, crushed
- 2 whole cloves

1. Put the chicken in a kettle and add the remaining ingredients.

2. Bring to the boil and simmer, partly covered, for about 35 minutes. Let the chicken stand in the broth until ready to bone and use.

YIELD: 1 poached chicken.

Note: This basic chicken can be used for sandwiches, salads, creamed dishes and so on. Skim the fat off the broth, strain and reserve it for use in other recipes.

Gai Yang

BARBECUED CHICKEN WITH FISH SAUCE

- 1 3- to 4-pound chicken, cut into serving pieces
- 1 teaspoon dried coriander seeds
- 1 large clove garlic
- ¼ teaspoon hot red pepper flakes
- 1 teaspoon freshly ground black pepper
- Juice of 1 large lime
- 1½ tablespoons fish sauce (see Note)

1. Put the chicken in a mixing bowl.

2. Put the coriander seeds, garlic, pepper flakes and black pepper in a

mortar and grind with a pestle. Add the lime juice and fish sauce and blend well.

3. Pour the spice blend over the chicken and stir to coat the pieces. Let stand at room temperature for 2 hours or longer.

4. Preheat a charcoal grill and preheat the oven to 350 degrees.

5. Arrange the chicken pieces in one layer in a baking dish. Place the dish in the oven and bake for 25 minutes.

6. Transfer the pieces to the grill and continue cooking, turning occasionally, for 5 to 10 minutes.

YIELD: 4 servings.

Note: Fish sauce, called nuoc mam or nam pla, is available in bottles in Oriental markets.

❧

Hominy and Chicken Casserole for a Crowd

- 2 tablespoons olive oil
- 3 cups finely chopped onion
- 3 tablespoons finely minced garlic
- 1½ pounds ground beef
- 3½ cups imported canned tomatoes
- ½ cup tomato paste
- 2 cups chicken broth from poached chicken thighs (see following recipe)
- ½ cup, more or less, finely chopped seeded fresh or canned jalapeño peppers
- 2 teaspoons crumbled dried oregano
- Salt to taste, if desired
- Freshly ground black pepper to taste
- 5 cups sauce suprême (see recipe page 402)
- 4 teaspoons butter
- 6 1-pound, 13-ounce cans hominy, drained, about 18 cups
- 6 cups shredded chicken made from poached chicken thighs (see following recipe)
- 6 cups grated sharp Cheddar cheese, about 1½ pounds

1. Heat the oil in a saucepan with a capacity of approximately 6 quarts and add the onion and garlic. Cook, stirring, until wilted. Add the beef, breaking up lumps with the side of a heavy metal spoon. Cook, stirring, until meat loses its raw look.

2. Add the tomatoes, tomato paste, chicken broth, peppers, oregano, salt and ground pepper. Cook, stirring often, for 30 or 40 minutes, or until thickened. Add the sauce suprême and stir.

3. Meanwhile, preheat the oven to 350 degrees.

4. Butter 2 8-quart casseroles and add a layer of hominy, a layer of chicken, a layer of sauce and a layer of cheese in each. Continue making layers, ending with a layer of cheese.

5. Place the casseroles in the oven and bake for 45 minutes, or until piping hot and bubbling throughout.

YIELD: 20 to 24 servings.

POACHED CHICKEN THIGHS

- 20 chicken thighs, about 6 pounds
- 2 cups water
- 2 bay leaves
- 1 teaspoon dried thyme
- 2 medium-sized onions, each stuck with 2 cloves
- 1¼ cups coarsely chopped celery
- 6 sprigs fresh parsley
- Salt to taste, if desired
- 14 whole black peppercorns

1. Combine the thighs, water, bay leaves, thyme, onions, celery, parsley, salt and peppercorns in a 3- or 4-quart kettle. Bring to the boil, partly covered, and simmer for 20 minutes.

2. Remove from the heat and let stand until ready to use. Remove the thighs, strain the broth and skim off the fat.

YIELD: 20 cooked thighs, plus 2 cups broth.

Pollo Pastacciata

CUBED CHICKEN WITH PEPPERS AND MUSHROOMS

- ½ cup dried Italian mushrooms, preferably porcini
- ½ cup peanut, vegetable or corn oil
- 1½ cups thinly sliced onion
- ½ cup diced sweet green or red pepper
- 1¼ pounds skinless, boneless chicken breast, cut into 1-inch cubes
- 3 tablespoons flour
- ½ cup dry white wine
- ¾ cup chicken broth
- ½ teaspoon hot red pepper flakes
- 1 cup heavy cream
- Salt and freshly ground black pepper to taste

1. Put the mushrooms in a mixing bowl and add warm water to cover. Let stand for an hour or longer.

2. Heat the oil in a large skillet and add the onion. Cook, stirring, for about 3 minutes. Add the diced pepper and cook, stirring, for about 1 minute.

3. Squeeze the mushrooms to extract most of the water. Add them to the onion and pepper mixture. Cook, stirring, for about 3 minutes.

4. Blend the chicken cubes with the flour. Push the vegetables to the side of the skillet. Add the chicken and cook over high heat, stirring, for about 3 minutes. Stir the chicken and vegetables together.

5. Add the wine and cook until most of it evaporates. Add the broth and pepper flakes. Stir. Add the cream and salt and pepper to taste. Cook quickly about 2 minutes.

6. When ready, the chicken will be cooked but still a trifle rare. Serve with hot polenta, if desired.

YIELD: 4 to 6 servings.

Ma-la Cold Chicken with Two Sauces

- 1 or 2 whole chicken breasts, about 1½ pounds total weight, poached and ice-chilled (see following recipe)
- 1 pound asparagus, the thinner the spears the better, or ¾ pound Chinese long beans
- 2½ tablespoons plus 1 teaspoon Chinese or Japanese sesame oil
- 2½ tablespoons corn or peanut oil
- 1½ tablespoons chopped scallions
- 2 slices of fresh ginger, ¼ inch thick
- ¼ teaspoon Sichuan peppercorns
- ⅛ to ¼ teaspoon hot red pepper flakes
- ¾ teaspoon thin (regular) soy sauce
- ⅓ to ½ cup mustard sauce (see following recipe)
- ⅓ to ½ cup smooth and zesty sesame sauce (see recipe page 164)

1. Poach and ice-chill the chicken breasts. Skin and bone the chicken. Cut the meat on the bias into ½-inch strips. Cut each strip into 2-inch thumb-size lengths. Place one length at a time on a flat surface and pound lightly to flatten slightly. Set aside.

2. Cut off the tough bottoms of the asparagus. Cut the tender spears on the diagonal into 1-inch lengths. Or, if the long beans are used, cut them into 3-inch lengths. Drop the asparagus or beans into boiling water. Simmer the asparagus for 30 seconds or the beans for 1 minute. Drain and chill under running cold water. Pat dry. Toss the vegetable lightly with 1 teaspoon of the sesame oil.

3. Combine in a small saucepan the remaining sesame oil and corn or peanut oil. Add a single piece of scallion and heat until the scallion piece starts to sizzle. Remove the oil from the heat and immediately add the remaining chopped scallions, ginger, peppercorns and red pepper flakes. Swirl the mixture to blend.

4. Arrange the asparagus or beans on a serving dish and arrange the chicken pieces neatly on top, leaving a green border.

5. Remove and discard the ginger rounds from the sauce. Add the soy sauce to the sauce and whisk briefly. Spoon this over the chicken, scattering bits of the chopped seasonings on top. Serve with mustard and sesame sauces in small separate bowls.

YIELD: 4 servings.

POACHED AND ICE-CHILLED CHICKEN

- 1 or 2 whole unskinned, unboned chicken breasts, about 1½ pounds total weight
- 2 thin slices fresh ginger
- 1 medium-sized scallion, trimmed and cut into 3-inch lengths

1. Put the chicken into a heavy pot in which it will fit snugly. Smash the ginger pieces and the scallion with the flat side of a cleaver and put them into the pot. Add enough cold water to cover the chicken to a depth of about 1 inch. Bring to the simmer over high heat.

2. Simmer gently for about 20 minutes. Drain. Thrust the chicken immediately into a bowl filled with ice water. Let stand for 15 minutes. Drain thoroughly.

YIELD: About 2 cups when skinned, boned and cut into pieces.

MUSTARD SAUCE

- ½ cup prepared mustard, preferably imported Dijon or Düsseldorf
- ½ cup Chinese or Japanese sesame oil
- 2 tablespoons rice vinegar
- 1 tablespoon plus 1 teaspoon shaoxing wine or dry sherry
- ¼ to ½ teaspoon salt, preferably fine sea salt

Put all the ingredients into the container of a food processor or blender and blend thoroughly. Or blend with a whisk. Let stand several hours to mellow. Or refrigerate overnight in a tightly capped jar.

YIELD: About 1 cup.

SMOOTH AND ZESTY SESAME SAUCE

- 3 to 4 large cloves garlic, peeled
- 2 tablespoons coarsely chopped fresh coriander leaves and upper stems
- 3 tablespoons Chinese sesame paste
- 1 tablespoon Chinese or Japanese sesame oil
- 2 tablespoons plus 2 teaspoons thin (regular) soy sauce
- 1 tablespoon plus 1 teaspoon shaoxing wine or pale dry sherry
- 2 teaspoons rice vinegar
- 1 tablespoon plus 1 teaspoon mild honey
- ¾ to 1 teaspoon hot chili oil
- ⅛ teaspoon roasted Sichuan pepper salt (see following recipe)

1. Put the garlic and coriander into the container of a food processor or blender. Blend to chop.

2. Add the remaining ingredients and blend to a smooth sauce. Bottle and cap tightly. Let stand for 1 hour before using or refrigerate overnight. This will keep indefinitely.

YIELD: About ⅔ cup.

ROASTED SICHUAN PEPPER SALT

- 1 tablespoon Sichuan brown peppercorns
- ⅛ teaspoon whole black peppercorns
- 2 tablespoons coarse kosher salt

1. Roast the peppercorns and salt in a dry skillet over low heat, stirring constantly, for about 5 minutes, until salt turns off-white. Adjust the heat so that the peppercorns smoke but do not burn.

2. Using a food processor or mortar and pestle, grind the peppercorns and salt to a fine powder.

3. Put the ground mixture through a fine sieve to remove any peppercorn husks. Serve sparingly as a seasoned salt. Store in an airtight container.

YIELD: About 2 tablespoons.

The very idea of cooking for a crowd of friends is enough to make many folks feel like taking to their beds. But there is no reason to be intimidated if one chooses to serve dishes that can be made a day in advance, then assembled just before the guests arrive. Here is one such recipe (you will find many others in this book), a distinguished casserole of chicken breasts in a tarragon cream sauce that can be made with a good bottle of brut champagne instead of white wine if the occasion is special. Either way, this dish, like most ragouts and stews, actually improves with a day of rest before serving.

Suprêmes de Volaille à la Crème et Estragon

CHICKEN BREASTS IN A TARRAGON CREAM SAUCE

- 15 whole chicken breasts, with skin and bones attached, about 15 pounds total weight
- 10 sprigs fresh tarragon, or 2 tablespoons dried tarragon tied in a cheesecloth bag
- 4 cups coarsely chopped onion
- 1 cup coarsely chopped celery
- 2 cups coarsely chopped carrots
- 2 large bay leaves
- 2 teaspoons whole black peppercorns
- Salt
- ½ teaspoon dried thyme
- 6 sprigs fresh parsley with stems
- 4 cups dry white wine or brut champagne
- 20 cups water, approximately
- 2 pounds mushrooms
- Juice of ½ lemon
- 16 tablespoons butter
- 1½ cups flour
- 3 cups heavy cream
- 2 tablespoons finely chopped fresh tarragon, or 1 tablespoon dried
- ¼ teaspoon Tabasco sauce
- ¼ teaspoon grated nutmeg
- Freshly ground black pepper to taste

1. Put the chicken breasts in a large kettle and add the tarragon, onion, celery, carrots, bay leaves, peppercorns, salt to taste, thyme, parsley, wine and enough water to barely cover. Bring to the boil. It may take 30 minutes or so to reach the boil. At the boil, simmer for 10 minutes. Remove from the heat and let stand until room temperature.

2. Remove the chicken breasts one at a time. Pull away and discard the skin of each breast. Carefully pull off, in one large piece, each breast half (one breast will obviously produce two pieces). As you remove the breast halves, arrange them in a pan and keep them covered with aluminum foil.

3. As you work, toss the skin and bones back into the kettle with the cooking liquid. Bring to the boil and simmer for about 2 hours. Strain. Discard the solids. There should be 13 or 14 cups of broth. Skim off and discard the fat on the top. Keep the broth at a simmer.

4. Rinse and drain the mushrooms. Leave the mushrooms whole, quarter them or slice them, depending on size. Put them in a saucepan with the lemon juice, 1 cup of the broth in which the chicken cooked, and salt to taste. Cover and simmer for about 3 minutes. Set aside.

5. You might want to do the following in two steps to prevent lumping. Melt the butter in a large saucepan. Add the flour, stirring with a wire whisk. Add 12 cups of the broth in which the chicken cooked and stir vigorously with the whisk.

6. Add 2 cups of the cream to the sauce and continue cooking about 15 minutes.

7. Meanwhile, add the remaining cup of cream to the mushrooms. Add the chopped tarragon. Bring to the boil and cook until the cream is reduced by half. Add this mixture to the sauce. Add the Tabasco, nutmeg and salt and pepper to taste.

8. Pour the sauce over the chicken to barely cover. Heat gently without cooking or the chicken will toughen. Serve with rice. Serve any additional sauce on the side.

YIELD: 30 servings.

Whenever we visit the meat counter of our favorite supermarket, we are always impressed with the fact that chicken breasts are one of the least expensive of all meats sold. We are doubly impressed by the fact that chicken breasts, throughout a long period of culinary history, have been considered one of the most elegant basics of cooking.

It is for these reasons that chicken breasts often wind up as the focal point of many dishes in our kitchen. They are incredibly versatile, gracefully accommodating almost any herb or spice or wine, red or white.

Suprêmes de Volaille au Vin Rouge

CHICKEN BREASTS IN RED WINE SAUCE

- 4 whole chicken breasts, split in half, skinned and boned but with skin and bones reserved
- Salt, if desired
- Freshly ground black pepper to taste
- 4 chicken wings, cut and chopped into small pieces (this may be done by the butcher)
- ½ cup chopped onion
- 3 tablespoons finely chopped shallots

- 3 cloves garlic, chopped
- ¼ cup flour
- 1 tablespoon Cognac
- 1 cup water
- 2¾ cups dry red wine
- ½ bay leaf
- ½ teaspoon dried thyme
- 6 sprigs fresh parsley
- 6 tablespoons butter
- 1½ cups thinly sliced mushrooms

1. Sprinkle the chicken breasts with salt and pepper and set aside.

2. Cut the reserved skin into small pieces and chop the bones into small pieces.

3. Put the chopped skin and bones and chicken wings in a heavy saucepan. Do not add butter, because the skin will give up a lot of chicken fat. Cook, stirring, for about ½ hour.

4. Add the chopped onion, 2 tablespoons of the chopped shallots, salt and pepper to taste and garlic. Cook, stirring frequently, for about 10 minutes longer.

5. Carefully pour off the fat from the solids. Sprinkle the bone mixture with flour and stir to distribute. Cook for about 5 minutes and add the Cognac. Stir in the water and 2½ cups of the wine. Bring to the boil and add the bay leaf, thyme and parsley.

6. Simmer the sauce for about 1 hour. Strain it through a fine sieve, pushing through as much of the soft solids as possible. Cook the sauce over low heat for about 15 minutes longer.

7. Melt 2 tablespoons of the butter in a skillet and add the chicken breasts. Cook for about 3 minutes on one side until they just start to brown. Turn the pieces and cook for 10 to 15 minutes, depending on the size of the breasts. Transfer to a platter and keep warm.

8. To the skillet add 2 more tablespoons of butter, the mushrooms and the remaining tablespoon of chopped shallots. Cook, stirring, until the mushrooms are wilted. Spoon the mushrooms over the chicken and cover with foil.

9. Add the remaining ¼ cup of wine to the skillet and stir to dissolve any brown particles that may cling to the bottom and sides of the skillet. Add this to the sauce. Pour any liquid that may have come from the chicken into the sauce. Swirl the remaining 2 tablespoons of butter into the sauce. Garnish each piece of chicken with mushrooms and pour the boiling sauce over. Serve hot.

YIELD: 8 servings.

Suprêmes de Volaille Farcies au Cari

CURRIED STUFFED CHICKEN BREASTS

- 2 large whole chicken breasts, about 2 pounds each, split in half
- 3 tablespoons seedless golden raisins
- 3 tablespoons butter
- ½ cup finely chopped onion
- ½ cup finely chopped celery
- ¼ teaspoon finely minced garlic
- 1 bay leaf
- 1 cup peeled and cored apple cut into ¼-inch cubes
- 3 tablespoons chutney
- Salt and freshly ground black pepper to taste
- ½ cup heavy cream
- 1 teaspoon curry powder

1. If possible, buy the breasts already boned but with the skin left on. Otherwise, using a paring knife and the fingers, remove and discard the bone or use it for soup. Set the boned chicken breasts aside.

2. Put the raisins in a small bowl and add warm water to cover. Set aside so the raisins will swell.

3. Preheat the oven to 425 degrees.

4. Melt 1 tablespoon of the butter in a skillet and add the onion, celery, garlic and bay leaf. Cook, stirring often, until the onion is wilted. Add the apple and stir. Cook for about 1 minute, stirring occasionally.

5. Squeeze the raisins to extract the liquid and add them. Add the chutney. Stir and remove from the heat. Let cool.

6. Place the chicken breasts skin side down on a flat surface. Pat lightly with a flat mallet or the bottom of a small, heavy skillet. Sprinkle with salt and pepper.

7. Spoon equal portions of the filling in the center of each breast. Bring up the edges of the breast, folding the edges over to enclose the filling and make a package.

8. Add the remaining 2 tablespoons of butter to a shallow, flameproof baking dish and melt the butter. Transfer the chicken breasts to the dish and brush the tops with the butter. Sprinkle with salt and pepper and place them seam side down.

9. Place the dish on top of the stove and cook for about 1 minute. Place the dish in the oven and bake for 10 minutes. Baste once as they bake.

10. Blend the cream and curry powder and pour this over the chicken breasts. Bake 10 minutes longer, basting occasionally.

YIELD: 4 servings.

Suprêmes de Volaille Farcies aux Foies de Poulets

CHICKEN BREASTS STUFFED WITH CHICKEN LIVERS

- 2 large whole chicken breasts, about 2 pounds each, split in half
- 3 tablespoons butter
- ¼ pound chicken livers, cut into ¼-inch pieces
- ¼ pound mushrooms, cut into ½-inch chunks, about 1½ cups
- ¼ cup finely chopped onion
- Salt and freshly ground black pepper to taste
- ½ cup cooked rice
- ¼ teaspoon grated nutmeg, optional
- 1 tablespoon Cognac
- ¼ cup heavy cream

1. If possible, buy the breasts already boned but with the skin left on. Otherwise, using a paring knife and the fingers, remove and discard the bone or use it for soup. Set the boned breasts aside.

2. Preheat the oven to 425 degrees.

3. Melt 1 tablespoon of the butter in a skillet and add the chicken livers. Cook over high heat, tossing and stirring the pieces so that they cook evenly.

4. Cook about 1 minute and add the mushrooms. Cook, tossing and stirring, for about 1 minute longer. Add the onion, salt and pepper and cook, stirring, for about 2 minutes. Remove from the heat and let cool slightly.

5. Add the rice and nutmeg.

6. Place the chicken breasts skin side down on a flat surface. Pat lightly with a flat mallet or the bottom of a small, heavy skillet. Sprinkle with salt and pepper.

7. Spoon equal portions of the chicken liver and mushroom filling in the center of each breast. Fold the sides of the breast over to enclose the filling. It is not necessary to tie the breasts to keep them sealed. But keep the edges of the breasts overlapping.

8. Add the remaining 2 tablespoons butter, melted, to a shallow flame-proof baking dish.

9. Arrange the breasts seam side down in the dish. Brush the top of the chicken breasts with the butter. Place the dish on top of the stove and cook for about 1 minute. Place the dish in the oven and bake for 15 minutes.

10. Add the Cognac and cream and return the dish to the oven. Bake 5 minutes longer and baste the chicken with the sauce. Serve piping hot.

YIELD: 4 servings.

Do not be put off by the pedestrian name of this next dish. It is a variation of chicken cutlet pojarski without the sour cream.

Chicken Burgers

- 2 pounds skinless, boneless chicken breasts
- Salt and freshly ground black pepper to taste
- ½ cup finely chopped parsley
- 1 cup fine fresh bread crumbs
- 1 teaspoon ground cumin
- ¼ cup chicken broth or water
- 4 tablespoons butter, approximately

1. Trim the breasts to remove all nerve fibers, cartilage and so on. Cut the chicken into cubes.

2. Put the prepared breast meat into the container of a food processor and process until fairly but not totally smooth.

3. Scrape the chicken into a mixing bowl. Add salt, pepper, parsley, bread crumbs, cumin and broth or water. Blend well with the hands.

4. Divide the mixture equally into 12 portions. Using dampened hands, pat the portions into flat round patties. Chill until ready to cook.

5. These patties are excellent when cooked on a preheated charcoal grill, about 4 minutes to a side. Or cook them in a little butter in a heavy skillet, 4 to 5 minutes to a side. Serve with a little melted butter poured over.

YIELD: 6 servings.

Bitokes de Volaille à l'Estragon

CHICKEN PATTIES WITH TARRAGON

- 3 whole skinless, boneless chicken breasts, about 1½ pounds
- ½ cup bread crumbs
- ⅛ teaspoon grated nutmeg
- Pinch of cayenne pepper
- Salt and freshly ground black pepper to taste
- 2 teaspoons plus 1 tablespoon chopped fresh tarragon, or half the amount dried
- ½ cup heavy cream
- 4 tablespoons peanut, vegetable or corn oil
- 2 cups fresh tomato sauce (see recipe page 407)

1. Trim off all fat, cartilage and membranes from the chicken. Cut the chicken into 1-inch cubes. Put the cubes into the container of a food processor. Process until the meat is coarse-fine. Do not overprocess it or it will be like pulp.

2. Put the ground chicken into a mixing bowl and add the bread crumbs, nutmeg, cayenne, salt and pepper to taste, 2 teaspoons chopped tarragon and the cream. Blend well by beating with a wooden spoon. Chill the mixture.

3. Shape the mixture into 12 patties.

4. Heat the oil in a skillet and add the patties. Cook until golden brown on one side, about 3 minutes. Turn and cook on the other side, for about 3 minutes.

5. Serve the patties with fresh tomato sauce and the remaining chopped fresh tarragon sprinkled over.

YIELD: 6 servings.

Curried Chicken Breasts

- 12 tablespoons butter
- 2 apples, peeled, cored and finely cubed, about 2 cups
- 1 cup finely chopped onion
- ¾ cup finely chopped celery
- 2 cloves garlic, finely minced, about 1½ tablespoons
- Salt, if desired
- Freshly ground black pepper to taste
- 3 tablespoons curry powder, or more to taste
- 1 tablespoon flour
- 1½ cups canned tomatoes, preferably Italian peeled tomatoes, crushed
- 1½ cups boiling chicken broth
- 4 whole chicken breasts, skinned, boned and split in half

1. Melt 4 tablespoons of the butter in a saucepan and add the apples, onion, celery, garlic, salt and pepper to taste. Cook, stirring frequently, until the onion is wilted.

2. Sprinkle with curry powder and flour and stir to blend well. Add the tomatoes, stirring, and bring to the boil. Add the chicken broth and cook, stirring frequently, for 40 minutes. If you do not stir, the sauce might stick on the bottom.

3. Put the sauce through a sieve and cook for about 15 minutes longer, stirring frequently.

4. Sprinkle the chicken pieces with salt and pepper.

5. Melt 4 tablespoons of the butter in a skillet and add the chicken pieces, skinned side down. Cook over moderate heat until that side is a light brown, 3 to 5 minutes. Turn the pieces. Cook for 8 to 10 minutes longer until the second side is lightly browned. Do not overcook.

6. Pour the sauce over the chicken breasts and cook for about 1 minute after it comes to the boil. Remove the chicken breasts and cook the sauce over high heat for about 1 minute, stirring. Immediately swirl in the remaining 4 tablespoons of butter. Serve the sauce over the chicken breasts.

YIELD: 8 servings.

Note: A nice accompaniment for this dish is deep-fried pine nuts sprinkled over the chicken before serving. To make them, bring about 1½ cups of oil almost but not quite to the point of smoking. Turn off the heat. Drop in ½ cup of pine nuts and let stand for 30 seconds. Drain immediately.

There is no concealing our keen appreciation of, if not a kind of predilection for, chicken wings. The reasons for this are all too obvious: The wings are vital proof that the nearer the bone the sweeter the meat. There is something succulent about well-cooked (but not overcooked) chicken wings. Besides which, they are both inexpensive and abundant.

The recipes outlined here are for baked wings seasoned in what might be called Italian style, with a generous grating of Parmesan cheese and one of the most Italian of all herbs, oregano; with the spiciness of mustard and Worcestershire sauce, or à la diable; and with a basting sauce of tomato ketchup, vinegar, honey and Worcestershire, or Southern style.

Chicken Wings Parmesan

- 24 chicken wings, about 5 pounds
- 1 cup melted butter
- 1 tablespoon prepared mustard, preferably imported Dijon or Düsseldorf
- ⅛ teaspoon Tabasco sauce
- 1 cup bread crumbs
- 1½ cups freshly grated Parmesan cheese
- 1 teaspoon crushed dried oregano
- 3 tablespoons finely chopped parsley
- 1 teaspoon finely minced garlic
- Salt to taste, if desired
- Freshly ground black pepper to taste
- 1½ cups fresh tomato sauce (see recipe page 407)

1. Preheat the oven to 350 degrees.

2. Fold the small tips of the chicken wings under the main wing bone so that the wings remain flat.

3. Pour the butter in to a mixing bowl or saucepan and add the mustard and Tabasco sauce.

4. Combine the bread crumbs, ½ cup of the cheese, the oregano, parsley, garlic, salt and pepper in a shallow dish. Dip each wing first in the butter mixture, then in the bread-crumb mixture. As the wings are prepared, arrange them fleshy side up in a baking dish.

5. Place the wings in the oven and bake, basting often with the pan drippings, for about 50 minutes. Pour off all the fat from the pan and continue baking for about 10 minutes. Spoon the tomato sauce over the wings and run under the broiler. Serve with the remaining grated cheese sprinkled over.

YIELD: 6 or more servings.

Ailes de Poulet à la Diable

DEVILED CHICKEN WINGS

- 16 to 18 chicken wings, about 3 pounds
- Salt to taste, if desired
- Freshly ground black pepper to taste
- 4 tablespoons butter
- 2 tablespoons prepared mustard, preferably imported Dijon or Düsseldorf
- 1 cup fresh or canned chicken broth
- 1 tablespoon Worcestershire sauce
- ⅔ cup fresh bread crumbs

1. Preheat the oven to 400 degrees.

2. Cut off and discard the small wing tip of each wing. Cut the main wing bone and second wing bone at the joint. Sprinkle the wing pieces with salt and pepper.

3. Melt the butter in a baking dish large enough to hold the wing pieces in one layer. Add the wing pieces and turn them in the butter to coat well. Place the wings skin side down in the dish and bake for 15 minutes.

4. Meanwhile, blend the mustard with ⅓ cup of the chicken broth and the Worcestershire sauce.

5. Pour the mustard mixture over all and sprinkle with ⅓ cup of the

bread crumbs. Shake the pan with the chicken pieces to keep the pieces loosened. Turn the pieces and bake for 15 minutes longer.

6. Turn the pieces once more. Bake for 15 minutes. Add the remaining chicken broth. Sprinkle with the remaining bread crumbs and bake about 10 minutes longer.

YIELD: 4 to 6 servings.

Oven-barbecued Chicken Wings

- 24 chicken wings, about 5 pounds
- Salt to taste, if desired
- 2 teaspoons medium-grind black pepper
- 3 teaspoons paprika
- ½ cup corn, peanut or vegetable oil
- 1 cup tomato ketchup
- ¼ cup honey
- 3 tablespoons red wine vinegar
- 3 tablespoons white vinegar
- 2 tablespoons Worcestershire sauce
- 1 teaspoon Tabasco sauce
- 1 tablespoon prepared mustard, preferably imported Dijon or Düsseldorf
- 1 tablespoon finely minced garlic
- 4 tablespoons butter
- 1 bay leaf

1. Preheat the oven to 400 degrees.

2. Fold the small tips of the chicken wings under the main wing bones so that the wings remain flat.

3. Arrange the wings in one layer in a baking dish so that they bake comfortably close together without crowding.

4. Sprinkle with salt, pepper and 2 teaspoons of the paprika. Pour half of the oil over all and turn the wings in the mixture so that they are evenly coated. Arrange them in one layer with the small wing side down.

5. Place in the oven and bake for 15 minutes.

6. Meanwhile, in a saucepan combine the ketchup, remaining oil, honey, vinegars, Worcestershire sauce, Tabasco sauce, mustard, garlic, butter, bay leaf and remaining paprika. Bring to a boil.

7. Brush the wings lightly with the sauce and turn them to the other side. Brush this side with sauce and continue baking for 15 minutes.

8. Brush the wings once more. Turn the pieces and brush this side once more. Continue baking for 15 minutes.

9. Continue turning, brushing and baking the chicken for 15 minutes longer or a total of about 1 hour.

YIELD: 6 or more servings.

French chefs and many serious home cooks often lament the fact that here they are unable to find the small poussins or young chickens that are so widely available in the markets of France. Poussins differ from just any young chickens in that they have reached maturity and developed flavor, yet they generally weigh only about one pound or slightly more. On rare occasions, one can buy these little chickens in rural areas where poultry farms exist. An excellent substitute for the small birds, however, is the Rock Cornish game hen, which is said to be a cross between a White Rock and a Cornish game bird. The word game, in the case of these hens, has long since lost its meaning, for the chickens do not smack in the least of a wild bird. Nonetheless, they are a delicacy and are remarkably easy to prepare. One unstuffed bird, roasted or grilled, will serve one. When filled with a meat stuffing, one bird will suffice for two servings.

❧

Cornish Hens à la Diable

- 4 Rock Cornish game hens, about 1¼ pounds each, split in half for broiling
- Salt and freshly ground black pepper to taste
- ¼ cup peanut, vegetable or corn oil
- 2 tablespoons prepared mustard, preferably imported Dijon or Düsseldorf
- 1 tablespoon dry white wine
- ½ cup fine fresh bread crumbs
- Sauce diable (see recipe page 406)

1. Preheat the broiler to high. If the oven has a separate temperature control, set the oven temperature to 450 degrees.

2. Place the split hens on a flat surface and pound lightly with a flat mallet. Sprinkle the hens on all sides with salt and pepper and the oil.

3. Combine the mustard and wine in a small bowl and set aside.

4. Arrange the halves neatly in one layer, skin side down, on a baking sheet and place under the broiler about 3 inches from the source of heat. Broil for 8 or 9 minutes and turn the halves.

5. Return to the broiler and broil for about 3 minutes. Remove the halves and brush the skin side with the mustard and wine mixture. Turn the halves and brush the second side with the mustard mixture. Brush with the pan drippings and sprinkle with the bread crumbs.

6. If the oven and broiler have dual heat controls, turn off the broiler and set the oven temperature to 450 degrees. Put the hens in the oven and bake for 15 minutes. Serve with sauce diable.

YIELD: 4 servings.

Cornish Hens Stuffed with Prosciutto and Giblets

- 2 Rock Cornish game hens with giblets, about 2 pounds each
- 2 ounces prosciutto or cooked ham
- ½ bay leaf
- 1 clove garlic, finely chopped
- ¼ teaspoon dried thyme, or ½ teaspoon chopped fresh thyme
- Salt and freshly ground black pepper to taste
- 1 tablespoon peanut, vegetable or corn oil

1. Preheat the oven to 375 degrees.

2. Remove the livers and hearts from the game hens and chop them finely.

3. Chop the prosciutto and bay leaf. Combine the chopped liver, heart and prosciutto, bay leaf, garlic, thyme and salt and pepper. Blend well.

4. Stuff the hens with equal portions of the mixture.

5. Arrange them in a shallow baking dish and sprinkle with salt and pepper and rub with oil. Scatter the necks and gizzards around the hens. Arrange the hens on their sides and place in the oven.

6. Bake for 20 minutes and turn the hens on their other side. Bake for 20 minutes and turn the hens on their backs and baste. Return to the oven and continue cooking, basting occasionally, for about 20 minutes. Total cooking time should be about 1 hour. Remove from the oven and serve hot or cold with the stuffing.

YIELD: 4 servings.

Yucatecan Chicken Escabeche

- 4 squab chickens or Rock Cornish game hens, 1 pound each, split for broiling
- Salt to taste, if desired
- Freshly ground black pepper to taste
- ¼ cup olive oil
- 2 tablespoons red wine vinegar
- ¼ cup lime juice
- 1 teaspoon crushed coriander seeds
- ½ teaspoon ground cumin
- ¼ cup coarsely chopped onion
- 1 bay leaf, broken
- ½ teaspoon dried thyme
- ¼ teaspoon hot red pepper flakes
- 3 cloves garlic, crushed
- 8 ¼-inch-thick slices seeded sweet green or red pepper
- 8 ¼-inch-thick slices raw onion
- 4 lemon halves, optional

1. Sprinkle the split birds on both sides with salt and a generous grinding of black pepper and put them in a large mixing bowl.

2. Combine all of the remaining ingredients except the peppers, onion slices and lemon halves. Pour this mixture over the birds. Stir to blend. Cover and refrigerate for 12 hours or longer. Turn the chicken halves occasionally.

3. When ready to cook, prepare a charcoal fire or preheat the broiler.

4. Place the chicken halves skin side down on a charcoal grill. Arrange the vegetable pieces around the chicken pieces. Cook for about 8 minutes. Or broil about 5 inches from the source of heat for about 8 minutes.

5. Turn the pieces, lower the grill hood and continue cooking for 8 minutes. Or broil the chicken and vegetables on the second side for about 8 minutes. Turn the pieces as they cook. The vegetables will cook faster than the chicken so remove them when they are cooked but still crisp-tender. Serve the chicken and vegetables with lemon halves, if desired.

YIELD: 4 servings.

Cordonices Escabechadas

QUAIL IN ESCABECHE

- 12 quail or 3 Rock Cornish game hens
- 6 tablespoons olive oil (see Note)
- 2 medium-sized onions, coarsely chopped
- 12 cloves garlic, peeled
- 2 tablespoons finely chopped shallots
- 4 carrots, scraped and cut into ⅛-inch rounds
- 1 peeled potato, cooked in water for about 5 minutes and drained
- 5 bay leaves
- 3 sprigs fresh parsley.
- 2 teaspoons dried thyme
- Salt to taste
- 20 whole black peppercorns
- ½ celery stalk with leaves
- Pinch of saffron
- ¾ cup red wine vinegar
- 3 cups dry white wine
- ¾ cup chicken broth, skimmed of all fat
- 1 lemon, thinly sliced
- 2 tablespoons finely chopped parsley

1. Truss the quail or have them trussed. If Cornish game hens are used, cut them in half or have them split.

2. Heat the oil in a large shallow casserole. Add the birds and cook over moderate heat until well browned on all sides. Transfer the birds to a platter.

3. To the casserole add the onions, garlic, shallots and carrots. Quarter the potato and add it. Cook, stirring, until the onions are wilted.

4. Add the bay leaves, parsley sprigs, thyme, salt, peppercorns, celery and saffron. Stir.

5. Add the vinegar, wine and broth. (Use only ½ cup vinegar if the Cornish game hens are used.)

6. Return the birds to the casserole. Cover and simmer for 45 minutes. Transfer the birds to a platter.

7. Cook down the liquid in the casserole for about 5 minutes. When ready, there should be enough liquid to cover the birds.

8. Pour the sauce into a deep casserole, preferably made of earthenware. Add the birds. Ideally, they should be covered with sauce.

9. Cover the casserole and refrigerate for 3 or 4 days. Place the birds and the marinade in a shallow serving dish. Garnish with lemon slices and chopped parsley.

YIELD: 6 servings.

Note: In Spain it is customary to prepare the oil before cooking the quail. This is done by heating the oil with a piece of lemon rind until the rind blackens. The oil is cooled immediately by adding a peeled raw potato to it.

Squabs, small pigeons that have never flown, are one of our favorite foods. They have a slightly gamier taste than other domestic fowl, and it is customary in most European countries to serve them slightly underdone. The squab served on a bed of endives is the creation of Alain Senderens, owner and chef of L'Archestrate, a distinguished three-star restaurant in Paris. The squab with apples and truffles was made in our kitchen by Eckart Witzigmann, chef of the Aubergine in Munich, which is the only restaurant in West Germany to be awarded three stars by the Guide Michelin.

Pigeon aux Endives Confites

SQUAB WITH ENDIVES

- 16 firm, unblemished endives, about 3 pounds
- 6 tablespoons butter
- Salt and freshly ground black pepper to taste
- ¼ cup sugar
- 4 fresh cleaned squabs, about 1 pound each
- ½ cup water

1. Trim off the ends of the endives and separate the leaves.

2. Bring enough water to the boil to cover the endive leaves when they are added. Add the endives, cover and cook exactly 4 minutes. Drain well.

3. Melt 4 tablespoons of the butter in a large, heavy skillet and, when it is very hot, add the endives. Sprinkle with salt, pepper and sugar. Cook over high heat, stirring and shaking the skillet so that the leaves cook evenly all over. The liquid will start to evaporate and the vegetable will become amber colored. Cook for about 20 minutes, or until the endives are caramel colored all over. Do not burn. Drain in a colander.

4. Meanwhile, preheat the oven to 525 degrees.

5. Cut off the wing tips and the second wing joints of each squab. Set these pieces aside.

6. Melt the remaining 2 tablespoons of butter in a heavy skillet large enough to hold the squabs in one layer without crowding.

7. Add the squabs and brown them on all sides, turning them often so that they brown evenly. Add the wing tips and second wing joints. Place in the oven and reduce the oven temperature to 425 degrees. Bake for 15 minutes. The squabs will be slightly undercooked. Transfer the squabs to a warm platter. Pour off the fat from the skillet. Set the skillet aside.

8. Spoon equal portions of the endives on each of four hot plates.

9. Carefully carve away the breast and leg meat from each side of the carcasses. Save the carcasses. Arrange 2 squab halves on each bed of endive.

10. Chop the carcasses into small pieces with a heavy cleaver. Add these pieces to the skillet and cook over moderately high heat until well browned. Add the water and cook down to about ¼ cup. Pour the liquid over the squabs and serve.

YIELD: 4 servings.

Pigeon aux Pommes Fruits et Truffes

SQUAB WITH APPLES AND TRUFFLES

- 4 ready-to-cook squabs, about ¾ pound each
- Salt and freshly ground black pepper to taste
- 2 tart green apples, preferably Granny Smith
- 3 tablespoons butter
- 1 tablespoon sugar
- 2 tablespoons dry white wine
- Juice of ½ lemon
- 1 tablespoon peanut or vegetable oil
- ½ cup sauce périgourdine (see recipe page 405)
- 8 slices truffle

1. Preheat the oven to 450 degrees.

2. Sprinkle the squabs inside and out with salt and pepper. Truss the squabs.

3. Remove the stems from each apple. Cut each apple into six wedges of equal size. Cut away the core of each wedge. Cut away the peel.

4. Melt 1 tablespoon of the butter in a skillet and add the sugar and wine. Add the apple wedges in one layer. Cook until the sugar starts to caramelize.

5. Remove the skillet from the heat and add the lemon juice. Turn the wedges in the skillet and continue cooking over gentle heat for about 1 minute, shaking the skillet.

6. Rub the squabs with the oil and remaining butter, which has been melted. Arrange the squabs breast side up in a shallow skillet and place in the oven. Roast, basting often, for about 15 minutes. If you wish them more fully cooked, continue roasting.

7. Remove the squabs from the roasting pan and untruss. Pour off the fat from the pan. Add the périgourdine sauce and any drippings that have gathered around the squabs to the pan. Bring to the boil, stirring.

8. Carve the breast meat away and cut away the legs (with thighs attached). Serve the squab pieces on each of four plates. Garnish with apple wedges.

9. Garnish the squab pieces with truffle slices and spoon the sauce over.

YIELD: 4 servings.

There are some foods that are not readily available in supermarkets and grocery stores throughout the country, though they have enormous appeal in areas where they can be found. This is increasingly true of something called Muscovy duck.

These ducks arrive at markets in late fall and are available throughout the winter, frequently at local poultry farms. Unlike most domestically raised birds, they should not be cooked until they are well done. They should be cooked to a rare or medium-rare state. Otherwise, the meat tends to become dry.

The choicest part of the Muscovy duck, which has a gamier flavor than regular duckling, is the breast. When the duck is done, transfer it to a carving board and neatly carve away half of its breast. Place the breast half skin side up on the board and cut it slightly on the bias, as with London broil. The thighs may be carved off the bone into thin slices. The thighs and legs tend to be a trifle tough.

A mystery of sorts exists over the origin of the duck's name. According to

Dr. Harold E. Nadler, director of the division of animal industry at the New York State Department of Agriculture and Markets, "Originally the duck was known simply as a musk duck, for no reason apparent to me. Somehow, someone apparently presumed musk to be short for Muscovy and started calling it that in error." It has nothing to do, he said, with Moscow. More than by the name, Dr. Nadler is fascinated by the fact that the Muscovy is one of the few ducks that can perch in trees.

Roast Muscovy Duck

- 1 4-pound Muscovy duck
- Salt, if desired
- Freshly ground black pepper to taste
- 1 teaspoon peanut oil
- ⅓ cup coarsely chopped celery
- ⅓ cup coarsely chopped onion
- ½ cup coarsely chopped carrot
- ½ bay leaf
- ½ teaspoon dried thyme
- 1 clove garlic, peeled and crushed
- ⅓ cup dry white wine
- ½ cup chicken broth
- 2 tablespoons butter

1. Preheat the oven to 475 degrees.

2. Cut off and reserve the wing tips and second wing joint of the duck. Leave the main wing bone intact. Remove the fat from inside the duck and rub it all over the duck.

3. Sprinkle the duck, inside and out, with salt and pepper. Brush the duck with the oil.

4. Arrange the duck breast side up in a roasting pan. Add the cut-off wing bones, gizzard and cavity fat. Bake for 30 minutes and pour off the fat from the roasting pan. Return the duck to the oven and scatter the celery, onion, carrot, bay leaf, thyme and garlic around the duck. Bake for 15 minutes longer if you wish the duck to be medium rare.

5. Transfer the duck to a warm platter. Pour the fat from the roasting pan, leaving the vegetables in the pan. Place the pan on the stove and cook the vegetables briefly, stirring. Add the wine and boil for 1 minute.

6. Add the broth and accumulated cavity drippings from the duck and cook, stirring, for about 5 minutes. Strain the broth and solids, pushing the solids with the back of a spoon to extract as much liquid as possible.

7. Melt the butter in a small saucepan, swirling it around until it takes on a nice hazelnut color. Do not burn. Pour the butter over the duck. Carve and serve with the hot pan sauce.

YIELD: 2 to 4 servings.

Although duck—gastronomically—is seldom thought of as America's national bird, it is without question one of the ten or twelve most popular dishes on French menus in this country, and deservedly so. Duck is a winged creature of many virtues, not the least of which is the richness of its flesh. While duck à l'orange is by far the best-known duck preparation in the French repertoire, there are scores more—including this superb dish with apples and Calvados.

Canards Normande

ROAST DUCK WITH APPLES

- 2 5½-pound ducks, hearts and gizzards reserved
- Salt and freshly ground black pepper to taste
- 1 cup coarsely chopped carrot
- ½ cup coarsely chopped celery
- ¾ cup coarsely chopped onion
- 1 small clove garlic, finely minced
- 3 pounds baking apples, such as McIntosh
- 3 tablespoons butter
- 3 tablespoons sugar
- ½ cup Calvados or applejack
- 1 cup fresh or canned chicken broth
- 3 tablespoons lemon juice
- 1½ cups heavy cream

1. Preheat the oven to 400 degrees.

2. Cut off the necks of the ducks and cut them into 1-inch lengths. Cut off the wing tips and the second joints of the wings, leaving the main wing bone intact.

3. Sprinkle the ducks inside and out with salt and pepper. Truss them and arrange them breast side down in a baking pan. Scatter the hearts, gizzards and neck pieces around the ducks.

4. Put the ducks in the oven and bake for 15 minutes. Turn the ducks back side down and continue roasting, turning them at 15-minute intervals. Pour off the fat as it accumulates. At the end of 1 hour, add the carrots, celery, onion and garlic. The total roasting time is 1½ to 2 hours, or until thoroughly tender.

5. Meanwhile, as the ducks roast, peel and core the apples. Cut them into quarters.

6. Melt the butter and pour it into a baking dish. (We used a dish that measured 11¾ by 7½ by 1¾ inches.) Arrange the apple quarters cored-side down on the dish and sprinkle with sugar. Bake for about 50 minutes and sprinkle with half of the Calvados.

7. When the ducks are done, remove them from the pan, lifting them up so that the juices run from the cavity. Set the ducks aside in a warm place and cover loosely with foil.

8. Pour off and discard the liquid and fat from the pan and return the neck pieces, gizzards and hearts to the pan. Sprinkle with remaining Calvados and cook for about 1 minute. Add the chicken broth and cook, stirring to dissolve the brown particles that cling to the bottom and sides of the pan. Pour the mixture into a saucepan and simmer for about 30 minutes. Add the lemon juice.

9. Strain the sauce and carefully skim off all fat. Reduce the sauce to about half its quantity and add the cream. Cook for about 10 minutes. Pour the sauce over the apples.

10. Carve the ducks and arrange the pieces skin side up on a baking dish. Run the duck briefly under the broiler to crisp up the skin a bit. Serve the duck with apples on the side, spooning a little of the sauce over both the duck pieces and the apples.

YIELD: 6 to 10 servings.

Caneton Roti au Jus

ROAST DUCK

- 3 5- to 6-pound ducks
- Salt and freshly ground black pepper to taste
- 6 celery stalks, trimmed
- ¼ cup peanut, corn or vegetable oil
- 2 medium-sized onions, peeled
- 1½ cups water
- 2 tablespoons butter

1. Preheat the oven to 450 degrees.

2. Remove the necks and giblets from each duck's cavity and set aside. Pat the ducks dry inside and out. Sprinkle the ducks inside and out with salt and pepper, and insert 2 celery stalks inside each duck.

3. Truss the ducks with string. Arrange the ducks breast side up in one or two shallow roasting pans. The ducks should not be touching. Rub the oil over the ducks so that they are evenly coated. Scatter the necks, gizzards, hearts and onions around the ducks. Place in the oven and bake for 1 hour.

4. Pour off the fat from each pan. (The fatness of ducks varies; if a great deal of fat accumulates in the pan before the hour is up, pour it off.) Leave the ducks in the pans and continue roasting for 30 minutes. Pour off any fat that has accumulated around the ducks.

5. Lift the ducks, one at a time, and let the juices in their cavities flow back into the pan or pans.

6. Cut and pull off the trussing strings. Transfer the ducks to a large platter and cover loosely with foil.

7. Pour or spoon off any fat from the roasting pans and combine the remaining juices in one pan. Add the water to the pan. Bring to the boil, stirring with a spoon to dissolve the brown particles that cling to the bottoms and sides of the pan. Let the sauce cook down over high heat for about 4 minutes, stirring constantly.

8. Strain through a fine sieve pressing to extract as much liquid from the solids as possible. There should be about 1½ cups of liquid.

9. Skim off any fat that rises to the surface. Set the sauce aside in a saucepan.

10. When ready to serve, return the ducks to an oven, preheated to 400 degrees, for 10 minutes. Carve the ducks (or simply split in two and serve half a duck per person). Heat the sauce and, at the last minute, melt the butter in a skillet, swirling it around and over the heat until it is browned a light hazelnut color. Pour the butter into the sauce and stir. Serve the sauce separately.

YIELD: 6 servings.

Caneton Grillé

GRILLED DUCK

- 1 5-pound duck
- Salt and freshly ground black pepper to taste
- 2 teaspoons peanut, vegetable or corn oil
- 2 tablespoons butter
- 1 teaspoon finely minced shallots
- 1 tablespoon raspberry vinegar
- 1 teaspoon finely chopped parsley
- Watercress leaves for garnish

1. Preheat the broiler.

2. Cut away the legs of the duck, leaving the thighs attached. Place legs fat side down. With a sharp knife, cut off all peripheral fat and skin from around the thighs. Sprinkle legs and thighs with salt and pepper. Brush all sides with oil.

3. Set the duck liver aside. Carve away the meat from each side of the breast. Using the fingers and a sharp knife, cut and pull off the fat skin, leaving only the two slabs of meat. Discard the carcass.

4. Arrange the legs and thighs on a broiler rack, skin side up. Place under the broiler about 3 inches from the source of heat.

5. Broil for about 5 minutes and turn the pieces. Broil for about 5 minutes on the other side.

6. Lower the broiler rack to about 12 inches from the source of heat. Cook the leg and thigh pieces another 5 minutes.

7. Brush the breast meat on both sides with a teaspoon of oil. Sprinkle with salt and pepper.

8. Turn the leg pieces skin side up. Arrange breast pieces alongside the leg pieces. Return the broiler rack to the upper part of the broiler so that leg and breast pieces are about 3 inches from the source of heat. Broil for about 2 minutes. Turn breast pieces and broil about 2 minutes longer. The breast meat should remain rare inside.

9. Meanwhile, cut the duck liver in half. Sprinkle with salt and pepper.

10. Melt 1 tablespoon of butter in a small skillet. Add the liver, cook for about 1 minute and turn the pieces. Cook for 1 minute longer. Remove the liver.

11. Add the remaining tablespoon of butter and the shallots to the skillet. Cook, stirring, for about 30 seconds. Add the vinegar and cook until almost evaporated.

12. Arrange one breast half and one leg with thigh attached on each of two plates. Arrange one piece of liver on the plate. Pour the vinegar sauce over. Sprinkle with chopped parsley and garnish with watercress leaves.

YIELD: 2 servings.

Red-cooked foods in Chinese cuisine are simmered in dark soy sauce with seasonings, which gives them a reddish-brown color. Duck cooked this way is delicious as is, or it can be used in the many flavor duck salad in the salad chapter.

Red-cooked Duck

- 1 5- to 6-pound duck
- 1 tablespoon plus ½ cup dark soy sauce
- ¼ cup light soy sauce
- 4 cups cold water
- ¼ cup shaoxing wine or dry sherry
- 2 ounces (about ¼ cup when cracked) Chinese rock sugar
- 2 slices fresh ginger
- 2 whole scallions
- 1 whole star anise
- 1 piece dried tangerine or orange peel

1. Preheat the oven to 400 degrees.

2. Cut away and discard the peripheral fat and skin from the duck. That is to say, the fat from the cavity, the excess skin around the neck and cavity opening and so on.

3. Brush the duck all over with 1 tablespoon of the dark soy sauce. Place on a rack breast side up and roast for 30 minutes.

4. Meanwhile, in a kettle combine the remaining dark soy sauce, the light soy sauce, cold water, shaoxing, rock sugar, ginger, whole scallions, star anise and tangerine peel. Set aside.

5. Remove the duck from the roasting pan and add it breast side down to the sauce. Bring the sauce to the boil, cover, lower the heat and simmer for 30 minutes.

6. Turn the duck in the sauce. Cover and return to the boil. Simmer for 30 minutes. Carve the duck and serve hot or cold.

YIELD: 2 to 4 servings.

Note: The sauce in which the duck is cooked may be kept indefinitely if it is strained and reheated, adding more ingredients as necessary to maintain the volume and flavor. You may cook more duck or other poultry, beef or pork in the sauce as you desire. Keep the strained sauce tightly covered and refrigerated until ready to use.

One dish on Italian menus consists of thinly sliced turkey breast, cut and cooked to resemble scaloppine of veal. In fact, the resemblance is so close that if one were blindfolded and offered a bite of both the veal and the turkey, it would be difficult to tell the difference. But where cost is concerned the difference is vast. Boneless veal cut from the leg is priced at about $8 a pound. Boneless turkey breast meat costs about $2 a pound. If you have an accommodating butcher, he may be willing to slice the turkey for you. If not, you can do it easily if you sharpen your slicing knife.

Preferably, you should buy a breast or half a breast that is skinless and boneless. A 1½-pound skinless, boneless turkey breast will yield 12 scaloppine of nice size. When cutting the breast, slice it on the bias, trying to cut pieces of about the same size and weight. Before cooking, place each slice between sheets of plastic wrap and, using a flat mallet, flatten them lightly and uniformly. Do not break the flesh.

Filetti di Tacchino Francese

TURKEY SCALOPPINE IN BATTER WITH LEMON

- 4 turkey scaloppine
- Salt and freshly ground black pepper to taste
- 1 egg, lightly beaten
- 2 tablespoons milk
- ¼ cup flour
- 7 tablespoons butter
- 4 thin slices lemon
- Juice of 1 lemon
- Chopped parsley for garnish

1. Sprinkle the scaloppine with salt and pepper.

2. Put the egg in a flat, shallow dish and beat it lightly. Add the milk and beat until well blended.

3. Put the flour plus a little salt and pepper in another shallow dish.

4. Dip the scaloppine first in flour to coat well, then in the beaten egg.

5. Select a skillet wide enough to accommodate 2 scaloppine at a time.

6. Melt 6 tablespoons of the butter in the skillet and add the scaloppine. Cook for about 1 minute, or until golden brown on one side. Turn and cook the other side. Transfer them to a warm serving dish.

7. Repeat with remaining scaloppine.

8. Garnish with lemon slices.

9. To the skillet add the lemon juice and remaining 1 tablespoon of butter. When the butter is melted, pour the sauce over the meat. Sprinkle with parsley and serve.

YIELD: 4 servings.

Filetti di Tacchino Beau Séjour

TURKEY SCALOPPINE WITH GARLIC AND BAY LEAVES

- 4 turkey scaloppine
- Salt and freshly ground black pepper to taste
- ¼ cup flour
- 5 tablespoons butter, approximately
- 4 cloves garlic, peeled and cut in half lengthwise
- 2 bay leaves, split in half
- ¼ cup dry white wine
- ¼ cup chicken broth

1. Sprinkle the scaloppine with salt and pepper. Dip them on both sides in the flour.

2. Select a skillet wide enough to accommodate 2 scaloppine at a time.

3. Melt 3 tablespoons of the butter in the skillet and, when it is hot, add the scaloppine. Scatter the garlic and bay leaves over and around the scaloppine.

4. Cook the scaloppine for about 1 minute, or until golden brown on one side. Turn and cook on the other side for about 1 minute. Transfer them to a warm serving dish.

5. Cook the remaining scaloppine, adding a bit more butter as necessary.

6. Add the wine to the skillet and cook until it has almost evaporated. Add the broth and cook briefly. Add salt and pepper to taste. Cook down briefly and pour the sauce over the scaloppine.

YIELD: 4 servings.

Filetti di Tacchino Viennese

BREADED TURKEY SCALOPPINE WITH ANCHOVY

- 4 turkey scaloppine
- Salt and freshly ground black pepper to taste
- 1 egg
- 2 tablespoons water
- 4 tablespoons plus 1 teaspoon peanut, vegetable or corn oil
- ¼ cup flour
- 2 cups bread crumbs
- 4 slices lemon
- 4 rolled anchovy fillets
- Finely chopped parsley for garnish
- 4 tablespoons butter

1. Sprinkle the scaloppine with salt and pepper to taste.

2. Put the egg in a flat, shallow dish and beat it lightly. Add the water, 1 teaspoon oil, salt and pepper and beat until well blended.

3. Put the flour in another shallow dish and the bread crumbs in a third.

4. Dip each scaloppine first in flour, then in beaten egg and finally in bread crumbs to coat on both sides. Place the scaloppine on a flat surface and pat lightly with the flat side of a knife to make the crumbs adhere.

5. Heat 2 tablespoons of oil in a heavy skillet and add one scaloppine. Cook for about 1 minute, or until golden brown on one side. Turn and cook on the other side for 1 minute. Remove to a warm platter.

6. Continue cooking scaloppine until all are done, adding more oil to the skillet, about a tablespoon at a time as necessary. About 4 tablespoons oil should be enough to cook them all.

7. To serve, place one lemon slice in the center of each scaloppine. Place one anchovy fillet in the center of the lemon slice. Sprinkle with parsley.

8. Melt the butter in a skillet, shaking it until it is hot and foamy. When the butter starts to turn brown, pour it over the scaloppine and serve.

YIELD: 4 servings.

One of the most elegant and delicate dishes in the French repertory is dindonneau en demi-deuil, which translates—in jest, of course—as turkey in half-mourning. Slices of truffles are inserted under the skin of the turkey and its stuffing is mousse-like in texture and intangibly subtle in flavor.

Dindonneau en Demi-deuil

TRUFFLED TURKEY WITH CREAM SAUCE

- 1 12-pound turkey
- 15 black truffle slices
- 2 pounds skinless, boneless chicken breasts
- 2 egg whites
- ¼ teaspoon grated nutmeg
- Salt and freshly ground black pepper to taste
- 1 tablespoon Cognac or Armagnac
- 1½ cups heavy cream
- ¼ cup finely diced black truffles
- 2 cups dry white wine
- 2 cups coarsely chopped carrot
- 1 cup coarsely chopped leeks, optional
- 2 cups coarsely chopped onion
- 1 cup coarsely chopped celery
- 2 cloves garlic
- 2 bay leaves
- ½ teaspoon dried thyme
- 6 sprigs fresh parsley
- Sauce suprême (see following recipe)

1. Using the fingers, separate the flesh of the turkey from the skin at the opening of the neck. Run the fingers toward the rear of the bird, loosening the skin totally as you go. Loosen it so that you can insert the lower part of your arm between the skin and the meat. Push the fingers to loosen the thigh and leg meat.

2. Push 1 truffle slice at a time between the skin and the meat of each leg. Push 1 truffle slice under the skin over each thigh. Place 9 truffle slices under the skin over the breast.

3. Slice away any nerve membranes on the chicken meat. Cut the chicken meat into 1-inch cubes and put them in the container of a food processor. Add the egg whites, nutmeg and salt and pepper to taste. Process to a fine purée.

4. Add Cognac and process briefly.

5. Continue processing while gradually adding the cream. Add the diced truffles and process for about 10 seconds.

6. Stuff the turkey cavity with the chicken mixture. Spoon some of the filling inside the neck and press the 2 remaining truffle slices against the neck filling. Cover the filling with the neck skin. Truss the turkey opening with string, making certain that the filling is well enclosed with skin.

7. Select a kettle large enough to hold the turkey compactly without crowding. Add water to barely cover, about 8 quarts. Add the wine, carrot, leeks, onion, celery, garlic, bay leaves, thyme and parsley.

8. Bring to the boil and cover. If the turkey skin should swell in the initial stages of cooking, make a tiny pinprick in the skin to release the air. Simmer slowly for about 2 hours and 45 minutes.

9. Transfer the turkey to a carving platter and keep it warm. Let stand for 20 minutes before serving. Use some of the broth to make the sauce suprême.

YIELD: 12 or more servings.

SAUCE SUPRÊME

A Turkey Cream Sauce

- 8 cups broth from the cooked turkey en demi-deuil
- 6 tablespoons butter
- 8 tablespoons flour
- 1½ cups heavy cream
- Salt and freshly ground black pepper to taste

1. Bring the broth to the boil in a saucepan and let it cook down to 4 cups.

2. Melt the butter in another saucepan and add the flour, stirring with a wire whisk. When it is blended, add the broth, stirring rapidly with the whisk.

3. When the sauce is blended and smooth, add the cream and salt and pepper. Continue stirring the sauce over a low heat, until it thickens, about 5 minutes.

YIELD: 12 or more servings.

MEATS

A WHILE ago, we judged a cooking contest sponsored by the March of Dimes in Pittsburgh, Pennsylvania, and one of the winning entries was spinach pancakes, the creation of Marty Allen, the comedian and a native of Pittsburgh. He served them with grilled steaks topped with zucchini in a tomato sauce, an admirable combination of flavors and textures. This is our version of Marty Allen's dish.

Steak Marty

- 2 zucchini, about ¾ pound total weight
- 1 onion, about ½ pound
- 2 tablespoons butter
- ½ cup finely chopped celery
- 1 teaspoon finely minced garlic
- 1 cup chopped tomatoes
- 2 tablespoons freshly grated Parmesan cheese
- 2 tablespoons fresh bread crumbs
- 4 thin, boneless shell steaks, about ½ pound each
- Spinach pancakes (see following recipe)

1. Trim off the ends of the zucchini and cut into ¼-inch-thick rounds. There should be about 3 cups.

2. Peel the onion and split it crosswise in half. Cut each half into ¼-inch-thick slices. There should be about 1½ cups.

3. Melt the butter in a skillet and add the onion and celery. Cook, stirring, until the onion is wilted. Add the zucchini and garlic. Cook, stirring occasionally, for about 5 minutes.

4. Add the tomatoes and cook for about 5 minutes. Add the cheese and bread crumbs. Stir and remove from the heat.

5. Grill the steaks over charcoal or cook them until golden brown on both sides in butter. Cook to the desired degree of doneness. Serve with the zucchini mixture on top. Serve the spinach pancakes on the side.

YIELD: 4 servings.

MARTY ALLEN'S SPINACH PANCAKES

- 1 pound fresh spinach purchased in bulk, or 1 10-ounce plastic bag of spinach (see Note)
- ½ cup heavy cream
- 6 tablespoons finely grated onion
- 3 tablespoons flour
- 2 eggs, lightly beaten
- Salt and freshly ground black pepper to taste
- ½ cup peanut, vegetable or corn oil, approximately

1. Pick over the spinach to remove any tough stems or any blemished leaves. Rinse the spinach well to remove all traces of sand. Drop the spinach into boiling water. Stir and cook for 1 minute.

2. Drain the spinach. When it is cool enough to handle, squeeze the spinach between the palms to extract most of the moisture. Chop the spinach. There should be about 1½ cups.

3. Put the spinach in a saucepan and add the cream and onion. Heat thoroughly. Sprinkle the flour over all and stir. Add the eggs, salt and pepper to taste and blend well.

4. Heat about 2 tablespoons of oil at a time in a skillet. Add 2 or 3 tablespoons of the pancake mixture. Cook 4 to 6 pancakes at a time, turning once. Cook until golden brown on one side, turn and cook until golden brown on the other side.

YIELD: 12 to 24 pancakes, depending on size.

Note: For this recipe, Marty Allen uses 2 packages of frozen creamed spinach, defrosted. If you use this, eliminate the fresh spinach and cream.

Emincé de Filet de Boeuf Sauté à l'Echalotes

SLICED FILLET OF BEEF WITH SHALLOTS

- 16 thin slices of fillet of beef, such as filets mignons, about 1½ pounds
- Salt and freshly ground black pepper to taste
- 4 tablespoons butter
- 4 tablespoons finely chopped shallots
- 1 tablespoon red wine vinegar
- Finely chopped parsley

1. Sprinkle the pieces of beef with salt and pepper.

2. Melt 2 tablespoons of the butter in a heavy skillet and add the beef

slices. Cook for about 30 seconds to a side, or until quickly browned on both sides. As the pieces cook, transfer them to a warm platter.

3. Add the remaining butter and the shallots to the skillet. Cook for about 30 seconds, swirling the shallots in the skillet. Add the vinegar. Bring to the boil. Pour this over the meat.

4. Serve sprinkled with finely chopped parsley.

YIELD: 4 to 6 servings.

Tamale Pie

THE BEEF

- 2 pounds very lean beef, preferably top sirloin
- 2 cups fresh or canned beef broth
- 3 cups water
- 2 cloves garlic, peeled but left whole

THE CORNMEAL MUSH

- 2 cups cornmeal
- Salt, if desired
- 5 cups cold beef broth or water
- 1½ tablespoons lard or vegetable oil

THE FILLING

- 2 tablespoons bacon fat
- 1 cup finely chopped onion
- 3 tablespoons finely minced garlic
- 1 cup finely chopped sweet green or red pepper
- 3 tablespoons chili powder
- 1 teaspoon ground cumin
- ½ teaspoon dried oregano
- ½ teaspoon ground coriander
- Salt, if desired
- Freshly ground black pepper to taste
- 2 cups canned tomatoes
- 1 cup whole kernel corn, fresh or canned
- 2 tablespoons chopped hot canned chilies
- 1 tablespoon butter

1. Put the meat in a large saucepan or small kettle. Add the broth, water and whole garlic. Bring to the boil and simmer for 2 hours, or until quite tender. Drain but reserve about ¼ cup of the cooking liquid. Shred the meat. If the meat is not tender enough, chop it in a food processor.

2. Put the cornmeal in a heavy saucepan and add the salt, broth and lard. Bring to the boil, stirring constantly with a wire whisk. Cook until thickened. Continue cooking, stirring, for about 5 minutes. Set aside. The mush should be slightly cooled, but do not let it get cold or it will not be manageable.

3. Preheat the oven to 400 degrees.

4. To make the filling, heat the bacon fat in a saucepan and add the onion, garlic and chopped pepper. Cook, stirring, until the vegetables are wilted. Add the shredded meat, chili powder, cumin, oregano, coriander, salt and pepper to taste, tomatoes, corn and hot chilies. Add the reserved ¼ cup of broth. Stir.

5. Butter a 10-cup baking dish.

6. Add enough of the mush to coat the bottom and sides of the dish. Leave enough mush to cover the top. Spread the mush in the dish as neatly as possible over and around the bottom and sides. Add the filling. Smooth it over. Add the remaining mush and smooth it over. Dot the top with butter. Place the dish in the oven and bake for 45 minutes, or until piping hot throughout and nicely browned on top.

YIELD: 8 servings.

Brochette de Boeuf

CUBED BEEF ON SKEWERS

1¼ pounds sirloin steak in one piece
16 1-inch squares of cored, seeded green pepper
2 tablespoons peanut, vegetable or corn oil
Salt and freshly ground black pepper to taste
Béarnaise sauce (see recipe page 401)

1. Heat the grill.

2. Cut the steak into cubes of about 1½ inches. There should be 48 pieces.

3. Arrange the pieces of beef on skewers, starting with one piece of green pepper. Add four pieces of beef, another green pepper, four of beef, another pepper piece, four more pieces of beef and finally a piece of pepper.

4. Repeat with three more skewers.

5. Place the skewered foods in a flat dish and brush all over with oil.

6. Place the brochettes on the grill and cook for 3 to 4 minutes on one side. Sprinkle all over with salt and pepper and turn the brochettes to cook on the other side, 3 to 4 minutes. Serve immediately with béarnaise sauce.

YIELD: 4 servings.

Beef Goulash

- ¾ pound boneless sirloin or shell steak
- 2 tablespoons peanut, vegetable or corn oil
- 2 cups finely chopped onion
- 2 teaspoons finely minced garlic
- 1½ cups finely chopped sweet green or red pepper
- 1 tablespoon sweet, mild or hot paprika, depending on individual taste
- 1 teaspoon caraway seeds
- Salt and freshly ground black pepper to taste
- 2 cups chopped fresh or canned tomatoes
- Sour cream, optional

1. Trim the meat of all gristle and fat. Cut the meat into ½-inch cubes.

2. Heat the oil in a large saucepan or casserole. Add the meat and cook, stirring often, until the meat starts to brown.

3. Add the onion, garlic and chopped peppers. Cook, stirring, for about 5 minutes. Add the paprika, caraway seeds, salt and pepper to taste and stir.

4. Add the tomatoes. Cover and cook, stirring occasionally, for about 1 hour. If desired, top each serving with a dollop of sour cream.

YIELD: 4 to 6 servings.

Paprika Beef Stew

- 3 pounds chuck or top round of beef
- ⅓ cup peanut, vegetable or corn oil or lard
- Salt and freshly ground black pepper to taste
- 3 cups coarsely chopped onion
- 1 tablespoon finely chopped garlic
- 4 teaspoons sweet, mild or hot paprika, depending on individual taste
- 1 tablespoon caraway seeds
- 1 tablespoon dried marjoram
- 1 cup chopped fresh or canned tomatoes
- 1 tablespoon tomato paste
- 1 cup beef broth
- 4 sweet green or red peppers

1. Cut the beef into 1½-inch cubes.

2. Heat the oil in a large casserole or Dutch oven. Add the cubed beef and cook, stirring often. When the meat is partly browned, add salt and pepper to taste.

3. Add the onion and cook until the onion is translucent. Add the garlic and stir. Add the paprika, caraway seeds and marjoram. Cook for about 10 minutes.

4. Add the tomatoes, tomato paste and beef broth. Bring to the boil and cover. Simmer slowly for about 1 hour. If necessary, add more broth as the stew cooks.

5. Split the peppers in half. Remove the seeds and the cores. Cut each pepper half lengthwise into four strips.

6. Scatter the pepper strips on top of the stew and cover. Cook for 1 hour longer.

YIELD: 8 servings.

When Amnuay Nethongkome came into our kitchen to cook his native Thai dishes, he was the saucier at Le Cirque, one of Manhattan's chicest dining establishments. Prior to that he had been at Maxwell's Plum under Jean Vergnes and at Luchow's—a long way from Bangkok. Mr. Nethongkome and his Thai-born wife regaled us with dishes made with things like lemon grass, dried lime leaves and that thin essence of anchovy called fish sauce, which they use in quantity. The Nethongkomes have subsequently opened a Thai restaurant in Miami.

Masman Beef Curry

- 4 large potatoes, about 1 pound, peeled and dropped into cold water
- 1 medium-sized onion, about ½ pound
- 2¾ cups coconut cream, preferably fresh (see instructions page 419) or canned (see Note)
- 2 pounds beef stew meat, cut into 1½-inch cubes
- 2 tablespoons curry powder
- 3 tablespoons fish sauce (see Note)
- ¼ cup sugar
- ¾ cup shelled peanuts
- 1½ cups canned, unsweetened coconut milk (see Note)
- 1½ cups water

1. Cut the potatoes into ½-inch-thick rounds and set aside in cold water.

2. Quarter the onion lengthwise. Cut the onion into lengthwise shreds. There should be about 1½ cups.

3. Heat the coconut cream in a large skillet and add the beef cubes. Bring to the boil and cook uncovered, stirring occasionally, for about 20 minutes, or until the liquid is thickened and sauce-like. Remove the pieces of meat and set aside. Add the curry powder and stir rapidly with a whisk.

4. Add the fish sauce and stir well. Add the sugar. Stir.

5. Return the meat to the sauce. Cook for 10 minutes.

6. Add the onions, drained potato rounds and peanuts. Add the canned coconut milk and water. Cover and bring to the boil. Cook for 45 minutes to 1 hour, until the meat is tender.

7. Spoon out the beef onto a warmed serving platter. Allow the sauce to rest for a minute, then skim off the surface fat and pour the sauce over the meat before serving.

YIELD: 10 servings.

Note: The preferred brand of coconut cream is a Philippine import packed in 10-ounce tins and with the Selecta brand label. The recommended brand of coconut milk is made in the Philippines and the brand is Newton. Fish sauce is available in Oriental markets and specialty food shops.

American cooks, by and large, have never been great experimenters with herbs and spices. Rosemary is not, as it is for the Italians, a basic part of our culinary heritage. And neither is tarragon, which could be called a herbal basic of the French kitchen. Cumin and coriander are foundations of Middle Eastern cooking, and ginger is an integral part of a good deal of Chinese food preparation.

But there is one herb that seems to be indigenous to the cooks of this nation, whether they are *cordons bleus* or neophytes. That herb is parsley, perhaps the most innocent of all herbs where flavor is concerned but also by far the most versatile. That is not to say parsley is without flavor, but it does not have the positive assertiveness of, say, coriander or mint.

That is one reason why we are fascinated with recipes and dishes in which parsley becomes a dominant factor. One of them is a Persian creation that we discovered many years ago in Iran, known as gormeh sabzee. It is a cubed meat dish made with lamb, beef or veal that calls for no less than 12 cups (the amount varies from kitchen to kitchen, but it is always an abundant quantity) of the herb.

Gormeh Sabzee

MEAT WITH BEANS AND PARSLEY PERSIAN STYLE

- 1 pound light red kidney beans
- 7 cups water
- Salt to taste, if desired
- Freshly ground black pepper to taste
- 1 medium-sized onion, peeled
- 2 whole cloves
- 6 tablespoons butter
- 12 cups finely chopped parsley
- 5 cups finely chopped scallions, green part and all
- 3 pounds veal, beef or lamb, cut into 1-inch cubes
- ⅓ cup lemon juice
- 1 lemon, cut into quarters

1. Put the beans in a large saucepan or kettle and add 4 cups of water and salt and pepper to taste. Stick the onion with the cloves and add it to the beans. Bring to the boil and let simmer, partly covered, for about 1 hour and 15 minutes, or until tender.

2. In a large casserole or Dutch oven, melt 4 tablespoons of the butter and add the parsley and scallions. Cook, stirring often, for about 5 minutes.

3. Melt the remaining 2 tablespoons of butter in a large skillet and add the meat. Add salt and pepper to taste. Cook, turning the cubes of meat often, until lightly browned. Add the parsley and scallion mixture and the remaining 3 cups of water. Add the lemon juice and the quartered lemon. Bring to the boil. Cover and simmer for 45 minutes to 1 hour, or until the meat is almost totally tender.

4. Add the beans and stir to blend. Continue cooking until the meat is tender, about 10 minutes longer.

YIELD: 8 or more servings.

Veal, Chicken and Wild Mushroom Meat Loaf

- 1 cup dried, imported mushrooms
- 1 pound skinless, boneless chicken breast
- 1 pound ground veal
- 2 tablespoons butter
- ½ cup finely chopped onion
- ½ teaspoon finely minced garlic
- 1 egg, lightly beaten
- 1 cup fine fresh bread crumbs
- ⅓ cup finely chopped parsley
- ¼ teaspoon grated nutmeg
- ¼ cup heavy cream
- Salt, if desired
- Freshly ground black pepper to taste

1. Put the mushrooms in a bowl and add warm water to cover. Let stand for 30 minutes or longer. Drain thoroughly, but reserve ¼ cup of the liquid.

2. Preheat the oven to 400 degrees.

3. Have the chicken breast ground by the butcher or grind it in a food processor. Put it in a bowl and add the veal.

4. Melt the butter in a saucepan and add the onion and garlic. Cook, stirring, until wilted. Add the mushrooms and cook, stirring, for about 1 minute. Let cool briefly.

5. Add the mushroom mixture and egg to the meat. Blend. Add the bread crumbs, parsley, nutmeg, cream, the reserved ¼ cup of mushroom liquid, salt and pepper to taste. Mix thoroughly.

6. Pack the mixture into a loaf pan measuring about 9 by 5 by 3 inches. Set the pan in a larger pan of water. Bring to the boil on top of the stove. Place both pans in the oven and bake for 1 hour (internal temperature should be 160 degrees). Let stand for about 15 minutes before slicing.

YIELD: 8 or more servings.

Gâteau de Viande

FRENCH MEAT LOAF

- 2 tablespoons butter
- 2 tablespoons finely chopped shallots
- 2 tablespoons chopped onion
- ½ teaspoon finely minced garlic
- ¼ pound mushrooms, finely diced, about 1½ cups
- Salt, if desired
- Freshly ground black pepper to taste
- ½ cup crushed fresh or canned tomatoes
- 2 pounds ground meat, preferably a combination of beef, veal and pork, although it could be all beef or all pork
- ¾ pound chicken livers
- 1 cup fine fresh bread crumbs
- 2 eggs, lightly beaten
- 3 tablespoons finely chopped parsley

1. Preheat the oven to 400 degrees.

2. Melt the butter in a saucepan and, when it is hot, add the shallots, onion and garlic. Cook, stirring, for about 5 minutes. Add the mushrooms, salt and pepper to taste. Cook, stirring frequently, for about 8 minutes. Add the tomatoes and cook for about 10 minutes. Let the mixture cool briefly.

3. Place the meat in a mixing bowl and add the onion and tomato mixture.

4. Chop the chicken livers until fine. (Do not chop them in a blender or they will be too fine.) Add them to the meat mixture. Add the remaining ingredients, plus salt and pepper to taste, and blend well.

5. Pack the mixture into a loaf pan measuring about 9 by 5 by 3 inches. Set the pan in a larger pan of water. Bring the water to the boil on top of the stove and then place both pans in the oven. Bake for 1 hour (internal temperature should be 160 degrees). Let stand about 15 minutes before slicing. Serve hot with tomato sauce or cold as an appetizer.

YIELD: 8 or more servings.

❧

Mushroom and Meat Loaf

- ½ pound mushrooms
- 1 tablespoon butter
- ½ cup finely chopped onion
- 1 pound ground very lean pork
- 1 pound ground very lean veal
- ⅛ teaspoon grated nutmeg
- ½ cup fresh bread crumbs
- ⅛ teaspoon hot red pepper flakes
- Freshly ground black pepper to taste
- 1 large egg, lightly beaten
- ¼ cup heavy cream
- 2 tablespoons finely chopped fresh dill
- ½ cup chopped fresh or canned tomatoes, drained
- 3 sprigs fresh dill

1. Preheat the oven to 400 degrees.

2. Slice the mushrooms on a flat surface. There should be 3 or 4 cups.

3. Melt the butter in a skillet and add the onion. Cook until wilted and add the mushrooms. Cook until the mushrooms give up their liquid. Cook until this liquid evaporates.

4. Put the pork and veal in a mixing bowl and add the mushroom and onion mixture. Add the nutmeg, bread crumbs, pepper flakes, a generous grinding of pepper, egg, heavy cream and chopped dill. Blend well with the hands.

5. Pack the mixture into a 9- by 5- by 3-inch loaf pan and smooth it over on top. Spoon the tomatoes on top and arrange the dill sprigs in the center.

6. Place the loaf pan in a larger pan and pour water around it. Bring the water to the boil on top of the stove and then place in the oven. Bake for 1 to 1½ hours, or until a meat thermometer in the center of the loaf registers 160 degrees.

YIELD: 6 to 8 servings.

Meat Loaf à la Chinoise

MEAT LOAF WITH GINGER AND GARLIC

- 1 pound ground lean pork
- 1 pound ground lean beef
- 2 tablespoons peanut, vegetable or corn oil
- 1 cup finely chopped onion
- 1 tablespoon finely minced garlic
- ½ cup finely chopped, drained water chestnuts
- ½ cup finely chopped parsley
- 2 tablespoons finely chopped fresh ginger
- ¾ cup finely chopped scallions
- 1 cup fine fresh bread crumbs
- 2 tablespoons soy sauce
- ⅓ cup dry sherry
- 1 egg, lightly beaten
- Salt, if desired
- Freshly ground black pepper to taste

1. Preheat the oven to 400 degrees.

2. Combine the pork and beef in a mixing bowl.

3. Heat the oil in a saucepan and add the onion and garlic. Cook, stirring, until the onion is wilted. Let cool briefly.

4. To the combined meats add the onion and garlic mixture, water chestnuts, parsley, ginger, scallions, bread crumbs, soy sauce, wine, egg, salt and pepper to taste. Blend well with the hands.

5. Pack the mixture into a loaf pan measuring about 9 by 5 by 3 inches. Set the pan in a larger pan of water. Bring to the boil on top of the stove. Place both pans in the oven and bake for 1 hour (internal temperature should be 160 degrees). Let stand about 15 minutes before slicing.

YIELD: 8 or more servings.

Polpette alla Romana

ITALIAN MEATBALLS

THE MEATBALLS

- 1¼ pounds ground beef
- ¼ pound prosciutto, finely chopped, about ¾ cup
- 1 cup fresh bread crumbs
- ½ cup milk
- ½ teaspoon finely minced garlic
- 3 tablespoons freshly grated Parmesan cheese
- 2 eggs, lightly beaten
- ⅛ teaspoon grated nutmeg
- ¼ cup finely chopped parsley
- Salt and freshly ground black pepper to taste
- 1 tablespoon olive oil

THE SAUCE

- ¼ cup olive oil, finely diced pancetta (salt-cured bacon), fresh bacon fat, salt pork or ham fat
- ¼ cup finely chopped onion
- ¼ cup finely diced carrot
- ¼ cup chopped celery
- ½ cup finely diced, unpeeled zucchini
- 1½ pounds fresh tomatoes, peeled and cored, or use 3 cups canned tomatoes
- Salt and freshly ground black pepper to taste
- 1 tablespoon chopped fresh basil

1. To make the meatballs, put the beef into a mixing bowl. Add the prosciutto and blend.

2. Combine the bread crumbs and milk in another bowl and blend well. Let stand a minute or so and add to the beef. Add the garlic, cheese, eggs, nutmeg and parsley. Add a little salt (the prosciutto is salty) and pepper.

3. Blend the mixture well. Shape into about 36 meatballs, each about 1½ inches in diameter.

4. To prepare the sauce, heat the oil or pancetta in a skillet and add the onion, carrot, celery and zucchini. Cook, stirring often, until the onion starts to brown.

5. Put the tomatoes into the container of a food processor or blender. Blend. There should be about 3 cups. Add this to the cooked vegetables. Cook for about 10 minutes. Add salt, pepper and basil.

6. When ready to cook the meatballs, heat the tablespoon of olive oil in a skillet and add the balls a few at a time. Do not crowd them. Brown them

all over, turning often so that they cook evenly. When one batch is cooked, remove it and cook another until all the balls are browned.

7. Add the meatballs to the sauce and simmer for about 15 minutes, turning the balls in the sauce occasionally.

YIELD: 4 to 6 servings.

Leftovers pose an undeniable challenge. What can a cook do when guests and family are fed to the teeth with sandwiches made from yesterday's roast beef, ham, chicken, fish, seafood, lamb or veal? The answer is simple: Chop the meat for croquettes. We offer here a foundation recipe for leftovers that could be called the "anything croquettes."

Croquettes

- 1 pound cooked meat, such as ham, veal, lamb, beef, pork, chicken or seafood, such as shrimp, crab and fish
- 4 tablespoons butter
- 3 tablespoons flour
- 1¼ cups milk
- 1 cup finely chopped celery
- ¾ cup finely chopped onion
- ½ teaspoon finely minced garlic
- ⅛ teaspoon grated nutmeg
- Salt and freshly ground black pepper to taste
- 3 egg yolks
- 1 egg
- 1 teaspoon oil
- ¼ cup water
- Flour for dredging
- Fresh bread crumbs for breading
- Fat for deep frying
- Sauce suprême (see following recipe)

1. If cooked solid meat such as ham, veal, lamb, beef, pork or shrimp is to be used, chop it. It is best to chop this with a heavy knife on a flat surface. Or it may be chopped in a food processor but it should not be too fine. As a last resort, it could be ground in a meat grinder. If crabmeat or fish is to be used, shred it. There should be about 3½ cups.

2. Melt 2 tablespoons of the butter in a saucepan and add the flour, stirring with a wire whisk. When blended, add the milk, stirring rapidly with the whisk. Stir constantly until thickened.

3. Heat the remaining butter in a skillet and add the celery, onion and garlic. Cook, stirring, until the vegetables are wilted. Add the chopped or shredded food. Stir until heated through.

4. Add the white sauce and stir to blend. Add the nutmeg, salt and pepper to taste. Add the egg yolks, stirring briskly. Heat thoroughly but do not cook. Remove from the heat.

5. Spoon and scrape the mixture into a flat dish to facilitate cooling. Chill.

6. Divide the mixture into 18 portions. Shape each portion by hand into any desired shape, pyramidal, round, oval and so on.

7. Beat the egg in a shallow, wide vessel with the teaspoon oil, water, salt and pepper to taste.

8. Dredge the croquettes first in flour, then in egg and finally in bread crumbs. Coat well.

9. Heat the fat for deep frying. Add the croquettes a few at a time and cook, turning in the fat, for 2 or 3 minutes, or until golden brown all over. Drain on absorbent paper towels.

10. Serve hot with sauce suprême.

YIELD: 6 to 8 servings.

SAUCE SUPRÊME

Cream Sauce

- 2 tablespoons butter
- 3 tablespoons flour
- 1½ cups rich broth (see Note)
- ½ cup heavy cream
- Salt and freshly ground black pepper to taste
- Juice of ½ lemon

1. Melt the butter in a saucepan and add the flour, stirring with a wire whisk. Add the broth, stirring rapidly with the whisk. When the mixture is thickened and smooth, add the cream. Continue cooking for about 5 minutes.

2. Add salt and pepper to taste. Add the lemon juice. Strain the sauce if desired.

YIELD: About 2 cups.

Note: Use beef broth for beef croquettes; chicken may be used for chicken, ham, veal, pork and so on; use fish stock for fish or seafood croquettes.

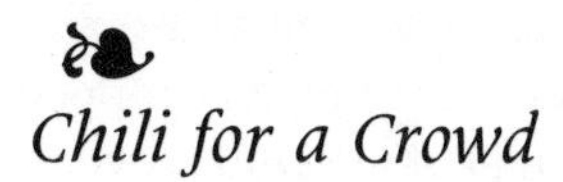

Chili for a Crowd

- 15 pounds very lean top round of beef in one or two pieces
- 1 cup refined sesame oil (available in health food stores), peanut or corn oil
- 1½ cups flour
- 1 to 2 cups chili powder
- ½ to 1 teaspoon cayenne pepper, or to taste
- ¾ cup finely chopped garlic
- 6 teaspoons whole cumin seeds, crushed with a mortar and pestle or ground in a spice mill
- 6 teaspoons dried oregano
- 5 cups fresh or canned beef broth
- 4 cups water
- ¼ cup red wine vinegar
- ¼ cup masa harina (available where Mexican food products are sold), optional
- Salt and freshly ground black pepper to taste
- Chili beans (see following recipe), optional
- Chili sauce to go with beans (see following recipe), optional

1. Trim the meat well to remove all trace of fat, membranes, veins and so on. Cut the meat into large slices about ½ inch thick. Make a stack of a few slices, then cut the slices into ½-inch-thick strips. Cut the strips into ½-inch cubes.

2. Heat the oil in a large casserole or kettle. Add the meat and cook, stirring, just until all the meat loses its raw look. Add the flour and stir. Add the chili powder, cayenne pepper, garlic, cumin and oregano and stir.

3. Add the beef broth, water and vinegar and bring to the boil. Stir in the masa harina. Add salt and pepper to taste. Let simmer gently, stirring often from the bottom to prevent sticking, for about 2 hours. Serve with rice, chili beans and chili sauce.

YIELD: 20 to 30 servings.

CHILI BEANS

- 3 pounds light red dried kidney beans or pinto beans
- 24 cups water
- 2 smoked ham hocks
- 2½ cups coarsely chopped onion
- 1 tablespoon finely minced garlic
- Salt and freshly ground black pepper to taste
- 1½ teaspoons dried oregano
- 3 tablespoons chili powder
- ¾ teaspoon hot red pepper flakes
- 1¼ cups tomato paste

1. Sort the beans to remove any stones or debris. Rinse well and drain. Put the beans in a kettle with the 24 cups of water, ham hocks, chopped onion, garlic, salt and pepper to taste, oregano and half of the chili powder.

2. Simmer for 1½ hours. Add the remaining chili powder, pepper flakes and tomato paste. Continue simmering for 30 minutes longer. Serve hot with chili.

YIELD: 30 servings.

CHILI SAUCE

- ¾ cup peanut, vegetable or corn oil
- ¾ cup flour
- 1½ teaspoons cumin seeds
- 6 cups tomato purée
- 3 tablespoons chili powder
- 1½ cups drained, chopped, canned, hot green chilies
- 3 cups water
- Salt to taste

1. Heat the oil in a saucepan and add the flour, stirring with a wire whisk. When blended and smooth, add the cumin seeds and stir.

2. Add the remaining ingredients and stir. Bring to the boil and simmer for about 5 minutes.

YIELD: 30 servings.

We have often voiced the opinion that chili con carne, rather than apple pie, might well be America's favorite dish. It is one of the tastiest—and easiest—of dishes to make, and anybody, regardless of age or ethnic background, can qualify as a chili expert, one who could declare that his, above all, is the greatest chili on earth.

This was called to mind recently when we read the International Chili Society's *Official Chili Cookbook* by Martina and William Neely (St. Martin's Press, $10.95). We admire the book, which offers a dazzling assortment of chili recipes, some of which have won championships in various chili-making contests. The authors make no claim to total purity in the presentation of the recipes; some call for very odd-sounding ingredients: canned tomato sauces, stuffed olives, whole kernel corn and eggplant. We decided to try several recipes chosen at random from the book and one in particular—with goat cheese—struck us as especially good. Here is our liberal adaptation of that recipe.

Carroll Shelby's Chili con Carne

- 1 pound round steak
- 1 pound chuck steak
- ½ cup peanut, vegetable or corn oil, or an equal amount of fat rendered from fresh suet
- 1 cup finely chopped onion
- 1 tablespoon finely minced garlic
- ¼ cup chili powder
- 1¼ teaspoons dried oregano
- ½ teaspoon paprika
- Salt, if desired
- 1 teaspoon ground cumin
- 1 cup tomato sauce
- 1½ cups beer (1 12-ounce can)
- ⅛ to 1 teaspoon cayenne pepper
- ¾ pound goat cheese, crumbled
- ½ teaspoon cumin seeds

1. Cut the meat into ¼-inch cubes.

2. Heat the oil in a skillet and cook the meat, stirring often, until browned.

3. Transfer the meat to a kettle and add the onion and garlic. Cook briefly and add the chili powder, oregano, paprika, salt to taste, cumin, tomato sauce and beer. Bring to the boil.

4. Cover closely and cook over very low heat for 1 hour. Add the cayenne pepper and cook for 2 hours longer. As the chili cooks, skim the fat from the surface.

5. Add the goat cheese and cumin seeds and simmer, stirring, for 30 minutes longer.

YIELD: 4 to 6 servings.

Plat de Côtes de Boeuf à la Diable

DEVILED SHORT RIBS OF BEEF

- 4 pounds short ribs of beef, the meatier the better, cut into 3- or 4-inch lengths
- 1 cup flour
- 1 teaspoon paprika
- Salt to taste, if desired
- 1 teaspoon freshly ground black pepper
- 2 tablespoons corn, peanut or vegetable oil
- 3 tablespoons imported mustard, the stronger the better
- 1 tablespoon dry white wine
- 1 teaspoon Worcestershire sauce
- 1½ cups fine fresh bread crumbs

1. Preheat the oven to 375 degrees.

2. Put the ribs of beef in a mixing bowl.

3. Blend the flour, paprika, salt to taste and pepper and spoon it over the ribs. Toss the ribs to coat well.

4. Select a baking dish large enough to hold the ribs in one layer without crowding. Add the oil. Add the ribs of beef and rub them all over with oil. Arrange the pieces neatly in the pan without letting them touch. Place in the oven and bake for about 1 hour, turning the pan in the oven occasionally so that the ribs cook evenly. Turn the pieces.

5. Reduce the oven temperature to 350 degrees. Continue baking the ribs for 20 to 30 minutes.

6. Pour off the fat from the baking pan.

7. Blend the mustard, wine and Worcestershire sauce in a mixing bowl. Use the mixture to brush the meaty part of the ribs all over. As they are brushed, use the fingers to sprinkle them liberally with the bread crumbs. Do not dip them in the crumbs or the crumbs in the bowl will become soggy.

8. As the ribs are crumbed, arrange them on a rack placed in a baking pan. Put the pan in the oven and continue baking for 30 minutes.

YIELD: 4 to 6 servings.

Plat de Côtes de Boeuf aux Légumes

SHORT RIBS OF BEEF WITH VEGETABLES

- 5 pounds short ribs of beef, the meatier the better, cut into 3- or 4-inch lengths
- 4 quarts water
- Salt to taste, if desired
- 2 onions, peeled and stuck with 2 cloves each
- 4 sprigs fresh thyme, or ½ teaspoon dried
- 1 bay leaf
- 12 whole black peppercorns, crushed
- 6 sprigs fresh parsley
- 1 cup coarsely chopped celery
- 1 3-pound head cabbage
- 2 large leeks, about ½ pound
- 4 carrots, about ¾ pound
- 4 to 6 white turnips, about ¾ pound
- Horseradish sauce (see recipe page 405), or freshly grated horseradish

1. Put the short ribs in a kettle and add cold water to cover. Bring to the boil and stir. Let boil for about 30 seconds. Drain well. Run cold water over the rib pieces until chilled.

2. Put the ribs back in a clean kettle and add the 4 quarts of water and salt to taste. Add the onions, thyme, bay leaf, peppercorns, parsley sprigs and celery. Bring to the boil and cook for 1½ hours.

3. Meanwhile, trim the cabbage to remove any blemished leaves and the bottom core. Cut the cabbage into eight wedges of equal size. Neatly trim the core portion.

4. Trim off the bottom of the leeks. Split them lengthwise halfway down on two sides. Rinse well between the leaves. Tie the leeks into a bundle with string.

5. Trim and scrape the carrots and cut into 1-inch lengths. Set aside.

6. Trim and peel the turnips. Cut into 1-inch cubes and set aside.

7. When the ribs have cooked 1½ hours, add the cabbage wedges and the bundle of leeks. Continue cooking for 20 minutes.

8. Add the carrots and turnips and continue cooking for about 30 minutes. Serve with horseradish sauce or freshly grated horseradish on the side.

YIELD: 6 to 8 servings.

Plat de Côtes de Boeuf au Carvi

BRAISED SHORT RIBS OF BEEF WITH CARAWAY

- 4 pounds short ribs of beef, the meatier the better, cut into 3- or 4-inch lengths
- ¼ cup flour
- Salt to taste, if desired
- Freshly ground black pepper to taste
- 2 tablespoons corn, peanut or vegetable oil
- 1 cup finely chopped onion
- 1 cup finely chopped carrot
- ½ cup finely chopped celery
- 2 cloves garlic, peeled and left whole
- 2 tablespoons crushed caraway seeds
- 1 bay leaf
- 3 sprigs fresh thyme, or ½ teaspoon dried
- ½ cup dry white wine
- 1½ cups imported canned tomatoes
- 3 tablespoons tomato paste
- 2 cups fresh or canned chicken broth
- 6 sprigs fresh parsley

1. Sprinkle the ribs with the flour and salt and pepper.

2. Heat the oil in a casserole or Dutch oven large enough to hold the ribs without crowding. When it is hot, add the ribs and cook, turning occasion-

ally so that they brown quite well and evenly on all sides, about 10 minutes.

3. Add the onion, carrot, celery, garlic, caraway seeds, bay leaf and thyme. Cook for about 3 minutes. Pour off all fat. Add the wine and cook briefly, stirring the ribs around. Add the tomatoes, tomato paste, broth, parsley, salt and pepper to taste. Cover closely and bring to the boil. Cook for 1 hour and 45 minutes to 2 hours, or until the rib meat is extremely tender.

4. Transfer the ribs to a platter. Pour the sauce into a bowl. Skim off and discard as much surface fat as possible.

5. Return the ribs to the casserole and pour the sauce over them. Bring to the boil and serve.

YIELD: 6 to 8 servings.

To many palates, oxtails are one of the finer, more gratifying delicacies of the table. One of the additional virtues of oxtails is that they are relatively inexpensive. On two recent occasions, we served dinner for four, and the cost of the oxtail as a main course for each menu was less than $5.

Oxtail soup is probably the best known dish in which these meaty bones appear, and, while this soup is excellent for early spring menus, there are other dishes that are equally appealing, including oxtail either grilled or braised.

Queue de Boeuf Braisée

BRAISED OXTAIL

- 2 well-trimmed oxtails, about 1½ pounds each and each cut into 8 crosswise pieces
- Salt and freshly ground black pepper to taste
- 2 tablespoons peanut, vegetable or corn oil
- 1 cup coarsely chopped onion
- ½ cup coarsely chopped carrot
- ½ cup coarsely chopped celery
- 1 bay leaf
- ½ teaspoon dried thyme
- ¼ cup flour
- 1 cup dry white wine
- 2 cups boiling water
- 1 cup chopped tomatoes
- 4 sprigs fresh parsley
- 4 carrots, trimmed and scraped, about ¾ pound
- ½ pound mushrooms
- 1 tablespoon butter
- ½ cup water

1. Sprinkle the pieces of oxtail with salt and pepper.

2. Heat the oil in a heavy casserole or Dutch oven and add the oxtails. Brown on all sides, about 10 minutes. Pour off all the fat from the casserole.

3. Add the onion, carrot, celery, bay leaf and thyme. Stir to distribute the vegetables. Cook, stirring, for about 2 minutes.

4. Sprinkle all the ingredients with flour and stir to distribute the flour evenly. Add the wine and stir. Add the boiling water, tomatoes and parsley sprigs and bring to the boil. Cover closely and cook for 2 hours.

5. Meanwhile, cut the carrots into 1½-inch lengths. Cut each length into quarters. Put the pieces in a saucepan with cold water to cover. Bring to the boil and simmer for about 5 minutes. Drain.

6. Cut the mushrooms into quarters, halves or slices, depending on size. There should be about 3 cups.

7. Melt the butter in a skillet and add the mushrooms. Cook, shaking the skillet and tossing, until the mushrooms give up their liquid. Cook until this liquid evaporates. Add the carrots and toss. Cook for about 5 minutes.

8. Transfer the pieces of oxtail to another casserole. Hold a sieve over the pieces and pour and scrape the sauce with the solids into the sieve. Press the solids with a spatula to extract any juices. Discard the solids. Add the ½ cup of water to the casserole. Bring to the boil.

9. Add the carrot and mushroom combination to the casserole. Cover and cook for 30 minutes.

YIELD: 4 to 6 servings.

Queue de Boeuf à la Diable

DEVILED OXTAIL

- 2 well-trimmed oxtails, about 3 pounds total
- 8 cups water
- ½ cup coarsely chopped onion
- ½ cup coarsely chopped carrot
- 1 clove garlic, finely minced
- ¼ cup coarsely chopped celery
- 1 bay leaf
- ½ teaspoon dried thyme
- 6 sprigs fresh parsley
- 6 whole black peppercorns
- Salt to taste
- 3 or 4 tablespoons prepared mustard, preferably imported Dijon
- 2 or 3 cups fine fresh bread crumbs
- 4 tablespoons butter

1. Cut each oxtail, or have the butcher cut each, into 8 pieces. Put the pieces in a kettle and add the water, onion, carrot, garlic, celery, bay leaf, thyme, parsley, peppercorns and salt to taste. Bring to the boil and simmer for 2½ hours, or until the meat is fork tender.

2. Drain the oxtails. The liquid may be reserved for a soup.

3. Preheat the oven to 450 degrees.

4. When the oxtails are lukewarm, brush the pieces all over generously with mustard. Dredge the pieces in bread crumbs until they are well coated. Pat the pieces to help the crumbs adhere. Put the pieces in one layer in a baking dish.

5. Melt the butter in a saucepan. Pour the butter evenly over the pieces.

6. Put the baking dish in the oven and bake for 15 minutes. Carefully turn the pieces and bake for 15 minutes longer, or until the oxtails are golden brown.

YIELD: 4 to 6 servings.

There are some quotations about food that are so exquisitely related to a subject at hand we find them irresistible. This is certainly true of a few lines pertaining to tripe that we discovered years ago in the *Wise Encyclopedia of Cookery*.

"Tripe," David B. Wise noted, "like certain alluring vices, is enjoyed by society's two extremes, the topmost and the lowermost strata, while the multitudinous middle classes of the world look upon it with genteel disdain and noses tilted. Patricians relished tripe in Babylon's gardens, plebeians have always welcomed it as something good and cheap, always the peasant cook has taught the prince how to eat it.

"No one can tell logically why so many persons despise the clean, white tissue of a steer's stomach that is called tripe. But some almost shudder at the word."

To that we say amen. We are so inordinately fond of the food that we cannot understand the general lack of enthusiasm that greets it. It is curious that tripe is looked upon far more favorably in European kitchens than in those of the United States.

❧

Trippa alla Fiorentina

TRIPE WITH TOMATOES AND CHEESE

- 6 pounds fresh beef tripe, trimmed of all fat
- 1 calf's foot, cut into 2-inch pieces, about 1½ pounds
- 12 cups water
- 1 onion, about 1 pound, peeled
- 2 celery stalks, trimmed and left whole
- 4 carrots, trimmed and scraped
- 6 sprigs fresh parsley, tied into a bundle
- 12 whole black peppercorns, crushed
- Salt to taste, if desired
- ½ cup olive oil
- 1 cup finely chopped onion
- ¾ cup finely diced celery
- ¾ cup finely diced carrot
- 2 tablespoons finely minced garlic
- ½ cup finely chopped fresh basil, or 1 tablespoon dried
- 2 teaspoons finely chopped fresh rosemary
- 2 large ripe tomatoes, about 1¼ pounds, peeled and chopped, about 3 cups, or use an equal volume of chopped, canned imported tomatoes
- 1 cup fresh or canned chicken broth
- 2 tablespoons butter
- 1 cup freshly grated Parmesan cheese

1. Cut the tripe lengthwise into strips, each about 2 inches wide. Cut the strips crosswise into ½-inch-thick strips. There should be about 12 cups.

2. Put the tripe and calf's foot pieces in a kettle and add cold water to cover. Bring to the boil and cook for 5 minutes. Drain well.

3. Return the tripe and calf's foot pieces to a clean kettle and add the water, whole onion, celery stalks, whole carrots, parsley sprigs, peppercorns and salt. Bring to the boil and simmer for 3 hours.

4. Using a slotted spoon, remove and discard the vegetables. Remove the calf's foot pieces. Cut away the gelatinous skin and discard the bones. Shred the skin and add it to the tripe.

5. Heat the oil in a heavy skillet and add the chopped onion. Cook, stirring, until the onion is wilted. Add the diced celery, diced carrots, minced garlic, basil and rosemary. Cook, stirring, for about 5 minutes. Add the tomatoes and chicken broth and cook for about 5 minutes.

6. Add this mixture to the tripe pot. Cook for 2 hours. Stir in the butter and cheese and serve.

YIELD: 10 or more servings.

Tripes à la Mode de Caen

BAKED TRIPE WITH CALVADOS

- 6 pounds fresh beef tripe, trimmed of all fat and cut into 2-inch squares, about 12 cups
- 1 calf's foot, about 1½ pounds, cut into 2-inch pieces
- 2 cups coarsely chopped onion
- 2 cups coarsely chopped leeks
- 1 cup finely chopped celery
- 4 cloves garlic, left whole
- 2 bay leaves
- 1 teaspoon dried thyme
- 2 whole cloves
- 6 sprigs fresh parsley
- 1 teaspoon crushed black peppercorns
- 4 whole carrots, trimmed and scraped
- 9 cups fresh or canned chicken broth
- 2 cups water
- 2 cups dry white wine
- Salt to taste, if desired
- ¼ cup Calvados

1. Preheat the oven to 350 degrees.

2. Put the tripe and calf's foot pieces in a kettle and add cold water to cover. Bring to the boil and cook for 5 minutes. Drain well.

3. Tie the onion, leeks, celery, garlic, bay leaves, thyme, cloves, parsley sprigs and peppercorns in a square of cheesecloth. Bring up the ends of the cloth and tie with string to make a bundle.

4. Put the tripe, calf's foot pieces, carrots, the cheesecloth bundle, 8 cups of the chicken broth, 2 cups of water, the wine and salt in a kettle and bring to the boil. Cover closely and place in the oven. Bake for 5 hours.

5. Skim off and discard most of the fat from the surface of the tripe. Remove and discard the cheesecloth bundle.

6. Remove the carrots and cut them into ¼-inch rounds. Add to the tripe.

7. Remove the calf's foot pieces. Cut away the gelatinous skin and discard the bones. Shred the skin and add it to the tripe. Add the remaining 1 cup of chicken broth. Bring to the boil. Add the Calvados. Return to the boil and serve.

YIELD: 10 or more servings.

Rôti de Veau Poêle au Romarin

BRAISED VEAL ROAST WITH ROSEMARY

- 1 2½-pound veal roast, tied
- Salt and freshly ground black pepper to taste
- 2 tablespoons butter
- ¾ cup finely cubed carrots
- ¾ cup finely diced onion
- 1 whole clove garlic, peeled
- 2 sprigs fresh rosemary, or 2 teaspoons dried
- ½ cup dry white wine
- 1 cup diced fresh or canned tomatoes
- 2 sprigs fresh parsley

1. Sprinkle the veal with salt and pepper.

2. Melt the butter in a heavy casserole in which the veal fits snugly but without crowding. Add the veal and brown on all sides over moderate heat for about 15 minutes, turning often.

3. Add the carrots, onion, garlic and rosemary. Stir the vegetables around in the bottom. Add the wine, tomatoes and parsley. Cover closely and cook over low heat for about 1¼ hours. Turn the meat.

4. Uncover and cook for about 15 minutes longer.

YIELD: 4 to 6 servings.

Rôti de Veau Estragon à la Crème

ROAST VEAL WITH TARRAGON CREAM SAUCE

- 1 boneless, fat-free roast rump of veal, about 2¼ pounds
- 2 tablespoons butter at room temperature
- Salt and freshly ground black pepper to taste
- 4 to 6 stems of fresh tarragon with leaves
- ¾ cup chopped onion
- ⅓ cup chopped celery
- ⅓ cup chopped carrots
- 1 large clove garlic, peeled
- 1 cup heavy cream
- 1 teaspoon chopped fresh tarragon leaves

1. Preheat the oven to 400 degrees.

2. Rub the roast all over with butter. Sprinkle all over with salt and pepper. Place the roast in a shallow roasting pan. Place in the oven and bake for 30 minutes.

3. As the meat roasts, remove the tarragon leaves from their stems. Save the stems and chop them coarsely along with about 20 leaves.

4. Scatter the onion, celery, carrots, garlic and chopped tarragon stems and leaves around the meat. Continue baking for 10 minutes. Cover the meat loosely with foil.

5. Continue roasting for about 20 minutes, basting often. The total roasting time should be about 1 hour.

6. Pour off into a small skillet all the liquid and the vegetables from around the roast, which should be kept covered with foil. Bring the liquid and vegetables to a boil and then let them cook down over moderate heat. This will concentrate the flavor of the sauce. When the sauce is reduced to about ¼ cup and no more, add the cream. Bring to the boil over high heat and cook for about 5 minutes. Shake the skillet often as the sauce cooks.

7. Strain the sauce through the finest sieve possible, preferably of the sort known in French kitchens as a chinois. Press the solids to extract as much of their juices as possible.

8. Pour the sauce into a saucepan. Cover and set aside.

9. When ready to serve, preheat the oven to 400 degrees. Place the foil-covered roast, along with any juices that have accumulated around it, in the oven and reheat for about 10 minutes. Add any drippings to the sauce. Heat the sauce and, just before serving, add the teaspoon of chopped fresh tarragon leaves. Serve the roast sliced with the cream sauce.

YIELD: 6 servings.

Côtes de Veau Farcies à l'Italienne

VEAL CHOPS STUFFED WITH SPINACH AND CHEESE

- 4 1½-inch-thick veal chops, about ¾ pound each, with a pocket for stuffing
- Salt to taste, if desired
- Freshly ground black pepper to taste
- 3 tablespoons butter
- ¼ cup finely chopped onion
- ½ teaspoon finely minced garlic
- ¼ pound clean, trimmed leaf spinach
- ¼ cup fine fresh bread crumbs
- 8 tablespoons freshly grated Parmesan cheese
- 1 egg, lightly beaten
- 2 tablespoons pine nuts
- ¼ cup flour
- 1 tablespoon corn, peanut or vegetable oil
- 3 tablespoons finely chopped shallots
- ½ cup dry white wine
- ½ cup fresh or canned chicken broth
- ½ cup finely chopped fresh or canned tomatoes

1. Preheat the oven to 400 degrees.

2. Sprinkle the chops on all sides and in the pocket with salt and pepper.

3. Melt 1 tablespoon of the butter in a saucepan and add the onion and garlic. Cook, stirring, until onion is wilted. Add the spinach and cook until spinach is wilted. Remove from the heat.

4. Add the bread crumbs, half of the cheese, egg, pine nuts and salt and pepper to taste. Stir to blend.

5. Stuff the chops with an equal portion of the filling. Close with toothpicks.

6. Dust the chops on all sides with flour and shake off any excess.

7. Heat the oil and 1 tablespoon of the butter in a large skillet and add the chops. Cook over medium heat for 3 to 4 minutes on each side. Lower the heat and cook for 5 to 6 minutes longer, turning occasionally.

8. Sprinkle each chop with 1 tablespoon of cheese. Place in the oven and bake for 15 minutes.

9. Transfer the chops to a warm serving platter. Pour the fat from the skillet. Place the skillet on the stove. Add the remaining 1 tablespoon of butter and the shallots. Cook, stirring, until the shallots are wilted. Add the wine. Cook, stirring with a wooden spoon to dissolve the brown particles that cling to the bottom and sides of the skillet. Cook down until reduced by half. Add the broth, tomatoes, salt and pepper to taste. Cook for about 5 minutes longer.

10. Hold a sieve over the chops. Put the sauce through the sieve, mashing the solids with a rubber spatula to extract as much liquid as possible. Discard remaining solids. Serve the chops with the sauce.

YIELD: 4 servings.

There is, we are convinced, a definite hierarchy or pecking order for foods. Ground meat dishes—which rank high on our list of preferences—belong to the baser and lesser order of things. Veal—and again, this is highly subjective—ranks among the most aristocratic and sophisticated of meats.

The trouble with veal is cost. The reason for the elevated price is natural. It simply requires more careful nurturing and coddling to produce the finest grade of veal, compared with the finest piece of beef or pork.

The cost of various cuts of the calf, of course, varies from one part of the animal to another. The most expensive part of the veal is the loin, from which come the rack, the saddle and the chops.

The least expensive is the breast of veal, and for this particular cut we have a special liking. It is juicy, meaty, flavorful and within the budget of most middle-class families in this country.

❧

Poitrine de Veau Farcie au Cresson

BREAST OF VEAL WITH WATERCRESS STUFFING

- 1 8- to 9-pound breast of veal with a pocket for stuffing
- 2 bunches fresh watercress, trimmed, about ½ pound
- 1 pound ground pork
- 2 cups finely chopped onion
- 2 cloves garlic, finely minced
- ½ pound mushrooms, finely chopped, about 4 cups
- 2 sprigs fresh thyme, finely chopped, or ½ teaspoon dried
- 1 bay leaf, chopped, about 1 teaspoon
- 1½ cups fresh bread crumbs
- 3 eggs, lightly beaten
- Salt, if desired
- Freshly ground black pepper to taste
- 3 tablespoons butter
- 4 or 6 celery stalks, cut into ½-inch cubes, about 1½ cups
- 2 green peppers, cored and cut into ¾-inch pieces
- 1 large onion, coarsely chopped
- 2 cloves garlic, coarsely chopped
- 1 whole bay leaf
- 2 sprigs fresh thyme, or 1 teaspoon dried
- 4 cups canned imported Italian tomatoes

1. Wipe the meat well with a damp cloth.

2. Rinse the watercress well and drop it into boiling water. Let stand for about 10 seconds. Drain well and, when cool enough to handle, squeeze it to extract excess moisture. Chop it and set aside.

3. Put the pork in a deep saucepan and add the 2 cups of chopped onion and the finely minced garlic. Cook, stirring, for about 5 minutes and add the mushrooms, chopped thyme and chopped bay leaf. Cook, stirring occasionally, for about 15 minutes. Add the chopped watercress and stir to blend well. Remove from the heat. Stir in the bread crumbs and add the beaten eggs, salt and pepper to taste. Stir and let cool.

4. Meanwhile, preheat the oven to 400 degrees.

5. Stuff the veal with the watercress mixture and sew up the pocket all around to enclose the filling. Sprinkle the meat on all sides with salt and pepper to taste.

6. Melt the butter in a heavy skillet or roasting pan and add the veal, skin side down and bone side up. Bake for 15 minutes and turn the meat skin side up. Bake for 15 minutes longer.

7. Scatter the celery, green peppers, coarsely chopped onion, coarsely chopped garlic, whole bay leaf, thyme sprigs and tomatoes around, but not on top of, the meat. Cover closely with foil and bake for 1 hour.

8. Reduce the oven temperature to 350 degrees. Uncover the meat and bake for 30 minutes longer. Let stand for about 10 minutes before slicing. Serve with vegetables in sauce surrounding the roast.

YIELD: 12 or more servings.

When we found ourselves the recipients of several batches of tree ears, that edible fungus used widely in Chinese cooking, the obvious suddenly occurred: Why not substitute these tasty, well-textured morsels in a classic French-style dish? Would they serve in dishes that call for the likes of expensive dried mushrooms such as morels and chanterelles? The results of our experiment were altogether elegant and more than worthwhile, although the tree ears do lack some of the depth of flavor of morels. An added bonus, in addition to cost, is that the Chinese have long regarded tree ears as a health food that enhances potency and longevity.

Escalopes de Veau les Cèpes aux Oreilles

VEAL SCALOPPINE IN CREAM SAUCE WITH TREE EARS

- 12 thin slices of veal, about 1½ pounds, cut as for scaloppine
- ¼ ounce (about 2½ tablespoons) dried tree ears
- 5 tablespoons butter
- 3 tablespoons finely chopped shallots
- 3 tablespoons plus ¼ cup white wine
- Juice of ½ lemon
- 1 cup heavy cream
- Salt to taste, if desired
- Freshly ground black pepper to taste
- ¼ cup flour
- ½ cup chicken broth
- 1 tablespoon Madeira or dry sherry

1. Put the slices of veal between sheets of plastic wrap and pound with a flat mallet without breaking the tissues. Set aside.

2. Meanwhile, put the tree ears in a small bowl and add hot water to cover. Let stand for 15 to 30 minutes. Drain. Cut off and discard the small hard base, if necessary. There should be about 1 cup.

3. Melt 1 tablespoon of the butter in a saucepan and add the shallots and tree ears. Cook, stirring, for about 1 minute. Add 3 tablespoons of the white wine and cook until it is almost evaporated. Sprinkle with lemon juice and add the cream, salt and pepper. Cook for 3 to 4 minutes, or until reduced and sauce-like. Remove from the heat.

4. Dredge the veal slices in flour seasoned with salt and pepper. Shake off any excess flour.

5. Melt the remaining butter in a large skillet (or use two skillets) and, when it is quite hot, add the veal slices. Cook until lightly golden, about 1½ minutes on each side.

6. Transfer the meat to a warm platter. Add the remaining ¼ cup of white wine and the broth to the skillet, and stir to dissolve the brown particles that cling to the bottom and sides of the pan. Stir in the Madeira.

7. Pour the tree ears in cream sauce over the veal. Pour the pan juices over all and serve.

YIELD: 4 to 6 servings.

Escalopes de Veau et Champignons Sautés Bordelaise

SCALOPPINE WITH MUSHROOMS

- 12 slices veal scaloppine, about 1¼ pounds
- ¾ pound mushrooms
- 2 tablespoons olive oil
- ¼ cup peanut, vegetable or corn oil
- ¼ cup flour
- Freshly ground black pepper to taste
- 2 tablespoons butter
- ⅓ cup finely chopped shallots
- ⅓ cup dry white wine
- ¼ cup finely chopped parsley

1. Pound the scaloppine on a flat surface with a flat mallet. Do not break the tissues. Set aside.

2. Slice the mushrooms thinly. There should be about 5 cups. Set aside.

3. Heat the olive oil in a large skillet. When it is hot and almost smoking, add the mushrooms. Cook over moderately high heat until the mushrooms give up their liquid. Cook until the liquid evaporates and the mushrooms are browned. Set aside.

4. Heat the peanut oil in a heavy skillet. Dredge the scaloppine in flour seasoned with pepper. Cook the scaloppine, a few at a time, on both sides until lightly browned, for about 45 seconds on each side. As they are cooked, transfer them to a warm platter.

5. Pour off the oil from the skillet in which the scaloppine cooked. Add the butter and, when it is hot, add the mushrooms. Cook briefly, shaking the skillet and turning the mushrooms. Add the shallots and cook briefly, stirring. Add the wine and cook, stirring to dissolve the brown particles that cling to the bottom of the skillet. Pour the mushrooms over the veal and serve sprinkled with chopped parsley.

YIELD: 4 to 6 servings.

❧

Vitello all'Uccelletto

VEAL AND ARTICHOKES

- 6 small artichokes, about 3½ pounds
- Juice of 1 lemon
- ¾ cup peanut, vegetable or corn oil
- 3 whole cloves garlic, peeled
- 2 teaspoons coarsely chopped garlic
- ½ cup dry white wine
- 1 pound thinly sliced veal, preferably from the leg
- 2 tablespoons flour
- ½ cup olive oil
- Salt to taste
- ½ teaspoon dried rosemary leaves

1. Pull away all the tough outer leaves from the artichokes. Carve away the stem from each artichoke and carve away the leaves around the base of each artichoke. Cut each artichoke bottom in half crosswise. Cut away the fuzzy choke from the center of each. Place the cut side of each bottom half on a flat surface and cut into thin slices. As each half is sliced, sprinkle with a little lemon juice and toss the slices so that they are lightly coated with lemon. This will prevent discoloration.

2. Use a large, heavy skillet and add peanut oil. Add the whole cloves of garlic and cook until browned. Discard the garlic.

3. Add the sliced artichokes to the skillet and cook, stirring, for about 5 minutes. Add the chopped garlic. Cook for about 1 minute and add the wine. Cook for about 1 minute; then simmer for about 5 minutes.

4. Meanwhile, stack the veal slices. Cut the veal into very thin ¼-inch strips. Put the flour in a shallow dish and toss the veal strips in the flour.

5. Use a clean wide skillet and add the olive oil.

6. Shake the excess flour from the veal strips.

7. When the olive oil is very hot, add the veal. Cook quickly over high heat, stirring. Sprinkle with salt and the rosemary. Continue stirring for about 4 minutes, or until the veal is lightly browned.

8. Add the artichokes and continue cooking for about 2 minutes longer. Serve with hot polenta, if desired.

YIELD: 4 to 6 servings.

Among our favorite foods are almost all stuffed and rolled meats, and we are equally fascinated by the names that they bear. In English, they are called veal birds, lamb rolls and beef bundles. They are also known as "birds" in France and Italy. French chefs speak not only of paupiettes but also of oiseaux sans tête, or birds without a head. Stuffed veal rolls in Italy are sometimes referred to as quagliette di vitello, or little veal quails. Italian cooks also refer to gli uccelli scappati, or birds that have escaped. And one encounters such terms as involtini, messicani, and braciolone and braciolette. One German word for stuffed meat rolls is rouladen.

We recently produced three stuffed meat rolls that we believe are characteristic of the traditions of three nations: France, Italy and Germany. All are uncommonly palatable and are very good as leftovers, served at room temperature.

Oiseaux sans Tête

VEAL ROLLS STUFFED WITH SAUSAGE AND HERBS

- 12 thin slices veal, about 1½ pounds, cut as for scaloppine
- 1 teaspoon plus 3 tablespoons butter
- 1 cup finely chopped onion
- 1½ teaspoons finely minced garlic
- ¾ pound lean bulk sausage meat
- ¼ cup finely chopped parsley
- 1 egg, lightly beaten
- Salt to taste, if desired
- Freshly ground black pepper to taste
- ¼ cup flour
- 2 tablespoons finely chopped shallots
- 1 bay leaf
- ½ teaspoon dried thyme
- ¾ cup finely diced carrot
- ¾ cup finely diced celery
- ½ cup dry white wine
- 1 cup crushed tomatoes

1. Put each slice of veal between sheets of plastic wrap and pound with a flat mallet without breaking the tissues. Set aside.

2. Melt 1 teaspoon of the butter in a saucepan and add ½ cup of the onion and ½ teaspoon garlic. Cook, stirring, until the mixture is wilted.

3. Spoon and scrape the mixture into a mixing bowl and add the sausage meat, parsley, egg, salt and pepper. Blend well.

4. Lay out the pieces of veal in one layer on a flat surface. Sprinkle with salt and pepper. Spoon an equal portion of the filling on each slice. Wrap the meat around the filling, folding and tucking in the ends in envelope fashion. Tie each roll neatly in two places with string. Sprinkle with salt and pepper. Dredge the rolls all over in flour and shake off any excess.

5. Select a heavy skillet large enough to hold the rolls in one layer without crowding them. Melt the remaining 3 tablespoons of butter and, when it is quite hot but not browned, add the rolls. Cook, turning occasionally, until they are nicely browned all over, 3 or 4 minutes.

6. Transfer the rolls to a warm platter.

7. Add the shallots, remaining ½ cup of onion, the remaining teaspoon of garlic, bay leaf, thyme, carrot and celery. Cook, stirring, for about 2 minutes. Add the wine and stir to dissolve the brown particles that cling to the bottom and sides of the skillet. Add the tomatoes and cook, stirring occasionally, for about 5 minutes.

8. Return the veal rolls to the skillet and turn to coat them with sauce. Cover closely and simmer for 30 minutes. Remove the strings and serve.

YIELD: 6 servings.

Messicani alla Milanese

VEAL ROLLS STUFFED WITH PROSCIUTTO AND CHEESE

- 12 thin slices veal, about 1½ pounds, cut as for scaloppine
- ¼ cup chopped prosciutto or cooked ham
- ½ pound ground lean pork
- 1 teaspoon plus 3 tablespoons butter
- ½ cup finely chopped onion
- ½ teaspoon finely minced garlic
- ½ cup fine fresh bread crumbs
- ⅛ teaspoon grated nutmeg
- Freshly ground black pepper to taste
- ½ teaspoon grated lemon rind
- 1 egg, lightly beaten
- ¼ cup freshly grated Parmesan cheese
- Salt to taste, if desired
- ¼ cup flour
- ½ cup dry white wine
- 1 cup fresh or canned chicken broth

1. Put the slices of veal between sheets of plastic wrap and pound with a flat mallet without breaking the tissues. Set aside.

2. Combine the prosciutto and pork in a mixing bowl.

3. Melt 1 teaspoon of the butter in a small skillet and cook the onion, stirring, until it is wilted. Add this to the mixing bowl. Add the garlic, bread crumbs, nutmeg, pepper, lemon rind, egg and cheese. Blend well.

4. Lay out the pieces of veal in one layer on a flat surface. Sprinkle with salt and pepper. Spoon an equal portion of the filling on each slice. Wrap the meat around the filling, folding and tucking the ends in envelope fashion. Tie each roll neatly in two places with string. Sprinkle with salt and pepper. Dredge the rolls all over in flour and shake off any excess.

5. Select a heavy skillet large enough to hold the rolls in one layer without crowding them. Melt the remaining 3 tablespoons of butter and, when

it is quite hot but not browned, add the veal rolls. Cook, turning occasionally, until they are nicely browned all over, 3 or 4 minutes. Reduce the heat and continue cooking over moderately low heat for about 15 minutes.

6. Add the wine and stir to dissolve the brown particles that cling to the bottom and sides of the pan. Add the chicken broth. Bring to the boil and let cook over high heat for about 5 minutes. Remove the strings and serve the veal rolls with the sauce spooned over.

YIELD: 6 servings.

Rouladen

BEEF ROLLS STUFFED WITH PORK AND DILL PICKLES

- 12 thin slices top round of beef, about 1½ pounds, cut as for scaloppine
- 12 teaspoons prepared mustard, such as imported Düsseldorf
- ½ pound ground lean pork
- 12 tablespoons plus ½ cup finely chopped onion
- Salt to taste, if desired
- Freshly ground black pepper to taste
- 3 dill pickles, quartered
- 3 tablespoons corn, peanut or vegetable oil
- ½ cup thinly sliced carrot
- ½ cup finely chopped celery
- 1 tablespoon paprika
- ½ cup dry white wine
- 1 cup fresh or canned chicken broth
- 2 teaspoons cornstarch or arrowroot
- 1 tablespoon cold water
- ½ cup sour cream

1. Put the slices of beef between sheets of plastic wrap and pound with a flat mallet without breaking the tissues.

2. Lay out pieces of beef in one layer on a flat surface. Spread the top of each with 1 teaspoon of mustard. Spoon an equal portion of the pork in the center of each piece. Flatten the pork over the center, leaving the margin uncovered. Sprinkle 1 tablespoon of chopped onion over each portion of pork. Sprinkle with salt and pepper, and cover with 1 strip of pickle. Wrap the meat around the filling, folding and tucking in the ends in envelope fashion. Tie each roll neatly in two places with string. Sprinkle with salt and pepper.

3. Select a skillet large enough to hold the meat rolls in one layer without crowding them. Heat the oil and, when it is quite hot but not smoking, add the rolls. Cook, turning occasionally, 3 to 5 minutes, or until nicely browned all over.

4. Transfer the rolls to a warm platter and pour off all the fat from the skillet. Return the skillet to the heat. Add the remaining ½ cup chopped onion, carrot and celery, and cook, stirring, until the onion is wilted. Sprinkle with paprika and stir. Add the wine and stir to dissolve the brown particles that cling to the bottom and sides of the skillet. Return the meat rolls to the skillet and add the chicken broth.

5. Cover and cook for 5 minutes. Transfer the meat rolls to a warm platter. Remove the strings.

6. Cook down the pan liquid with vegetables until reduced to about 2 cups. Blend the cornstarch or arrowroot with water and stir it into the sauce. Cook, stirring, for about 10 seconds. Remove from the heat.

7. Stir in the sour cream. Strain the sauce, pushing with a wooden spoon to extract as much liquid from the solids as possible. Serve the meat rolls with the sauce spooned over.

YIELD: 6 servings.

Veal Burgers Cordon Bleu

- 1 pound ground lean veal
- 1 small onion
- ¼ cup finely chopped fresh dill or parsley
- ½ cup fine fresh bread crumbs
- ¼ cup milk
- ¼ teaspoon grated nutmeg
- Salt, if desired
- Freshly ground black pepper to taste
- 8 circles thinly sliced prosciutto, each about 1½ inches in diameter
- 8 thin circles Gruyère or Swiss cheese, each about 1½ inches in diameter
- 2 tablespoons corn, peanut or vegetable oil
- 5 tablespoons butter
- Juice of ½ lemon

1. Put the veal into a mixing bowl.

2. Grate the onion. Put the grated onion in a square of cheesecloth and squeeze to extract about 1 tablespoon of juice. Add the juice to the meat. Discard onion.

3. Add the dill or parsley, bread crumbs, milk, nutmeg, salt and pepper to taste.

4. Divide the meat into eight portions of equal weight. Shape each portion into a thin patty. Arrange one layer of prosciutto on each of four patties. Cover with a circle of cheese, another round of prosciutto and another circle of cheese. You must leave a clear margin of meat around the

prosciutto and cheese layers. Cover each neatly with a second veal patty. Press around the edges to seal.

5. Heat the oil and 1 tablespoon of the butter in a skillet and, when it is hot, add the veal patties. Cook on one side until lightly browned, about 2 minutes. Turn. Continue cooking, turning the patties carefully so that they cook evenly, about 10 minutes.

6. Melt the remaining butter in a skillet, swirling it around until it is hazelnut brown.

7. Sprinkle the patties with lemon juice. Pour the butter over and serve hot.

YIELD: 4 servings.

Emincé de Foie de Veau aux Avocats

CALF'S LIVER SAUTÉ WITH AVOCADO

- 1½ pounds thinly sliced calf's liver
- 2 avocados
- Juice of ½ lemon
- 4 tablespoons butter
- 2 tablespoons finely chopped shallots
- 1 bay leaf
- 1 tablespoon Cognac
- 1 cup crème fraîche or heavy cream
- Salt and freshly ground black pepper to taste
- 1 tablespoon prepared mustard, preferably imported Dijon or Düsseldorf

1. If there are any membranes or nerves in the liver, cut them away and discard. Put each liver slice on a flat surface and cut it into ¼-inch-wide strips (julienne).

2. Peel the avocados and cut them in half. Remove and discard the pits. Cut the avocados into thin wedges. Cut each wedge crosswise in half. Add the lemon juice and toss to prevent discoloration.

3. Melt 3 tablespoons of the butter in a large, heavy skillet and add the liver strips, stirring quickly over high heat to cook evenly. Add the shallots and bay leaf and cook for 2 minutes or less.

4. Have ready another large skillet and in this melt the remaining tablespoon of butter.

5. Using a slotted spoon, transfer the drained strips of liver to the second skillet. Cook briefly and add the avocados. Let cook gently as you complete the dish.

6. Let any pan liquid from the first skillet cook down for about 1 minute

and add the Cognac. Add the crème fraîche and cook down over high heat for about 2 minutes. Add salt and pepper to taste.

7. Strain the cream sauce over the liver and avocado. Add the mustard and stir. Heat thoroughly and serve hot.

YIELD: 4 to 6 servings.

Fegato di Vitello alla Crema di Cipolle

CALF'S LIVER WITH CREAM OF ONIONS

- 1½ pounds calf's liver, cut into ¼-inch-thick slices
- ½ cup milk
- ½ teaspoon anise seeds
- 10 tablespoons butter
- 1 tablespoon finely chopped pork fat
- 2½ cups finely chopped onion
- 6 sage leaves, preferably fresh
- ½ teaspoon dried rosemary leaves
- 1¾ cups fresh tomatoes cut into small wedges
- Salt to taste
- 3 tablespoons finely chopped parsley
- ½ cup dry white wine
- Freshly ground black pepper to taste
- 1 small clove garlic, thinly sliced
- ⅓ cup peanut, vegetable or corn oil
- 6 tablespoons flour
- 1 cup chicken broth

1. Put the liver in a dish and add the milk and anise seeds. Let stand for an hour or until ready to cook.

2. Melt 4 tablespoons of the butter in a heavy casserole and add the pork fat and onion. Cook over low heat, stirring often, for about 10 minutes, or until golden brown.

3. Add the half cup of milk from the liver. Cook over very low heat, stirring often, for about 5 minutes.

4. Add the sage, rosemary, tomatoes and salt. Continue cooking, stirring often, until the onions are almost a purée, about 5 minutes. Add 1 tablespoon of the parsley, the wine and pepper to taste and continue cooking for about 10 minutes over very low heat. Do not let the mixture stick or burn. When the mixture is ready, it will be moist-dry. There should be about 1½ cups. Add the garlic.

5. Heat the oil in one or two large, heavy skillets. Lightly dredge each slice of liver in flour without patting it on. Add the liver slices to the hot oil without crowding. Cook for about 1½ minutes on one side, or until golden brown. Turn and cook for about 1½ minutes on the other side. Let cook over gentle heat for 1 minute.

6. Sprinkle lightly with salt and shake the skillet.

7. Add 4 tablespoons of the butter. When it melts, add the onion mixture and broth. Stir and bring to the simmer and cook over high heat for about 1 minute.

8. Sprinkle with remaining chopped parsley. Remove from the heat and stir in the remaining 2 tablespoons of butter.

YIELD: 6 to 8 servings.

Brochette de Rognons de Veau

VEAL KIDNEYS ON SKEWERS

- 2 veal kidneys, trimmed of all fat
- 8 slices bacon
- 2 tablespoons peanut, vegetable or corn oil
- Salt and freshly ground black pepper to taste
- Béarnaise sauce (see recipe page 401)

1. Heat the grill.

2. Place the kidneys on a flat surface and carefully cut away and discard part but not all of the white core that runs down the center. Cut the kidneys crosswise into cubes. There should be about 48 pieces.

3. Cut the bacon into 1½-inch pieces.

4. Arrange the kidney pieces on skewers, interlarding each 2 pieces with a piece of bacon.

5. Place the skewered foods in a flat dish and brush all over with oil.

6. Place the brochettes on the grill and cook for 3 to 4 minutes on one side. Sprinkle all over with salt and pepper to taste and turn the brochettes to cook on the other side, for about 3 to 4 minutes. Serve immediately with béarnaise sauce.

YIELD: 4 servings.

Although Americans are, by and large, a nation of sausage eaters, we are not a nation that indulges in a vast variety of them. Most sausages consumed in this country are made with pork. And yet one of the grandest of all is made not with pork but with the fine flesh of veal. This is the boudin blanc, or white pudding sausage, and it is traditionally served in French homes for year-end holidays, particularly New Year's Eve. Two sausage recipes are outlined here. One is for that delicate white pudding sausage made with veal. Another is a well spiced chaurice sausage as made by the Lee Barnes Cooking School in New Orleans.

Boudins Blancs

WHITE VEAL SAUSAGES

- 1½ pounds lean veal, cut into 1-inch cubes
- 1 pound pork fat (the firmer the better), cut into 1-inch cubes
- 2 cups milk
- 1 bay leaf
- ½ teaspoon dried thyme
- 2 sprigs fresh parsley
- ⅓ cup chopped celery
- ⅓ cup chopped carrot
- ½ cup chopped onion
- 6 eggs
- ¼ cup Madeira or port wine
- ¼ teaspoon freshly ground white pepper
- ½ teaspoon grated nutmeg
- Salt
- ¼ cup finely chopped black truffles, optional
- 5 or 6 prepared casings (see instructions for preparing)

1. To prepare this recipe, it is necessary to use a food processor. The sausage filling should be made in two batches. Divide the veal and pork fat into two batches.

2. Combine the milk, bay leaf, thyme, parsley, celery, carrot and onion in a saucepan. Bring to the boil and simmer for 5 minutes. Strain. Discard solids.

3. Add half the veal and pork fat to the container of a food processor. Add half of each of the following: the eggs, Madeira, pepper and nutmeg. Add 1 teaspoon salt. Blend to a fine purée. While blending, gradually pour half of the hot milk mixture through the funnel. When ready, the batch will look like a very thick soup.

4. Repeat, using the remaining identical ingredients and procedure.

5. Combine the two batches in a bowl. Add the chopped truffles and stir to blend.

6. Outfit an electric grinder or a sausage-making machine—either hand-cranked or electric—with a sausage attachment. Pour or feed the mixture into the feeder of the machine. If you have a large sausage maker, you can pour all of the mixture into the machine's cylinder.

7. Slide one prepared sausage casing onto the attachment and tie the end. Start grinding to partly fill the casing. To shape the first sausage length, simply twist the sausage casing about 6 inches from the tied end of the casing. Continue filling and twisting the casings at 6-inch intervals. As you work, always twist the casing in alternate directions.

8. When you deem it necessary (after a yard or so of sausages has been filled and twisted), cut off the sausage casing and tie the end. Continue

preparing sausages until all the filling has been used. Inspect the sausages. If you find any air bubbles, use a needle and prick the casings at the point where the bubbles occur. There should be about 16 sausages.

9. Bring enough water to the boil in a wide casserole to cover the sausages when added. Add salt to taste. Add the sausages. They must be immersed in the water. Bring slowly to the boil. Simmer for about 10 minutes. Remove from the heat. Let stand for about 30 minutes. Drain well.

10. Arrange the sausages on a platter and cover with plastic wrap. Chill before using. The sausages may be broiled or grilled.

YIELD: About 16 sausages.

HOW TO PREPARE SAUSAGE CASINGS

1. Sausage casings are normally preserved in salt. When ready to use, put them in a basin of cold water and let stand for about 30 minutes.

2. Drain and return to a basin of cold water.

3. To determine if the casings have holes in them, fill with water and examine for leaks. Discard sections with holes and use the partial casing.

Note: Sausage casings are available in pork stores in metropolitan areas.

Lee Barnes's Chaurice Sausages

- 1½ pounds lean pork, trimmed of all fat
- ⅔ pound fatback or hardest pork fat available
- 1 cup finely chopped onion
- ½ cup finely chopped parsley
- 1½ tablespoons finely minced garlic
- 2 tablespoons finely chopped fresh hot red chilies, or use 1 teaspoon or more hot dried chilies
- 2½ teaspoons powdered hot pepper or cayenne
- 2 teaspoons freshly ground black pepper
- 1 teaspoon dried thyme
- ½ teaspoon ground allspice
- 1 tablespoon salt
- ⅛ teaspoon saltpeter, optional
- 5 or 6 prepared sausage casings (see previous instructions for preparing)

1. Grind the lean pork and pork fat, using a meat grinder.

2. Add the onion, parsley, garlic, fresh chilies, hot pepper, black pepper, thyme, allspice, salt and saltpeter. Blend well.

3. Test the mixture by making a small batch into a patty and cooking on both sides until done. Adjust the seasonings according to taste.

4. Put the mixture through the meat grinder a second time.

5. Stuff the sausage casings, using a pastry bag or a sausage stuffer. Use the same instructions outlined in the recipe for boudins blancs for stuffing.

6. When ready to cook, prick the sausages all over with a fork to prevent bursting. Fry in a little oil.

YIELD: About 16 sausages

One reference work has observed that if Robinson Crusoe had been cast on that island without benefit of chests, casks, ropes, food, gunpowder and other necessities of life, he could have managed a happy existence if he had access to a coconut tree. Its fruit would have provided him with milk and nutrition. And, culinary lore has it, the roots of the tree can be ground and used like tea or coffee. Besides, half a coconut shell could have given him one of the nicer amenities of life, a cup from which to sip.

Those with better facilities than Crusoe had can enjoy coconut in an Indonesian creation made with pork and a sweetened soy sauce (the Indonesian word for this special bottled sauce is ketjap benteng manis) plus coconut milk. The coconut milk that is used in cooking is not, by the way, that clear liquid that drains from the coconut when it is cracked. This genuine coconut milk or coconut cream is made by blending grated coconut with water and squeezing to extract the liquid.

Indonesian Pork Roast with Coconut

- 1 2½-pound lean, boneless pork roast
- Salt and freshly ground black pepper to taste
- 2 tablespoons peanut, vegetable or corn oil
- ½ cup finely chopped onion
- 2 tablespoons finely minced garlic
- 1 tablespoon finely minced fresh ginger
- 2 teaspoons sambal oelek (see Note), or ½ teaspoon hot red pepper flakes
- ¾ cup ketjap benteng manis (see Note), or use an equal amount of soy sauce plus 1 tablespoon sugar
- ¾ cup coconut milk (see instructions for making coconut milk page 419)

1. Sprinkle the pork with salt and pepper.

2. Heat the oil in a heavy Dutch oven or casserole and add the pork. Cook, turning often, until nicely browned all over, about 30 minutes.

3. Pour off most of the oil from the Dutch oven.

4. Combine the onion, garlic, ginger and sambal oelek in the container of a blender or food processor. Or use a mortar and pestle. Grind as finely as possible. Add this to the fat remaining in the Dutch oven. Cook, stirring, briefly.

5. Add the ketjap benteng manis and coconut milk. Cover and bring to the boil. Simmer slowly until quite tender, about 1½ hours. Serve sliced with fluffy rice.

YIELD: 6 servings.

Note: Ketjap benteng manis and sambal oelek are widely available in food specialty shops that deal in fine imported products.

One interesting facet of bourgeois or family-style cookery is known as en cocotte, which consists of a main dish plus vegetables cooked together. These dishes, also known as en casserole, are hearty fare for winter menus.

Carré de Porc en Cocotte

PORK LOIN WITH VEGETABLES

- 1 4½-pound loin of pork
- 1 large clove garlic, peeled
- Salt and freshly ground black pepper to taste
- 2 tablespoons peanut, vegetable or corn oil
- 4 small turnips, about ¾ pound
- 5 small carrots, about ¾ pound
- 4 medium-sized potatoes, about 1 pound
- 3 medium-sized onions, about 1 pound
- 6 mushrooms, about 6 ounces
- 2 whole cloves garlic, unpeeled
- 2 sprigs fresh thyme, or ½ teaspoon dried
- 1 bay leaf
- ½ cup water
- 1 tablespoon rosemary leaves

1. Cut off most of the top fat from the loin but leave a thin layer.

2. Cut the peeled garlic clove into 6 slivers. Make 6 gashes close to the bone of the pork and insert the garlic slivers. Sprinkle the meat all over with salt and pepper.

3. Heat the oil in a heavy casserole large enough to hold the pork loin comfortably and without crowding. Add the pork, fat side down, and brown slowly. Turn the pork, cooking over low heat, until it is browned on all sides, about 10 minutes. Cover and cook 1 hour.

4. Peel the turnips and cut each crosswise in half. Cut each half into three wedges. Set aside.

5. Trim and scrape the carrots. Cut each carrot crosswise into 1½-inch lengths. Set aside.

6. Peel the potatoes and cut each in half lengthwise. Cut each half into three wedges. Drop into cold water.

7. Peel the onions and cut them into quarters.

8. Combine the onions, drained potatoes, turnips and carrots in a large saucepan. Add cold water to cover and bring to the boil. Simmer for about 1 minute and drain.

9. Rinse the mushrooms and drain. If they are small, leave them whole; otherwise, cut them in half or in quarters. Add them to the vegetables.

10. When the pork has cooked for 1 hour, uncover and add the unpeeled garlic cloves, thyme, bay leaf, vegetables and the water.

11. Cover and cook for 1 hour longer. Toward the end of the cooking, sprinkle with rosemary. Serve the pork sliced with the natural gravy and vegetables.

YIELD: 8 to 10 servings.

Côtes de Porc Farcies au Carvi

PORK CHOPS STUFFED WITH RYE BREAD

- 4 pork chops, each about 2 inches thick, about 3 pounds total
- 1 tablespoon butter
- ⅓ cup finely chopped onion
- ⅓ cup finely chopped celery
- ⅓ cup finely chopped green pepper
- 1 teaspoon finely minced garlic
- ¾ cup fine fresh rye bread crumbs
- ½ teaspoon caraway seeds
- 4 tablespoons finely chopped parsley
- Salt to taste, if desired
- Freshly ground black pepper to taste
- 1 egg, lightly beaten
- 1 tablespoon corn, peanut or vegetable oil
- ¼ cup dry white wine
- 2 teaspoons tomato paste
- ½ cup chicken broth

1. Preheat the oven to 350 degrees.

2. To make pockets for stuffing, cut a slit down the center of each chop all the way to the bone, or have this done by the butcher. Place the chops on a flat surface and open up the flaps. Pound each flap lightly without breaking the meat.

3. Melt the butter in a saucepan and add the onion, celery, green pepper and garlic. Cook, stirring, until the mixture is wilted. Add the bread crumbs, caraway seeds, 2 tablespoons of the chopped parsley, salt and pepper to taste and the egg. Blend well. Let cool.

4. Open up the flaps once more and add equal portions of the stuffing. Bring the flaps together to enclose the stuffing. Fasten the edges with toothpicks. Sprinkle the chops on both sides with salt and pepper to taste.

5. Heat the oil in a heavy skillet large enough to hold the stuffed chops in one layer. Add the chops and cook until nicely browned on one side, about 3 minutes. Turn and brown well on the second side. Cover closely with a lid. Place in the oven and bake for 30 minutes.

6. Uncover and continue baking for 30 minutes.

7. Transfer the chops to a warm serving dish.

8. Heat the pan liquids and add the wine and tomato paste, stirring. Add the broth and cook for about 5 minutes, or until reduced to about 1 cup. Strain the sauce over the chops and sprinkle with the remaining chopped parsley. Serve hot.

YIELD: 4 servings.

Carne de Porco com Amêijoas

A PORTUGUESE CASSEROLE OF PORK WITH CLAMS

- 2 large, unblemished sweet red peppers
- 1 medium-sized onion
- 1½ pounds pork, cut into ¾-inch cubes
- 1 cup dry white wine
- 1 tablespoon paprika
- 3 cloves garlic, crushed
- 1 bay leaf, crumbled
- Salt and freshly ground black pepper to taste
- 3 tablespoons olive oil
- 1 cup chicken broth
- 2 teaspoons finely chopped garlic
- 1 cup tomatoes, drained and chopped
- ¼ teaspoon hot red pepper flakes
- ½ teaspoon saffron stems, optional
- 3 dozen littleneck clams, rinsed well and drained
- 3 tablespoons finely chopped cilantro (Chinese parsley)
- 1 lemon, cut into quarters

1. Preheat the broiler.

2. Place the red peppers under the broiler. Cook them, turning often on all sides until the skin is blackened. Put the peppers in a brown paper bag and close tightly. Let stand for 20 minutes, or until cool enough to handle. Pull off the outside peel. Core and seed the peppers. Cut the peppers into ½-inch strips.

3. Cut the onion in half lengthwise. Slice each half lengthwise into thin strips. Set aside.

4. Combine the pork, wine, paprika, crushed garlic, bay leaf and salt and pepper to taste in a bowl. Let stand for 2 hours.

5. Drain the pork well but save the marinating liquid. Discard the garlic and bay leaf.

6. Heat 1 tablespoon of oil in a large, heavy skillet. When it is quite hot, add the pork cubes. Cook, stirring often, until the pork is nicely browned.

7. Transfer the pork pieces to a bowl.

8. Add the marinating liquid to the skillet and add the chicken broth. Cook over high heat until reduced by half. Pour this over the pork.

9. Heat the remaining oil in a casserole and add the onion and chopped garlic. Cook, stirring, until the onion is wilted. Add the tomatoes, pepper flakes, pepper strips and saffron, and cook for about 5 minutes. Add the pork and the liquid. Cook for about 30 minutes, stirring occasionally.

10. Add the clams and cover closely. Cook over high heat until the clams open. As each clam opens, remove it to prevent overcooking. When all the clams are open, return them to the casserole and stir. Sprinkle with the cilantro. Serve piping hot with rice and lemon wedges.

YIELD: 4 servings.

Brochette de Porc au Romarin

BROCHETTES OF PORK WITH ROSEMARY

- 1¼ pounds lean, boneless pork
- 1 cup dry white wine
- 1 tablespoon finely minced garlic
- 1 tablespoon dried rosemary leaves
- 2 tablespoons finely chopped parsley
- 1 teaspoon grated lemon rind
- Salt and freshly ground black pepper to taste
- 2 tablespoons olive oil
- 2 tablespoons white wine vinegar
- Melted butter

1. Cut the pork into 1½-inch cubes and put the meat in a mixing bowl.

2. Add the wine, garlic, rosemary, parsley, lemon rind, salt and pepper to taste, olive oil and vinegar. Blend well and marinate for 2 to 4 hours.

3. Drain the meat. Arrange equal portions of meat on each of 6 to 8 skewers.

4. Preheat a charcoal grill.

5. Place the brochettes on the grill and cook, turning the pieces often, for 15 to 20 minutes, or until the pork is thoroughly cooked but not dry.

6. Serve with melted butter poured over.

YIELD: 6 to 8 servings.

❧

Crépinettes de Porc

PORK PATTIES WITH TOMATO SAUCE

1 pound lean pork, cut into cubes
½ pound pork fat, cut into cubes
Pinch of cayenne pepper
¼ teaspoon freshly ground black pepper
Pinch of ground cinnamon
Pinch of ground allspice
2 teaspoons salt
¼ cup dry white wine
2 sheets caul fat, about ¾ pound (see Note)
¼ cup finely chopped parsley
Tomato sauce with peppers (see recipe page 409)

1. Put the pork and pork fat in a bowl and add the cayenne, black pepper, cinnamon, allspice, salt and wine. Blend well. Refrigerate for 10 minutes or longer.

2. Put the pork mixture into the container of a food processor. This may have to be done in two steps. Process the pork until the meat looks like sausage meat. Do not overprocess or the meat will become mushy.

3. Divide the meat into six portions. Flatten each portion to make a patty. Lay out the caul fat, one sheet at a time. Cut the caul fat into rectangles large enough to enclose one patty with the edges of the fat overlapping.

4. Place 1 teaspoon of parsley in the center of each rectangle. Top the parsley with a pork patty. Dot the center of the patty with another teaspoon of parsley. Enclose the patty with caul fat, letting the edges overlap. Continue until all the patties are wrapped.

5. Heat a skillet and cook the patties (about four at a time) for about 10 minutes to a side, turning often, until the pork is cooked through. Drain thoroughly. Serve with tomato sauce.

YIELD: 6 servings.

Note: Caul fat is available in Italian and Oriental markets, as well as many butcher shops.

Leslie Newman is one of the most dedicated and talented home cooks we have ever encountered. There are very few cuisines about which she cannot speak with authority, including Indian, Creole, Thai, French, Tex-Mex and Chinese, and which serve as the focal point for her ambitious New Year's buffets for 200 guests. In real, hardworking life, Mrs. Newman turns out scripts for such epics as *Superman, Superman II* and *Superman III.* Her husband, David, is a film director and also worked on the *Superman* scripts. Mrs. Newman makes dishes, such as this Chinese roast pork and the following bean curd in spicy meat sauce, in several batches when she is cooking for a large gathering.

Chinese Roast Pork

- 2¼ pounds lean pork loin, cut into six lengthwise strips
- 1 tablespoon bourbon, Cognac or rum
- ½ cup sugar
- 6 tablespoons light soy sauce
- 1 tablespoon sesame paste
- 2 tablespoons bean sauce, available in Oriental markets
- 1 cup honey
- 1 teaspoon five-spice powder, commercially prepared or homemade (see following recipe)

1. Put the pork strips in a mixing bowl.
2. Combine the remaining ingredients and pour over the pork, turning the pieces until the meat is coated.
3. Preheat the oven to 450 degrees.
4. Place a rack on top of a roasting pan. The rack should be about 2 inches above the bottom of the pan. Arrange the pieces of meat parallel to each other but without the sides touching. Bake for 30 minutes, basting, then turn each piece of meat and bake for 15 minutes longer. Continue baking and turning the pieces often, basting, for about 15 minutes longer.

YIELD: 8 to 12 servings.

FIVE-SPICE POWDER

- 60 whole black peppercorns
- 4 whole star anise
- 2 teaspoons fennel seeds
- 1 teaspoon ground cinnamon
- 12 whole cloves

Blend all the ingredients in a spice mill to a fine powder.

YIELD: About 3 tablespoons.

❧

Bean Curd in Spicy Meat Sauce

- 4 tablespoons corn, peanut or vegetable oil
- 1⅓ cups cored, seeded sweet red pepper cut into ½-inch cubes
- 1⅓ cups cored, seeded sweet green pepper cut into ½-inch cubes
- 2 pounds ground pork, preferably not too lean
- ½ cup brown bean sauce, available in Oriental markets
- 4 teaspoons bottled chili paste with garlic
- 4 teaspoons sugar
- 4 tablespoons dry sherry
- 2 cups plus 3 tablespoons chicken broth
- 4 tablespoons cornstarch
- 12 squares bean curd, each cut into 16 pieces
- 1 cup finely chopped scallions, green and white parts combined
- 1 teaspoon ground roasted Sichuan peppercorns (see Note page 124)
- 1½ teaspoons sesame oil
- Hot chili oil, optional

1. Heat half of the oil in a wok and, when it is hot but not quite smoking, add half of the red and green peppers. Cook, stirring and pressing them against the side of the wok so that they blacken a bit without burning. Using a slotted spoon, remove them while they are still crisp and set aside. Leave the oil in the wok.

2. To the wok add half of the pork and cook over high heat, stirring and chopping down to break up any lumps. Cook only until the pork loses its raw look.

3. Add half of the bean sauce, half of the chili paste with garlic, half of the sugar and 1 tablespoon of the sherry, blending thoroughly. Add 1 cup of the chicken broth and bring to the simmer.

4. Blend half of the cornstarch with 1 tablespoon of sherry and 1½ tablespoons chicken broth.

5. Stir this into the simmering meat sauce. When thickened, spoon and scrape the sauce into a large mixing bowl.

6. Wipe out the wok. Repeat the procedure using the remaining oil, peppers, pork, bean sauce, chili paste with garlic, sugar, sherry, chicken broth and cornstarch. Add the second batch of peppers to the first and let cool. Add the second batch of meat sauce to the first batch and let cool. Refrigerate overnight or until ready to use. Refrigerate the peppers separately.

7. When ready to serve, return the meat sauce to room temperature. Return the sauce to large saucepans or casseroles and bring to the boil.

8. Carefully add the bean curd pieces to the meat sauce. Stir and heat

gently so as not to break up the bean curd pieces more than necessary. Add the cooked red and green pepper cubes. Heat briefly.

9. Add the chopped scallions, ground peppercorns and sesame oil. Stir gently and serve. Serve with hot chili oil on the side, if desired, to be added by those who enjoy very spicy foods.

YIELD: 20 to 25 servings.

Edna Lewis, the Virginia-born granddaughter of a onetime slave, learned to cook in the days when there were no movies and no television and young women didn't "learn" how to cook—"you were just born knowing how." She arrived in New York when she was in her thirties and ended up by chance as the cook when the Café Nicholson opened and was in its heyday. She subsequently has written a cookbook that brought her fame as a regional food authority. At a picnic Mrs. Lewis gave for a group of friends in Central Park, we feasted on such Southern specialties as Virginia ham with biscuits and liver pudding, one of her favorite family dishes that was made when the hogs were first butchered.

❧

Liver Pudding

- 1½ pounds pork liver (see Note), preferably in one piece
- 1½ pounds fresh pork jowl (see Note), or use 1½ pounds fresh unsalted pork belly or uncured bacon
- 1 onion, about ½ pound, peeled
- Salt and freshly ground black pepper to taste
- 1 teaspoon finely chopped fresh sage, or half the amount dried

1. Put the liver and pork in a kettle and add the onion and water to cover. Bring to the boil. Cover and cook for about 2 hours.

2. Preheat the oven to 275 degrees.

3. Remove the meats and onion from the kettle. There should be 2 cups of broth. If there is more, skim off the clearest top portion, leaving the bottom portions with its meat residue.

4. Cut the meats into small chunks. Using a meat grinder or food processor, grind the meat and onion coarsely. Spoon and scrape into a mixing bowl. Stir in the 2 cups of reserved broth. The mixture will be quite thin.

5. Stir in the salt, pepper and sage. Mix well and pour into a heavy tin loaf pan or 2-quart casserole. Place in the oven and bake for 2½ hours. The

long cooking helps develop the flavor of the pudding and makes it easy to slice. When cool, place in a cold place or in the refrigerator.

YIELD: 6 to 8 servings.

Note: Fresh pork liver and pork jowl are available in many pork stores in metropolitan areas and on request from many butchers.

Gigot d'Agneau à l'Anglaise

LEG OF LAMB WITH CAPER SAUCE

THE LAMB

- 1 7½-pound leg of lamb
- Water to cover, about 14 cups
- Salt to taste, if desired
- 1 teaspoon lightly crushed black peppercorns
- 1 cup coarsely chopped onion
- ½ cup trimmed sliced carrot
- ½ cup trimmed chopped celery
- 1 bay leaf
- 2 cloves garlic, each cut in half
- 4 sprigs fresh parsley
- ½ teaspoon dried thyme

THE SAUCE

- 7 tablespoons butter
- 3 tablespoons flour
- 1½ cups liquid in which lamb cooked
- 3 egg yolks
- 2 tablespoons lemon juice
- ½ cup drained capers

1. Trim the lamb well. Using a boning or other knife, run it carefully all around the chine bone of the leg. Sever it from the main leg bone and remove the chine bone. Leave the main leg bone intact. When trimmed and with bone removed, the lamb will weigh about 6 pounds.

2. Put the lamb in a large kettle, casserole or Dutch oven in which it will fit compactly but without crowding. Add the water, salt to taste, peppercorns, onion, carrot, celery, bay leaf, garlic, parsley and thyme. Bring to the boil.

3. Cover and let the lamb simmer for about 1½ hours. At this point, the lamb when sliced will be slightly pink in the center. If well-done lamb is desired, continue cooking.

4. To make the sauce, melt 3 tablespoons of the butter in a saucepan and add the flour, stirring with a wire whisk. When blended and smooth, add the liquid, stirring rapidly with the whisk. Simmer, stirring often, for about 10 minutes.

5. Beat the egg yolks with the lemon juice and gradually add about ¼ cup of the hot sauce. Add the yolk mixture to the remaining sauce in the saucepan.

6. Stir in the remaining 4 tablespoons of butter and add the capers. Place the saucepan over gentle heat for a brief period. Do not let boil or the sauce may curdle.

7. Serve the lamb sliced with the sauce on the side.

YIELD: 8 to 10 servings.

Roast Leg of Lamb with Orzo

- 1 5- to 6-pound leg of lamb
- Salt and freshly ground black pepper to taste
- 2 cloves garlic, peeled and cut in half
- 1½ cups thinly sliced onions
- 4 tablespoons butter
- 4 cups canned plum tomatoes
- 1 cup water
- 5 cups rich chicken broth (see recipe page 418)
- 2 cups orzo
- Freshly grated Parmesan cheese

1. Preheat the oven to 400 degrees.

2. Cut away most of the surface fat from the lamb. Rub the lamb all over with salt and pepper to taste and garlic cloves.

3. Place the lamb in a shallow roasting pan (one that measures about 12 inches by 15 inches is ideal). Scatter the slices of onion around it. Melt the butter and pour it over the meat.

4. Place the lamb in the oven and bake for about 20 minutes, or until browned.

5. Lower the oven temperature to 350 degrees. Add the tomatoes and water and cook, basting often, for about 1½ hours, or until cooked to the desired degree of doneness.

6. Remove the lamb to a heated platter and cover loosely with foil.

7. Add the chicken broth and orzo to the roasting pan and stir. Continue baking until the orzo is tender and most of the liquid has been absorbed, 15 to 20 minutes.

8. Carve the lamb and serve with orzo. Serve grated Parmesan cheese to sprinkle over the orzo.

YIELD: 6 to 8 servings.

Those who deal in coffee lore tell us that coffee was consumed as a food before it was a beverage. Coffee cherries, which contain the beans, were crushed and blended with animal fat, then shaped into balls and popped into the mouth. And, at one point, the cherries were used to produce a fermented wine. Today, coffee has a host of uses in cookery. It is most widely used as a flavoring for desserts, but far more unusual is its use as a basting liquid for roast lamb.

❧

Swedish Roast Lamb with Coffee Cream

1 7-pound untrimmed leg of lamb, or 1 6-pound ready-to-roast leg
Salt and freshly ground black pepper to taste
1 tablespoon softened butter
1 cup coarsely chopped onion
¾ cup thinly sliced carrot
½ cup finely diced celery
½ cup lamb or chicken broth (see Note)
¾ cup strong coffee
⅓ cup heavy cream
¾ tablespoon sugar
1 tablespoon finely chopped dill, optional

1. Preheat the oven to 425 degrees.

2. If the lamb is not trimmed, here is how to go about it. Cut off the nonmeaty tip of the leg or shank bone about 3 inches from the end. Trim and set aside.

3. Using a sharp boning knife, cut around the chine and rib bone and remove it. Cut off excess fat and set aside.

4. Trim off and discard most but not all of the skin and fat from the surface of the lamb. The leg should now weigh about 6 pounds.

5. Sprinkle the lamb with salt and pepper and rub the surface all over with butter. Place the lamb skin side down in a roasting pan. Scatter the onion around it. Arrange the lamb bones around it and place in the oven. Bake for 30 minutes, then turn the lamb skin side up. Continue baking for about 15 minutes.

6. Remove the lamb from the oven. Lift the lamb and skim off most of the surface fat. Lower the leg and scatter the carrot and celery around it.

7. Reduce the oven temperature to 375 degrees and continue roasting the lamb for 30 minutes more. Add the broth and continue roasting for about 15 minutes.

8. Blend the coffee, cream and sugar and add it to the pan sauce. Continue roasting, basting often, for about 50 minutes.

9. Remove the lamb to a warm platter. Strain the pan juices into a saucepan and discard the solids. Stir the dill into the sauce. Carve the lamb and serve it with the hot sauce.

YIELD: 8 to 10 servings.

Note: To make lamb broth, do not use the lamb bones as indicated. That is to say, do not scatter them around the lamb as it roasts. Put the uncooked lamb bones in a small kettle with water to cover and add salt and pepper to taste. Add a small peeled onion, 1 bay leaf and ½ cup of chopped carrot and simmer about 45 minutes. Strain.

Lamb Curry with Yogurt

- 1 tablespoon peanut, vegetable or corn oil
- 2 tablespoons butter
- 4 pounds cubed lamb, preferably from the leg
- 2 cups finely chopped onion
- 1 tablespoon finely chopped garlic
- 2 tablespoons finely chopped fresh ginger
- 1 tablespoon curry powder
- ¼ teaspoon ground cinnamon
- 1 teaspoon ground cumin
- ½ teaspoon ground turmeric
- 1 teaspoon ground coriander
- ½ teaspoon ground cardamom
- 2 bay leaves
- 1 cup plain yogurt
- Salt and freshly ground black pepper to taste
- 2 tablespoons finely chopped fresh coriander

1. Heat the oil and butter in a heavy casserole. Add the lamb, onion, garlic and ginger. Cook, stirring, until the meat loses its raw look and onion is wilted.

2. Add the curry powder, cinnamon, cumin, turmeric, ground coriander, cardamom, bay leaves, ½ cup yogurt, salt and pepper to taste. Bring to the boil.

3. Cover and cook, stirring often, for about 1 hour and 10 minutes, or until the lamb is fork-tender. Add the remaining yogurt and chopped fresh coriander. Heat briefly and serve with hot rice.

YIELD: 6 to 8 servings.

Brochettes d'Agneau à l'Estragon

LAMB BROCHETTES WITH TARRAGON

- ½ leg of lamb, 3½ to 4 pounds
- 1 cup dry red wine
- Salt and freshly ground black pepper to taste
- 1 tablespoon dried tarragon
- 2 tablespoons red wine vinegar
- 2 tablespoons olive oil
- 2 teaspoons finely minced garlic
- 12 to 16 mushroom caps
- Melted butter
- Fresh lemon juice

1. Bone the leg of lamb or have it boned. Have all the fat and skin removed. Cut the meat into 1½-inch cubes. There should be about 2¼ pounds of meat. Put the meat in a mixing bowl.

2. Add the wine, salt and pepper to taste, tarragon, vinegar, oil and garlic. Stir. Let stand for 4 hours. Drain.

3. Arrange 1 mushroom cap on each of 6 or 8 skewers. Arrange equal portions of meat on each of the skewers. Add 1 more mushroom cap.

4. Preheat a charcoal grill.

5. Place the brochettes on the grill and cook, turning often, for about 10 minutes. Serve with melted butter and a squeeze of lemon juice sprinkled over.

YIELD: 6 to 8 servings.

Carré d'Agneau Rôti aux Poivres Verts

ROAST RACK OF LAMB WITH GREEN PEPPERCORNS

- 2 untrimmed 7- or 8-rib racks of lamb, about 2½ pounds each
- Salt to taste, if desired
- Freshly ground black pepper to taste
- 10 small sprigs fresh thyme, broken into small pieces, or 1 teaspoon dried
- 10 whole, unpeeled cloves garlic
- 7 tablespoons butter
- 2 cups water
- 2 egg whites
- ¼ cup finely chopped parsley
- 2 tablespoons drained green peppercorns
- 2 tablespoons strong Dijon mustard
- 2 tablespoons fine fresh bread crumbs

1. Preheat the oven to 500 or 525 degrees.

2. Have the butcher hack away the chine bone of each rack. Take care that all scraps of meat and bone are reserved. Cut the chine bones into 2-inch pieces and set aside. There is a top coating of fat on top of each rack. At one side of each rack there is a small, cartilage-like half-moon-shaped shoulder blade between the meat and the top coating of fat. Have this removed.

3. Using a sharp knife, make deep diamond-shaped scorings down to the bottom of the top layer of fat. Neatly trim the bottom of each rib to make them French style, which is to say neatly trimmed of all meat and fat. They should be trimmed about 1 inch from the bottom. Sprinkle the racks with salt and pepper and cover the French-style ends of the chops with aluminum foil to prevent burning.

4. Scatter the scraps of meat and bones over the bottom of a shallow roasting pan large enough to hold the racks in one layer. Scatter the thyme and garlic cloves over the scraps. Arrange the racks, fat side up, in the baking dish. Put 2 tablespoons of the butter on top of each rack.

5. Put the lamb in the oven and bake for 20 minutes. Turn the racks and continue roasting for about 15 minutes.

6. Transfer the racks to a warm platter. Put the roasting pan on top of the stove and heat the pan liquids. Add the water. Let simmer for 10 minutes.

7. Meanwhile, remove the garlic cloves and remove the outer coatings. Chop the garlic to a fine purée and set aside.

8. Beat the whites until stiff. Add the parsley, green peppercorns and mustard. Blend well.

9. Discard the foil from the lamb racks. Smear half the beaten white mixture on top of each rack. Sprinkle each rack with an equal amount of the bread crumbs. Pat the crumbs lightly to make them adhere.

10. Melt the remaining 3 tablespoons of butter in a small saucepan. Dribble the butter on top of the racks.

11. Return the lamb to the oven and bake 5 minutes or less, until the top of lamb coating starts to brown. Place the lamb briefly under the broiler to give a nice brown glaze.

12. Strain the pan juices from the roasting pan into a saucepan. Add the reserved chopped garlic. Stir and reheat briefly.

13. Carve the lamb, slicing between each two ribs, and serve with pan juices.

YIELD: 4 to 6 servings.

Barcelona, the political capital of Catalonia, has long been known as a gastronomic capital as well and when Montse Guillen, one of the best cooks in the Catalan region, was in New York we invited her to prepare some dishes in our kitchen. The heart of her quintessentially Catalan menu was a magnificent meat dish built around lamb chops and accompanied by escalibada, an elaborate yet easily made side dish of vegetables. The food was served with four sauces, the most famous of which is a romescu, a pungent garlic sauce, that Mrs. Guillen said was a staple in Catalan homes and served with grilled pork, fish or chicken or steamed seafood as well as lamb chops.

Lamb Chops with Four Garlic Sauces

- 8 small lamb chops (see Note), each about 2 inches thick, trimmed of almost all fat
- ½ teaspoon chopped fresh or dried thyme
- ½ teaspoon chopped fresh or dried rosemary
- Salt to taste, if desired
- Freshly ground black pepper to taste
- 1 tablespoon olive oil
- 1 tablespoon butter
- Romescu sauce (see following recipe)
- Garlic sauces (see following recipes)

1. The chops may be cooked over charcoal or baked; if grilled, preheat grill; if baked, preheat oven to 500 degrees.

2. Place each chop on a flat surface and pound lightly with a flat mallet. Place them in a baking dish in which they fit snugly without crowding. Add the thyme, rosemary, salt, pepper and olive oil. Turn the chops in the mixture to coat them well.

3. If the chops are to be baked, dot the top of each with equal portions of butter. Place in the oven and bake for about 7 minutes. Turn and continue baking for 10 to 12 minutes. Preheat the broiler to high and run the chops briefly under the broiler until lightly browned on top. If the chops are to be grilled, cook on each side for about 5 minutes. Serve with one or more garlic sauces and escalibada, or baked vegetables (see recipe page 322).

YIELD: 4 servings.

Note: It is best if the chops are cut from racks of lamb, well trimmed of almost all surface fat and each with two ribs.

ROMESCU

All-purpose Roast Garlic and Toasted Nut Sauce

- 3 large cloves garlic
- 1 large tomato, about ¾ pound
- ¼ pound pine nuts, about ½ cup, toasted
- ¼ pound blanched, skinless hazelnuts, about ¾ cup, toasted
- ¼ pound blanched, skinless almonds, about ¾ cup, toasted
- 1 tablespoon water
- 2 tablespoons Cognac
- ⅛ teaspoon paprika
- ¼ teaspoon Tabasco sauce
- 6 tablespoons olive oil
- Salt to taste, if desired
- Freshly ground black pepper to taste

1. Preheat the oven to 500 degrees. Arrange the unpeeled garlic cloves and tomato on a foil-lined baking sheet. Bake the tomato, turning occasionally, for about 30 minutes. Bake the garlic cloves for 45 minutes. Let cool slightly before peeling.

2. Put nuts into the container of a food processor or electric blender. Blend briefly and add the water. Continue blending until a paste forms.

3. Peel the garlic and add to the nut paste.

4. Peel the tomato. Discard peel and core. Chop. There should be about ¾ cup. Add to the nut paste.

5. Add the remaining ingredients one at a time, blending after each addition. Let stand 1 hour before using.

YIELD: About 2¼ cups.

HONEY AND GARLIC MAYONNAISE

- 1 tablespoon finely chopped garlic
- ½ egg yolk
- ½ cup corn, peanut or vegetable oil
- Salt to taste, if desired
- 2 tablespoons honey

1. Crush the garlic to a paste. It is best to use a mortar and pestle.

2. Put the garlic in a small mixing bowl and add the egg yolk.

3. Start beating with a wire whisk while adding the oil in a very thin stream. Continue beating until all oil is added. Add salt to taste and beat in the honey.

YIELD: Slightly more than ½ cup.

SAUCE OF APPLES AND GARLIC

- 3 Golden Delicious apples, about 1½ pounds
- 1 tablespoon finely chopped garlic
- Salt to taste, if desired
- ½ cup corn, peanut or vegetable oil

1. Peel the apples. Cut away and discard stems and cores. Cut into quarters.

2. Put the apples in a casserole and add water to cover, about 8 cups. Bring to the boil and let cook, uncovered, for about 10 minutes. Drain. Let cool.

3. Meanwhile crush the garlic to a paste. It is best to use a mortar and pestle.

4. Put apples into the container of a food processor or electric blender and blend to a purée like applesauce.

5. Add the garlic and salt. Gradually add the oil while blending.

YIELD: 2 cups.

CATALAN GARLIC MAYONNAISE

- 1 tablespoon finely chopped garlic
- 1 egg yolk
- ½ cup corn, peanut or olive oil
- Salt to taste, if desired

1. Crush the garlic to a paste. It is best to use a mortar and pestle.

2. Put the garlic in a small mixing bowl (see Note) and add the egg yolk.

3. Start beating with a wire whisk while adding the oil in a very thin stream. Continue beating until all the oil is added. Add salt to taste.

YIELD: Slightly more than ½ cup.

Note: Mrs. Guillen prepares this sauce wholly in a mortar using a pestle. When the garlic is mashed to a paste she adds the yolk, stirring with the pestle. She then adds the oil quite gradually, stirring with the pestle.

We have never felt that the basic flavor and goodness of a dish should be sacrificed for dramatic flair. There is one theatrical dish, however, that we cordially recommend for home cooks, and that is a crown roast of lamb. It is not only dramatic to the eye, but it is easy to prepare.

Curiously, as far as we can tell, this dish was created in American kitchens; it is rarely, if ever, found on French tables.

Although the dish requires two racks of lamb, which are expensive, the feast is extended in its use of ground lamb. The two racks, when shaped into a crown and baked, will serve six or more.

Crown Roast of Lamb with Ground Lamb and Pine Nuts

- 1 ready-to-cook crown roast of lamb, 3 to 4 pounds
- Salt, if desired
- Freshly ground black pepper to taste
- 1 tablespoon olive oil
- 1½ cups finely chopped onion
- 1 tablespoon finely chopped garlic
- ¼ pound mushrooms, finely chopped, about 1½ cups
- ⅓ cup pine nuts
- 1 pound ground lamb
- ½ teaspoon finely chopped dried rosemary
- ½ cup finely chopped parsley
- 1 cup plus 1 tablespoon fine fresh bread crumbs
- 1 egg, lightly beaten
- ¼ cup coarsely chopped onion
- ¼ cup coarsely chopped carrot
- ¼ cup coarsely chopped celery
- 1 bay leaf
- 2 sprigs fresh thyme, or ½ teaspoon dried
- 1 cup fresh or canned chicken broth

1. Preheat the oven to 425 degrees.

2. Sprinkle the lamb inside and out with salt and pepper.

3. Heat the oil in a small skillet and add the finely chopped onion and garlic. Cook, stirring, until the onion is wilted. Add the mushrooms and cook, stirring, until the mushrooms give up their liquid. Cook until liquid evaporates.

4. Meanwhile, put the pine nuts in a small skillet and cook, shaking the skillet, until they are lightly browned. Add the ground lamb, stirring and chopping down with the side of a heavy metal kitchen spoon to break up lumps. Cook until the meat loses its raw look. Add salt and pepper to taste. Transfer the mixture to a mixing bowl.

5. Add the rosemary, parsley, 1 cup of the bread crumbs and the egg. Add the mushroom mixture and a generous grinding of pepper. Blend well.

6. Place the crown roast on a sheet of aluminum foil. Fill the center with the stuffing, smoothing it over in a rounded fashion with a spatula. Sprinkle with the remaining tablespoon of bread crumbs.

7. Lift up the foil, keeping the roast neatly intact, and transfer it to a shallow roasting pan. Keep the stuffed lamb as neatly intact as possible. If there are any lamb bones, scatter them around the roast.

8. Scatter the coarsely chopped onion, carrot, celery, bay leaf and thyme around the roast. Place in the oven and bake for 1 hour.

9. Transfer the stuffed lamb to a serving dish. Remove and discard the foil.

10. Add the chicken broth to the baking pan with the bones. Bring to the boil, stirring. Strain the sauce around the lamb. Carve the lamb, serving two to four ribs, plus a generous helping of the stuffing, for each portion.

YIELD: 6 or more servings.

HOW TO PREPARE A CROWN ROAST OF LAMB FOR STUFFING

If the butcher will not prepare a crown roast of lamb, here is how to go about it. Buy two racks of lamb, about seven ribs each. Have them neatly trimmed, removing almost all the surface fat. Cut and pull away the skin, but leave the single thin layer of fat beneath the skin. The ribs should measure about four inches in length. Using a sharp knife, make a slight slit between each rib and the meaty end.

Place the ribs together, matching the ribs and meat of the joining racks. Using a heavy needle and string, tie the ends of the racks neatly together. If there are any spare lamb bones, save them for the roasting process.

Julie Sahni's Sookha Keema

DRY-COOKED, SPICY GROUND MEAT

- 2 tablespoons peanut, vegetable or corn oil
- ⅔ cup finely chopped onion
- 4 teaspoons finely minced garlic
- 1½ tablespoons chopped fresh ginger
- 1 teaspoon finely chopped fresh hot green chilies, seeded
- 1 pound ground lean lamb or beef
- ¼ cup hot water
- 2 teaspoons garam masala (see Note)
- 2 teaspoons lemon juice
- 2 tablespoons chopped fresh coriander leaves

1. Heat the oil in a heavy skillet and add the onion. Cook, stirring, for about 10 minutes, or until the onions are caramel colored. Do not burn.

2. Add the garlic, ginger and green chilies. Cook, stirring for about 2 minutes longer.

3. Add the lamb and, using the side of a heavy metal spoon, chop and stir the meat to break up any lumps. When the meat loses its raw, red look, sprinkle the mixture with turmeric and salt to taste. Stir briefly and add the water. Reduce the heat and cover. Cook for about 25 minutes. Stir often to prevent burning.

4. Remove from the heat and stir in the garam masala, lemon juice and coriander. Serve.

YIELD: 4 servings.

Note: Garam masala is a basic blend of Indian spices and varies from Indian cook to Indian cook. One mixture is made with ground cardamom pods, cinnamon, cloves, peppercorns, cumin and coriander seeds. It is available in bottles and tins from specialty food shops.

Middle East Meatballs with Cheese

- ½ cup raw rice
- 1 pound ground lamb
- 1 teaspoon butter
- ½ cup finely chopped onion
- ½ teaspoon finely minced garlic
- ⅓ cup finely chopped parsley
- ½ cup freshly grated Parmesan cheese
- 2 tablespoons finely chopped dill
- Salt, if desired
- Freshly ground black pepper to taste
- 2 eggs, lightly beaten
- ¼ cup water
- ½ cup flour
- ½ cup peanut, vegetable or corn oil
- Tomato sauce (see following recipe)

1. Bring enough water to the boil to cover the rice by at least half an inch above the top level of the rice. Add the rice and cook for 15 minutes. Drain.

2. Put the lamb in a mixing bowl and add the rice.

3. Melt the butter in a small saucepan or skillet. Add the onion and garlic and cook until wilted. Add this to the lamb mixture.

4. Add the parsley, cheese, dill, salt and pepper to taste. Blend well with the hands.

5. Shape the meat mixture into about 24 balls of equal size. Roll each into an egg-shape patty about 2 inches long.

6. Beat the eggs lightly in a shallow dish and add the water. Coat the patties with the egg mixture, then roll in flour.

7. Heat the oil in a skillet and add half of the patties. Cook for about 5 minutes, shaking the pan and turning the patties so that they cook evenly. Remove and drain on paper towels. Cook the second batch and drain. Put the meatballs into the tomato sauce and bring to the boil. Serve hot with the sauce.

YIELD: 4 to 6 servings.

TOMATO SAUCE WITH CINNAMON

- 3 cups canned imported tomatoes with basil
- ¼ cup olive oil
- ⅓ cup finely chopped onion
- 1 tablespoon finely chopped garlic
- 1 1-inch piece stick cinnamon, or ½ teaspoon ground
- Salt, if desired
- Freshly ground black pepper to taste
- 1 bay leaf
- ½ teaspoon sugar

1. Put the tomatoes and their liquid into the container of a food processor or electric blender. Process finely.

2. Heat the oil in a saucepan and add the onion and garlic. Cook, stirring, until wilted. Add the tomatoes, cinnamon, salt and pepper to taste, bay leaf and sugar. Bring to the boil and simmer for about 30 minutes. Remove and discard the bay leaf and cinnamon stick, if used.

YIELD: 4 to 6 servings.

Casserole of Lamb and Eggplant

- 1 large eggplant, about 1½ pounds
- ¼ cup olive oil
- 1 cup finely minced onion
- 1 teaspoon finely minced garlic
- 1½ pounds ground lamb
- Freshly ground black pepper to taste
- ½ teaspoon ground cinnamon
- 1 bay leaf
- 1 dried hot red pepper
- 4 cups tomatoes with tomato paste
- 1 cup bread crumbs
- ½ cup freshly grated Parmesan or Gruyère cheese

1. Preheat the oven to 425 degrees.

2. If the eggplant is not young and tender, peel it. Otherwise, leave the skin intact.

3. Cut the eggplant into 1-inch-thick lengthwise slices. Cut the slices into strips 1 inch wide. Cut the strips into 1-inch cubes. There should be about 6 cups.

4. Heat the oil in a casserole and add the onion and garlic. Cook, stirring, until the onion is wilted. Add the lamb, chopping down with the side of a heavy metal spoon to break up lumps. Add the eggplant and cook, stirring often, for about 5 minutes.

5. Add the pepper, cinnamon, bay leaf, hot pepper and tomatoes. Cook, stirring, for 5 minutes.

6. Spoon and scrape the mixture into a casserole or baking dish. Sprinkle with a mixture of crumbs and cheese. Place in the oven and bake 15 minutes.

YIELD: 4 to 6 servings.

Shanks, whether they be lamb, veal or pork, have a tenderness, a gelatinous texture that makes them, to some palates, far superior to the more luxurious cuts of meat such as tenderloins, fillets and the like. Shanks, too, are exceptionally easy to cook. Other than an occasional basting, they require little attention once they are placed in the oven. The flavors of these three recipes for shank dishes are all influenced by herbs—mint, basil and parsley—and offer a delightful change of pace in winter dining.

Lamb Shanks with Mint

- 2 lamb shanks, about 1¼ pounds each
- Salt and freshly ground black pepper to taste
- 1 cup coarsely chopped onion
- 2 bay leaves
- 2 cloves garlic, coarsely chopped
- 1 sprig fresh thyme, or ¼ teaspoon dried
- 1 tablespoon crumbled dried mint leaves
- 2 cups cored ripe tomatoes cut into 1-inch cubes
- 1 cup fresh or canned chicken broth

1. Preheat the oven to 425 degrees.

2. Sprinkle the shanks with salt and pepper. Place in a baking dish. If a few spare lamb bones are available, scatter them around the shanks. Place in the oven and bake for 25 minutes. Turn the shanks and continue baking.

3. When the shanks have cooked 5 minutes longer, or a total of ½ hour, reduce the oven temperature to 350 degrees.

4. Pour off all the fat from the pan. Scatter the onion, bay leaves, garlic, thyme and mint around the shanks. Return to the oven and bake for 15 minutes.

5. Scatter the tomatoes over the lamb and add the broth. Cover the pan closely with foil. Continue baking for 1 hour and 15 minutes longer. Total baking time is 2 hours.

YIELD: 2 servings.

Veal Shank with Fresh Basil

- 1 3-pound veal shank taken from the hind leg (see Note)
- 2 cloves garlic, peeled and cut lengthwise into 4 pieces
- Salt and freshly ground black pepper to taste
- 2 tablespoons olive oil
- 1 cup coarsely chopped onion
- 1 cup coarsely chopped celery
- 2 large carrots, scraped, quartered and cut into 2-inch lengths
- 2 cloves garlic, finely minced
- 1 tablespoon finely chopped fresh basil, or 2 teaspoons dried
- ½ cup dry white wine
- ½ cup fresh or canned chicken broth

1. Preheat the oven to 425 degrees.

2. Wipe the shank with a damp, clean cloth. Pierce the meaty part of the shank in eight places and insert the garlic slivers. Sprinkle the shank with salt and pepper to taste.

3. Place the shank in an ovenproof casserole and pour the oil over the shank. Turn the shank in the oil to coat completely. Place in the oven and bake for 15 minutes. Turn the shank and continue cooking.

4. When the shank has cooked 15 minutes longer, or a total of 30 minutes, reduce the oven temperature to 350 degrees.

5. Remove the shank and pour off the fat from the pan. Return the shank to the pan and add the onion, celery, carrots, minced garlic and basil. Return the shank with vegetables to the oven and bake for 30 minutes. Add

the wine and broth and cover the pan closely with foil. Return to the oven and bake for 1 hour longer. Total baking time is 2 hours.

6. Place the pan on the stove and remove the foil. Bring the pan juices to the boil and reduce slightly, stirring occasionally, about 4 minutes. Serve, sliced, with buttered noodles.

YIELD: 3 to 4 servings.

Note: Veal shanks are available from fine butchers. It may be necessary, however, to order them in advance.

Pork Hocks with Parsley Jelly

- 4 pork hocks (see Note)
- 4 cups cold water
- 1 large onion stuck with 2 cloves
- 1 cup chopped green part of leeks
- 2 celery stalks, each cut in half
- 2 carrots, scraped and cut in half or quartered
- 1 bay leaf
- 3 sprigs fresh thyme, or ½ teaspoon dried
- 1 tablespoon coriander seeds
- 2 cloves garlic, peeled
- 2 sprigs fresh parsley
- 6 whole black peppercorns
- Salt
- 4 tablespoons finely chopped parsley
- ½ teaspoon finely minced garlic
- 1 teaspoon finely chopped shallots
- 2 tablespoons red wine vinegar

1. Put the pork hocks (or hocks and feet if the trotters are used) in a deep saucepan or small kettle. Cover with cold water and bring to the boil. Drain well and rinse to chill.

2. Return the pork pieces to a clean kettle. Add the 4 cups of water, onion stuck with cloves, leeks, celery, carrots, bay leaf, thyme, coriander seeds, peeled garlic cloves, parsley sprigs, peppercorns and salt to taste. Bring to the boil and cook for 1 hour. Cover and continue cooking 2 hours.

3. Remove the hocks (and/or pigs' feet). Set aside to cool. Strain the liquid into a saucepan.

4. When cool enough to handle, remove all the meat from the bones. Discard the bones. Do not chop the meat but leave it as it comes from the bones.

5. Add the meat to the strained liquid in the saucepan. Add the chopped parsley, minced garlic, shallots and vinegar. Return to the heat. Bring to the boil and test seasoning. If desired, add more salt, pepper, garlic or whatever.

6. Pour the mixture into a 6-cup mold. Let cool to room temperature. Refrigerate overnight or until set. Serve sliced. Serve, if desired, with mustard and cornichons (sour pickles) on the side.

YIELD: 8 or more servings.

Note: If available, you may substitute 2 whole pork trotters, which include the shanks and pigs' feet in one piece, for the pork hocks. The shanks and feet should be chopped in two and both pieces used from each trotter.

FISH AND SHELLFISH

Poisson de Mer à l'Estragon

BAKED SALTWATER FISH WITH TARRAGON

- 1 3½-pound (cleaned weight, gills removed) fish, such as weakfish, striped bass or red snapper
- 6 tablespoons butter
- 1 cup finely chopped onion
- 1 cup finely chopped leeks
- 1 teaspoon finely minced garlic
- 4 cups peeled, cored and cubed tomatoes
- Salt and freshly ground black pepper to taste
- 1 tablespoon finely chopped fresh tarragon, or half the amount dried
- 1 cup dry white wine
- 1 bay leaf
- 12 scrubbed littleneck clams
- Chopped fresh basil or parsley

1. Preheat the oven to 425 degrees.

2. Wipe the fish and pat it dry inside and out.

3. Melt 2 tablespoons of the butter in a large skillet and add the onion, leeks and garlic. Cook briefly, stirring, until the onion is wilted. Add the tomatoes and salt and pepper. Cook for about 5 minutes.

4. Add half of the tarragon, all of the wine and bay leaf. Simmer, stirring occasionally, for about 5 minutes.

5. Rub a baking dish large enough to hold the fish with 2 tablespoons of the butter. Sprinkle with salt and pepper.

6. Put the fish in the baking dish. Pour and scrape the tomato sauce around the fish. Sprinkle the fish with salt and pepper. Sprinkle the remaining tarragon over the fish. Dot with the remaining 2 tablespoons of butter.

7. Cover the dish closely with foil and place in the oven. Bake for 15 minutes, basting occasionally. Scatter the clams around the fish and cover once more with foil.

8. Continue baking for 10 to 15 minutes, or until the clams open, basting occasionally.

9. Pour and scrape the tomato sauce into a skillet or casserole. Cook down to about half.

10. Transfer the fish to a warm serving dish. Arrange the clams around the fish. Pour the tomato sauce over the fish. Sprinkle with chopped basil or parsley and serve.

YIELD: 4 to 6 servings.

I asked Gerard Boyer, whose three-star restaurant is in the Champagne region, to prepare at least one dish with champagne when he visited my kitchen. My purpose was to find out whether champagne, which loses its sparkle when heated, was preferable to any fine white wine. Mr. Boyer mulled the question over and admitted to a certain prejudice. "The difference may be minuscule," he said, "but I feel that a dish has more elegance and finesse if it is made with champagne rather than a still white wine." He added that in his own restaurant 45 percent of the wine sold is a champagne. "And in creating a dish in the kitchen, you should always use a wine that is in rapport with what is being drunk in front." His striped bass with zucchini was, indeed, elegant.

Bar Rayé aux Courgettes

STRIPED BASS WITH ZUCCHINI

- 2 skinless, boneless striped bass fillets, about 1¼ pounds total weight (see Note)
- 1 firm, unblemished zucchini, about 6 ounces
- 1 firm ripe tomato, about ⅓ pound
- 10 tablespoons plus 3 teaspoons butter, approximately
- 2 tablespoons finely chopped shallots
- ¼ cup brut champagne
- 1 cup fish stock (see recipe page 419)
- 1 cup heavy cream
- Salt to taste, if desired
- 1 teaspoon lemon juice
- Freshly ground pepper, preferably white, to taste

1. Place each fillet on a flat surface. Slice each on the bias to produce four pieces, about 2 ounces each. Place each piece between sheets of clear plastic wrap and pound lightly with a flat mallet (or use the bottom of a small, clean, heavy saucepan) without breaking the flesh.

2. Trim the zucchini. Cut it into thin, ⅛-inch-thick rounds. Stack the rounds and cut them into thin ⅛-inch slivers (julienne). There should be about 2 cups. Set aside.

3. Core, peel and seed the tomato. Cut it into ¼-inch cubes. There should be about ½ cup. Set aside.

4. Melt 1 tablespoon of the butter in a saucepan and add the shallots. Cook, stirring, until wilted. Add the champagne and fish stock. Bring to the boil and cook down over high heat until reduced to ⅓ cup. Add the cream and salt.

5. Add 7 tablespoons of the butter, a little at a time, stirring constantly. When the sauce starts to simmer, remove from the heat. Add the lemon juice and pepper.

6. Melt 2 tablespoons of butter in a small skillet and add the zucchini slivers. Cook, stirring, about 15 seconds, or until crisp-tender. Add salt to taste and stir. Drain well. Add this to the sauce. Add the tomato.

7. Sprinkle the fish pieces on both sides with salt and pepper.

8. Melt approximately 1 teaspoon of butter in a skillet, preferably a non-stick pan. Add 2 or 3 pieces of the fish and cook for 1 minute or less to a side or until done. Take care not to overcook. Transfer the pieces to a warm serving dish. Continue cooking, adding small amounts of butter as necessary, until all the pieces are cooked.

9. Serve the fish pieces with the sauce spooned over.

YIELD: 8 servings.

Note: Chef Boyer worked from one whole 2½-pound striped bass with head on, total weight, to produce the fillets and bones for the fish stock.

Poisson aux Épices

FISH WITH SPICES

- 2 striped bass, about 1½ pounds each, cleaned weight
- ½ cup peanut oil
- 2 cups water
- 2 teaspoons ground ginger
- 2 teaspoons ground turmeric
- 2 teaspoons ground cumin
- 1 teaspoon paprika
- ¼ teaspoon cayenne pepper
- Salt to taste, if desired
- 4 tablespoons butter
- 6 tablespoons lemon juice
- 1 cup finely chopped parsley
- 6 thin, seeded lemon slices
- 6 round slices of cherry tomatoes

1. Cut off the heads of the fish and neatly trim the end of each tail.

2. Select a flameproof oval baking dish large enough to accommodate both fish. Do not add the fish. Select six pieces of bamboo (cut-off chopsticks may be used). Arrange them crosswise, evenly spaced, over the bottom of the baking dish to support the fish and prevent them from lying directly on the bottom of the dish.

3. Add the oil, water, ginger, turmeric, cumin, paprika, cayenne and salt. Bring to the boil on top of the stove.

4. Arrange the fish in the dish. Baste the fish for about 3 minutes with the simmering sauce.

5. Cover closely with foil and continue cooking for 20 minutes. Uncover and add the butter and lemon juice. Continue cooking for 10 minutes and sprinkle the parsley on top of each fish. Arrange the lemon and tomato slices on the fish and baste with the sauce. Serve.

YIELD: 6 servings.

Poached Striped Bass with Sauce Chevillot

- 1 striped bass, 3½ pounds cleaned weight, with head and tail on
- 5 quarts water
- 1 onion, peeled and thinly sliced
- 4 carrots, scraped and cut into cubes, about 1½ cups
- 1½ cups coarsely chopped celery with leaves
- 4 cloves garlic, peeled and crushed
- 6 sprigs fresh parsley
- 1 teaspoon dried thyme
- 24 whole cloves
- 4 bay leaves
- ¼ cup whole black peppercorns
- 1 bottle dry white wine
- Sauce Chevillot (see following recipe)

1. The bass must be scrupulously clean of scales. Using scissors, cut off and discard the back and side fins. Leave the head and tail intact.

2. If available, use a fish cooker. In the cooker combine the water, onion, carrots, celery, garlic, parsley, thyme, cloves, bay leaves, peppercorns and wine. Do not add salt. Do not add the fish.

3. Cover and place on the stove. Bring the liquid to the boil and cook for 20 minutes.

4. Uncover, add the fish and let it simmer for 13 minutes. Remove from the heat and let rest for about 5 minutes before draining and serving.

5. Remove the skin from the fish and serve boneless pieces with sauce Chevillot.

YIELD: 4 servings.

SAUCE CHEVILLOT

- 2 tablespoons finely chopped shallots
- Salt and freshly ground black pepper to taste
- 3 tablespoons red wine vinegar
- ½ pound cold butter

1. Put the shallots in a heavy saucepan and add salt, pepper and vinegar.
2. Cut the butter into ½-inch cubes. Set aside.
3. Put the saucepan on the stove and cook until the vinegar is reduced by half. Pour off the vinegar but leave the shallots in the saucepan.
4. Add the butter to the shallots and reduce the heat immediately. Stir rapidly with a whisk and cook just until butter is hot and melted. Do not allow the butter to boil or it will separate.

YIELD: About ¾ cup.

It has always struck us odd that so many Americans seem intimidated by the cooking of fish, for, to us at least, it is one of the easiest of all forms of cookery. In the baked fish recipe outlined here, for example, the fillets are simply brushed with mustard, sprinkled with bread crumbs and dotted with butter before cooking. In the sautéed fish recipe, a simple breading technique is used and the fillets, once cooked, may be served as is or, even better—but more complicated—with a mustard hollandaise. Easiest of all is to steam or poach the fillets, then serve with that delicious butter sauce called beurre blanc.

Filets de Poisson au Four

BAKED FISH FILLETS

- 4 fillets striped bass, fluke, flounder or sole, 1½ to 2 pounds
- 4 tablespoons plus 6 teaspoons butter
- Salt, if desired
- Freshly ground black pepper to taste
- 2 tablespoons finely chopped shallots or scallions
- ½ cup dry white wine
- 2 teaspoons prepared mustard, preferably imported Dijon or Düsseldorf
- 6 tablespoons fresh bread crumbs
- ¼ cup finely chopped parsley
- Lemon wedges

1. Preheat the oven to 400 degrees.

2. Cut each fillet into three pieces.

3. Butter a baking dish large enough to hold the pieces in one layer with the 4 tablespoons of butter. Sprinkle with salt and pepper and shallots.

4. Arrange the fish pieces over the shallots and sprinkle with half of the wine. Blend the remaining wine with the mustard and brush the tops of the fish with the mixture. Sprinkle each piece of fish with 1½ teaspoons of the bread crumbs and dot each piece with ½ teaspoon of butter. Bake in the oven for 5 minutes.

5. Turn the broiler to high and run the baking dish under it. Broil until the fish flakes easily when tested with a fork. Do not overcook. Sprinkle with chopped parsley. Serve each portion with a lemon wedge.

YIELD: 4 servings.

Filets de Poisson à l'Anglaise

BREADED FISH FILLETS

- 2 pounds fish fillets, such as striped bass, sole or flounder
- ¾ cup flour
- Salt, if desired
- Freshly ground black pepper to taste
- 1 egg, lightly beaten
- 3 tablespoons plus 1 teaspoon peanut, vegetable or corn oil
- 2 tablespoons water
- ¾ cup fresh bread crumbs
- 1 tablespoon butter
- Lemon wedges
- Mustard hollandaise (see recipe page 401), optional

1. Cut the fish into serving pieces.

2. Combine the flour, salt and pepper to taste.

3. Beat the egg with 1 teaspoon of oil, the water, salt and pepper to taste.

4. Coat the fish pieces all over in the seasoned flour. Dip them well into the egg, then coat them all over with the crumbs.

5. In a heavy skillet, heat the remaining 3 tablespoons of oil and the butter and cook the fish pieces until golden brown on one side. Turn and cook on the other side, basting frequently with the oil and butter in the skillet. It is impossible to give an exact cooking time, because it depends on the thickness of the fish. Cooking time may range from 5 minutes for flounder to 10 minutes for bass. Serve with lemon wedges or mustard hollandaise. Accompany the fish with steamed potatoes.

YIELD: 4 to 6 servings.

Poached Fish with Beurre Blanc

- 1½ pounds fresh skinless, boneless fish fillets, such as cod, flounder, whitefish, tilefish or striped bass
- 2 cups water
- ½ cup milk
- 2 whole cloves
- 1 bay leaf
- Salt
- Beurre blanc (see recipe page 400)

1. There is a small center line of bones down the center of each fillet. Cut this away, trimming the line on either side. Discard the bone line.

2. Place the fillets in an oval heatproof dish and add the water, milk, cloves, bay leaf and salt to taste. Cover and bring to the simmer, spooning the liquid over the fish. Cook for about 1 minute or less. Turn off the heat.

3. Drain and serve with beurre blanc.

YIELD: 4 servings.

Paupiettes de Sole au Vermouth

ROLLED SOLE FILLETS IN VERMOUTH SAUCE

- 12 small, skinless, boneless fillets of sole or flounder, about 2¼ pounds
- Salt, if desired
- Freshly ground black pepper to taste
- 1 pint fresh scallops, preferably bay scallops
- 1 egg white
- ½ cup heavy cream
- 3 drops Tabasco sauce
- 1 tablespoon butter
- ½ cup dry white vermouth
- 1 cup heavy cream
- Juice of ½ lemon
- 1 tablespoon finely chopped parsley

1. Preheat the oven to 400 degrees.

2. Arrange the fillets skinned side up on a flat surface. Sprinkle lightly with salt and pepper.

3. Put the scallops into the container of a food processor or blender. Add the egg white and start blending. Gradually pour in the cream. Add salt and pepper to taste and Tabasco and blend.

4. Spoon an equal portion of the scallop mixture on each fillet. Fold over the ends of the fillet to enclose the mixture.

5. Select a shallow, flameproof baking dish large enough to hold the folded fillets in one layer. Rub it with the butter. Arrange the fillets, seam side down, in the dish. Sprinkle lightly with salt and pepper. Pour the vermouth over all.

6. Place the dish on top of the stove and bring the liquid to the simmer. Cover closely with aluminum foil and place in the oven. Bake for 15 minutes.

7. Transfer the fish fillets to a hot serving platter and cover with foil to keep warm. Pour the pan liquid from the fish into a saucepan.

8. Bring the liquid in the saucepan to the boil over high heat and cook down. As the liquid boils, add any liquid that accumulates around the fish. Continue cooking down to ⅓ cup. Add the cream and cook down over high heat for about 4 minutes. There should be about 1 cup. Line a mixing bowl with a strainer. Add the sauce and scrape to extract all the liquid from any solids in the sauce. Return the sauce to a saucepan and reheat.

9. Add the lemon juice and pour the sauce over the fish. Serve sprinkled with parsley.

YIELD: 6 servings.

Filets de Poissons à la Vapeur au Beurre Blanc

STEAMED FISH FILLETS WITH WHITE BUTTER SAUCE

4 boneless fish fillets, such as striped bass, red snapper and so on, about ½ pound each
Salt to taste, if desired
Freshly ground black pepper to taste
1 tablespoon finely chopped herbs, such as fresh basil or tarragon
Beurre blanc (see recipe page 400)

1. Place the fish fillets skin side down in the top of a steamer. Sprinkle with salt and pepper. Sprinkle with chopped basil or tarragon.

2. Pour water in the bottom of the steamer and bring to a high boil.

3. Place the steamer top securely over the boiling water and cover closely. Let steam for 3 to 5 minutes. Steaming time will depend on the thickness of the fillets.

4. Serve with hot white butter sauce.

YIELD: 4 servings.

Americans have a long-standing enthusiasm for stuffed vegetables such as green or red peppers, zucchini, eggplant and especially cabbage. There is a good reason for this appreciation: Stuffed vegetables can offer an uncommon versatility in flavor and texture. They are also relatively inexpensive as main courses and they provide a practical and palate-pleasing way to use leftovers.

Curiously, lettuce as a vegetable for stuffing is little known or understood in this country, though it makes an admirable base for fillings of various sorts. For example, the leaves of Boston lettuce—this variety works best—may be unfolded (after they have been blanched) and stuffed a few at a time; or the entire head of lettuce may be split down the center and stuffed. An excellent filling is this sole and duxelles recipe.

Filets de Sole Enrobés de Laitues

SOLE-STUFFED LETTUCE

- 3 to 6 heads Boston lettuce (see Note)
- ¾ pound mushrooms, rinsed well and drained
- 4 tablespoons butter
- 2 tablespoons finely chopped onion
- 3 tablespoons finely chopped shallots
- Juice of ½ lemon
- 2 tablespoons finely chopped parsley
- ¼ cup fine fresh bread crumbs
- Salt and freshly ground black pepper to taste
- 6 small fillets of sole, about 1 pound total weight
- ½ cup dry white wine
- 1¼ cups heavy cream

1. Soak the heads of Boston lettuce in cold water, stem side up, for 1 hour. Drain, shaking each head to remove the excess water.

2. Bring to the boil enough water to cover the lettuce when it is added. Add the lettuce and push the heads down so that they are submerged when added. Cover. When the water returns to the boil, simmer, uncovered, for 1 or 2 minutes. Drain well. Run under cold water to cool. Drain again. Squeeze each head of lettuce between the hands to extract most of the liquid.

3. Preheat the oven to 400 degrees.

4. Put the mushrooms on a flat surface and chop them finely. Or chop them in a food processor. Put the mushrooms in a clean towel and bring up the ends to make a sack. Twist tightly to squeeze out most of the mushrooms' natural liquid.

5. Melt 1 tablespoon of the butter in a saucepan and add the onion and 1 tablespoon of the shallots. Add the mushrooms and the lemon juice. Stir. Bring to the boil and cook, stirring occasionally, for about 2 minutes. Most of the moisture should have evaporated from the mixture. Add the parsley, bread crumbs and 1 tablespoon of butter. Add salt and pepper to taste. This mixture is called a duxelles.

6. Place the sole on a flat surface. There may be a thin bone line running halfway up the center of each. Cut away this bone line, but do not cut the sole entirely in half.

7. Spoon equal portions of the duxelles in the center of each fillet of sole. Bring up the ends of the sole and fold the ends over to enclose the stuffing.

8. Lay a large outside lettuce leaf on a flat surface, stem end away from you. Lay a second lettuce leaf slightly overlapping the first leaf, stem end toward you. Repeat this, placing each leaf at an opposite angle, slightly overlapping, the stem ends going in opposite directions. Place 2 or 3 broken leaves in the center.

9. Place the fish roll in the center. Bring up and fold over the ends of the lettuce to make a package. Turn the package seam side down. Continue making packages until all 6 fillets are enclosed.

10. Rub a flameproof baking dish large enough to hold the packages in one layer with 1 tablespoon of butter. Sprinkle with remaining 2 tablespoons of chopped shallots. Arrange the packages in the dish, seam sides down. Dot with the remaining 1 tablespoon of butter divided among the 6 packages.

11. Add the wine and bring to the boil on top of the stove.

12. Place the baking dish in the oven. Bake for 15 minutes.

13. Transfer the stuffed lettuce to a serving dish.

14. Pour the cooking liquid into a saucepan. Bring to the boil and cook down until almost totally reduced. Add the cream and bring to the boil. Cook over high heat until reduced to about 1 cup. As the cream cooks, add any additional juices that accumulate around the stuffed lettuce.

15. Pour the sauce over the stuffed lettuce and serve hot.

YIELD: 6 servings.

Note: You will probably need 1 large head of lettuce for 2 stuffed sole fillets. If the heads are small or medium-sized, you may need 1 head for each fillet.

Since my first bite of fish au vin blanc on the *Île de France* back in the 1950s (tourist class), I have been persuaded that it is conceivably the greatest fish preparation in the world. Curiously enough, it is not one of the more complicated preparations in the French repertory. When Pierre Franey collaborated on this dish recently in my home kitchen, he reminded me that sole au vin blanc was one of the great specialties of Le Pavillon restaurant when he was in charge of the kitchen there. It was made with imported English sole and was listed on the menu as sole Pavillon. The sauce for this particular dish was made with tomatoes and mushrooms.

Filets de Sole Pavillon

FILLETS OF SOLE WITH A TOMATO AND MUSHROOM SAUCE

- 8 small, skinless, boneless fillets of sole or flounder, about 2 pounds
- 1 teaspoon plus 2 tablespoons butter
- 3 tablespoons finely chopped shallots
- ½ pound mushrooms, thinly sliced, about 2 cups
- 1 cup drained canned tomatoes, preferably imported
- Salt and freshly ground black pepper to taste
- ½ cup dry white wine
- 1 cup fish stock (see recipe page 419)
- ¾ cup fish velouté (see recipe page 418)
- 1 cup heavy cream
- 2 tablespoons finely chopped parsley
- 1 egg yolk

1. Preheat the oven to 400 degrees.

2. Run the fingers lengthwise down the center of each fillet. There may be a tiny bone line at the end near the center base of each fillet. If there is, use a small paring knife and cut on either side to remove it. Arrange the fillets skinned side up on a flat surface.

3. Split each fillet down the center lengthwise.

4. Rub the bottom of a baking dish with 1 teaspoon of the butter. Scatter the shallots over it. Scatter the mushrooms over the dish and arrange the tomatoes evenly over the mushrooms. Sprinkle with salt and pepper.

5. Fold each piece of fillet in half. Arrange the folded fillet pieces neatly and compactly in one layer over the tomatoes. Sprinkle with salt and pepper. Pour the wine over all. Cover closely with a round of wax paper.

6. Place the baking dish on top of the stove and bring to the simmer.

7. Place in the oven and bake for 5 minutes.

8. Using a spatula, transfer the pieces of fillet to a warm ovenproof serving dish. Cover with foil and keep warm.

9. Bring the pan sauce with the mushroom slices to the boil. Add the fish stock. Cook down over high heat until reduced to about 1½ cups. Stir in the velouté.

10. Add ¾ cup of the cream and bring to the boil. Cook, stirring, for about 5 minutes. Off the heat, swirl in the remaining 2 tablespoons of butter. Add the parsley.

11. Whip the remaining ¼ cup of heavy cream until it holds peaks but is not stiff. Beat in the egg yolk. Add 6 tablespoons of the whipped cream mixture to the sauce. Discard the rest (it is almost impossible to whip less than ¼ cup of cream).

12. Preheat the broiler to high.

13. Spoon the sauce over the fish fillets. Place under the broiler and leave the door open. Let stand under the broiler heat for 2 or 3 minutes until golden brown and bubbling on top.

YIELD: 4 servings.

Stir-fried Fish with Tree Ears

- 3 tablespoons dried tree ears
- 1 pound skinless, boneless gray sole fillets
- 4 tablespoons shaoxing wine or dry sherry
- ½ cup plus 1½ tablespoons cornstarch
- 1½ cups fresh or canned chicken broth
- Salt to taste
- 1 tablespoon sugar
- 1 cup peanut, vegetable or corn oil
- 1 tablespoon melted chicken fat

1. Put the tree ears in a mixing bowl and add boiling water to cover. Let stand for at least 30 minutes.

2. Cut each fillet in half lengthwise. Cut each fillet half on the diagonal into 2-inch pieces.

3. Put the fish in a bowl and add 1 tablespoon of the wine.

4. Put ½ cup of the cornstarch on a plate. Dredge each piece of fish on both sides in the cornstarch. Set aside.

5. Blend a little of the chicken broth with the remaining cornstarch, salt to taste and the sugar. Blend with the remaining broth and set aside.

6. Drain the tree ears and put them in a saucepan. Add cold water to cover. Bring to the boil and simmer for 1 minute. Drain. Squeeze to extract excess moisture. Set aside.

7. Heat the oil in a wok and, when it is very hot, add 2 or 3 pieces of fish at a time. Cook over very high heat for about 15 seconds and remove. The fish pieces should not brown. Do not overcook.

8. Pour off all but 1 teaspoon of oil from the wok. Add the broth mixture and the remaining 3 tablespoons of wine. Cook, stirring, until thickened.

9. Add the tree ears and fish and cook, stirring gently, for about 1 minute. Transfer to a hot serving dish. Spoon the chicken fat over the dish and serve hot.

YIELD: 8 servings with other Chinese dishes.

Fish Mousse

- 1½ pounds skinless, boneless, fresh (never frozen) fish fillets, such as flounder, grey sole, lemon sole, weakfish, red snapper or salmon
- Salt and freshly ground black pepper to taste
- Pinch of cayenne pepper
- ⅛ teaspoon grated nutmeg
- 1 egg yolk
- 2 cups heavy cream
- Sauce portugaise (see recipe page 409)

1. Preheat the oven to 375 degrees.

2. There may be a fine bone line running down the center of each fillet. If so, cut it away and discard. Cut the fish into 2-inch cubes and put the pieces into the container of a food processor. Put the container in the freezer until very cold, but do not let the fish freeze.

3. Remove from the freezer and return to the food processor. Add salt, pepper, cayenne, nutmeg and egg yolk. Start processing and, when the mixture is coarse-fine, gradually add the heavy cream, pouring it through the funnel.

4. Butter the bottom and sides of a 4-cup mold.

5. Spoon and scrape the mousse into the mold and pack it down, smoothing over the top.

6. Cover closely with foil, pressing it snugly around the sides of the mold.

7. Set the mold in a baking dish and pour boiling water around it. Bring the water to the boil on top of the stove. Then bake for 1 hour, or until the internal temperature registers 130 degrees on a meat thermometer. The mousse can be served now or reheated later.

8. If reheated later, reheat the oven to 400 degrees. Place the mousse back in the oven and bake for 10 minutes or slightly longer. Remove the foil and unmold on a round dish. Slice and serve with the hot sauce portugaise.

YIELD: 6 servings.

Sautéed Fresh Roe

- 1 pound fresh roe from flounder, herring, weakfish or other fish
- Salt and freshly ground black pepper to taste
- Flour for dredging
- 2 tablespoons butter
- 1 teaspoon finely minced garlic
- Juice of ½ lemon
- Finely chopped parsley for garnish
- Lemon wedges for garnish

1. The size of the roe may vary greatly from 2 to 6 or more inches in length. Prick the roe in several places with a needle or pin.
2. Sprinkle with salt, pepper and flour. Shake to remove any excess flour.
3. Melt the butter in a skillet large enough to hold the roe in one layer. When the butter is quite hot, add the roe. Reduce the heat. Cook until nicely golden on one side. Cooking times will vary depending on the size of the roe, from 3 to 8 minutes to a side. Turn the roe and cook over gentle heat until golden and cooked through.
4. Remove the roe to a serving dish. Add the garlic to the skillet and cook briefly without browning. Add the lemon juice, stir and pour the pan sauce over the roe. Serve sprinkled with chopped parsley and lemon wedges.

YIELD: 4 or more servings.

Like most Southerners, I adore catfish. I'm not certain that my mother ever prepared catfish at home, however. She was too aristocratic for that. Red snapper, yes; but catfish was too common, something to be enjoyed outdoors on Sunday outings. Eating deep-fried catfish was a ritual and the menu was always the same: the cornmeal-coated catfish with its golden brown crusty exterior and moist white inner flesh; deep-fried hush puppies; deep-fried potatoes, and coleslaw. And tomato ketchup. Deep-fried catfish without ketchup is like a hot dog without mustard. Now that catfish are being raised in fresh water ponds, they are available frozen all over the country and can be used in any recipe calling for a white nonoily fish. Even after freezing and defrosting, catfish remain snow white and as firm as when taken from the water.

Sybil Arant's Catfish Baked with Cheese

- 6 to 8 catfish fillets, about 2 pounds
- ½ cup freshly grated Parmesan cheese
- ¼ cup flour
- Salt to taste, if desired
- Freshly ground black pepper to taste
- 1 teaspoon paprika
- 1 egg, lightly beaten
- 1 tablespoon milk
- 8 tablespoons melted butter
- ¼ cup sliced almonds

1. Preheat the oven to 350 degrees.
2. Wipe the catfish dry.
3. Blend together the cheese, flour, salt, pepper and paprika.
4. Combine the egg and milk in a flat dish.
5. Dip the fillets in the egg mixture and then coat with the cheese mixture. Arrange the fillets in one layer in a baking dish and pour the butter over all. Sprinkle with the almonds. Place in the oven and bake for 20 minutes.

YIELD: 6 to 8 servings.

Catfish Fillets in White Wine Sauce

- 6 catfish fillets, about 2 pounds
- 5 tablespoons butter
- ½ cup dry white wine
- ½ pound mushrooms, thinly sliced, about 2 cups
- Salt to taste, if desired
- Freshly ground black pepper to taste
- 2 tablespoons flour
- ½ cup milk
- Juice of ½ lemon
- 2 tablespoons freshly grated Parmesan cheese
- 2 tablespoons finely chopped parsley

1. Preheat the oven to 400 degrees.

2. Pat the catfish pieces dry. Rub a baking dish (a dish measuring about 2 by 13 by 8 inches is ideal) with 1 tablespoon of the butter. Arrange the fillets in the buttered dish in one layer.

3. Add the wine. Scatter the mushrooms over all and sprinkle with salt and pepper to taste. Place in the oven and bake for 10 minutes.

4. Meanwhile, melt the remaining butter in a saucepan and add the flour, stirring with a wire whisk. Add the milk, stirring with the whisk. When blended and smooth, remove from the heat.

5. Pour the liquid from the baked fish into the sauce, stirring. Bring to the boil and cook, stirring often, for about 5 minutes. Stir in the lemon juice. Pour the sauce over the fish and bake for 10 minutes longer. Sprinkle with Parmesan cheese and parsley. Serve hot.

YIELD: 6 servings.

❧

Deep-fried Catfish

Fresh corn oil to cover
3 catfish fillets, about 1 pound
½ cup white cornmeal
Salt to taste, if desired
Freshly ground black pepper to taste
Lemon halves
Tomato ketchup
Hush puppies (see recipe page 387)

1. Heat the oil for deep frying.

2. Cut each fillet in half crosswise.

3. Combine the cornmeal, salt and pepper.

4. Dredge the fillets in the cornmeal. Pat to make the cornmeal adhere. Drop the fillets in the oil and cook 5 to 10 minutes, or until crisp and brown. Serve with lemon halves, ketchup and hush puppies.

YIELD: 2 to 4 servings.

❧

Mustard-fried Catfish

Follow the recipe for deep-fried catfish but brush the pieces on all sides with mustard before dredging in cornmeal.

Fricassée de Flétan au Coulis de Tomates

HALIBUT FRICASSEE WITH TOMATO SAUCE

- 1 pound skinless, boneless halibut fillets, cut 1 inch thick
- 6½ tablespoons butter
- ½ teaspoon finely chopped shallots
- Salt and freshly ground black pepper to taste
- 1 teaspoon lemon juice
- 1 cup diced, seeded and peeled tomatoes
- 2 tablespoons dry white wine
- 1 tablespoon heavy cream
- 2 tablespoons shredded fresh basil

1. Cut the fish fillets into two pieces of equal size.

2. Melt 1 tablespoon of the butter in a small casserole large enough to hold the fish in one layer and add the shallots. Cook briefly and add the fish in one layer.

3. Sprinkle with salt, pepper and lemon juice and set aside.

4. Meanwhile, melt 1½ tablespoons of butter in a saucepan and add the tomatoes, salt and pepper. Cook until thickened, about 2 minutes.

5. Spoon the wine over the fish. Bring to the boil. Simmer for about 1 minute. Turn each piece of fish and simmer for about 1 minute.

6. Carefully transfer the fish to another saucepan. To the liquid remaining in the casserole, add the heavy cream. Bring to a simmer and add the remaining butter, little by little, beating rapidly with a wire whisk. Add 3 tablespoons of the tomato sauce (you may save the remaining sauce for another use). Add the basil and stir.

7. Spoon the sauce over the fish pieces and reheat gently.

YIELD: 4 servings.

Paul Prudhomme is that rarity in the world of food—a celebrated, internationally known chef who just happens to have been born in the United States. With his wife, Kay Hinrich, Mr. Prudhomme is the owner of K. Paul's Louisiana Kitchen, which has become one of the most popular eating places in New Orleans. Mr. Prudhomme recently visited my kitchen to demonstrate numerous Louisiana specialties, including jambalaya and chicken gumbo, dirty rice, red beans with rice and his own invention, this specialty of specialties, blackened redfish. Because there were no redfish or red snapper in our local market, he chose tilefish, and it worked admirably as a substitute.

❧

Blackened Redfish

- 3 teaspoons salt, optional
- ½ teaspoon cayenne pepper
- ½ teaspoon freshly ground white pepper
- ¼ teaspoon freshly ground black pepper
- ¼ teaspoon dried thyme
- ¼ teaspoon dried basil
- ¼ teaspoon dried oregano
- 2 teaspoons paprika
- 8 skinless, boneless fillets of fish, preferably redfish, pompano or tilefish, about ¼ pound each (see Note)
- 8 tablespoons melted butter

1. Combine the salt, cayenne, white pepper, black pepper, thyme, basil, oregano and paprika in a small bowl.

2. Dip the fish pieces on both sides in butter. Sprinkle on both sides with the seasoned mixture.

3. Heat a black iron skillet over high heat for about 5 minutes or longer (the skillet cannot get too hot) until it is beyond the smoking stage and starts to lighten in color on the bottom.

4. Add two or more fish pieces and pour about a teaspoon of butter on top of each piece. The butter may flame up. Cook over high heat for about 1½ minutes. Turn the fish and pour another teaspoon of butter over each piece. Cook for about 1½ minutes. Serve immediately. Continue until all the fillets are cooked.

YIELD: 4 servings.

Note: Redfish and pompano are ideal for this dish. If tilefish is used, you may have to split the fillets in half. Place the fillet on a flat surface, hold the knife parallel to the surface and split in half through the center from one end to the other. The weight of the fish may vary from 1 to 1½ pounds, depending on your skillet, but they must not be more than about 1½ inches thick.

Almost all the fish flourishing in American waters are associated with the seasons: cod in the winter, trout in the spring and so on. If ever a fish smacked gloriously of summer, it is the elegantly pink, seductively flavored salmon. It is one of the very few fish that seem to team well with a red wine sauce. Perhaps it is the color. Saumon Chambord, named for the largest château of the Loire Valley, is the greatest of all fish-in-red-wine-sauce dishes when made with a well-rounded and not-too-tart but dry red wine, preferably a smooth and suitably aged Burgundy.

❧

Saumon Chambord

SALMON IN RED WINE SAUCE

- 2 pounds salmon with skin and bone (this may be a whole salmon or a portion, such as the tail or a center cut)
- Salt and freshly ground black pepper to taste
- 4 tablespoons butter
- ½ cup thinly sliced onion
- ¼ cup finely chopped shallots
- ½ cup thinly sliced mushrooms
- 2 sprigs fresh parsley
- 1½ cups dry red wine, preferably a Burgundy
- ¼ teaspoon dried thyme
- 1 bay leaf
- 2 teaspoons flour
- 4 whole mushrooms
- Juice of ½ lemon

1. Preheat the oven to 350 degrees.

2. Sprinkle the salmon with salt and pepper.

3. Use 1 tablespoon butter to grease a flameproof baking dish large enough to hold the salmon comfortably.

4. Place the salmon in the dish and scatter around it the onion, shallots, sliced mushrooms, parsley, wine, thyme and bay leaf.

5. Cover the dish closely with foil. Place the dish on top of the stove and bring the cooking liquid to the boil. Place the dish in the oven and bake for 30 minutes. Remove the foil.

6. Transfer the fish to a warm platter. Pour and scrape the cooking liquid and vegetables into a saucepan and bring to the boil. Cook the liquid down to about ¾ cup. Pour the liquid and vegetables into a strainer. Press the solids to extract as much liquid as possible. Discard the solids. Pour the liquid into a saucepan.

7. Carefully pull off and discard the skin of the fish. Scrape away and discard the dark flesh that coats the pink flesh of the salmon. When turning the fish, turn it carefully so that the flesh does not break.

8. Transfer the fish to a serving dish.

9. Bring the cooking liquid to the boil.

10. Blend 2 tablespoons of butter and the flour in a small mixing bowl.

11. Meanwhile, put the whole mushrooms in a small saucepan and add water to cover and the lemon juice. Bring to the boil. Simmer for 1 minute. Drain.

12. Add the butter-flour mixture to the cooking liquid, stirring constantly. Cook until smooth and thickened, about 1 minute. Remove from the heat and swirl in the remaining 1 tablespoon of butter.

13. Arrange the whole mushrooms in the center of the salmon. Spoon the sauce over and serve.

YIELD: 4 to 6 servings.

❧

Grilled Salmon and Tuna with Anchovy Butter

- 1 pound fillet of fresh tuna, available in fish markets and markets that sell Japanese products
- 1 pound fillet of fresh salmon
- 2 tablespoons olive oil
- Grilled onion slices (see following recipe)
- ¾ cup anchovy butter (see following recipe), at room temperature
- 12 whole anchovy fillets, optional

1. Preheat a charcoal grill to very hot.

2. Cut the tuna across the grain into six equal portions, each about ¾ inch thick.

3. Cut the salmon into six individual portions.

4. Combine the tuna and salmon in a mixing bowl and add the oil. Stir to coat the fish pieces with oil.

5. Put the fish pieces on the grill and cook for about 1 minute on one side. Turn and cook the fish on the other side for 1 to 2 minutes longer.

6. Scatter the onions (broken into rings) over a hot serving dish. Arrange the fish pieces over the onions. Smear the anchovy butter on top. Garnish, if desired, with whole anchovy fillets and serve.

YIELD: 6 servings.

GRILLED ONION SLICES

1. Preheat a charcoal grill to very hot. Trim off the ends of 3 or 4 medium-sized red onions. Peel the onions and cut into ¼-inch-thick slices. Put the slices in a bowl and add ¼ cup olive oil. Set aside until ready to cook.

2. Put the onion slices on the grill and cook for about 45 seconds. Turn them with a spatula or tongs. They will probably divide into rings. Cook until tender, 2 or 3 minutes, turning often.

YIELD: 6 servings.

ANCHOVY BUTTER FOR GRILLED FISH

- 3 whole anchovies packed in salt (see Note), or use 6 to 8 anchovy fillets packed in oil and drained
- 6 tablespoons butter, at room temperature
- Juice of ½ lemon
- Freshly ground black pepper to taste

1. If anchovies packed in salt are used, fillet them with the fingers. Discard the bones. Rinse the anchovy halves under cold running water and pat dry. Pound the fillets, whether packed in salt or oil, in a mortar and pestle or chop as finely as possible.

2. Put the anchovies in a small bowl and add the butter, lemon juice and pepper. Blend well.

YIELD: ¾ cup.

Note: Anchovies packed in salt are available in many specialty shops where imported Italian and Greek groceries are sold.

The availability of shad in this country usually begins early in February in the rivers around Florida. The fish travels up the Altamaha and Ogeechee rivers in Georgia, through the waters of the Carolinas, then the Chesapeake and the Delaware and, eventually, it is found in some unpolluted sections of the Hudson (shad will neither swim nor spawn in polluted waters for lack of oxygen). The season ends in Connecticut near the end of May. So we always take advantage of the short season for this glorious fish and its roe. One of the best preparations for shad roe is to be found at times on the menu of La Caravelle in Manhattan, listed as les quatres oeufs au beurre blanc.

L'Alose Marinée aux Herbes

GRILLED MARINATED SHAD WITH HERBS

- 1 boneless fillet of shad
- Salt to taste, if desired
- Freshly ground black pepper to taste
- 2 tablespoons olive oil
- 2 tablespoons lemon juice
- ½ teaspoon finely crumbled bay leaf
- ½ teaspoon dried thyme
- ¼ teaspoon paprika
- Lemon wedges for garnish

1. Put the fillet on a platter and sprinkle it with salt and pepper. Add the oil and turn the fish to coat it.

2. Add the lemon juice, bay leaf and thyme and spread around. Cover and let stand for 1 hour.

3. Preheat the broiler to high.

4. Remove the shad from the platter and arrange it skin side down in a baking dish. Pour the marinade into a small saucepan and keep it warm. Sprinkle the fish with paprika and brush the top to coat it evenly. Place under the broiler about 4 inches from the source of heat and broil for about 5 minutes. Cut the fish in half lengthwise.

5. Transfer the fish to two hot serving dishes. Spoon a little of the marinade over each serving. Serve with lemon wedges.

YIELD: 2 servings.

Filet d'Alose Riviera

SHAD WITH MUSHROOMS AND TOMATOES

- 1 boneless fillet of shad
- Salt to taste, if desired
- Freshly ground black pepper to taste
- ¼ cup milk
- ½ cup flour
- ¼ cup corn, peanut or vegetable oil
- ¼ pound mushrooms
- 3 tablespoons olive oil
- 1 teaspoon finely minced garlic
- 1 tablespoon butter
- ½ cup imported canned tomatoes, crushed
- 2 tablespoons finely chopped parsley

1. Split the fillet in half crosswise. Sprinkle the pieces with salt and pepper and place in a small flat basin of milk. Remove the fish pieces from the milk without draining. Put the pieces in flour to coat on both sides.

2. Heat the corn or other oil in a frying pan and add the fish pieces skin side up. Cook 1½ to 2 minutes over high heat, or until golden brown on one side. Carefully turn the pieces and continue cooking on the second side over moderately low heat for 3 to 4 minutes. Transfer the pieces to two warm serving plates.

3. Slice the mushrooms thin. There should be about 2 cups.

4. Heat the olive oil in a skillet and add the mushrooms and salt and pepper to taste. Cook, stirring, for about 2 minutes. Add the garlic and butter and swirl and stir around until the butter melts.

5. Meanwhile, heat the tomatoes in a small saucepan and cook down for about 5 minutes.

6. Spoon half of the tomatoes onto each fish piece. Pour mushrooms over and sprinkle with parsley.

YIELD: 2 servings.

❧

La Caravelle's Les Quatre Oeufs au Beurre Blanc

SHAD ROE WITH CAVIAR

- 1 pair shad roe
- 6 tablespoons butter
- 2 tablespoons finely chopped shallots
- Salt to taste, if desired
- Freshly ground black pepper to taste
- ½ cup dry white wine
- ¼ cup heavy cream
- 1 teaspoon lemon juice
- 2 tablespoons sieved hard-boiled egg
- 1 tablespoon black caviar, optional
- 1 tablespoon salmon roe (red caviar)
- 2 tablespoons finely chopped parsley

1. Preheat the oven to 400 degrees.

2. Trim off excess membranes from the roe. Do not split the roe, although they might separate as they cook. Puncture the roe in several places with a pin.

3. Rub a small baking dish with 2 tablespoons of butter. Sprinkle the dish with shallots, salt and pepper to taste. Arrange the roe over the shallots and sprinkle with salt and pepper. Pour the wine over the roe.

4. Place the dish on the stove and bring to the boil. Transfer to the oven and bake for 8 to 10 minutes, depending on the size of the roe.

5. Remove roe to a serving dish and cover with foil to keep warm.

6. Cook down the liquid in the baking dish until it is reduced to about 3 tablespoons. Add the cream and bring to a rolling boil. Gradually add the remaining 4 tablespoons of butter, stirring rapidly with a wire whisk. As the butter starts to melt, remove the sauce from the heat but continue stirring vigorously until the butter is melted.

7. Strain the sauce into a small saucepan, pressing the solids to extract as much liquid as possible. Add the lemon juice, sieved egg, black caviar and salmon roe.

8. If the shad roe has not split, divide in two carefully. Transfer the roe to two hot plates. Spoon half of the sauce over each serving. Sprinkle with parsley and serve hot.

YIELD: 2 servings.

Perhaps we find portents in curious places but why is it that trout figures more often in English poetry than any other fish? Lord Byron spoke of "trout not stale." And trout, according to Shakespeare, "must be caught with tickling." Tennyson spoke of "here and there a lusty trout." We prefer to think it has more to do with the elegant taste of the fish than with iambic pentameter and such.

We would by all means nominate trout as one of the supreme beings of lakes, creeks and rivers. It has a sweet delicacy of flavor, an uncommon texture that makes it, in our minds, the rival of carp, tuna, cod and weakfish (which sometimes goes by the fancy name of sea trout, yet is unrelated to the true trout) and other fine foods with fins that swim in ocean waters.

Truite Farcie aux Crevettes

SHRIMP-STUFFED TROUT

- 2 tablespoons butter
- 3 tablespoons finely chopped shallots
- ¾ cup thinly sliced mushrooms
- ½ pound raw shrimp, shelled, deveined and finely chopped
- ½ cup plus 1 tablespoon dry white wine
- ½ cup fine fresh bread crumbs
- 1 egg
- 2 tablespoons finely chopped parsley
- Salt and freshly ground black pepper to taste
- 4 5-ounce or slightly larger boneless, ready-to-stuff trout (see Note)
- ½ cup heavy cream
- Finely chopped parsley for garnish

1. Preheat the oven to 400 degrees.

2. Melt 1 tablespoon of the butter in a small skillet and add 2 tablespoons of the shallots and all of the mushrooms. Cook briefly and add the chopped shrimp. Stir and cook for about 10 seconds. Stir in 1 tablespoon wine.

3. Spoon and scrape the mixture into a small bowl. Add the bread crumbs, egg and 2 tablespoons parsley. Add salt and pepper to taste and blend well.

4. Open up the trout for stuffing. Stuff each with equal portions of the mixture. Tie each trout with string in two places. Sprinkle the trout with salt and pepper.

5. Butter a shallow baking dish with the remaining tablespoon of butter. Scatter the remaining tablespoon of shallots over it. Arrange the stuffed trout in the dish. Bring the remaining ½ cup wine to the boil in a small saucepan, then pour it around the fish.

6. Place the trout in the oven and bake for 15 minutes.

7. Pour the cream around the trout and continue baking for 5 minutes longer. Baste occasionally with the cream. Remove the string and serve sprinkled with chopped parsley.

YIELD: 4 servings.

Note: Boneless, ready to stuff trout can sometimes be purchased frozen. If the trout are whole, have them boned by the fishman.

There are scores, if not hundreds, of fish swimming around in American waters that are all but unknown on the American table, often because fishermen toss them back into the sea. But some are startlingly good and can be purchased in season in fish markets. One of the greatest and tastiest fish known to man is skate, known in France as raie. Raie au beurre noir, or skate with black butter sauce, is a supreme invention. Another fish with excellent texture and flavor is known variously as bellyfish, monkfish or anglerfish. Bellyfish is delectable in fish soups, and we recently cooked bellyfish meunière and in red wine and both were excellent.

Raie au Beurre Noir

SKATE WITH BLACK BUTTER

- 2 poached skate wings (see following instructions)
- ½ cup white vinegar
- 1 teaspoon crushed black peppercorns
- 2 bay leaves
- 2 sprigs fresh thyme, or ½ teaspoon dried
- Salt and freshly ground black pepper to taste
- 8 tablespoons butter
- 4 tablespoons drained capers
- 1 tablespoon red wine vinegar
- 2 tablespoons finely chopped parsley

1. After draining and trimming the skate as indicated in the preparation instructions, transfer the wings to a wide utensil that will hold them in one layer.

2. Add water to cover, white vinegar, peppercorns, bay leaves and thyme. Bring just to a gentle, rolling boil and turn off the heat.

3. Drain the fish and transfer it to a hot platter. Sprinkle with salt and pepper.

4. Melt the butter in a large skillet and cook, shaking the skillet and swirling the butter around over high heat. When the butter becomes quite brown, watch it carefully. Continue cooking until the butter starts to become a very dark brown (black). Add the capers and wine vinegar. Shake the skillet to blend and pour this over the skate. Sprinkle with parsley and serve with hot boiled potatoes.

YIELD: 4 servings.

HOW TO PREPARE SKATE FOR COOKING

Leave the skate wings whole; cut off and discard the connecting tail portion. Put the wings in a large, wide utensil and add water to cover. Bring the fish to the boil and simmer for 2 minutes. Drain quickly and run under cold water until cold.

Remove the wings to a flat surface lined with absorbent paper toweling. Using a knife, gently and carefully scrape away the skin from one side. Discard it. Turn the wings and scrape away the skin from the second side. Also scrape away any red streaks across the center of one side.

Using a heavy knife, chop and trim off the tips of the outside bones that rim the wings. Return the wings to the utensil and refrigerate until ready to use.

Lotte Meunière

SAUTÉED BELLYFISH OR MONKFISH

- 10 thin slices skinless, boneless bellyfish fillets, cut on the bias, about 1 pound
- Salt and freshly ground black pepper to taste
- ¼ cup flour
- 2 tablespoons milk
- ¼ cup peanut, vegetable or corn oil
- 8 thin seedless lemon slices
- Juice of 1 lemon
- 4 tablespoons butter
- 2 tablespoons finely chopped parsley

1. Sprinkle the fish slices on both sides with salt and pepper.

2. Dredge in flour and shake off any excess. Dip the slices in milk, turning them to moisten all over.

3. Dredge the slices in flour again, shaking off any excess.

4. Heat the oil in a skillet large enough to hold the slices in one layer. Add the slices.

5. Cook over high heat for 3 or 4 minutes, or until golden brown on one side. Turn to cook the other side about 2 minutes, or until golden brown. Transfer the pieces to a warm platter.

6. Pour off the fat from the skillet and discard. Wash and dry the skillet.

7. Garnish the cooked slices with lemon slices. Sprinkle with lemon juice. Melt the butter in the skillet, swirling it around until it starts to turn brown. Pour this sauce over the fish. Sprinkle with chopped parsley and serve.

YIELD: 4 servings.

Lotte en Matelote

BELLYFISH OR MONKFISH IN RED WINE

- 2 pounds skinless, boneless bellyfish
- 4 tablespoons butter
- ½ cup chopped onion
- 2 tablespoons coarsely chopped shallots
- ⅓ cup coarsely chopped carrot
- 2 teaspoons finely minced garlic
- 4 tablespoons flour
- 3 cups dry red wine
- 1 cup fish stock (see recipe page 419)
- 4 sprigs fresh parsley
- 1 bay leaf
- 3 whole cloves
- 1 sprig fresh thyme, or ½ teaspoon dried
- 6 whole black peppercorns
- Salt to taste
- ½ pound mushrooms, thinly sliced or quartered, about 3 cups
- Freshly ground black pepper to taste
- 2 tablespoons finely chopped shallots
- 1 tablespoon Cognac

1. Take care that all the fish bones are trimmed away, including random small fish bones. Cut the fish into 2-inch cubes and set aside.

2. Melt 2 tablespoons of the butter in a heavy saucepan and add the onion, coarsely chopped shallots, carrot and half the garlic. Cook, stirring occasionally, until the onion is wilted.

3. Sprinkle the vegetables with half the flour, stirring with a wire whisk. Add the wine and fish stock, stirring rapidly with the whisk.

4. Add the parsley, bay leaf, cloves, thyme, peppercorns and salt to taste. Bring to the boil and let the sauce simmer for about 30 minutes.

5. Meanwhile, melt the remaining 2 tablespoons of butter in a large skillet or casserole and add the mushrooms and salt and pepper to taste. Cook, stirring, for about 2 minutes and add the finely chopped shallots and remaining garlic. Add the fish and stir briefly. Sprinkle with the remaining flour and stir to coat the pieces. Strain the sauce over the fish and stir. Discard the solids. Add salt and pepper to taste. Cover closely and simmer over low heat for about 30 minutes.

6. Add the Cognac and stir. Serve piping hot.

YIELD: 6 servings.

We were recently feasting on an assortment of skewered foods—beef, kidneys and seafood—hot off a charcoal grill and we were discussing with Charles Chevillot the principles and virtues of grilling and barbecuing. He is a scion of the family that has owned the Hôtel de la Poste in Burgundy and is the proprietor of two estimable restaurants in Manhattan, La Petite Ferme and Les Tournebroches, the latter of which specializes in grilled dishes. "The trouble with a ketchup sauce," he said, "is that it tends to disguise flavors, so much so that you can't taste the natural flavor of the foods." When he grills meats or seafood en brochette, he does not marinate the foods even briefly. He coats the foods lightly with a neutral oil simply to prevent them from sticking. Salt and pepper are added at the last moment. He prefers white pepper to black pepper since it is less forceful in flavor. And he serves the grilled foods with béarnaise sauce.

Brochettes de Fruits de Mer

SEAFOOD ON SKEWERS

12 jumbo shrimp, peeled and deveined
8 large sea scallops
16 1½-inch cubes bellyfish or monkfish, about ½ pound
16 1½-inch cubes swordfish, about ½ pound
2 tablespoons peanut, vegetable or corn oil
Salt and freshly ground pepper to taste
Sauce béarnaise (see recipe page 401)

1. Heat the grill.

2. On each of four metal skewers, arrange alternately 3 shrimp, 2 scallops, 4 pieces of bellyfish and 4 pieces of swordfish.

3. Place the skewered foods in a flat dish and brush all over with oil.

4. Place the brochettes on the grill and cook for 4 to 5 minutes on one side. Sprinkle all over with salt and pepper to taste. Turn the skewers and cook for 4 to 5 minutes on the other side. Turn often as necessary, but take care not to overcook. Serve immediately with béarnaise sauce.

YIELD: 4 servings.

Paul Prudhomme's Seafood Gumbo

- ¾ cup peanut, vegetable or corn oil
- 1 cup flour
- 2 tablespoons butter
- 3½ cups finely chopped onion
- 3 cups finely chopped green peppers
- 2 cups finely chopped celery
- 1 tablespoon finely minced garlic
- 1½ pounds Polish sausage (kielbasa), cut into ½-inch cubes (see Note)
- ¼ teaspoon dried oregano
- ½ teaspoon dried thyme
- 2 bay leaves
- ½ teaspoon cayenne pepper
- ¼ teaspoon freshly ground white pepper
- ½ teaspoon freshly ground black pepper
- Salt, if desired
- 2 cups chopped fresh or canned imported tomatoes
- 2 quarts seafood stock (see following recipe)
- 4 live blue crabs, optional
- 2 pounds shrimp, shelled and deveined (use the shells for seafood stock)
- 1 pound lump crabmeat

1. Put the oil and flour in a heavy kettle. Cook, stirring with a wire whisk or flat wooden spoon, until the flour goes through several changes of color: beige, light brown, dark brown, light red and a slightly darker red. You must keep stirring constantly. The cooking will take 5 minutes or slightly longer. This is a roux. Set aside.

2. Melt the butter in a saucepan and add the onion, green peppers, celery and garlic. Cook, stirring, until the vegetables are wilted. Add the sausage and stir.

3. Add the oregano, thyme, bay leaves, cayenne, white and black peppers, salt to taste, tomatoes and seafood stock. Bring to the boil and simmer for 15 minutes.

4. Add the tomato and sausage mixture to the roux. Bring to the boil, stirring, and cook for 1 hour.

5. If the blue crabs are used, pull off and discard the apron at the base on the underside of each crab. Cut the crabs in half and pull off and discard the

spongy "dead man's fingers." Cut each crab half in two and add to the kettle. Simmer for 1 minute.

6. Add the shrimp and crabmeat. Stir. Cover and set aside for 15 minutes. Serve with rice.

YIELD: 8 or more servings.

Note: To be genuinely authentic, the sausage should be a smoked andouillete, which is common in Louisiana.

SEAFOOD STOCK

- 4 pounds fish bones, preferably with head on but gills removed
- 3 quarts water
- 1½ cups coarsely chopped onion
- 1½ cups coarsely chopped celery
- 2 cups cored, coarsely chopped tomatoes
- Shells from 2 pounds of shrimp

1. Combine all the ingredients in a kettle. Bring to the boil. Cook the stock down until about 2 quarts of liquid are left.

2. Cook for 5 to 7 hours longer, but always keep the liquid replenished so that it remains at approximately 2 quarts. Strain and discard the solids.

YIELD: 2 quarts.

Seafood Jambalaya

- 1 pound sausages, preferably kielbasa, cut into 1-inch pieces
- 1 pound smoked ham, cut into ½-inch cubes
- 2 cups finely chopped green pepper
- 1 cup finely chopped celery
- 2 cups finely chopped onion
- ½ cup tomato purée
- 1 cup ripe tomatoes, or use imported canned tomatoes
- 7 cups fish stock (see recipe page 419)
- ¾ teaspoon dried thyme
- 1 teaspoon dried oregano
- 1 teaspoon freshly ground white pepper
- 1½ teaspoons cayenne pepper
- ¾ teaspoon freshly ground black pepper
- ½ teaspoon dried basil
- Salt to taste
- 1½ cups raw rice
- 35 large shrimp, peeled and deveined, about 2 pounds
- 2 cups shucked oysters
- 1 pound crabmeat, picked over
- 1 cup chopped scallions

1. Heat a large skillet and add the sausage pieces. Cook over high heat for about 10 minutes, stirring often. Add the ham and continue cooking, stirring often, for about 10 minutes.

2. Add the green pepper, celery and onion. The vegetables will stick to the bottom of the skillet and turn brown. Scrape up this brown part as it cooks. This is essential to the flavor. Cook for about 15 minutes, stirring often.

3. Add the tomato purée and cook, stirring, about 3 minutes. Add the tomatoes and cook, scraping the brown particles on the bottom.

4. Add the fish stock and bring to the boil. Add the thyme, oregano, white pepper, cayenne, black pepper, basil and salt. Cook over low heat for about 1 hour.

5. Add the rice and cover. Cook for about 15 minutes and add the shrimp, oysters and crabmeat. Stir to blend well.

6. Cook for 5 minutes. Add the scallions and stir them in. Serve.

YIELD: 8 or more servings.

One of the most gratifying and interesting of all dishes in the nouvelle cuisine is one I first dined on about fifteen years ago at the Taillevent restaurant in Paris. It is a cervelas aux fruits de mer, or seafood sausage, poached and served hot and sliced with a white butter sauce. To me this is a dish of awesome inspiration. This is Pierre Franey's and my version.

Cervelas aux Fruits de Mer

SEAFOOD SAUSAGE

- ¾ pound fresh bay or sea scallops
- ¾ pound striped bass, bellyfish, sole or freshwater fish, such as yellow pike
- Salt and freshly ground black pepper to taste
- 1 egg yolk
- Dash of Tabasco sauce
- ¼ teaspoon grated nutmeg
- 1 cup heavy cream
- 6 medium-sized shrimp, shelled and deveined
- ½ tablespoon butter
- 1 tablespoon finely chopped shallots
- ¾ cup cooked lobster meat, cut into ½-inch cubes
- ¼ cup finely chopped white part of leeks
- Prepared sausage casing (see Note)
- Beurre blanc (see recipe page 400) if dish is to be served hot
- Sauce verte (see recipe page 403) if dish is to be served cold

1. Cut ½ pound of the scallops in half. Cut ½ pound of the fish into 1-inch cubes. Put these in the container of a food processor and add salt, pepper, egg yolk, Tabasco sauce and nutmeg.

2. Start blending while pouring the cream gradually through the funnel of the processer.

3. Spoon and scrape the mixture into a mixing bowl. Chill thoroughly.

4. Cut the remaining scallops and fish into ½-inch cubes.

5. Cut the shrimp into ½-inch cubes.

6. Melt the butter in a small skillet and add the shallots. Cook briefly and add the cubed scallops and fish. Cook briefly until the fish loses its raw look and any liquid has evaporated. Add the shrimp and cook, stirring, about 10 seconds. Place a sieve in a mixing bowl and pour the mixture in. Let drain.

7. Combine the shrimp and fish with the lobster and chill thoroughly.

8. Combine the chilled lobster mixture, the chilled scallop and fish mixture and the leeks. Blend well.

9. Outfit a hand or electric sausage machine with a sausage-stuffing cylinder. Slip a 3-foot length of prepared sausage casing over the cylinder. Grind the seafood mixture, holding the casing to permit free entry of the filling into the casing. Fill the casing. When the filling has been added, pinch off the casing and make a knot at each end.

10. Put the sausage ring into a casserole with cold water to cover and salt to taste. Bring to the boil, then reduce the heat and cook the sausage in barely simmering water for 4 minutes; turn the sausage in the water and let simmer for about 4 minutes longer. Remove from the heat and let stand without draining for 10 minutes.

11. Drain and serve hot or cold, sliced on the bias. Serve hot with beurre blanc or cold with sauce verte.

YIELD: 6 to 8 servings.

Note: The sausage casings we used in preparing this recipe were natural beef round casings, 40 to 43 millimeters. See instructions on page 230 for preparing the casings.

Poo Chah

DEEP-FRIED CRAB AND PORK BALLS

- 5 cloves garlic with a few peelings left on
- 3 stem or root ends (not the leaves) of fresh coriander
- 2½ cups thinly sliced mushrooms
- Salt and freshly ground black pepper to taste
- ¾ pound ground pork
- ½ pound lump or backfin crabmeat
- 2 tablespoons fish sauce (see Note)
- ½ teaspoon monosodium glutamate, optional
- 3 eggs
- Oil for deep frying

1. Combine the garlic, coriander stems and ½ cup mushrooms in the container of an electric blender or food processor and blend.

2. Scrape the mixture into a mixing bowl and add the salt and pepper. Add the pork and blend slightly.

3. Add the crabmeat.

4. Blend the remaining mushrooms in a food processor until finely chopped. Do not overblend or they will become mushy. Add them to the crab mixture.

5. Add the fish sauce and monosodium glutamate and blend well with the hands. Shape into 28 or 30 round balls.

6. Line one or more steamers (such as a Chinese bamboo steamer) with a round of aluminum foil. Arrange the crab balls over each layer and cover. Steam over simmering water for about 5 minutes. Remove and let cool.

7. Beat the eggs until well blended. Drop the crab balls into the egg mixture and coat well.

8. Heat the oil for deep frying and drop the crab balls in, one at a time. Cook in batches about 25 seconds in all. Drain on paper toweling.

9. When all the balls are fried, dip the fingers into the egg batter and quickly scatter the batter into the oil. The batter will stick together. Cook a few seconds until brown and remove with a strainer. Drain well and use as a garnish for the crab balls.

YIELD: 10 servings.

Note: Fish sauce, called nuoc mam or nam pla, is available in Oriental groceries and supermarkets.

Crabes Farcis

CRAB SHELLS STUFFED WITH CREAMED CRAB AND TARRAGON

- 4 tablespoons butter
- 2 tablespoons flour
- 1 cup milk
- Salt to taste, if desired
- Freshly ground black pepper to taste
- ⅛ teaspoon grated nutmeg
- ¾ cup heavy cream
- ¼ to ½ cup edible, nonmeaty parts of crab such as coral or liver from freshly picked-over crabs, optional
- 3 tablespoons finely chopped shallots
- 1 pound fresh crabmeat (see following recipe), or canned lump crabmeat, picked over
- 2 tablespoons Cognac
- 1 tablespoon finely chopped fresh tarragon, or 1 teaspoon dried
- 4 to 6 crab shells for stuffing, or use individual heatproof ramekins
- Tarragon sprigs for garnish

1. Preheat the oven to 400 degrees.

2. Melt half the butter in a saucepan and add the flour, stirring with a wire whisk. Add the milk, stirring vigorously with the whisk. When thickened and smooth, add the salt, pepper and nutmeg. Let simmer, stirring often, about 5 minutes. Stir in the cream and the edible, nonmeaty portions of the crabs, if used. If the nonmeaty parts of the crabs are used, strain this sauce through a sieve, pushing to extract as much liquid as possible from the solids. Discard the solids.

3. Meanwhile, melt the remaining 2 tablespoons of butter in a saucepan and add the shallots. Cook briefly, stirring, and add the crabmeat. Do not cook, but stir gently just to heat through. Add the Cognac and tarragon and stir gently to blend.

4. Add half of the sauce to the crabmeat and blend.

5. Fill the crab shells with the crab mixture. Place in the oven and bake for 5 minutes. Bring the remaining sauce to the boil and spoon equal portions of it over the stuffed crabs. Garnish each serving with tarragon sprigs. Serve immediately.

YIELD: 4 servings.

CRABES POCHÉS
Poached Crabs

- 4 large hard-shell blue crabs, about 1¼ pounds each
- 1 quart water
- ½ teaspoon ground allspice
- 4 whole cloves
- 1 tablespoon whole black peppercorns
- 4 hot dried red peppers
- 1 teaspoon celery seeds
- Salt to taste, if desired

1. Set the crabs aside until ready to cook.

2. Put the water, allspice, cloves, peppercorns, peppers, celery seeds and salt in a kettle and bring to a boil.

3. Put in the crabs and cover closely. Cook for 10 minutes. Drain and set the crabs aside until cool enough to handle.

YIELD: 4 boiled crabs that, when picked over, will yield a pound of meat plus more edible, nonmeaty portions such as the coral, liver and roe.

❧

Homard à la Nage
LOBSTER AND VEGETABLES IN COURT BOUILLON

- 1 small onion
- 2 stalks heart of celery
- 1 small carrot
- 1 cup thinly sliced green part of leeks
- ½ cup coarsely chopped onion
- ½ cup coarsely chopped celery
- ½ cup coarsely chopped carrot
- 2 cups water
- 1 cup dry white wine
- ½ teaspoon dried thyme
- 1 bay leaf
- 6 sprigs fresh parsley
- 6 whole black peppercorns, crushed
- Salt to taste
- 2 1½-pound live lobsters
- 2 tablespoons butter

1. Peel the onion and cut it lengthwise in half. Cut each half crosswise into very thin slices. There should be about ½ cup. Set aside.

2. Trim the celery and cut it crosswise into ⅛-inch slices. Set aside.

3. Trim and peel the carrot. Use a lemon peeler to make lengthwise ridges around the carrot. Cut the carrot into thin rounds. Set aside.

4. Combine in a large kettle half of the leeks, the coarsely chopped onion, coarsely chopped celery, coarsely chopped carrot, water, wine, thyme, bay leaf, 2 parsley sprigs, peppercorns and salt. Cover and bring to the boil. Simmer for 15 minutes.

5. Add the lobsters and cover closely. Cook for exactly 7 minutes.

6. Remove the lobsters. Strain the cooking liquid. Discard the solids.

7. Put the thinly sliced onion, celery slices and carrot rounds in a saucepan. Add the remaining leeks. Add the strained cooking liquid. Bring to the boil and cook over high heat for about 5 minutes.

8. Split the lobsters in half. Remove and discard the tough sac near the eyes. Crack the claws. Arrange a lobster half and 1 claw in a soup bowl.

9. Pluck off enough small bits of parsley leaves from each of the remaining sprigs to make ½ cup.

10. To the vegetables and liquid add the butter bit by bit, swirling it into the sauce. Cook for about 1 minute. Add the parsley bits.

11. Pour the sauce over the lobster and serve hot.

YIELD: Four servings.

Under the old rules of French haute cuisine, one rarely heard of a blanquette that was not made with veal or chicken. Nouvelle cuisine, in which lobster is a prized ingredient, has no such rules, and thus this adaptation of a recipe by Serge Coulon, proprietor of the Serge Restaurant in La Rochelle, France, who is one of the many new young chefs to visit America. Crème fraîche, of course, is another hallmark of the nouvelle cuisine.

Blanquette de Homard

LOBSTER AND MUSHROOMS IN A WINE AND CREAM SAUCE

- 4 lobsters, about 1¼ pounds each
- 12 small shallots
- 16 small mushrooms
- 2 tablespoons olive oil
- Salt and freshly ground black pepper to taste
- 4 tablespoons butter
- 10 sprigs fresh parsley
- 1 bay leaf
- 2 sprigs fresh thyme, or ½ teaspoon dried
- 1 cup dry white wine, preferably a Muscadet
- ⅓ cup Cognac
- 1 cup crème fraîche (see recipe page 407)

1. Place the lobsters on their backs and quickly sever the spinal cord by plunging a sharp knife through to the back shell where the body and tail of the lobster are joined.

2. Chop off the main claws and pincers of each lobster. Put the pieces in a bowl.

3. Chop off the tail of each lobster. Chop each tail section crosswise into three pieces. Add these to the bowl.

4. Cut each carcass in half lengthwise. Remove and discard the tough sac near the eyes of the lobsters. Remove and set aside the coral and liver of each lobster in a separate small bowl. Add the carcass pieces to the claws and tail.

5. Peel the shallots and set them aside. Trim off the stems of each mushroom. If the mushrooms are small, leave them whole; if large, cut them in half.

6. Heat the oil in a large, heavy casserole or Dutch oven. When it starts to smoke, add all the lobster pieces. Do not add the coral and liver. Sprinkle with salt and pepper. Cook, stirring often, until the lobster shells turn quite red, about 5 minutes. Remove the tail pieces and set aside in a bowl.

7. Transfer the other pieces of lobster to another bowl and set aside.

8. When cool enough to handle, remove the meat from the lobster tails and set aside.

9. Crack all the other meaty pieces of lobster and remove the meat. Add this to the tail meat.

10. Melt the butter in a clean, heavy casserole or Dutch oven and add the peeled shallots. Cook, stirring briefly.

11. Add the mushrooms and lobster meat.

12. Tie the parsley sprigs, bay leaf and thyme in a cheesecloth bundle and add it. Cover closely and cook for about 2 minutes. Uncover, add the wine and Cognac. Bring to the boil. Cook over high heat for 10 minutes.

13. Add the crème fraîche and cook over high heat for 5 minutes.

14. Meanwhile, place a sieve in a mixing bowl. Pour in the coral and liver and push through the sieve.

15. Remove the lobster preparation from the heat and remove the herb bundle. Stir in the coral and liver. Serve immediately.

YIELD: 4 servings.

Homards Grillés à l'Estragon

BROILED LOBSTERS WITH TARRAGON

- 4 lobsters, about 1¾ pounds each
- ½ cup fine fresh bread crumbs
- 4 tablespoons butter at room temperature
- 2 tablespoons finely chopped fresh tarragon, or 1 tablespoon dried
- ¼ cup heavy cream
- Salt and freshly ground black pepper to taste
- ⅓ cup peanut, vegetable or corn oil
- Parsley sprigs for garnish
- ¼ pound butter, melted
- Lemon wedges

1. Preheat the broiler.

2. Place each lobster, shell side up, on a flat, heavy surface. Plunge a sharp heavy kitchen knife into the midsection of the lobster where the tail and body meet, then cut the lobster in half lengthwise, cutting first through the tail, then through the body. Discard the tough sac near the eyes.

3. Remove the soft liver and coral from the body of the lobsters and put it in a small mixing bowl. Set aside.

4. Arrange the lobster halves cut side up on a baking dish.

5. To the coral and liver add the bread crumbs, butter, tarragon, cream and salt and pepper to taste. Blend well.

6. Spoon equal portions of the filling into the cavity of each lobster half.

7. Sprinkle each lobster half with salt and pepper. Brush the tops of each lobster half, filling included, with oil.

8. Place the lobsters under the broiler, about 6 inches from the source of heat. It may be necessary to use two racks to do this. In that case, place one baking dish under the broiler about 6 inches from the source of heat. Place the other on a second rack below. Bake and broil, alternating the placement of the dishes on the racks, for about 5 minutes.

9. Turn the oven temperature to 400 degrees and continue baking for 10 minutes longer. Garnish with parsley sprigs. Serve with melted butter and lemon wedges.

YIELD: 4 to 8 servings.

Homards Farcis Clarence

CURRIED STUFFED LOBSTERS

- 4 cooked lobsters, 1¼ to 1½ pounds each (see following recipe)
- 2 tablespoons butter
- 2 tablespoons flour
- 1 tablespoon curry powder
- 1 cup milk
- 1¼ cups heavy cream
- Salt to taste, if desired
- Freshly ground black pepper to taste
- 1⅓ cups cooked rice
- ½ cup thinly sliced truffles, optional (see Note)

1. Preheat the oven to 400 degrees.

2. Remove the large lobster claws. Crack the claws and remove the meat. Cut the meat into bite-sized pieces. Set aside in a bowl.

3. Cut the small feelers from the lobsters and put them in a bowl.

4. Split each lobster in half lengthwise. Discard the small, tough sac near the eyes. Remove the soft coral and liver and add them to the bowl with the feelers. Set aside.

5. Remove the tail meat from the lobsters. Cut it into bite-sized medallions. Add the medallions to the bowl with the claw meat. Set aside.

6. Arrange the lobster shells split side up on a baking sheet.

7. Melt the butter in a saucepan and add the flour and curry powder, stirring with a wire whisk. Add the milk, stirring with the whisk.

8. Scrape the coral and livers along with the feelers into the container of a food processor. Blend until coarsely fine. Pour and scrape the mixture into a saucepan and add the cream. Bring to the boil. Pour the mixture into a sieve, preferably the sort known in a French kitchen as a chinois. Pass it through, pressing with a wooden spoon to extract as much liquid from the solids as possible. Add this to the curry sauce, stirring. Discard the solids. Add salt and pepper to taste.

9. Spoon equal portions of the rice into each lobster shell. Add equal portions of the lobster meat blended with truffle slices. Spoon enough curry sauce over the top of each serving to cover. The remaining sauce will be served on the side. Place the lobsters in the oven and bake for about 5 minutes until piping hot. Serve the stuffed lobster halves with the remaining heated curry sauce on the side.

YIELD: 4 servings.

Note: Truffles are traditional in this recipe, but they are not essential for an excellent dish.

HOMARDS POCHÉS

Poached Lobsters

- 3 quarts water
- 1 bay leaf
- ½ teaspoon dried thyme
- ½ teaspoon whole black peppercorns
- Salt to taste, if desired
- 4 live lobsters, 1¼ to 1½ pounds each

Put the water, bay leaf, thyme, peppercorns and salt in a kettle and bring to the boil. Add the lobsters and cover with a tight-fitting lid. Let cook for about 10 minutes. Remove from the heat.

YIELD: 4 poached lobsters.

Lobster? Vanilla? It would seem to be one of the least compatible flavor liaisons conceivable. If the reflexive reaction to such a dish was a grimace, it was quickly dispelled when Alain Senderens, owner and chef of L'Archestrate in Paris, prepared a droll and captivating menu on a visit to our kitchen. Like many nouvelle cuisine dishes, this is a triumph of taste over logic.

Homards Rôtis à la Sauce Vanille

ROAST LOBSTERS WITH VANILLA SAUCE

- 5 tablespoons butter
- 2 tablespoons finely chopped shallots
- ¼ cup dry white wine
- 2 2-inch lengths plus 1 1-inch length of vanilla bean
- ½ cup fish stock (see recipe page 419)
- 1 cup heavy cream
- Salt and freshly ground black pepper to taste
- 4 live lobsters, 1½ pounds each
- 1 pound spinach
- 1 large bunch watercress

1. Preheat the oven to 525 degrees.

2. Put 1 tablespoon of the butter in a saucepan and add the shallots. Cook briefly, stirring. Add the wine and the 2-inch lengths of vanilla bean. Cook down, stirring, until the wine is almost evaporated. Add the fish stock and cook down over high heat, stirring, until reduced by half.

3. Add the cream and cook the mixture about 2 minutes, or until reduced to about 1 cup. Split the remaining piece of vanilla bean and add it.

4. Strain the sauce through a fine sieve, pressing with the back of a wooden spoon or rubber spatula to extract most of the juices from the solids. Discard the solids.

5. Return the sauce to a saucepan. Add salt and pepper to taste and bring to the boil. Remove from the heat and swirl in 2 tablespoons of butter.

6. Place the live lobsters close together in a casserole and place in the oven. Bake for 15 minutes.

7. Meanwhile, pick over the spinach to remove and discard any tough stems or blemished leaves. Pick over the watercress to remove the leaves. Discard the stems.

8. Melt the remaining 2 tablespoons of butter in a skillet and add the spinach and watercress. Cook, stirring, until wilted.

9. Split the hot lobsters lengthwise down the center. They will not be

fully cooked at this point. Arrange the halves split side up on a baking dish and return to the oven for about 1½ minutes.

10. Crack the claws and arrange them in another baking dish. Bake about 2 minutes.

11. Remove the meat from the lobster tails. Spoon the spinach into the center of a serving dish. Arrange the lobster tail meat over the spinach. Arrange the cracked claws around in a symmetrical pattern. Garnish, if desired, with one lobster carcass split in half. Spoon some of the sauce over the lobster tails and serve the rest on the side.

YIELD: 4 to 8 servings.

Homard à l'Américaine

LOBSTER IN A TOMATO, TARRAGON AND COGNAC SAUCE

- 3 1½-pound live lobsters
- Salt and freshly ground black pepper to taste
- ¼ cup peanut, vegetable or corn oil
- 4 tablespoons butter
- ½ cup finely minced onion
- ¼ cup finely minced shallots
- ¼ cup finely diced celery
- ½ cup finely diced carrot
- 1 teaspoon finely minced garlic
- 6 tablespoons Cognac
- ¼ cup dry white wine
- 1 cup chopped fresh or canned tomatoes
- 1 cup tomato purée
- 1 cup clam juice or fish stock
- 1 bay leaf
- ½ teaspoon dried thyme
- 1 tablespoon dried tarragon
- ¼ teaspoon cayenne pepper
- 10 sprigs fresh parsley
- 2 teaspoons finely chopped fresh tarragon, or 1 teaspoon dried

1. Kill the lobsters instantly by plunging a knife in the point where the tail and body meet. Then chop off the claws of each lobster and set aside in a large mixing bowl.

2. Chop off the tail of each lobster and add to the bowl.

3. Cut the carcass lengthwise in half. Remove and discard the tough sac near the eyes of the lobster. Scrape out and reserve all the coral and liver from the carcass. Put this in a small bowl. Chop the carcass pieces crosswise into 2-inch lengths and add these to the large mixing bowl. Sprinkle with salt and pepper to taste.

4. Heat the oil and 1 tablespoon of the butter in a large casserole or kettle. When it is hot and almost smoking, add the lobster pieces. Do not

add the coral and liver. Cook, shaking the casserole and stirring, for about 2 minutes. Cover and pour off the oil.

5. Uncover and add the onion, shallots, celery, carrot and garlic. Cook, stirring, for about 1 minute. Add 4 tablespoons of the Cognac and the wine, tomatoes, tomato purée, clam juice, bay leaf, thyme, 1 tablespoon dried tarragon, cayenne pepper and parsley sprigs. Cover and cook for 8 minutes.

6. Remove and reserve the large claws and tails. Set aside briefly.

7. Remove the other pieces of carcass and all other solids. Chop these pieces on a flat surface. Put the chopped pieces into a food mill (this cannot be done in a food processor) and press to extract as much liquid as possible. Add this to the sauce remaining in the casserole. Discard the solids. Cook this sauce down to exactly 2 cups.

8. Meanwhile, crack the claws and remove all the meat from the claws and the tails. Cut the meat into bite-sized morsels. Put them in a small casserole. Sprinkle with the remaining 2 tablespoons of Cognac. Ignite the Cognac and let the flame burn down. Add the sauce and stir.

9. Add 2 tablespoons of the butter to the reserved coral and liver. Blend thoroughly. Add this to the lobster in sauce. Add the chopped fresh tarragon. Heat, shaking the casserole and stirring. Swirl in the remaining tablespoon of butter and serve.

YIELD: 4 to 6 servings.

Moules Vinaigrette

MUSSELS VINAIGRETTE

- 6 quarts (6 pounds) mussels, well scrubbed
- 2 cups coarsely chopped red onion
- ½ teaspoon freshly ground black pepper
- Sauce vinaigrette (see following recipe)
- ½ cup finely chopped parsley

1. Put the mussels in a large, heavy metal casserole and scatter half the onions over all. Sprinkle with pepper. Do not add salt or liquid.

2. Put the casserole on the stove and cover. Cook over high heat for 6 to 10 minutes, or until the moment the steam starts to escape from the casserole. Shake the casserole so that the mussels are redistributed. Remove from the heat as soon as the mussels are open. Take care not to overcook or

the mussels will fall out of the shells. Pour off the cooking liquid immediately. Let stand, uncovered, until ready to serve.

3. When ready to serve, put the mussels in a large salad bowl and scatter the remaining onion over all.

4. Spoon the sauce over the mussels and toss with finely chopped parsley.

YIELD: 4 servings.

LA PETITE FERME'S SAUCE VINAIGRETTE

- 2 tablespoons prepared mustard, preferably imported Dijon or Düsseldorf
- 6 tablespoons red wine vinegar
- 6 tablespoons peanut oil
- 6 tablespoons olive oil
- Salt and freshly ground black pepper to taste

Spoon the mustard into a mixing bowl and add the vinegar. Start beating with a wire whisk and gradually beat in the oils. Add salt and pepper to taste.

YIELD: About 1¼ cups.

Moules Ravigote au Vermouth

MUSSELS IN OIL AND VINEGAR SAUCE WITH VERMOUTH

THE MUSSELS

- 3 pounds well-scrubbed, debearded mussels
- ½ cup finely chopped white onion
- 1 bay leaf
- 1 sprig fresh thyme, or ½ teaspoon dried
- 1 sprig fresh parsley
- ½ cup dry white wine
- Freshly ground black pepper to taste

THE SAUCE

- 2 tablespoons prepared mustard, preferably imported Dijon
- 4 tablespoons finely chopped red onion
- 2 tablespoons dry white vermouth
- 2 tablespoons red wine vinegar
- ½ cup corn oil
- Salt, if desired
- Freshly ground black pepper to taste
- 4 tablespoons finely chopped parsley

1. Combine the mussels, chopped onion, bay leaf, thyme, parsley, wine and pepper in a large kettle. Cover and bring to the simmer. Cook until mussels are opened, 5 minutes or less. Drain. When the mussels are cool enough to handle, remove the top shell. Arrange the mussels in a layer on a serving dish.

2. To make the sauce, put the mustard, onion, vermouth and vinegar in a mixing bowl. Gradually add the oil, beating constantly with a wire whisk. Add salt and pepper to taste.

3. Spoon the sauce over the mussels, sprinkle with the parsley and serve.

YIELD: 4 to 8 servings.

Whenever considering oysters, my thoughts turn to one of the finest books that I have encountered about a single food—*The Glorious Oyster,* printed in England and edited by Hector Bolitho.

One learns from the book, for example, that the oyster is the most tranquil of animals and can be rather eccentric. It tells of an oyster that learned to whistle, another that became a mousetrap, and it explains that in certain lands oysters grow on trees. It is their talent for laziness that makes them, as one expert put it, the most tender and delicate of seafoods.

Oysters, apparently, know no national boundaries, provided the land is surrounded by saltwater. And their culinary uses, of course, know no bounds. We enjoy them Southern style, coated with cornmeal and deep-fried, blended with spinach and turned into a French pâté destined to be served with a mushroom and white wine sauce, or in any of the following ways.

❧

Oysters Fried in Cornmeal

- 24 large, shucked oysters with their liquor
- ½ cup cornmeal, preferably yellow although white may be used
- ½ teaspoon freshly ground black pepper
- ⅛ teaspoon cayenne pepper
- ⅛ teaspoon paprika
- Salt to taste, if desired
- Corn, peanut or vegetable oil for deep frying

1. Drain the oysters briefly.

2. Combine the cornmeal, black pepper, cayenne pepper, paprika and salt. Blend well.

3. Heat the oil to 375 degrees.

4. Dredge the oysters in the cornmeal mixture. Drop them, a few at a time, into the hot fat and cook, stirring often, until they are golden brown all over, less than 2 minutes depending on size. Do not overcook. Remove and drain.

5. Let the fat return to the proper temperature before adding successive batches. Serve, if desired, with tartar sauce, mayonnaise, or, Southern style, with tomato ketchup flavored with Worcestershire sauce, a dash of Tabasco and lemon juice.

YIELD: 2 servings.

Pâté Chaude aux Huîtres et Épinards

OYSTER AND SPINACH PÂTÉ

- 2 pounds fresh spinach in bulk, or 2 10-ounce packages of spinach in plastic
- 4 tablespoons butter plus butter for greasing the pan
- 1 cup finely chopped onion
- ½ teaspoon finely minced garlic
- 2 cups finely chopped heart of celery
- 1 cup heavy cream
- 3 cups fine fresh bread crumbs
- 3 eggs, lightly beaten
- Salt to taste, if desired
- Freshly ground black pepper to taste
- ⅛ teaspoon grated nutmeg
- 1 cup coarsely chopped drained oysters
- Sauce bonne femme (see recipe page 403), optional

1. Preheat the oven to 375 degrees.

2. Rinse the spinach well. Tear off and discard any tough stems and blemished leaves. Set aside.

3. Melt the 4 tablespoons of butter in a large skillet and add the onion, garlic and celery. Cook, stirring, until the mixture is wilted. Add the spinach and cook until the spinach is wilted.

4. Add the cream and continue cooking, stirring often, for about 5 minutes. Put the mixture into a mixing bowl. Add the bread crumbs, eggs, salt, pepper, nutmeg and oysters. Blend thoroughly.

5. Butter a loaf pan measuring about 9 by 5 by 2¾ inches. Pour in the spinach and oyster mixture and smooth over the top.

6. Set the loaf pan in a larger pan of hot water. Bring the water to the boil on top of the stove. Place in the oven and bake for 1 hour. Serve, if desired, with sauce bonne femme.

YIELD: 6 to 8 servings.

Huîtres Chaudes aux Blancs de Poireaux

HOT OYSTERS WITH LEEKS

- 18 oysters in the shell
- 2 leeks
- 4 tablespoons butter
- Salt and freshly ground black pepper to taste
- 2 teaspoons water
- ¼ cup finely chopped shallots
- ¼ cup red wine vinegar
- ½ cup plus 2 tablespoons white wine

1. Preheat the oven to 350 degrees.

2. Open the oysters, reserving their liquor and half of the shells. Set the shells aside. Put the oysters and their liquor in a saucepan.

3. Place the oyster shells on a baking dish and bake in the oven 10 minutes.

4. Cut off the ends of the leeks. Cut off and save for another use the green part of the leeks. Cut the white part of the leeks crosswise into 2-inch lengths. Cut the leeks in half and then into quarters. Cut the lengths of leeks into the finest possible julienne shreds. There should be about 3 cups loosely packed.

5. Heat 1 tablespoon of the butter in a heavy saucepan. Add the leeks and salt and pepper. Stir and add the water. Continue cooking and stirring about 5 minutes, or until the leeks are wilted and lose their raw taste. Set aside.

6. To make a beurre blanc, melt 1 tablespoon of the butter in a saucepan and add the shallots. Cook, stirring often, for about 1 minute. Add the vinegar and cook down totally. Add ½ cup of the wine. Cook down, stirring often, until the wine is almost but not totally evaporated.

7. Over low heat, beat in the remaining butter piece by piece and remove from the heat. Stir in the leeks.

8. Heat the oysters and their liquor with the remaining 2 tablespoons of wine. Cook briefly until the edges of the oysters curl. Carefully transfer the oysters to a small platter. Cook the liquid down over high heat to 2 tablespoons. Add this to the leek and butter sauce. Add the oysters. Heat gently without boiling.

9. Spoon equal portions of the oyster mixture into the oyster shells. Use one oyster per shell. Arrange them on a baking dish.

10. Place the oysters in the oven and bake for 30 seconds and serve.

YIELD: 3 to 6 servings.

Huîtres et Crevettes au Beurre de Poireaux

OYSTERS AND SHRIMP WITH LEEK BUTTER

- 9 tablespoons butter
- 3 tablespoons finely chopped shallots
- ½ cup oyster liquor
- ¼ cup dry white wine
- 30 small oysters, about 1¼ cups
- 2 cups finely shredded leeks cut into 1-inch lengths
- 1 pound shrimp, about 16, shelled and deveined
- ½ cup heavy cream
- Salt to taste, if desired
- Freshly ground black pepper to taste

1. Melt 1 tablespoon of the butter in a skillet and add the shallots. Cook briefly, stirring. Add the oyster liquor and wine and cook over high heat until reduced to about ⅓ cup.

2. Add the oysters and let them cook briefly, just until the edges curl. Hold a strainer over a saucepan and pour in the oysters with the cooking liquid. Pour the oysters into a mixing bowl.

3. Return the cooking liquid to the skillet and add the leeks. Cook, stirring, for about 1 minute.

4. Add the shrimp and cook for about 30 seconds on one side. Turn the shrimp and cook for about 30 seconds on the second side, or just until the shrimp lose their raw look. Transfer the shrimp to the mixing bowl with the oysters.

5. Add the cream, salt and pepper to the skillet. Cook for about 1 minute. Swirl in the remaining 8 tablespoons of butter. Add the shrimp and oysters to the sauce and stir briefly. Serve immediately.

YIELD: 4 to 6 servings.

New Orleans Oyster Loaf

- 1 loaf crusty French or Italian bread, preferably about 10 or 12 inches long
- 2 to 4 tablespoons melted butter
- 24 oysters fried in cornmeal (see recipe page 300)
- 2 to 4 tablespoons mayonnaise
- Tabasco sauce to taste

1. Preheat the oven to 400 degrees.

2. Split the loaf in half lengthwise as for making sandwiches. Wrap it in foil and bake for about 10 minutes.

3. Preheat the broiler. Brush each half of the bread on the split sides with melted butter and toast until golden on the split side.

4. Pile the oysters on one half of the bread. Spoon the mayonnaise on top and add a few dashes of Tabasco sauce. Cover with the second half of the bread. Split in half crosswise and serve.

YIELD: 2 servings.

Scallops are, conceivably, my favorite bivalve, with an incredible versatility where preparation is concerned. Recently at lunch I asked a very young neighbor as he speared his fork into a large platter of broiled scallops what it was that he admired so much about the bay scallops. With scarcely a pause he answered, "No bones." Now that is putting it simplistically.

Coquilles St. Jacques, by the way, is the French name for scallops as well as for a preparation made with scallops in a thickened butter sauce. One of the great categories of French food is that called à la nage. This culinary expression literally means "in the swim," and refers to the fact that the seafood is swimming in a flavorful, rich buttery broth.

Coquilles St. Jacques à la Nage

SCALLOPS AND VEGETABLES IN COURT BOUILLON

- 1 pint fresh bay scallops or sea scallops cut in half
- 1 small onion
- 2 stalks heart of celery
- 1 small carrot
- 4 sprigs fresh parsley
- 4 tablespoons butter
- ½ cup thinly sliced leeks
- ½ bay leaf
- Salt and freshly ground black pepper to taste
- ½ cup dry white wine
- ½ cup heavy cream
- Pinch of cayenne pepper

1. Pick over the scallops, if necessary, to remove any bits of shell.

2. Peel the onion and cut it in half lengthwise. Cut each half crosswise into very thin slices. There should be about ½ cup. Set aside.

3. Trim the celery stalks and cut them crosswise into ⅛-inch slices. Set aside.

4. Trim and scrape the carrot. Use a lemon peeler to make lengthwise ridges around the carrot. Cut the carrot into thin rounds. Set aside.

5. Pluck off bits of parsley leaves from each sprig. There should be about ½ cup. Set aside.

6. Melt 2 tablespoons of the butter in a small skillet and add the onion, celery, carrot, leeks, bay leaf, salt and pepper to taste. Cook, stirring often, until the vegetables are tender. Do not brown. The vegetables must remain a bit crisp.

7. Add the wine and cook until the wine is reduced almost by half.

8. Add the cream and cook until the cream is reduced by half. Add the scallops and more freshly ground pepper to taste. Add the cayenne. Cook over high heat for about 1½ minutes, stirring often. The scallops should barely cook, but they should not be raw.

9. Add the parsley bits. Swirl in the remaining butter and serve.

YIELD: 4 servings.

Coquilles St. Jacques Orientale

SCALLOPS IN A TOMATO AND GARLIC SAUCE

- 2 or 3 large ripe tomatoes, totaling about 1 pound
- 4 tablespoons olive oil
- 1 tablespoon finely minced garlic
- 2 tablespoons lemon juice
- 2 cups (1 pint) fresh bay scallops
- ½ teaspoon paprika
- Salt and freshly ground black pepper to taste
- ½ cup finely chopped parsley
- ¼ teaspoon hot red pepper flakes
- 4 thin seeded lemon slices
- Chopped parsley for garnish

1. Drop the tomatoes into boiling water to cover and let stand for exactly 12 seconds. Drain and peel.

2. Cut away and discard the cores of the tomatoes. Cut each tomato in half and squeeze gently to extract most of the seeds and the soft pulp containing them.

3. Cut each tomato into ½-inch cubes. There should be about 2½ cups.

4. Heat the oil in a skillet and add the garlic. Cook briefly, stirring, about 30 seconds. Add the tomatoes and lemon juice and cook over high heat for about 6 minutes, or until the sauce is quite thick. Remember that the scallops when added will give up a considerable amount of liquid.

5. Meanwhile, combine the scallops, paprika and salt and pepper.

6. Add the scallops to the tomato sauce. Add the ½ cup chopped parsley and the pepper flakes. Cook for about 1½ minutes. Do not overcook.

7. Pour the mixture into a serving dish. Cover with overlapping lemon slices. Sprinkle with chopped parsley for garnish.

YIELD: 4 servings.

Navarin de Coquilles St. Jacques

A SCALLOP AND VEGETABLE STEW

- 1 small to medium-sized zucchini
- 1 medium-sized carrot, trimmed and scraped
- 1 small turnip, peeled
- 2 cups very small mushrooms, about 6 ounces
- 1 tablespoon butter
- 3 tablespoons finely chopped shallots
- ½ cup dry white wine
- 1 sprig fresh thyme, or ½ teaspoon dried
- 1 bay leaf
- 2 sprigs fresh parsley
- 1 cup heavy cream
- Salt and freshly ground black pepper to taste
- ⅛ teaspoon cayenne pepper
- 2 cups (1 pint) fresh bay scallops
- 1 tablespoon lemon juice
- 2 tablespoons finely chopped parsley

1. Cut the zucchini into 1½-inch lengths. Cut each length into ¼-inch-thick slices. Stack the slices and cut them into sticks ¼ inch wide. There should be about 1 cup.

2. Cut the carrot into strips to match the zucchini pieces in size. There should be about 1 cup.

3. Cut the turnip into pieces the same size as the zucchini and carrot.

4. Rinse the mushrooms and pat them dry.

5. Put the carrots in a saucepan with water to cover. Bring to the boil and simmer for about 5 minutes. Add the turnip and zucchini and cook about 45 seconds. Drain and set aside.

6. Melt the butter in a skillet and add the mushrooms and shallots. Cook, stirring, for about 1 minute. Add the wine, thyme, bay leaf and parsley sprigs. Cook until the liquid evaporates totally.

7. Add the cream, salt, pepper and cayenne pepper and cook for about 1 minute.

8. Add the drained vegetables and cook until the sauce is quite thick, stirring often, about 5 minutes. Add the scallops and stir. Cook for about 1 minute. Stir in the lemon juice and chopped parsley.

YIELD: 4 to 6 servings.

Gratin de Coquilles St. Jacques

BREADED SCALLOPS IN SHELLS

- 8 tablespoons butter at room temperature
- 1 cup thinly sliced mushrooms
- 3 tablespoons finely chopped shallots
- 1 tablespoon finely chopped garlic
- 2 cups (1 pint) fresh bay scallops
- ½ cup bread crumbs
- ½ cup finely chopped parsley
- Salt and freshly ground black pepper to taste

1. Preheat the oven to 450 degrees.

2. Melt 4 tablespoons of the butter in a small skillet and add the mushrooms. Cook, stirring often, until mushrooms are wilted and give up their liquid. Add the shallots and garlic and cook briefly.

3. Spoon the mushroom mixture into a mixing bowl. Let cool briefly. Add 2 tablespoons soft butter, scallops, bread crumbs, parsley and salt and pepper. Blend well.

4. Use the mixture to fill 6 seafood shells.

5. Arrange the filled shells on a baking dish. Pour the remaining butter, melted, over the scallops and place in the oven. Bake for 10 minutes. Run the scallops under the broiler until nicely browned on top, about 1 minute.

YIELD: 6 servings.

Coquilles St. Jacques Grillées

BROILED SCALLOPS

- 2 cups (1 pint) fresh bay scallops
- 2 tablespoons melted butter
- Salt and freshly ground black pepper to taste
- ¼ teaspoon paprika

1. Preheat the broiler to high.

2. Combine the scallops, butter, salt, pepper and paprika in a mixing bowl. Stir to blend.

3. Pour and scrape the scallop mixture into a fairly large baking dish. Place the scallops about 4 inches from the source of heat. They should not

press close together or they will not brown properly. Cook the scallops, shaking the dish often so they cook evenly, for about 5 minutes or less, depending on the size of the scallops.

YIELD: 4 servings.

If we were to be asked to single out one shellfish as our favorite, it would certainly be shrimp. Apparently, we are not alone in this preference, for we have been told by many fish experts that it is also the favorite of the nation.

The principal reason for the popularity of shrimp is undoubtedly its taste and texture. But it is also one of the most versatile and easiest to cook of things that come in a shell. Shrimp are delectable hot or cold, as a first course, main course, side dish or salad. Our favorite plain method of cooking shrimp is in beer with peppercorns and allspice. A somewhat fancier favorite is this dish of shrimp cooked briefly in a cream sauce with mushrooms and dill.

❧

Crevettes et Champignons au Fenouil Bâtard

SHRIMP AND MUSHROOMS IN DILL SAUCE

- 1 pound medium-sized raw shrimp, about 26
- 1 tablespoon butter
- ¼ pound mushrooms, thinly sliced
- Salt and freshly ground black pepper to taste
- 3 tablespoons Cognac
- 1 cup plus 3 tablespoons heavy cream
- 1 egg yolk
- ⅛ teaspoon cayenne pepper
- Juice of ½ lemon
- ¼ cup finely minced fresh dill

1. Shell and devein the shrimp. Run them under cold water and drain well.

2. Melt the butter in a saucepan and add the mushrooms. Cook until wilted, about 2 minutes, stirring. Add the shrimp and sprinkle with salt and pepper. Cook for about 3 minutes, stirring frequently, and sprinkle with Cognac. Ignite it.

3. Remove the shrimp with a slotted spoon and set aside. Add 1 cup of cream and cook over high heat for about 6 minutes to reduce the liquid. Blend the remaining 3 tablespoons of cream with the egg yolk and stir the

mixture into the sauce. Cook briefly, stirring rapidly, and add the shrimp and salt to taste. Add the remaining ingredients and serve piping hot with hot rice.

YIELD: 4 to 6 servings.

❧

Shrimp Balls with Tree Ears and Snow Peas

- 3 tablespoons dried tree ears
- ⅛ pound unsalted pork fat
- 1 pound shrimp
- 2 tablespoons water
- 1 tablespoon plus 1 teaspoon cornstarch
- 2 egg whites
- Salt to taste
- ¾ teaspoon sugar
- ¼ teaspoon monosodium glutamate, optional
- 12 drained water chestnuts
- 1 teaspoon finely chopped fresh ginger
- 2 tablespoons finely chopped scallions
- 7 tablespoons peanut, vegetable or corn oil
- 40 snow peas
- ¾ cup chicken broth
- 2 tablespoons shaoxing wine or dry sherry

1. Put the tree ears in a mixing bowl and add boiling water to cover. Let stand for at least 30 minutes.

2. Put the pork fat into a small saucepan and add cold water to cover. Bring to the boil and cook for 30 minutes. Drain and chop. There should be about ¼ cup.

3. Peel and devein the shrimp. Put the shrimp into the container of a food processor. Add the water, 1 tablespoon of the cornstarch, egg whites, salt to taste, ¼ teaspoon sugar and monosodium glutamate. Process to a fine paste.

4. Spoon and scrape the mixture into a mixing bowl. Add the ¼ cup of chopped pork fat.

5. Chop the water chestnuts finely. There should be about 1 cup. Add the chopped chestnuts, ginger and scallions to the shrimp mixture. Blend well with the hands.

6. Using dampened fingers and palms, pick up about 1½ tablespoons of the mixture at a time. Shape each portion into a ball and then flatten into a biscuit shape.

7. Heat 3 tablespoons of the oil in a skillet. Add the shrimp pieces, a few at a time. Cook about 1½ minutes on one side until golden brown. Turn

and continue cooking 1½ to 2 minutes or until golden brown on the second side. Continue cooking the shrimp pieces until they are all cooked.

8. Meanwhile, string the snow peas and set aside.

9. Drain the tree ears. Squeeze them to extract any excess liquid. There should be about 1 cup.

10. Put the tree ears in a saucepan and add cold water to cover. Bring to the boil and simmer for 1 minute. Drain well, pressing to extract any excess moisture.

11. Blend the chicken broth with remaining ½ teaspoon sugar, salt to taste and remaining 1 teaspoon cornstarch. Set aside.

12. Heat the remaining 4 tablespoons of oil in a wok and, when it is very hot, add the snow peas. Cook for about 30 seconds and add the wine, shrimp balls and tree ears, stirring. Cook for about 30 seconds and add the chicken broth mixture. Cook, stirring constantly, for about 1 minute. Transfer the mixture to a serving dish.

YIELD: 8 servings with other Chinese dishes.

Crevettes Farcies Orientale

SHRIMP STUFFED WITH PORK AND GINGER

- 18 large shrimp, about 1½ pounds
- Salt to taste, if desired
- Freshly ground black pepper to taste
- 2 tablespoons butter
- ½ cup finely chopped onion
- ½ teaspoon finely chopped garlic
- ½ pound ground lean pork
- 1 tablespoon finely chopped fresh ginger
- 3 tablespoons soy sauce
- ⅓ cup finely chopped scallions
- 1 cup fine fresh bread crumbs
- 1 egg, lightly beaten
- ½ teaspoon sugar
- ¼ teaspoon hot red pepper flakes
- ½ cup heavy cream, optional

1. Preheat the oven to 425 degrees.

2. Split the shrimp down the back and shell and devein them but leave the last tail segment intact. Split each shrimp partly down the back. Place the shrimp on a flat surface, split side up, and pound lightly without breaking the flesh. Place them on a baking dish and sprinkle with salt and pepper.

3. Melt the butter in a skillet and add the onion and garlic. Cook, stirring, until wilted. Add the pork and cook, chopping down to break up any

lumps. Cook for about 2 minutes. Add the ginger, soy sauce, scallions, bread crumbs, egg, sugar and pepper flakes. Stir to blend.

4. Using a small spoon, add neat equal portions of the pork mixture to each opened-up butterflied shrimp. Shape the fillings into neat, smooth mounds. Pour the cream over the filling.

5. Bake for 5 minutes. Heat the broiler to high and put the shrimp under the heat. Broil for 2 minutes and serve.

YIELD: 4 or more servings.

Croquettes de Crevettes

SHRIMP CROQUETTES

- 1 pound shrimp cooked in the shell (see following recipe)
- 2 tablespoons butter
- ½ cup finely chopped onion
- ¼ cup plus 3 tablespoons flour
- ½ teaspoon paprika
- 1 cup milk
- ½ cup liquid in which shrimp were cooked
- 2 egg yolks
- 2 tablespoons dry sherry
- 2 cups fine fresh bread crumbs
- Salt, if desired
- Freshly ground black pepper to taste
- Pinch of cayenne pepper
- 1 egg
- 3 tablespoons water
- Oil for deep frying
- Sauce Newburg (see following recipe), optional

1. Peel and devein the shrimp. Chop them finely. There should be about 2 cups. Set aside.

2. Melt the butter in a saucepan and add the onion. Cook until wilted, stirring with a wire whisk. Add 3 tablespoons of the flour and the paprika, stirring. Add the milk and shrimp liquid, stirring rapidly with the whisk.

3. When thickened and smooth, continue cooking for about 2 minutes. Add the chopped shrimp, egg yolks and sherry. Cook briefly, about 30 seconds, stirring.

4. Add half of the bread crumbs, salt and pepper to taste and the cayenne. Blend well. Let stand until thoroughly cooled.

5. Divide the mixture into 16 equal portions. Shape each portion into a ball. Roll the balls in the remaining ¼ cup of flour. Mold them into the desired form: spheres, cylinders, pyamids or flat cakes.

6. Beat the egg with the water. Roll the croquettes in the egg mixture and then in the remaining bread crumbs. Press to help crumbs adhere. Shake off any excess.

7. Heat the oil for deep frying. Add the croquettes a few at a time and cook for about 4 minutes, or until golden brown. Serve, if desired, with sauce Newburg.

YIELD: 4 servings.

CREVETTES POCHÉES

Boiled Shrimp

- 1 pound medium to large shrimp
- ½ cup dry white wine
- ⅓ cup water
- ½ bay leaf
- 2 sprigs fresh thyme, or ½ teaspoon dried
- 12 whole black peppercorns
- Salt to taste, if desired
- 4 sprigs fresh parsley

Combine all the ingredients in a saucepan and bring to the boil. Let simmer for about 1 minute and remove from the heat.

YIELD: 1 pound cooked shrimp.

SAUCE NEWBURG

- 2 tablespoons butter
- 2 tablespoons finely chopped shallots
- 1 teaspoon paprika
- 2 tablespoons flour
- 1 cup milk
- ½ cup heavy cream
- Salt, if desired
- Freshly ground black pepper to taste
- 2 tablespoons dry sherry

1. Melt the butter in a saucepan and add the shallots and paprika. Cook, stirring, until the shallots are wilted. Sprinkle the mixture with flour and stir with a wire whisk.

2. Add the milk, stirring vigorously with the whisk. Add the cream and salt and pepper. Strain the sauce through a sieve, preferably of the sort known in French kitchens as a chinois. Press with a spatula to extract as much liquid as possible from the shallots. Reheat and add the sherry.

YIELD: About 1½ cups.

We offer two easily made shrimp dishes for a score or more guests, each with a sauce that can be made ahead and refrigerated or frozen. The sauce américaine is an enormously simplified version of the real thing, which involves cooking lobsters in the shell, crushing and pressing the shells in a sieve and so on. But it is equally delectable.

Shrimp Américaine

- 15 pounds raw shrimp in the shell
- 14 cups sauce américaine (see following recipe)
- ¾ pound butter
- ¾ cup finely chopped shallots
- Salt and freshly ground black pepper to taste
- ¼ teaspoon cayenne pepper, optional
- 1 cup Cognac
- ½ cup finely chopped fresh tarragon, or half the amount dried
- 3 tablespoons Cognac, optional
- 2 tablespoons arrowroot or cornstarch, optional

1. Peel and devein the shrimp. Rinse well and drain thoroughly.

2. Bring the sauce to the boil, but do not let it cook.

3. Melt 8 tablespoons of the butter in a large kettle or casserole. Add the shallots and cook briefly, stirring.

4. Add the shrimp and sprinkle with salt and pepper and cayenne pepper. Cook the shrimp, stirring gently, for about 5 minutes, or until they lose their raw look. Sprinkle with 1 cup of Cognac and ignite it (if it does not flame, do not worry). Stir and add half of the tarragon. Stir.

5. Add the sauce and stir to blend. Bring to the boil. Do not cook more than a minute. It is important, however, that the dish be piping hot throughout.

6. The liquid from the shrimp will probably thin the sauce. Thicken the sauce by blending the additional 3 tablespoons of Cognac with the arrowroot. Stir in gently.

7. Dot the mixture with the remaining butter and stir gently until it is melted and blended. Stir in the remaining tarragon and serve.

YIELD: 30 servings.

SAUCE AMÉRICAINE

- 4 tablespoons butter
- 1½ cups finely chopped onion
- ½ cup finely chopped shallots
- 2 teaspoons finely minced garlic
- 1 cup finely chopped celery
- 1 cup finely diced carrots
- ¼ cup flour
- 2 cups dry white wine
- 2 cups fish stock (see recipe page 419), or bottled clam juice
- 10 cups fresh or canned imported Italian tomatoes, crushed
- ¼ cup tomato paste
- 1 teaspoon dried thyme
- 1 bay leaf
- ⅓ cup packed fresh tarragon leaves, or 1 teaspoon dried
- Salt and freshly ground black pepper to taste
- ¼ teaspoon cayenne pepper

1. Melt the butter in a kettle or large casserole. Add the onion, shallots, garlic, celery and carrots. Cook, stirring, for about 5 minutes. Sprinkle with flour and stir to coat the vegetables evenly.

2. Add all of the remaining ingredients, stir and bring to the boil. Cook, stirring, for about 20 minutes.

3. Put the sauce through a food mill, pressing to extract as much of the liquid from the solids as possible.

YIELD: 14 cups.

Curried Shrimp

- 6 pounds raw shrimp, peeled and deveined, about 10 cups
- 2 tablespoons butter
- Salt to taste, if desired
- Freshly ground black pepper to taste
- 1 tablespoon curry powder
- 3 cups curry sauce (see following recipe)
- Yogurt and vegetables (see following recipe)
- Chutney

1. Prepare the shrimp and set aside.

2. Melt the butter in a 4- to 5-quart kettle and add the shrimp. Add salt and pepper. Sprinkle with curry powder and cook briefly, stirring, just until the shrimp lose their raw look.

3. Add the curry sauce and cook, stirring constantly from the bottom to prevent sticking, 3 to 5 minutes, until piping hot throughout. If desired, the sauce may be thinned a little with chicken broth or heavy cream. It should not be necessary, however. Serve with rice, yogurt and vegetable side dish and chutney.

YIELD: 24 servings.

CURRY SAUCE

- 4 tablespoons butter
- 2 cups finely chopped onion
- 1 cup finely chopped celery
- 2 tablespoons finely minced garlic
- 2 bay leaves
- 4 to 6 tablespoons curry powder
- 1 tablespoon ground turmeric
- ½ cup flour
- 5 cups rich chicken broth (see recipe page 418)
- 3 tablespoons tomato paste
- Salt to taste if desired
- Freshly ground black pepper to taste
- 2 bananas, peeled and mashed, about 1¼ cups
- 2 apples, peeled, cored and finely diced, about 2 cups

1. Select a large, heavy kettle, preferably one with a 9-quart capacity. Melt the butter in the kettle and add the onion, celery and garlic. Cook, stirring, until wilted. Add the bay leaves, curry powder, turmeric and flour and stir with a wire whisk.

2. Add the broth and tomato paste, stirring rapidly with the whisk. Add salt and pepper. Let simmer for about 5 minutes.

3. Add the bananas and apples and stir. Cook for about 20 minutes, stirring often from the bottom.

4. Put the sauce through a food mill, pressing to extract as much liquid as possible from the solids. Or, less preferably, purée the sauce using a food processor or a blender.

YIELD: About 8 cups.

YOGURT AND VEGETABLES

- 3 medium-sized cucumbers
- 3 cups plain yogurt
- 1 tablespoon sugar
- ¾ cup chopped scallions
- ¾ teaspoon ground cumin
- Salt to taste, if desired
- Freshly ground black pepper to taste
- 1½ cups peeled, seeded and cubed tomatoes

1. Peel the cucumbers. Cut them in half lengthwise and scrape out the center seeds.

2. Cut the cucumber into 1½-inch lengths. Slice the pieces lengthwise into thin slices. Stack the slices and cut them lengthwise into very thin strips. There should be about 5½ cups.

3. Combine the yogurt, cucumber and remaining ingredients.

YIELD: 24 servings.

Shrimp and Eggplant à la Grecque

- 1½ pounds eggplant
- Flour for dredging
- Salt and freshly ground black pepper to taste
- ½ cup olive oil, approximately
- 24 raw shrimp, shelled and deveined
- 2 cups fresh tomato sauce (see recipe page 407)
- 1 teaspoon dried oregano
- Juice of 1 lemon

1. Preheat the oven to 400 degrees.

2. Cut the eggplant into 12 slices, each about ¾ inch thick. Cut each slice into rounds about 3 inches in diameter.

3. Dredge the slices on all sides in flour seasoned with salt and pepper.

4. Heat about ¼ cup of the oil in a heavy skillet and, when it is hot and almost smoking, add the eggplant slices. Cook quickly until golden on one side and turn to brown the other. It may be necessary to add a little more oil to prevent burning or sticking. Drain the slices and set aside.

5. Arrange the slices in one layer in a baking dish. Arrange 2 shrimp on each slice and spoon equal amounts of tomato sauce over the shrimp. Sprinkle with oregano, lemon juice and ¼ cup additional oil.

6. Bake for 30 minutes and serve piping hot.

YIELD: 6 servings.

Crevettes en Brochettes au Beurre Blanc

GRILLED SHRIMP WITH WHITE BUTTER SAUCE

- 32 shrimp, about 1¼ pounds, peeled and deveined
- Salt to taste, if desired
- Freshly ground black pepper to taste
- 2 tablespoons prepared mustard, preferably imported Dijon or Düsseldorf
- 2 tablespoons corn, peanut or vegetable oil
- Beurre blanc (see recipe page 400)

1. Preheat a charcoal grill or preheat the boiler to high.

2. Sprinkle the shrimp with salt and pepper. Arrange 8 of them neatly on

each of four skewers so that they lie flat and touching. Brush on both sides with mustard.

3. Arrange them on a baking dish. Brush the shrimp on both sides with oil.

4. Place the skewered shrimp on the grill or the broiler about 5 inches from the source of heat. Grill or broil for about 1½ minutes on one side and turn. Continue grilling or broiling from 1½ to 2 minutes.

5. Serve with hot white butter sauce.

YIELD: 4 servings.

Americans seem to have a very small appetite for squid, a delicacy that I would place in the highest category of good things to eat from the sea. They are often referred to as voracious predators because they enthusiastically consume large and small fish as well as other squid. I feel equally voracious when faced with a platter of deep-fried squid rings or squid stuffed with a delicate shrimp mousse.

Friture de Calmar

FRENCH-FRIED SQUID

- 2 pounds squid, cleaned (see following instructions)
- ½ cup milk
- 2 cups flour
- Salt to taste, if desired
- Freshly ground black pepper to taste
- 6 cups oil
- Juice of ½ lemon

1. Cut squid bodies into ½-inch rounds and the tentacles into bite-sized pieces. There should be about 3 cups.

2. Put the squid in a bowl. Pour the milk over the squid.

3. Put the flour in a flat dish and add salt and pepper. Blend well. Drain the squid lightly and add to the flour. Dredge thoroughly, shaking off excess flour.

4. Pour oil—about 1 inch deep—into a heavy skillet. Heat the oil until it is quite hot but not smoking (375 degrees). Add the squid pieces, a few at a time, to the skillet without crowding. Cook until crisp and lightly golden, about 2 minutes for each batch. Remove squid pieces and drain on paper toweling. Continue cooking in batches until all the pieces are cooked. Serve sprinkled with lemon juice.

YIELD: 4 to 6 servings.

HOW TO CLEAN SQUID

1. Twist and pull off the head of the squid. As you do this you will also pull out much of the interior of the body. This may include an ink sac, which is used in many European recipes but not for the recipes given here. Discard the pulled-out material.

2. Pull out and discard the semi-hard translucent, sword-shaped pen.

3. Using a knife, cut off the tentacles from the head of the squid (just in front of the eyes).

4. Using the fingers, pop out the round, hard beak in the center of the tentacles. Discard the beak.

5. The tentacles are wholly edible. If they are long, you may want to cut them in half or into smaller lengths.

6. Rub off the brown skin of the squid, holding the squid under cold running water. Use coarse salt while rubbing and pulling with the fingers.

7. Rinse the squid inside and out to remove any remaining material from inside the body. Drain the squid thoroughly and set aside.

Squid Stuffed with Shrimp Mousse

- 8 to 12 squid, about 3 pounds before cleaning
- ¾ pound raw shrimp in the shell
- 1 egg
- Pinch of cayenne pepper
- ⅛ teaspoon grated nutmeg
- Salt to taste, if desired
- Freshly ground black pepper to taste
- 1½ cups heavy cream
- 2 tablespoons butter
- 2 tablespoons finely chopped shallots
- ¾ cup crushed fresh or canned tomatoes
- 1½ cups dry white wine
- ¾ cup heavy cream

1. Preheat the oven to 400 degrees.

2. Clean the squid and set aside.

3. Shell and devein the shrimp. Put them into the container of a food processor and add the egg, cayenne pepper, nutmeg, salt and pepper. Blend. Gradually pour the cream through the funnel while blending.

4. Outfit a pastry bag with a round No. 8 pastry tube. Fill the bag with the shrimp mixture and pipe equal portions of the mousse mixture into the

squid bodies. Partly fill each body; the stuffing will expand as it cooks. Sew up the opening of each body with a needle and thread or secure the openings with toothpicks.

5. Rub with butter a baking dish large enough to hold the stuffed squid in one layer. Sprinkle the bottom with shallots, crushed tomatoes, salt and pepper to taste. Arrange the stuffed squid neatly inside the pan. Scatter the tentacles around the stuffed squid. Sprinkle wine over all.

6. Cover closely with foil. Bring to the boil on top of the stove. Place in the oven and bake for 10 minutes. If any of the stuffing runs out, it can be served with the squid. Transfer the squid to a warm platter. Remove and discard the thread or toothpick from each squid.

7. Pour and scrape the cooking liquid into a saucepan and bring to the boil. Cook the liquid down to ¾ cup. Add the cream and return to a boil. Cook over high heat until the liquid is reduced to 1 cup. Pour the sauce over the squid and serve.

YIELD: 6 servings.

VEGETABLES

CROQUETTES, crisp and crunchy on the outside, moist within, are usually composed of leftover meats, poultry or fish. But one of our favorites is made with chopped fresh vegetables and cooked rice. The croquettes are an ideal accompaniment to meat, poultry and fish dishes and do not require a sauce.

Croquettes de Légumes

VEGETABLE CROQUETTES

- 1 small eggplant, about ¾ pound, peeled
- 1 small zucchini, about ½ pound, ends trimmed
- 1 sweet red or green pepper, cored and seeded
- 2 tablespoons peanut, vegetable or corn oil
- 1 cup finely chopped onion
- 1 teaspoon finely minced garlic
- 1 cup peeled and seeded ripe tomatoes cut into ¼-inch cubes
- 1 bay leaf
- ½ teaspoon dried thyme
- 1 cup cooked rice
- 3 tablespoons butter
- 5 tablespoons plus ¼ cup flour
- 1 cup chicken broth
- ½ cup milk
- 4 egg yolks
- Salt, if desired
- Freshly ground black pepper to taste
- ½ cup finely chopped fresh parsley
- 1 teaspoon grated fresh ginger
- 1 egg
- 3 tablespoons water
- 1 cup fine fresh bread crumbs
- Oil for deep frying

1. Cut the eggplant into ¼-inch cubes. There should be about 3 cups.
2. Cut the zucchini into ½-inch cubes. There should be about 2 cups.
3. Cut the pepper into ½-inch pieces.
4. Heat the 2 tablespoons of oil in a large, heavy skillet and add the onion, garlic and sweet pepper pieces. Cook, stirring, until wilted.

5. Add the eggplant, zucchini, tomato, bay leaf and thyme and cook, stirring, about 5 minutes, or until the liquid from the tomato has evaporated. Do not brown the vegetables. Add the rice.

6. Melt the butter in a saucepan and add the 5 tablespoons of flour, stirring with a wire whisk. Add the broth and milk, stirring vigorously with the whisk. When blended and smooth, cook for about 5 minutes, stirring. Add the egg yolks and cook, stirring, for about 30 seconds. Add the salt and pepper.

7. Stir the sauce into the vegetable mixture. (Remove the bay leaf.) Add the parsley and fresh ginger. Let stand until thoroughly cooled.

8. Divide the mixture into 20 equal portions. Shape each portion into a ball. Roll the balls in the remaining ¼ cup of flour. Mold them into the desired form: spheres, cylinders, pyramids or flat cakes.

9. Beat the egg with the water. Roll the croquettes in the egg mixture and then in the bread crumbs. Press to help the crumbs adhere. Shake off any excess.

10. Heat the oil for deep frying. Add the croquettes a few at a time and cook for about 4 minutes, or until golden brown.

YIELD: 4 to 6 servings.

Macedoine de Légumes

SAUTÉED CARROTS, TURNIPS AND SNOW PEAS

- 2 large carrots, about ½ pound
- 2 large white turnips, about ½ pound
- ½ pound fresh snow peas
- 2 tablespoons butter
- Salt and freshly ground black pepper to taste
- 1 tablespoon red wine vinegar

1. Scrape and trim the carrots. Cut the carrots crosswise into 1½-inch lengths. Cut the pieces into ¼-inch slices. Cut slices into batons about ¼ inch wide. There should be about 1½ cups.

2. Trim and scrape the turnips. Cut the turnips in half. Cut each half crosswise into ¼-inch-thick slices. Stack the slices; cut them into batons about the same size as the carrots. There should be about 2 cups.

3. Trim off and discard the tips of the snow peas. There should be about 1 cup of peas.

4. Melt the butter in a heavy skillet. Add the carrots and turnips. Cook the vegetables, stirring, for about 1 minute. Add the snow peas and cook, stirring, for about 5 minutes until crisp-tender.

5. Add salt and pepper to taste and the vinegar. Cook briefly and stir well.

YIELD: 4 servings.

Escalibada

BAKED VEGETABLES, CATALAN STYLE

8 large leeks, about 2½ pounds
3 eggplants, about 2 pounds
3 or 4 large onions, about 2 pounds
5 large sweet green or red peppers, about 1¾ pounds
Salt to taste, if desired
Freshly ground black pepper to taste
8 tablespoons olive oil

1. Preheat the oven to 500 degrees.

2. Cut off the thread-like root ends of the leeks. Trim off portions of the upper green stems of each leek, leaving about 12 inches, including white bottom portions plus part of green. Leave leeks whole but rinse away as much sand and soil as possible from between inner leaves. Pat dry. Line a baking dish with aluminum foil and arrange the leeks in one layer.

3. Line a second large baking dish with foil. Arrange whole eggplants, onions and peppers in one layer.

4. Place both baking dishes in the oven and bake for 1 hour, turning the vegetables at 15 minute intervals so they bake evenly.

5. At the end of the hour, check the vegetables. If the green peppers are tender and slightly browned, remove them. Or continue cooking until they are tender and can be peeled.

6. If at the end of the hour the leeks are slightly charred and are tender, remove them. Wrap in foil and let stand for ½ hour or so until they can be handled.

7. Let the onions continue to bake up to 1½ hours, or until the inner flesh is tender to the touch.

8. Peel the peppers, cutting or pulling away and discarding the core and seeds. Cut the flesh of each pepper lengthwise into strips, each about ½ inch wide. Arrange the strips in a small serving dish.

9. Peel the eggplants. Discard peel and seeds. Cut the flesh into strips about the same size as the peppers. Arrange the strips in a second serving dish.

10. Remove and discard the browned outer skin of each onion. Cut the onions into strips about the same size as the eggplants and peppers. Stack the strips in a third serving dish.

11. Remove the leeks from the foil. Trim off and discard the tough browned outer leaves. Split the tender inner portions of each in half lengthwise. Cut crosswise in half. Arrange the strips in a fourth serving dish.

12. Sprinkle the vegetables lightly with salt. Sprinkle with pepper to taste. Spoon equal amounts of oil over each vegetable. Serve as a side dish with grilled meats or fish. Leftover vegetables are excellent.

YIELD: 4 to 8 servings.

Carciofi Ripieni di Maiale

PORK- AND SAGE-STUFFED ARTICHOKES

- 4 large artichokes prepared for stuffing (see instructions)
- 2 tablespoons olive oil
- 1 cup finely chopped onion
- 2 teaspoons finely minced garlic
- 1 cup finely chopped mushrooms
- ½ pound ground lean pork
- ½ cup finely chopped parsley
- 1 tablespoon rubbed sage
- 1 egg, lightly beaten
- ¼ cup freshly grated Parmesan cheese
- ¼ teaspoon hot red pepper flakes, optional
- Salt to taste
- Freshly ground black pepper to taste
- 1 cup coarsely chopped imported canned tomatoes
- 1 cup water
- 1 bay leaf

1. Prepare the artichokes for stuffing and set aside.

2. Heat half the oil in a saucepan and add half the onion and half the garlic. Cook, stirring, until wilted. Add the mushrooms and cook until wilted.

3. Put the pork in a mixing bowl and add the mushroom mixture, parsley, sage, egg, cheese, pepper flakes, salt and pepper. Blend well.

4. Stuff the artichokes with equal portions of the mixture.

5. Select a kettle large enough to hold the artichokes when placed snugly together. Add the remaining oil, onion and garlic, tomatoes, water, bay leaf, salt and pepper.

6. Arrange the artichokes close together, stuffed side up, in a kettle. Bring to the boil. Cover closely and cook over low heat for 45 minutes to 1 hour. To test for doneness, pull off an outside leaf; if it comes off easily, the artichokes are done.

YIELD: 4 servings.

HOW TO PREPARE WHOLE ARTICHOKES FOR STUFFING

Cut off the stems of the artichokes, using a sharp knife, to produce a neat, flat base. Rub any cut surfaces with lemon. Slice off the top "cone" of the artichoke about 1 inch from the tip. With kitchen scissors, cut off the sharp tips of the leaves about ½ inch down.

Use a melon ball cutter to hollow out the choke in the center, pulling and scraping away the tender center leaves above. Turn the artichokes upside down and press down to open the center, facilitating stuffing. Turn right side up and stuff.

Ardishawki Mihshi

LAMB-STUFFED ARTICHOKES, SYRIAN STYLE

- 4 large artichokes prepared for stuffing (see instructions)
- 1 tablespoon olive oil
- 1½ cups finely chopped onion
- 1 teaspoon finely minced garlic
- 1 cup finely chopped mushrooms
- ½ pound ground lamb
- ½ cup finely chopped scallions
- ¼ cup finely chopped parsley
- 2 tablespoons finely chopped fresh dill
- ¼ cup toasted pine nuts
- Salt to taste, if desired
- Freshly ground black pepper to taste
- Juice of ½ lemon
- 1½ cups plus 1 tablespoon water
- 1 teaspoon cornstarch or arrowroot

1. Prepare the artichokes for stuffing and set aside.

2. Heat the oil in a saucepan and add half the onion and half the garlic. Cook, stirring, until wilted. Add the mushrooms and cook until wilted.

3. Put the lamb in a mixing bowl and add the mushroom mixture, scallions, parsley, dill, pine nuts, salt and pepper. Blend well.

4. Stuff the artichokes with equal portions of the mixture.

5. Select a kettle large enough to hold the artichokes when placed snugly together. Add the remaining onions and garlic, lemon juice and 1½ cups water.

6. Arrange the artichokes close together, stuffed side up, in the kettle. Bring to the boil. Cover closely and cook over gentle heat for about 45 minutes.

7. Remove the artichokes to a warm serving dish and pour the cooking liquid into a saucepan. Bring to the simmer.

8. Blend the cornstarch with the remaining tablespoon cold water. Stir into the simmering liquid. When thickened, pour the sauce over the artichokes and serve.

YIELD: 4 servings.

Three Mile Harbor Stuffed Sweet and Sour Cabbage

- 1 large or 2 small cabbages, about 3 pounds total
- 1 pound ground chuck
- 1 teaspoon peanut or vegetable oil
- 2 cups finely chopped onion
- 1 clove garlic, finely minced
- 1 cup fine fresh bread crumbs
- 1 egg, lightly beaten
- ¼ cup finely chopped parsley
- 1 cup drained imported canned tomatoes
- Salt and freshly ground black pepper to taste
- 1 28-ounce can tomatoes with tomato paste
- ½ cup white vinegar
- ¼ cup sugar
- 1 teaspoon paprika

1. Cut the core from the cabbage and drop the cabbage into a kettle of cold water to cover. Bring to the boil and cook for 5 minutes. Drain well.

2. Put the meat in a mixing bowl and set aside.

3. Heat the oil in a small skillet and add the onion and garlic. Cook, stirring, until wilted. Remove from the heat and let cool slightly.

4. Add half the onion mixture to the beef. Add the bread crumbs, egg and parsley. Add the 1 cup of tomatoes and salt and pepper. Blend thoroughly with the hands.

5. Separate the leaves of the cabbage. Place one large leaf on a flat surface and cover the center with a small leaf. Add about 3 tablespoons of the meat mixture to the center and fold the cabbage leaves over, tucking in the ends. There should be about 18 cabbage rolls in all.

6. Do not drain the tomatoes with tomato paste but crush them.

7. Add half the crushed tomatoes to the bottom of a baking dish large enough to hold the stuffed cabbage rolls close together, in one layer.

8. Cover the tomato layer with the stuffed cabbage.

9. Blend the remaining crushed tomatoes with remaining onion mixture, vinegar and sugar. Spoon this over the stuffed cabbage. Sprinkle with paprika.

10. Preheat the oven to 350 degrees.

11. Cover the dish closely and bring to the boil on top of the stove. Bake for 1 hour and 15 minutes. Uncover and bake for about 20 minutes longer.

YIELD: 6 to 8 servings.

Ruth Stefanycia's Stuffed Cabbage in a Mold

- 2 medium-sized Savoy cabbages, about 3½ pounds
- ½ pound ground veal
- ½ pound ground pork
- ½ pound ground beef
- 1 tablespoon peanut, vegetable or corn oil
- 2 cups finely chopped onion
- 1 teaspoon finely minced garlic
- 2 cups bread cut into 1-inch cubes
- ½ cup water or milk
- 1 large egg, lightly beaten
- Salt and freshly ground black pepper to taste
- ½ teaspoon grated lemon rind
- 2 tablespoons lemon juice
- ¼ cup finely chopped parsley
- 1 teaspoon dried marjoram
- ¼ teaspoon dried thyme
- Fresh tomato sauce (see recipe page 407)

1. Cut away the white inner core of each cabbage and cut each cabbage into quarters. Put the quarters in a large kettle with cold water to cover. Bring to the boil and simmer for 5 minutes. Drain well in a colander.

2. Combine the ground meats in a mixing bowl and set aside.

3. Heat the oil in a skillet and add the onion. Cook, stirring occasionally, until wilted. Add the garlic and stir. Cool briefly.

4. Meanwhile, soak the bread cubes in the water and let stand briefly. Squeeze dry.

5. Add the squeezed-out bread, egg, salt and pepper, lemon rind, lemon juice and parsley to the meat. Add the onion mixture, marjoram and

thyme. Blend well with the hands. To test for seasonings, fry a small amount in a skillet. Add more seasonings to the basic mixture, if desired.

6. Select a 9- or 10-cup mold (preferably a charlotte mold measuring about 5 inches high and 7 inches in diameter).

7. Lightly grease the bottom and sides of the mold with oil. Line the bottom and sides of the mold with cabbage leaves, filling with layers of meat mixture as you go to support the leaves against the sides of the mold.

8. Between the layers of meat add some of the cabbage leaves, coarsely chopped. Fill the mold almost to the top with the meat and pack in the remaining cabbage.

9. Preheat the oven to 400 degrees.

10. Cover the top of the mold closely with foil. Place the mold in a large deep pan of water. Water should be poured into the pan so that it reaches halfway up the mold. Bring the water to the boil on top of the stove.

11. Place the pan in the oven and bake the cabbage for 2 hours.

12. Hold a plate over the mold and invert the mold over the plate. Unmold the cabbage and meat but save the juices if desired. The juices may be added to the tomato sauce. Serve sliced in wedges with tomato sauce on the side.

YIELD: 12 servings.

Chou au Lard

CABBAGE WITH BACON

- 1 head young cabbage, about ¾ pound
- 6 ounces bacon, preferably thick-sliced
- Salt and freshly ground black pepper to taste
- ½ teaspoon dried thyme

1. Pull off and discard any tough outer and blemished leaves of the cabbage.

2. Cut the cabbage into quarters. Cut away and discard the center core. Drop the quarters into cold water and rinse well. Drain thoroughly. Cut the cabbage into fine shreds. There should be 10 or 11 cups.

3. Cut the bacon into very thin crosswise strips.

4. Bring enough water to the boil to cover the shredded cabbage.

5. Put the bacon into a skillet and cook until rendered of fat. Do not cook until crisp. Pour off the fat but reserve both the fat and bacon.

6. Drop the cabbage shreds into the boiling water and let stand for 1 minute. It is not necessary that the water return to the boil. Drain immediately.

7. Use a skillet large enough to accommodate all the cabbage and add 3 tablespoons of the reserved bacon fat. When hot, add the cabbage. Sprinkle with salt and pepper. Toss and stir the cabbage so that it cooks evenly.

8. When the cabbage has cooked for about 1 minute, sprinkle with the bacon pieces. Toss and stir. Sprinkle with thyme and toss again. The cooking time for the cabbage with bacon is about 10 minutes. Take care not to overcook. The cabbage strands must remain *al dente,* or slightly resilient to the bite.

9. Rub the inside of 6 small but deep individual ovenproof molds with bacon fat. Spoon in the cabbage and pack it down loosely.

10. Preheat the oven to 400 degrees.

11. Set the molds in a metal pan and pour water around them. Bring to the boil on top of the stove and bake for 20 minutes.

YIELD: 6 servings.

❧

Friture de Chou-fleur

BATTER-FRIED CAULIFLOWER

1 cauliflower, about 1¼ pounds
Salt
1 recipe for fritter batter (see recipe page 110)
Oil for deep frying
Tomato sauce, French style (see recipe page 408)

1. Break the cauliflower into flowerets.

2. Drop the cauliflower into boiling water with salt to taste. When the water returns to the boil, cook for about 2 minutes. Drain and run under cold water. Drain well and set aside.

3. Add the cauliflower to the fritter batter, turning to coat well.

4. Heat the oil for deep frying and, when it is quite hot, add the batter-coated cauliflower pieces one at a time. Do not crowd the pieces in the oil. Cook, turning the pieces occasionally, for about 2 minutes, or until crisp outside and golden brown.

5. Remove with a slotted spoon and drain on paper toweling.

6. Add the remaining cauliflower pieces and cook until done. Sprinkle with salt to taste. Serve hot with tomato sauce.

YIELD: 4 to 8 servings.

Chayotes enjoy considerable popularity on the tables of Louisiana in general and New Orleans specifically, where they are known as mirlitons. They resemble a pale green quince and are available everywhere there are markets that sell South American or West Indian foods. This squash has a pleasant crunchy texture like that of a not-too-ripe melon and its flavor makes it a natural for almost any assertive flavors you wish to employ.

Mirlitons Farcis aux Crevettes

CHAYOTES STUFFED WITH SHRIMP

- 3 chayotes, ¾ to 1 pound each
- Salt to taste, if desired
- ¾ pound raw shrimp in the shell
- 4 tablespoons butter
- 1 cup finely chopped onion
- 1 teaspoon finely minced garlic
- 2 tablespoons flour
- 1 cup milk
- 2 teaspoons finely chopped fresh ginger, optional
- ¼ cup finely chopped scallions
- 1 egg yolk
- Freshly ground black pepper to taste
- ½ cup fine fresh bread crumbs
- ¼ cup finely chopped parsley
- ½ cup grated Cheddar cheese

1. Split the chayotes lengthwise in half. Put in a kettle of cold water and add salt to taste. Bring to the boil and simmer about 10 minutes. Do not overcook or the vegetables will become mushy. Drain and run briefly under cold water. Drain again.

2. Using a spoon or melon ball cutter, scoop out the flesh and seeds of each half, leaving a shell of about ⅛ inch thick or slightly thicker. Set the shells aside. Chop flesh and seeds fine. There should be about 1 cup. Set aside.

3. Peel and devein the shrimp and chop coarsely. There should be about 1¼ cups. Set aside.

4. When ready to cook, preheat the oven to 425 degrees.

5. Melt half the butter in a saucepan and add the onion and garlic. Cook, stirring, until wilted. Sprinkle with flour and stir to distribute evenly. Add the milk, stirring rapidly with a wire whisk.

6. When the sauce is thickened and smooth, add the chopped pulp. Bring to the boil, stirring, and add the ginger and scallions.

7. Remove from the heat and stir in the egg yolk. Let stand to room temperature. Stir in the shrimp, salt, pepper, ¼ cup of the bread crumbs and the parsley.

8. Use the mixture to stuff chayote halves. Pile up and smooth over.

9. Blend the remaining ¼ cup of bread crumbs and cheese. Sprinkle the tops with the mixture, patting to help it adhere. Dot with the remaining 2 tablespoons of butter.

10. Arrange the stuffed halves in a lightly buttered baking dish and bake for 20 minutes.

YIELD: 6 servings.

❧

Chayotes Rellenos al Queso

CHAYOTES STUFFED WITH CHEESE

- 3 chayotes, ¾ to 1 pound each
- Salt to taste, if desired
- 1½ cups fine fresh bread crumbs
- 2½ cups finely grated Muenster cheese
- 1 egg, lightly beaten
- 2 teaspoons finely minced garlic
- ¼ cup finely chopped scallions
- ¼ teaspoon hot red pepper flakes
- Freshly ground black pepper to taste
- 2 tablespoons butter

1. Split the chayotes lengthwise in half. Put them in a kettle of cold water with salt to taste. Bring to the boil and let simmer about 10 minutes. Do not overcook or the vegetable will become mushy. Drain and run briefly under cold water. Drain again.

2. Using a spoon or melon ball cutter, scoop out the flesh and seeds of each half, leaving a shell about ⅛ inch thick or slightly thicker. Set the shells aside. Chop flesh and seeds fine. There should be about 1 cup.

3. When ready to cook, preheat the oven to 425 degrees.

4. In a mixing bowl, combine the chopped pulp with 1 cup of bread crumbs, 2 cups of cheese, egg, garlic, scallions, pepper flakes, salt and pepper to taste.

5. Use this mixture to fill the chayote halves. Pile the filling up and smooth it over.

6. Combine the remaining ½ cup of cheese with the remaining ½ cup of bread crumbs. Sprinkle the tops with the mixture, patting to help it adhere. Dot the tops of each half with butter.

7. Arrange the stuffed halves in a lightly buttered baking dish and bake for 20 minutes.

YIELD: 6 servings.

Eggplant used to be called *mala insana,* mad apple, and it was thought to cause insanity. But that was a long time ago. We happen to be crazy about the vegetable ourselves, because it is earthy yet elegant. It has a pronounced and seductive flavor and marries exceedingly well with any number of delectable fillings.

Lamb-stuffed Eggplant

- 2 medium to large eggplants, about 1¼ pounds each
- Salt
- 1 tablespoon olive oil
- 1 teaspoon finely chopped garlic
- 1½ cups finely chopped onion
- 1¼ pounds ground lean lamb
- ¾ cup cubed fresh tomatoes
- ½ cup rice
- Juice of 1 lemon
- ¼ cup finely chopped fresh dill
- ¼ cup chopped parsley
- Freshly ground black pepper to taste
- 8 tablespoons chopped feta cheese, or 4 tablespoons freshly grated Parmesan cheese

1. Preheat the oven to 400 degrees.

2. Split the eggplants in half lengthwise. Run a sharp paring knife around the inside perimeter of each half, about an inch from the skin. Do not penetrate the skin. Score the insides of each half with the paring knife, running it to within about ½ inch of the bottom skin. The scoring should have a diamond pattern.

3. Sprinkle the tops of each half with salt. Place the halves, cut side up, in a baking dish and bake for about 15 minutes.

4. Heat the oil in a skillet and add the garlic and onion. Cook until the onion wilts, about 5 minutes. Add the lamb, stirring and chopping down with the side of a heavy metal spoon to break up any lumps.

5. Add the tomatoes and cover. Continue cooking for about 10 minutes. Uncover.

6. Meanwhile, bring about 4 cups of water to the boil. Add the rice and cook, stirring occasionally, for about 10 minutes. Drain.

7. When the eggplants are ready, remove from the oven and reduce the temperature to 375 degrees. Using a spoon, scoop out the center scored portion, leaving the ½-inch-thick shell. Chop the center pulp. There should be about 1½ cups.

8. Add the pulp to the lamb mixture and continue cooking for about 1 minute. Add the drained rice and stir. Add the lemon juice, dill, parsley, salt and pepper to taste.

9. Arrange the eggplant shells in a baking dish. Fill with the lamb mixture, piling it up until all is used. Sprinkle the top of each eggplant half with chopped feta cheese or 1 tablespoon grated Parmesan cheese.

10. Place the dish in the oven and bake for 30 minutes.

YIELD: 4 servings.

Eggplant with Ham Stuffing

- 4 tablespoons butter
- 1½ cups finely chopped onion, about ½ pound
- 1 clove garlic, minced
- 1 pound fresh mushrooms, finely chopped, about 4 cups
- Juice of 1 lemon
- Salt and freshly ground black pepper to taste
- 3 tablespoons finely chopped parsley
- 1 teaspoon finely chopped fresh thyme, or ½ teaspoon dried
- 2 tablespoons finely chopped fresh basil
- ½ pound boiled, sliced ham, finely chopped
- 10 tablespoons fresh bread crumbs
- 7 tablespoons freshly grated Parmesan cheese
- 2 large or 3 medium-sized eggplants, about 2½ pounds
- Flour for dredging
- 1 cup peanut, vegetable or corn oil, approximately
- Fresh tomato sauce (see recipe page 407)

1. Melt the butter in a skillet and add the onion and garlic. Cook, stirring, until the onion is wilted, about 5 minutes. Add the mushrooms, lemon juice, salt and pepper, parsley, thyme and basil. Cook over relatively high heat, stirring frequently, until the liquid has almost completely evaporated, 8 to 10 minutes.

2. Add the ham and cook, stirring, for about 4 minutes. Add 6 tablespoons of the bread crumbs and 3 tablespoons of the grated Parmesan cheese.

3. Trim off the ends and cut each eggplant into ½-inch slices. (We used 3 eggplants cut into 16 slices.)

4. Pour the flour onto a baking dish and add salt and pepper to taste. Dredge the eggplant slices in the mixture on both sides, shaking off the excess.

5. Heat about ¼ cup of oil in a large, heavy skillet and add as many eggplant slices as the skillet will hold. Cook until golden brown on one side, 1½ to 2 minutes, adding more oil, little by little. The point is to add as

much oil as necessary but as little as possible. Turn the slices, cook until golden on that side and drain on paper toweling. Continue adding slices and oil as necessary until the slices have been cooked on both sides.

6. Select a rectangular, square or oval baking dish. (We used a No. 6 Pyrex glass dish that measured 11¾ inches by 7½ inches by 1¾ inches.) Arrange the smaller slices of eggplant, sides touching, on the bottom of the dish. Spoon the filling into the center, spreading it out almost but not quite to the edges and mounding it in the center. Cover with the remaining slices, overlapping as necessary.

7. Blend the remaining bread crumbs and Parmesan cheese and sprinkle it over all.

8. When ready to cook, preheat the oven to 400 degrees. Bake for 35 to 40 minutes or longer. Remove the dish and pour off the fat that will have accumulated on top and around the edges. Let cool slightly. Serve with tomato sauce.

YIELD: 6 to 10 servings.

Barbara Tropp, whose expertise in Chinese cooking came about by way of studying Chinese poetry and art in Taiwan, explained to us that this dish comes from the word "guai," which in Chinese poetry can mean odd or weird. In cooking, however, strange flavor refers to an ineffable and delicious blend of flavors—spicy, subtle, sweet, tart and tangy all at the same time.

❧

Strange Flavor Eggplant

- 1½ pounds eggplant, preferably the Chinese long variety, available in Oriental supermarkets and grocery stores
- 1 tablespoon finely minced garlic
- 1 tablespoon finely chopped fresh ginger
- 1 large scallion, trimmed and cut into 1-inch lengths
- ¼ to ½ teaspoon hot red pepper flakes
- 2½ tablespoons thin (regular) soy sauce
- 2½ to 3 tablespoons loosely packed light brown sugar
- 1 teaspoon rice vinegar
- 2 tablespoons hot water
- 2 tablespoons corn or peanut oil
- 1 teaspoon Chinese or Japanese sesame oil
- 1 tablespoon chopped scallion, or sprigs of fresh coriander for garnish

1. Preheat the oven to 475 degrees.

2. Rinse the eggplants and pat dry. Prick them all over with a fork.

3. Arrange the eggplants on a baking dish or cookie sheet. Put the dish in the center of the oven and bake until eggplants are wilted and collapse when pressed. Turn once as they bake. This will take 20 to 40 minutes or longer. Let stand until cool enough to handle.

4. Pull off and discard the skin of each eggplant. Cut the flesh into pieces and put in the container of a food processor or blender. Blend until smooth. Scrape the eggplant into a bowl.

5. Add the garlic, ginger and 1-inch lengths of scallion to the container of a food processor or blender. Blend thoroughly. Scrape into a bowl and add the pepper flakes.

6. Combine the soy sauce, sugar, vinegar and water, stirring to dissolve the sugar.

7. Heat a wok and add the corn oil. Add the garlic mixture and cook, stirring, for about 20 seconds. Do not burn.

8. Add the sugar mixture and stir. When the liquid boils, add the eggplant. Stir to blend. Bring to the simmer.

9. Add the sesame oil and stir. Scrape the mixture into a serving dish. Garnish with chopped scallion or sprigs of fresh coriander. Serve hot, cold or lukewarm.

YIELD: 4 servings.

Baked Stuffed Eggplant Rolls

- 1 large eggplant, about 1½ pounds
- 2 tablespoons peanut, vegetable or corn oil
- 3 tablespoons plus 1 teaspoon butter
- 4 tablespoons flour
- 2 cups milk
- 2 tablespoons finely chopped onion
- Freshly ground black pepper to taste
- ½ cup grated Parmesan or Gruyère cheese
- 1 tablespoon finely chopped parsley
- 1 egg, lightly beaten

1. Preheat the oven to 400 degrees.

2. If the eggplant is not young and tender, peel it. Otherwise, leave the skin intact.

3. Cut the eggplant into very thin lengthwise slices, each about ¼ inch thick. There should be about 14 slices. Arrange the slices in one layer on one or two baking sheets and brush lightly with oil. Place the baking sheet in the oven and bake about 5 minutes.

4. Meanwhile, melt 3 tablespoons of the butter in a saucepan and add the flour, stirring with a wire whisk. Add the milk, stirring rapidly with the whisk. When blended and smooth, let simmer for 1 minute. Remove from the heat.

5. Melt the remaining 1 teaspoon of butter in a saucepan and add the onion. Sprinkle with pepper and cook briefly, stirring. Add 6 tablespoons of the sauce, half of the cheese and the parsley. Blend.

6. Arrange the eggplant slices on a flat surface. Spoon an equal amount of the filling on top of each and smooth it over. Roll up the eggplant slices, starting at the small end, to enclose the filling.

7. Butter a baking dish and arrange the rolls close together in it.

8. To the sauce in the saucepan add the beaten egg. Blend well and heat to the bubbling point. Spoon the sauce over the eggplant rolls. Sprinkle with the remaining cheese and place in the oven. Bake for 10 minutes. Run briefly under the broiler to glaze.

YIELD: 4 to 6 servings.

Among the handful of vegetables and salad greens that most appeal to our palates is one of the most difficult to cultivate, Belgian endive. Endive is cultivated by hand, as it has been for the past 125 years, on the Flemish flatlands that surround Brussels. The vegetable defies harvesting by machine. The seeds are sown by hand and, when they produce roots at the end of six weeks, the roots must be dug up and replanted in a blend of sand and soil that offers both heat and humidity, plus total darkness. It is this combination of factors that produces a premature, straight, smooth and fragile-crisp endive.

As if this were not labor enough, the endive is then harvested, replanted and covered with deep-layered mounds of loamy earth. Weeks later, the ready-to-market endive is again brought to the surface by hand, washed, spun-dried and packaged to be sold at home or shipped overseas.

An average harvest is estimated at about 80,000 tons a year; of this, more than 550 tons are exported to the United States for the delectation of those who cherish the finer things of the table. Although endive is best known and enjoyed in this country as a salad ingredient, it is a remarkably versatile vegetable, as the following recipes demonstrate.

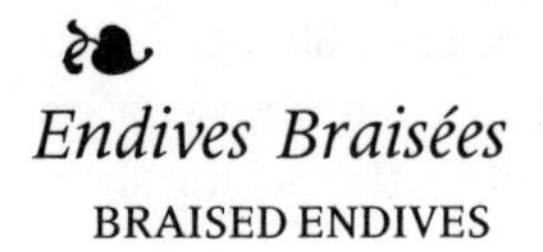

Endives Braisées

BRAISED ENDIVES

- 8 firm, perfect, unblemished endives, about 1½ pounds
- 1 tablespoon butter
- Juice of ½ lemon
- ½ cup water
- 1 teaspoon sugar
- Salt to taste, if desired
- Freshly ground black pepper to taste

1. Trim off the darkened ends of each endive. Put the endives in one layer in a heavy skillet.

2. Add the butter, lemon juice, water, sugar, salt and pepper and cover closely. Bring to the boil and simmer for 25 minutes.

YIELD: 4 servings.

Endives et Poulet au Gratin

ENDIVES AND CHICKEN AU GRATIN

- 8 firm, perfect, unblemished endives, about 1½ pounds
- 2½ cups fresh or canned chicken broth
- Juice of ½ lemon
- Salt to taste, if desired
- Freshly ground black pepper to taste
- 3 tablespoons butter
- ¼ cup flour
- 1 cup heavy cream
- 3 cups diced cooked chicken
- 1 egg yolk
- 2 tablespoons freshly grated Parmesan cheese
- 1 tablespoon fine fresh bread crumbs

1. Trim off the darkened ends of the endives. Split the endives in half lengthwise and cut the pieces crosswise into 1-inch lengths. There should be about 8 cups.

2. Put the pieces in a casserole and add ½ cup of the chicken broth, the lemon juice, salt and pepper. Cover, bring to a boil and cook for about 15 minutes. The liquid should have evaporated. If there is liquid, uncover and cook until the liquid evaporates.

3. Meanwhile, melt the butter in a saucepan and add the flour, stirring with a wire whisk. When blended, add the remaining 2 cups of chicken

broth, stirring rapidly with the whisk. Continue cooking, stirring often with the whisk, for about 10 minutes. Add the cream, salt and pepper, and continue cooking for about 5 minutes, stirring often.

4. Add the chicken to the endives and 2 cups of the sauce. Stir to blend.

5. Add the egg yolk to the remaining sauce and blend.

6. Preheat the oven to 375 degrees.

7. Spoon the creamed chicken mixture into a baking dish (an oval dish measuring 14 by 8½ by 2 inches is ideal). Spoon the remaining sauce over all, and sprinkle with the cheese and bread crumbs. Bake for 30 minutes, or until piping hot and golden brown on top.

YIELD: 6 to 8 servings.

Endives au Parmesan

BAKED ENDIVES WITH PARMESAN CHEESE

- 8 cooked, well-drained endives (see recipe for braised endives)
- 2 tablespoons butter
- ¼ cup freshly grated Parmesan cheese

1. Preheat the oven to 425 degrees.

2. Drain the endives well on paper toweling.

3. Using 1 tablespoon of the butter, lightly butter the bottom and sides of a baking dish large enough to hold the endives close together in one layer. Add the endives. Sprinkle with the cheese and dot with the remaining butter.

4. Bake for 15 minutes. Run briefly under the broiler until browned and nicely glazed.

YIELD: 4 servings.

One of the most abundant, curiously neglected and oddly named foods in America is the Jerusalem artichoke. It is not an artichoke at all, as we know the more sophisticated globe artichoke. The Jerusalem version is actually related to the sunflower, called girasole in Italian. And, at least according to folk etymology, girasole through some slip of nomenclature turned into Jerusalem. In today's French kitchens it is known as a topinambour, again for an unusual reason: At approximately the same time that it was introduced into that country, there was an exhibition featuring a tribe from Brazil known as *topinambours.* The vegetable was thus christened and the name stuck. Whatever it is called (most recently sun chokes), it is delicious and, when in season, readily available from California.

Topinambours au Gratin

JERUSALEM ARTICHOKES OR SUN CHOKES AU GRATIN

- 1 pound Jerusalem artichokes or sun chokes, about 8 to 10
- Salt to taste, if desired
- 4 tablespoons butter
- 4 tablespoons flour
- 1½ cups milk
- Freshly ground black pepper to taste
- ⅛ teaspoon grated nutmeg
- 2 tablespoons finely chopped onion
- ¼ cup heavy cream
- Pinch of cayenne pepper
- 1 cup grated Swiss or Gruyère cheese
- 1 egg yolk

1. Preheat the broiler.

2. Using a small regular or swivel-bladed paring knife, peel the artichokes. If the artichokes are very large, cut them in half. Ideally, the artichokes or pieces of artichoke should be of uniform size or the size of the smallest whole artichoke.

3. Put the artichokes in a saucepan. Add cold water to cover and salt to taste. Bring to the boil. Simmer for 10 to 15 minutes, or until tender but still a little crisp. Drain well.

4. Meanwhile, melt 3 tablespoons of the butter in a saucepan; add the flour, stirring with a wire whisk. Add the milk, stirring rapidly with the whisk. Add the salt, pepper and nutmeg.

5. Cut the hot artichokes into not-too-small bite-sized cubes or wedges. There should be about 2 cups.

6. Melt the remaining 1 tablespoon of butter in a saucepan and add the onion. Cook until wilted. Add the artichoke pieces, cream and cayenne. Bring to a boil and add the white sauce. Blend well. Bring to a simmer. Add ¾ cup of the grated cheese and stir until melted. Add the egg yolk and simmer for about 15 seconds.

7. Pour and scrape the mixture into a baking dish. Sprinkle with the remaining cheese.

8. Place under the broiler until bubbling and nicely glazed on top.

YIELD: 6 servings.

Topinambours Provençale

JERUSALEM ARTICHOKES OR SUN CHOKES WITH TOMATOES

- 1 pound Jerusalem artichokes or sun chokes, about 8 to 10
- 3 tablespoons olive oil
- 1 tablespoon finely minced garlic
- 1 cup drained, imported canned tomatoes
- 2 tablespoons finely chopped parsley
- Salt to taste, if desired
- Freshly ground black pepper to taste

1. Using a small regular or swivel-bladed paring knife, peel the artichokes. Cut them into ¼-inch-thick slices. There should be about 3 cups.

2. Heat the oil in a saucepan and add the artichoke slices. Cook, stirring and tossing in the oil, for about 2 minutes. Add the garlic and cook, stirring and tossing, for about 30 seconds. Add the tomatoes, parsley, salt and pepper to taste. Stir and cover. Cook for 8 to 10 minutes and serve.

YIELD: 4 servings.

If we had to produce a list of our favorite vegetables for cold weather, it would certainly include the leek, that delectable green and white root of such a hearty nature that it can be left in the ground all winter if the temperature does not drop beyond 10 below. Although it is a member of the onion family, it has a subtle, irresistible flavor and certainly leaves no aftertaste.

Poireaux au Gratin

LEEKS AU GRATIN

- 3 pounds leeks, about 8 small leeks
- 2 tablespoons butter
- Salt, if desired
- Freshly ground black pepper to taste
- ⅛ teaspoon grated nutmeg
- 1 cup heavy cream
- ½ cup freshly grated Parmesan cheese

1. Trim off the stem end of each leek. Cut off enough of the green part to leave a main section of about 7 inches. Split the leeks in half lengthwise. Cut the split leeks crosswise into 1½-inch lengths. There should be about 8 cups loosely packed. Rinse thoroughly in cold water. Drain.

2. Put the leeks in a heavy skillet and add the butter, salt, pepper and nutmeg. Cook, stirring, for about 1 minute. Add the cream and bring to the simmer. Cover and cook for 15 minutes.

3. Preheat the broiler.

4. Spoon the hot leeks into a baking and serving dish and smooth over the top. Sprinkle the top with cheese and place under the broiler until nicely glazed. Serve hot.

YIELD: 6 servings.

Purée de Poireaux

LEEK PURÉE

- 3 pounds leeks, about 8 small leeks
- Salt, if desired
- Freshly ground black pepper to taste
- 4 tablespoons butter
- ⅛ teaspoon grated nutmeg

1. Trim off the stem end of each leek. Cut off enough of the green part to leave a main section of about 7 inches. Split the leeks in half lengthwise. Cut the split leeks crosswise into 1½-inch lengths. There should be about 8 cups loosely packed. Rinse thoroughly in cold water. Drain.

2. Put the leeks in a saucepan or kettle and add enough water to cover. Bring to the boil and simmer, uncovered, for about 15 minutes, or until tender. Drain thoroughly.

3. Put the leeks into the container of a food processor or blender and purée until fine. Scrape the mixture into a saucepan and start beating. Add the salt, pepper, butter and nutmeg. Stir until piping hot.

YIELD: 6 to 8 servings.

If you are reasonably well versed in Chinese cookery, you will know that tree fungus is more often than not listed as tree ears or tree ear mushrooms. If you have ever eaten those staples of a Chinese menu, hot and sour soup and moo-shu-ro, you have undoubtedly sampled tree ears, whether you knew it or not. And we have recently learned the happy news from a scientist at the University of Minnesota that tree ears may be one reason why people in China have far less heart disease than Westerners. The summer oyster mushrooms in this recipe are sometimes called abalone mushrooms, both names referring to their shape and texture.

Summer Oyster Mushrooms with Tree Ears and Corn

- ¼ cup dried tree ears
- 5 dried black Chinese mushrooms
- 1 10-ounce can summer oyster mushrooms (see Note)
- 1 8-ounce can young corn—this is baby corn on the cob (see Note)
- ¾ cup chicken broth
- 2 teaspoons cornstarch
- 1½ teaspoons sugar
- Salt to taste
- ¼ cup peanut, vegetable or corn oil
- 2 tablespoons shaoxing wine or dry sherry
- 2 scallions, trimmed and cut into 2-inch lengths

1. Put the tree ears and dried black mushrooms in separate bowls. Add boiling water to cover each. Let stand for at least 30 minutes.

2. Drain the summer oyster mushrooms and the young corn and set aside.

3. Blend the chicken broth, cornstarch, ½ teaspoon sugar and salt and set aside.

4. Drain the tree ears and mushrooms. Squeeze to extract any excess liquid.

5. Put the tree ears in a saucepan and add cold water to cover. Bring to the boil and simmer for 1 minute. Drain.

6. Heat the oil in a wok and add the black mushrooms and tree ears. Cook, stirring, for about 10 seconds.

7. Add the oyster mushrooms and cook, stirring, for about 10 seconds. Add the remaining teaspoon sugar, salt to taste and the wine.

8. Add the corn and cook, stirring, for about 10 seconds. Add the chicken broth mixture and cook, stirring, for about 1 minute. Add the scallions. Cook for about 10 seconds, stirring. Transfer to a hot platter and serve.

YIELD: 8 servings.

Note: The Chinese ingredients listed in this recipe are available in Oriental groceries and supermarkets.

Braised Chinese Mushrooms for a Crowd

- 48 large to 60 medium-sized unbroken dried Chinese mushrooms (preferably Botan brand Yellow Label)
- ¾ pound shrimp, peeled, deveined and finely chopped
- ¾ pound ground pork, preferably not too lean and not too finely ground
- 6 water chestnuts, preferably fresh, finely minced, about ½ cup
- ¼ cup finely chopped scallions, green and white parts combined
- 2 teaspoons finely minced fresh ginger
- 3 tablespoons light soy sauce
- 3 tablespoons shaoxing wine or dry sherry
- 3 tablespoons cornstarch
- ¾ teaspoon plus ¼ teaspoon sugar
- 1 teaspoon sesame oil
- Salt to taste, if desired
- Freshly ground black pepper to taste
- 6 tablespoons corn, peanut or vegetable oil
- 1½ cups fresh or canned chicken broth
- 1½ tablespoons oyster sauce

1. Put the mushrooms in a large bowl and add hot water to cover. Let stand for 1 hour or longer.

2. Rinse and dry the mushrooms. Cut off and discard stems.

3. In a mixing bowl, combine the shrimp, pork, water chestnuts, scallions, ginger, soy sauce, shaoxing, cornstarch, ¾ teaspoon sugar, sesame oil, salt and pepper. Blend well.

4. Fill each mushroom cap with an equal portion of the mixture, mounding and smoothing over the tops.

5. Heat 3 tablespoons of the oil in each of two large skillets. Add the mushrooms, stuffing side down, and brown lightly. Turn the mushrooms carefully in both skillets and carefully pour off the oil from both skillets.

6. Blend the broth, oyster sauce and the remaining ¼ teaspoon sugar. Pour an equal portion of this into each skillet. Bring the liquid to the simmer and cover closely. Cook over low heat for about 15 minutes, basting once during cooking. If the liquid starts to evaporate, add a few drops of water and continue cooking.

7. Give the mushrooms one final basting. Transfer them to a dish in one layer. Pour the remaining liquid over all. Let cool uncovered. Cover and refrigerate.

8. When ready to serve, preheat the oven to 300 degrees. Heat the mushrooms in their cooking liquid for 15 minutes. These mushrooms are good even at room temperature.

YIELD: 20 to 25 servings.

Funghi alla Marsala

MUSHROOMS IN MARSALA WINE

- 1 ounce dried mushrooms, preferably imported Italian boletus mushrooms, or use one ¾-ounce package
- 1 cup lukewarm water
- ¼ cup olive oil
- ½ teaspoon finely minced garlic
- ½ teaspoon dried rosemary
- 1 pound mushrooms, thinly sliced, about 6 cups
- ½ cup Marsala wine

1. Soak the mushrooms in lukewarm water for 30 minutes. Line a small sieve with cheesecloth and add the mushrooms. Strain and reserve the soaking liquid. Squeeze the mushrooms in the sieve to extract their juices.

2. Heat the oil in a casserole and add the soaked, drained mushrooms, garlic and rosemary. Cook, stirring, for about 1 minute. Add the reserved soaking liquid and cook down over high heat until most of the liquid evaporates.

3. Add the fresh mushrooms and cook, stirring often, until the mushrooms are wilted. Add the Marsala and cook, stirring occasionally but gently, until the wine is almost but not quite evaporated. Serve hot or at room temperature.

YIELD: 4 servings.

Onions à la Grecque

- 48 small white onions, about 1¾ pounds
- ¼ cup olive oil
- ¼ cup lemon juice
- 1 teaspoon finely minced garlic
- 1 teaspoon fennel seeds
- 1 teaspoon coriander seeds
- 1 bay leaf
- 1 teaspoon whole black peppercorns
- ½ teaspoon dried thyme
- 2 tablespoons white vinegar
- ½ cup water
- ½ cup diced celery

1. Peel the onions and put them in one layer in a skillet or casserole.

2. Add the remaining ingredients and bring to the boil. Simmer for about 30 minutes, or until onions are tender yet firm. Let cool. Serve at room temperature.

YIELD: 6 to 8 servings.

Kay Ahuja's Indian Okra and Onions

- 1 pound fresh baby okra
- ¼ cup peanut, vegetable or corn oil
- 2½ cups thinly sliced onion
- Salt and freshly ground black pepper to taste
- ¼ teaspoon cayenne pepper
- ¼ teaspoon ground turmeric
- ½ teaspoon ground coriander
- ¾ teaspoon ground cumin

1. Rinse the okra in cold water and drain well. If the stem ends are tough, cut them off and discard. Cut the okra into ½-inch lengths. There should be about 4 cups.

2. Heat the oil in a skillet and add the onion. Cook over medium heat, stirring, until wilted. Continue cooking until somewhat caramelized but not burned.

3. Add the salt, pepper, cayenne, turmeric, coriander and cumin.

4. Add the okra and cover closely. Cook over low heat until tender, for 5 to 10 minutes.

YIELD: 4 servings.

Oignons Farcis

STUFFED ONIONS

- 6 large onions, about 3 pounds
- 3 tablespoons butter
- 1 cup finely chopped mushrooms
- 1 teaspoon finely minced garlic
- ½ pound ground veal, pork or beef
- ¼ cup fine fresh bread crumbs
- 1 egg, lightly beaten
- ¼ cup finely chopped parsley
- 6 tablespoons freshly grated Parmesan cheese
- 1 cup unsalted chicken broth

1. Peel the onions. Cut off a slice from the top of each onion. The diameter of the top of the onion should be about 2½ inches. Reserve the slices.

2. Cut off a thin slice from the bottom of each onion so that they will sit flat in a baking dish when stuffed. Reserve the slices.

3. Put the reserved slices in the container of a food processor or blender and process to a fine purée. There should be about 2½ cups.

4. Using a melon ball cutter, scoop out a portion of each onion, leaving a shell about ½ inch thick. Put the onions in a kettle and add cold water to cover. Bring to the boil and simmer for 5 minutes. Drain thoroughly.

5. Melt 1 tablespoon of the butter in a heavy saucepan and add the mushrooms and garlic. Cook briefly and add the meat and puréed onions. Cook, stirring often, for about 15 minutes, or until the filling is quite thick. Stir in the bread crumbs, egg and parsley.

6. Melt the remaining 2 tablespoons of butter in a baking dish large enough to hold the onions compactly without crowding.

7. Stuff each onion with an equal portion of the filling and arrange them in the baking dish. Sprinkle with the cheese.

8. Preheat the oven to 400 degrees.

9. Place the onions in the baking dish and pour the chicken broth around them. Bake for 20 minutes.

10. Reduce the oven temperature to 350 degrees and continue baking for 30 to 40 minutes, or until the onions are quite tender but firm. Baste and serve with the natural sauce.

YIELD: 6 servings.

Puréed Parsnips and Carrots

- 4 medium-sized parsnips, about 1 pound, trimmed and scraped
- 4 to 5 carrots, about ½ pound, trimmed and scraped
- Salt, if desired
- Freshly ground black pepper to taste
- 2 tablespoons butter
- ½ cup milk
- ⅛ teaspoon grated nutmeg

1. Cut the parsnips in half lengthwise. Cut each half crosswise into ½-inch-thick pieces. There should be about 3 cups.

2. Cut the carrots crosswise into rounds about ¼ inch thick. Combine the carrots and parsnips in a saucepan. Add water to cover and salt and pepper to taste. Bring to the boil and cook for about 5 minutes, or until tender. Do not overcook.

3. Drain thoroughly. Put the vegetables into the container of a food processor and process or, preferably, into a conical food mill and pass the vegetables through into a saucepan.

4. Reheat while stirring the butter, milk, salt to taste and nutmeg into the mixture. When piping hot, remove from the heat and serve.

YIELD: 6 or more servings.

Crème de Petits Pois Parfumé à la Menthe

PURÉED FRESH PEAS WITH MINT

- 4 tablespoons butter
- 1 tablespoon finely chopped onion
- ⅛ teaspoon sugar
- 2 cups shelled fresh green peas
- Salt to taste
- 2 cups water
- 8 fresh mint leaves
- ½ cup heavy cream

1. Melt 2 tablespoons of the butter in a saucepan and add the chopped onion. Cook, stirring, until wilted. Add the sugar, green peas, salt, water and 1 mint leaf. Bring to the boil and cook for about 3 minutes or longer until the peas are tender. The cooking time will depend on the age and size of the peas.

2. Pour the peas and liquid into the container of a food processor and purée as finely as possible. Spoon and scrape the mixture into a saucepan. Add the cream and bring to the boil. Simmer for 5 minutes, stirring.

3. Finely shred the remaining mint leaves and add them.

4. Swirl in the remaining butter.

YIELD: 4 to 6 servings.

If anyone were to study our enthusiasms, they would find a well-defined fondness for stuffed vegetables. There is every reason to presume that the first version came about through some fortuitous deployment of a leftover food, such as a roast. Chances are that the result was so eminently delectable that the stuffing became an end in itself, as with these three Tex-Mex-inspired fillings for sweet peppers.

Picadillo-stuffed Sweet Peppers

- 6 large red or green sweet peppers
- 2 tablespoons olive oil
- ⅓ cup whole blanched almonds
- 1½ cups finely chopped onion
- 1 tablespoon finely chopped garlic
- 1 pound lean ground beef
- 1 tablespoon chili powder, optional
- 1 tablespoon chopped canned jalapeño pepper with seeds
- 1 cup fresh tomato sauce (see recipe page 407), or use 1 cup drained canned tomatoes
- Salt and freshly ground black pepper to taste
- ¼ teaspoon ground cinnamon
- ⅛ teaspoon ground cloves
- ¼ to ½ cup seedless raisins
- 3 tablespoons ground blanched almonds

1. Split the peppers in half lengthwise and remove the cores. Bring a large quantity of water to the boil and add the peppers. Cook for about 30 seconds and drain well.

2. Heat 1 tablespoon of the olive oil in a saucepan and add the whole almonds. Cook, shaking the skillet and stirring, until the almonds are golden brown. Remove with a slotted spoon and set aside.

3. To the oil remaining in the saucepan, add the onions and garlic. Cook until wilted. Add the meat and cook, stirring and chopping down with the side of a metal spoon to break up the lumps. Add the chili powder, chopped jalapeños, tomato sauce, salt and pepper, cinnamon, cloves and raisins. Cook for about 3 minutes and add the reserved whole almonds.

4. Rub the bottom of a large baking dish with the remaining tablespoon of olive oil. Arrange the peppers over it, split side up. Sprinkle inside lightly with salt and pepper. Fill the cavities with the picadillo. Sprinkle the fillings with the ground almonds.

5. When ready to cook, preheat the oven to 375 degrees. Bake for about 15 minutes.

YIELD: 4 to 6 servings.

Chili-stuffed Green Peppers

- 4 large, unblemished green peppers, about 1 pound
- ¾ cup elbow macaroni
- 1 tablespoon olive oil
- 1½ cups finely chopped onion
- ¼ cup finely chopped celery
- ¾ pound ground beef
- 1 tablespoon minced garlic
- 1 tablespoon chili powder
- ½ teaspoon ground cumin
- ½ teaspoon ground coriander
- 2 tablespoons tomato paste
- Salt and freshly ground black pepper to taste
- ¼ teaspoon hot red pepper flakes
- 1 tablespoon butter
- ¾ cup chopped tomatoes

1. Carefully cut off a very thin slice from the end of each pepper. This will permit them to stand upright. Cut away and discard the core of each pepper and scoop out and discard the white inner veins. Set the peppers aside.

2. Cook the macaroni in boiling water until tender. Drain.

3. Heat the oil in a skillet and add 1 cup of the chopped onion and the celery. Cook until the onion is wilted.

4. Add the beef and cook, stirring and breaking up the lumps in the meat with the sides of a heavy metal spoon. Sprinkle with the garlic, chili powder, cumin and coriander. Add the tomato paste, salt and pepper to taste and the red pepper flakes. Cook for about 10 minutes. Stir in the macaroni.

5. Meanwhile, bring a large quantity of water to the boil. Add the green peppers and let the water return to the boil. Let simmer for about 1 minute. Drain thoroughly.

6. Preheat the oven to 400 degrees.

7. With the 1 tablespoon of butter, grease a baking dish large enough to hold the stuffed peppers in one layer. Scatter the remaining ½ cup of chopped onion and the chopped tomatoes over it.

8. Stuff the peppers and arrange them stuffed side up in the dish. Bake for 25 minutes.

YIELD: 2 to 4 servings.

Tamale-style Stuffed Peppers

- 4 sweet red or green peppers, about 1½ pounds
- 1 cup chopped ripe tomatoes, or use imported canned tomatoes
- ¼ cup yellow cornmeal
- 3 tablespoons olive oil
- 1 cup finely chopped onion
- 1 tablespoon finely minced garlic
- 1 pound ground lean beef
- ¼ cup chili powder, more or less to taste
- 1 teaspoon ground cumin
- ½ teaspoon ground coriander
- Salt to taste, if desired
- Freshly ground black pepper to taste
- 1 cup cooked corn cut from the cob, or use canned drained whole kernel corn
- 2 tablespoons chopped fresh coriander leaves, optional
- ½ cup grated Cheddar cheese

1. Split the peppers lengthwise in half. Remove and discard the seeds and veins. Drop them into a saucepan or kettle of boiling water. When the water returns to the boil, drain the peppers.

2. Put the tomatoes in a saucepan and cook them for about 3 minutes, stirring and breaking up lumps. Add the cornmeal, stirring constantly. Let cook over low heat for about 10 minutes, stirring often to prevent lumping.

3. Heat 2 tablespoons of the olive oil in a saucepan and add the onion and garlic. Cook, stirring, until the onion is wilted. Add the beef and chop

down with a heavy metal spoon to break up any lumps. Add the chili powder, cumin, ground coriander, salt and pepper. Add the tomato-cornmeal mixture, the corn and chopped fresh coriander. Blend well.

4. Preheat the oven to 350 degrees.

5. Select a baking dish large enough to hold the peppers in one layer. Rub with the remaining 1 tablespoon of olive oil. Stuff the pepper halves with equal portions of the filling.

6. Sprinkle each stuffed pepper with 1 tablespoon of grated cheese. Bake for 30 minutes.

YIELD: 4 servings.

Butternut Squash Américaine

BUTTERNUT SQUASH WITH MINTED GREEN PEAS

- 2 butternut squash, about 1½ pounds each
- 2 tablespoons melted butter
- ¼ cup brown sugar
- 1 teaspoon confectioners' sugar
- 1 teaspoon ground ginger
- 1 10-ounce package frozen small green peas
- 1 tablespoon butter
- 2 teaspoons chopped fresh mint, or 1 teaspoon dried
- Salt, if desired
- Freshly ground black pepper to taste

1. Preheat the oven to 375 degrees.

2. Split the squash, lengthwise or crosswise, in half. Scrape out and discard the seeds. Cut off a thin slice from the bottom of each half so that it will rest firmly upright in a pan.

3. Brush the rims and cavity of each squash with the melted butter.

4. Blend the sugars and ginger and sprinkle each half, rim and cavity, with equal portions of the mixture. Arrange the halves on a baking sheet and bake for 1 hour.

5. Meanwhile, put the peas into a sieve and run hot water over them for 15 seconds, or until defrosted. Put the peas in a small skillet. Add the 1 tablespoon of butter, mint, salt and pepper to taste. Cook briefly until heated throughout. Do not overcook. Fill the squash halves with the peas and serve immediately.

YIELD: 4 servings.

Curry-stuffed Tomatoes

- ⅓ cup dark raisins
- 8 ripe but firm tomatoes, about 4 pounds
- 2 tablespoons butter
- ¼ cup finely chopped celery
- ¾ cup finely chopped onion
- 1 teaspoon minced garlic
- 2 tablespoons curry powder
- 2 bay leaves
- 1 pound finely ground lean lamb
- Salt and freshly ground black pepper to taste
- ¼ cup fine bread crumbs

1. Put the raisins in a bowl and add warm water to cover. Set aside for 30 minutes.

2. Slice about half an inch off the tops of the tomatoes. Set the tops aside.

3. Using a melon ball cutter or a spoon, scoop out the inside of each tomato, leaving a shell about ⅓ inch thick. Reserve and chop the scooped-out pulp.

4. Melt 1 tablespoon of the butter in a wide saucepan and add the celery, ½ cup of the onion and the garlic and cook, stirring, until the onion is wilted. Add the curry powder and bay leaves. Add the lamb and cook, stirring and breaking up the lumps in the meat with the side of a heavy metal spoon.

5. Add the chopped tomato pulp and salt and pepper to taste. Cook, stirring often, for about 30 minutes.

6. Drain the raisins and add them. Cook for 5 minutes longer.

7. Preheat the oven to 400 degrees.

8. Butter a baking dish large enough to hold the tomatoes in one layer with the remaining butter. Sprinkle with the remaining ¼ cup chopped onion. Chop the reserved tops of the tomatoes, cutting away and discarding the cores. Sprinkle the chopped tomatoes over the onions.

9. Sprinkle the inside of the tomatoes with salt and pepper to taste. Stuff the tomatoes with the curried lamb.

10. Arrange the stuffed tomatoes over the chopped tomatoes and onion. Sprinkle the tops of the stuffed tomatoes with bread crumbs.

11. Place the tomatoes in the oven and bake for 30 minutes.

YIELD: 4 to 8 servings.

Tomatoes Stuffed with Keema

- 8 to 10 medium to large ripe, unblemished tomatoes, about 3 pounds
- 4 tablespoons olive oil
- 1½ cups finely chopped onion
- 4 teaspoons finely minced garlic
- 1 tablespoon curry powder
- 1 teaspoon ground cumin
- 2 tablespoons chopped fresh ginger, or 1 teaspoon ground ginger
- ¼ teaspoon ground turmeric
- 1 pound ground lamb, pork or beef
- ¼ teaspoon hot red pepper flakes
- 2 tablespoons finely chopped fresh coriander leaves, or 1 teaspoon ground coriander
- Juice of ½ lime
- Salt to taste, if desired
- Freshly ground black pepper to taste
- 2 bay leaves

1. Preheat the oven to 350 degrees.

2. Cut off a slice, ½ inch or less, from the top of each tomato and set aside. Using a spoon or melon ball cutter, scoop out the pulp from the inner part of the tomato, leaving a substantial shell at least ¼ inch thick for stuffing. Chop the pulp and set it aside.

3. Heat 2 tablespoons of the oil in a skillet and cook 1 cup of the chopped onion, the garlic, the curry powder, cumin, ginger and turmeric until wilted.

4. Put the meat in a mixing bowl and add the onion mixture, pepper flakes, coriander, lime juice and ½ cup of the reserved chopped tomato pulp. Add salt and pepper to taste. Blend well.

5. Select a baking dish large enough to hold the tomatoes in one layer. Put the remaining 2 tablespoons of olive oil, the remaining ½ cup of chopped onion, the remaining chopped tomato pulp, the bay leaves, salt and pepper in the baking dish.

6. Fill each tomato with an equal portion of the meat mixture; round it on top. Place 1 cut-off tomato slice on top of each serving. Arrange the tomatoes in the baking dish.

7. Place the dish in the oven and bake for 1 hour. Serve the tomatoes with the pan mixture.

YIELD: 4 or 5 servings.

Of all the vegetables that have come into our kitchen over the last few decades, zucchini has been the most fascinating, for we watched it evolve from an obscure squash to an American favorite. When we published our first zucchini recipe in the early 1960s, it was a considerable oddity. In fact, it was necessary to define it as "green Italian squash."

Today, the number of zucchini admirers and the recipes they develop increase every day. No matter how often we use zucchini throughout the summer, we are never bored with it.

Chicken-stuffed Zucchini

- 6 unblemished zucchini, about 1½ pounds
- 2 tablespoons plus 1 teaspoon butter
- 2 tablespoons flour
- ¾ cup rich chicken broth (see recipe page 418)
- ½ cup milk
- ⅛ teaspoon grated nutmeg
- Salt and freshly ground black pepper to taste
- ¼ pound grated Cheddar cheese
- 1 tablespoon finely chopped shallots
- 1½ cups cooked chicken or turkey cut into ½-inch cubes
- 3 tablespoons freshly grated Parmesan cheese

1. Split the zucchini in half lengthwise. Using a melon ball cutter, scoop out the centers of each half, leaving a shell about ¼ inch thick. Reserve the scooped-out portion.

2. Bring a large quantity of water to the boil and add the zucchini shells. Let the water return to the boil and drain the shells.

3. Melt 1 tablespoon of the butter in a saucepan and add the flour, stirring with a whisk. When blended, add the broth and milk, stirring rapidly with the whisk. When blended and smooth, add the nutmeg, salt and pepper. Add the Cheddar cheese and stir until melted. Set the cheese sauce aside.

4. Melt 1 tablespoon of the butter in a saucepan and add the shallots. Cook briefly. Chop the reserved scooped-out zucchini into fine dice. There should be about 1 cup. Add it to the shallots and stir. Cook for about 3 minutes.

5. Add the chicken to the chopped zucchini mixture. Add about two thirds of the cheese sauce. Blend.

6. Butter the bottom of a baking dish large enough to hold the zucchini in one layer with the remaining butter. Neatly fill the zucchini halves with the chicken mixture.

7. Spoon a little of the remaining sauce over each stuffed zucchini half. Sprinkle with the Parmesan cheese.

8. When ready to cook, preheat the oven to 375 degrees. Bake for about 15 minutes.

YIELD: 4 to 6 servings.

❧

Stuffed Zucchini, Turkish Style

- 8 medium-sized zucchini, about 4 pounds
- 2 teaspoons peanut, vegetable or corn oil
- 1 cup finely chopped onion
- 1 teaspoon finely minced garlic
- ½ pound ground lamb
- 2 teaspoons grated lemon rind
- 1 cup chopped ripe tomatoes, fresh or canned
- 4 tablespoons rice
- 2 tablespoons finely chopped dill
- 4 tablespoons finely chopped parsley
- ¼ teaspoon ground cinnamon
- Salt to taste, if desired
- Freshly ground black pepper to taste
- 2 tablespoons olive oil
- 2 cups chicken broth, approximately
- 3 tablespoons lemon juice, optional
- 1 egg, optional

1. Preheat the oven to 350 degrees.

2. Cut off the ends of each zucchini, about 1 inch from each end. Save the cut-off pieces.

3. Using a small spoon, scoop out the center seeded portion from each cavity to make a tunnel for filling. The shell should be only about ¼ inch thick. Trim the end pieces to fit into each end to act as plugs.

4. Heat the peanut oil in a saucepan and add the onion and garlic. Cook, stirring, until wilted.

5. Put the meat in a bowl and add the cooked onion mixture, the lemon rind, tomatoes, rice, dill, parsley, cinnamon, salt and pepper. Blend well.

6. Fill the tunnels of each zucchini with the meat mixture. Stop each end with a plug. Select a baking dish large enough to hold the zucchini in one layer. Brush it with 1 tablespoon of the olive oil. Add the zucchini and brush them with the remaining oil. Pour 2 cups of chicken broth around the zucchini and place in the oven. Bake for 1½ hours.

7. You may serve the zucchini as they come from the oven or you may make a sauce as follows: Pour the cooking liquid into a glass measuring cup. Pour off all the fat. Add enough chicken broth to make ½ cup. Bring to the simmer in a saucepan. Beat the lemon juice and egg together until frothy. Add salt and pepper to taste. Pour this into the simmering sauce, stirring vigorously with a wire whisk. Cook for about 10 seconds. Take care not to overcook or the sauce will curdle. Pour the sauce over the stuffed zucchini and serve.

YIELD: 8 servings.

❧

Courgettes Farcies Marocaine

SAUSAGE-STUFFED ZUCCHINI

- 3 medium-sized zucchini, about 1 pound
- 6 small link sausages
- ½ teaspoon cayenne pepper
- ¼ cup peanut oil
- ¼ teaspoon ground anise seeds
- ¾ cup water, approximately
- 1 teaspoon ground turmeric
- 1 teaspoon ground cumin
- ½ teaspoon paprika
- Salt to taste, if desired
- 1 teaspoon finely chopped fresh coriander
- 3 whole cloves garlic, peeled
- ¼ cup peeled, seeded and diced tomato

1. Trim off the ends of each zucchini. Cut the center portions of each zucchini into 2-inch lengths. Cut the remaining ends into ½-inch rounds.

2. Using a knife or melon ball cutter, hollow out the centers of each length of zucchini. The hollowed-out portions should be just large enough to hold 1 small link of sausage; reserve the hollowed-out pulp.

3. Roll the link sausages in the cayenne pepper.

4. Heat the oil in a skillet and add the sausages. Cook, turning often, until browned and cooked through. Sprinkle with anise, coating them evenly.

5. Stuff 1 sausage inside each piece of zucchini. Put the stuffed pieces back into the skillet. Add the small rounds and hollowed-out pulp.

6. Combine the ¾ cup of water, turmeric, cumin, paprika, salt, coriander, garlic and tomato. Pour it over the zucchini. Cook, turning the zucchini pieces, for about 5 minutes. Cover closely and continue cooking for 30 minutes. Turn the pieces often in the cooking liquid so that they

cook evenly. If, as the zucchini cook, the water becomes too little, add up to ½ cup more. When ready, the zucchini should be very tender and the sauce cooked down to about ⅓ cup. Remove the cloves of garlic. Serve hot or cold.

YIELD: 6 servings.

Tian de Courgettes et Tomates

ZUCCHINI AND TOMATO CASSEROLE

- 3 medium-sized red peppers, about ½ pound, optional
- 6 medium-sized zucchini, about 1¾ pounds
- 4 large ripe tomatoes, about 2½ pounds
- 1 large onion, about ½ pound
- ⅓ cup plus ¼ cup olive oil
- ½ cup water
- 1 tablespoon finely minced garlic
- Salt to taste, if desired
- Freshly ground black pepper to taste
- 1 teaspoon dried thyme, or 4 sprigs fresh thyme broken into small pieces

1. If the peppers are to be used, preheat the broiler. Place the peppers under the broiler and roast until they are burnt on one side. Turn and roast on the other side. Continue turning until roasted all over, top and bottom. Put in a plastic bag to cool. Peel. Discard the stems and seeds. Cut the peppers into thin strips. There should be about ¾ cup.

2. Trim off the ends of the zucchini. Using a swivel-bladed vegetable cutter, trim off the sides of each zucchini, leaving intervals of green to make a pattern. Cut the zucchini on the bias into ¼-inch slices. There should be about 7 cups.

3. Remove the cores from the tomatoes. Cut each tomato into slices about ⅓ inch thick.

4. Peel the onion and cut it in half crosswise. Cut each half into very thin slices. There should be about 2 cups. Put the onion in a heavy saucepan.

5. Add ⅓ cup of oil and the water to the onion. Bring to the boil and cook over relatively high heat for 10 or 12 minutes. When ready, the onion will be nicely glazed and lightly browned. Do not burn.

6. Preheat the oven to 350 degrees.

7. Spoon the onion over the bottom of an oval or rectangular baking dish (a dish that measures about 13½ by 8 by 2 inches is ideal). Sprinkle the garlic and pepper strips over the onion.

8. Arrange a layer of tomatoes, letting them lean at an angle against the sides of the baking dish. Arrange a layer of zucchini against the tomatoes. Continue making layers until all the tomatoes and zucchini are used. Sprinkle with salt and pepper to taste and the thyme. Dribble the remaining ¼ cup of oil over all.

9. Place in the oven and bake for 30 minutes. Increase the oven temperature to 475 degrees and continue baking about 45 minutes. At this point the top of the vegetables will be quite dark. Press the vegetables down with a flat pancake turner. Return to the oven and continue baking for 15 minutes. Serve hot or cold.

YIELD: 4 to 6 servings.

Baked Zucchini with Herbs and Cheese

- 3 or 4 medium-sized zucchini, about 1¾ pounds
- Salt and freshly ground black pepper to taste
- ⅓ cup plus 2 tablespoons olive oil
- 1 clove garlic
- 1 cup white bread trimmed of crust and cut into 1-inch cubes
- 6 sprigs fresh parsley
- ½ teaspoon dried rosemary leaves
- ⅓ cup freshly grated Parmesan cheese

1. Preheat the oven to 400 degrees.

2. Trim off the ends of the zucchini and cut the zucchini on the bias into ½-inch slices.

3. Sprinkle the slices with salt and pepper. Heat ⅓ cup of the oil in a skillet and cook the slices until golden brown on one side. Turn and brown on the other. This may take several steps. Arrange the slices slightly overlapping on a baking dish in which they will fit neatly.

4. Blend the garlic, bread, parsley and rosemary in a food processor or blender. Sprinkle this over the zucchini and sprinkle with the cheese. Dribble the remaining oil over all and bake for 20 minutes, or until bubbling. If desired, run under the broiler to brown further.

YIELD: 6 to 8 servings.

PASTA, RICE AND OTHER GRAINS

WITH America in the throes of what has been called the "pastarization" of the nation, we invited the owners of three of the best known Italian restaurants in Manhattan to our home to discuss what is right and what is wrong in cooking and eating pasta. Cheese with seafood pasta? Never! Well, maybe. A fork plus a spoon for eating pasta? Spoons are for children, amateurs and people with bad table manners. The best cheese for pasta? Imported Parmigiano-Reggiano, which must be at least two years old before it is exported. The experts were Adi Giovanetti, proprietor of Il Nido; Sirio Maccioni, owner of Le Cirque; Luigi Nanni, proprietor and chef of both Nanni's and Il Valetto. Mr. Nanni cooked, preparing the pasta with field mushrooms and pasta with sauce militare.

Pasta alla Funghi Prataioli

PASTA WITH FIELD MUSHROOMS

- 1¼ pounds mushrooms, preferably field mushrooms (see Note)
- ¾ cup olive oil
- ½ pound butter
- ¾ cup thinly sliced, lightly chopped shallots
- 2¼ cups rich chicken broth (see recipe page 418)
- ½ pound imported Fontina cheese at room temperature, cut into ¼-inch cubes, about 1¼ cups
- ¼ pound freshly grated Parmesan cheese
- ¼ cup finely chopped fresh basil
- 1 teaspoon dried thyme
- 1½ pounds pasta (penne, fettuccine, ditalini, pappardelle), cooked to the desired degree of doneness
- ½ cup coarsely chopped fresh basil

1. If necessary, rinse the mushrooms and pat them dry. Cut them into bite-sized pieces.

2. Heat the oil in a large skillet and add the mushrooms, stirring. Cook about 5 minutes and add half the butter and the shallots. Cook over high heat for about 5 minutes.

3. Add the chicken broth and bring to the boil. Add the Fontina cheese and cook over high heat for 5 or 6 minutes. Add the remaining butter and toss. Add the Parmesan and toss. Add the ¼ cup finely chopped basil and the thyme and toss.

4. Serve with cooked pasta garnished with the coarsely chopped basil.

YIELD: 6 main-course servings or 12 first-course servings.

Note: Field mushrooms, known as prataioli in Italian and pleurotes in French, are available at times in shops that import fresh foods from Europe. Cultivated mushrooms may be substituted.

Pasta alla Militare

PASTA WITH TOMATOES, BASIL AND HOT PEPPERS

- 4 pounds ripe tomatoes, peeled
- ½ cup olive oil
- 1 cup thinly sliced, lightly chopped shallots
- 10 fresh basil stems tied in a bundle
- Salt to taste, if desired
- 2 or more dried hot red peppers, crushed
- ¼ pound butter
- 2 pounds pasta (ditalini, penne, spaghetti, fettuccine), cooked to the desired degree of doneness
- 3 cups freshly grated Parmesan cheese
- 30 fresh basil leaves

1. Cut the tomatoes into small wedges. There should be about 12 cups.

2. Heat the oil in a large skillet and add the shallots. Cook, stirring, until golden brown. Add the basil stems and tomatoes. Add salt to taste and hot red peppers.

3. Cook, stirring, for about 7 minutes and add the butter. Cook for 2 minutes and remove from the heat.

4. Put the pasta in a large hot bowl. Remove the bundle of basil stems and add three quarters of the sauce. Add 2 cups of the cheese and toss. Garnish with basil leaves and serve with the remaining sauce and Parmesan cheese on the side.

YIELD: 6 main-course servings or 12 first-course servings.

Kidneys and Mushrooms with Bucatini

- 1½ pounds veal or lamb kidneys
- Salt and freshly ground black pepper to taste
- ¼ cup peanut, vegetable or corn oil
- 2 tablespoons butter
- ½ pound mushrooms, quartered or thinly sliced
- ¼ cup finely chopped shallots
- ½ cup Marsala wine
- 1½ cups heavy cream
- 2 tablespoons prepared mustard, preferably imported Dijon or Düsseldorf
- 1 pound bucatini, perciatelli or spaghetti, cooked according to taste
- Freshly grated Parmesan cheese

1. Split the kidneys lengthwise through the center. Cut away and discard the center core. Cut the kidneys into ½-inch cubes. Sprinkle with salt and pepper and set aside.

2. Heat the oil in a heavy skillet and, when it is quite hot and almost smoking, add the kidneys. Cook, stirring, for about 1½ minutes. Drain thoroughly in a colander, discarding the oil.

3. Add the butter to the skillet and, when it is hot, add the mushrooms. Add salt to taste. Cook, stirring, for about 2 minutes.

4. Add the shallots and wine. Cook until the wine has reduced by half and add the cream. Bring to a rolling boil and add the mustard. Turn off the heat and add the kidneys and blend.

5. Serve with cooked bucatini and grated Parmesan cheese on the side.

YIELD: 6 to 8 servings.

Nico Girolla's Orechiette al Gorgonzola

- ¼ pound butter
- ¼ pound Gorgonzola cheese
- 1 cup half-and-half
- 1 ounce Cognac
- 3 tablespoons tomato purée
- ½ cup coarsely chopped shelled walnuts, or blanched, shelled pistachios
- 1 pound orechiette or small pasta shells (No. 22)
- 2 cups freshly grated Parmesan cheese
- ½ cup coarsely chopped fresh basil

1. Melt the butter in a skillet and add the Gorgonzola. When melted, add the half-and-half, Cognac, tomato purée and nuts.

2. Cook the orechiette or shells according to taste and toss with the sauce and half of the Parmesan cheese.

3. Serve immediately garnished with the chopped basil and with the remaining Parmesan cheese on the side.

YIELD: 4 servings.

One of the great revelations to come about within the past few years is the awakening in the American public's consciousness that pasta in all its multifarious forms—spaghetti, linguine, ziti and so on—need not invariably be served with tomato sauce or meat sauce.

Among the most gratifying, interesting and delicate sauces with which to enrobe pasta are those made with fish or seafood of one variety or another.

Spaghetti with Whiting Sauce

- 3 cleaned whiting, without heads, about 1¼ pounds
- 1 bay leaf
- 1 sprig fresh thyme, or ¼ teaspoon dried
- 3 sprigs fresh parsley
- Salt and freshly ground black pepper to taste
- ¼ cup olive oil
- 1 teaspoon finely minced garlic
- 3 tablespoons finely chopped parsley
- ¼ teaspoon grated lemon rind
- 1 pound spaghetti or spaghettini, cooked according to taste

1. Place the whiting close together in one layer in a casserole. Add water to cover, the bay leaf, thyme, parsley, salt and pepper.

2. Bring to the boil and let barely simmer for about 5 minutes. Remove from the heat. Drain, but reserve ¼ cup of the cooking liquid.

3. When the fish is cool enough to handle, carefully remove the skin and discard. Take the flesh from the bone in large lumps. There should be from 1½ to 2 cups.

4. Heat the oil in a skillet and add the garlic. Cook gently without browning. Remove from the heat. Add the chopped parsley, lemon rind and the reserved ¼ cup of cooking liquid.

5. Add the fish to the sauce. Handle gently. Stir to barely blend. Serve the sauce with spaghetti.

YIELD: 4 servings.

Spaghetti with Smoked Salmon in Cream

- ¼ pound smoked salmon cut into thin slices
- ½ cup green peas, preferably fresh
- Salt
- 1 tablespoon butter
- ¾ cup heavy cream
- Freshly ground black pepper to taste
- ⅛ teaspoon grated nutmeg
- 2 tablespoons loosely packed, shredded, fresh basil leaves
- 1 pound spaghetti or spaghettini, cooked according to taste

1. Stack the salmon slices. Cut the slices into 1-inch cubes. Set aside.

2. Cook the peas briefly in boiling salted water. When just tender, drain. Set aside.

3. Melt the butter in a skillet and, when it is hot, add the salmon cubes. Cook quickly, stirring. Add the cream and cook over high heat for about 1 minute.

4. Add the peas, pepper, nutmeg and basil leaves.

5. Heat the sauce briefly and serve with the spaghetti.

YIELD: 4 servings.

Spaghetti con Cozze

SPAGHETTI WITH MUSSELS, SICILIAN STYLE

- 2 quarts mussels, well scrubbed
- ¼ cup dry white wine
- 2 sprigs fresh thyme, or ½ teaspoon dried
- 1 bay leaf
- 2 sprigs fresh parsley
- Freshly ground black pepper to taste
- ¼ cup olive oil (see Note)
- 1 teaspoon finely chopped garlic
- 2 tablespoons drained capers
- ¼ cup pitted black olives, preferably imported
- ¼ cup finely chopped parsley
- Salt
- ½ teaspoon hot red pepper flakes
- 1 pound spaghetti or spaghettini, preferably imported, cooked according to taste

1. Put the mussels in a kettle and add the wine, thyme, bay leaf, parsley sprigs and black pepper. Cover tightly and cook until the mussels open,

tossing occasionally as they cook, about 5 minutes. Remove from the heat. Strain the mussel liquid and set aside.

2. Heat the oil in a saucepan and add the garlic. Cook briefly and add the capers and olives. Remove from the heat. Stir in the chopped parsley and ¼ cup of the reserved mussel liquid. Add pepper to taste and a little salt. Add the hot red pepper flakes.

3. Remove the mussels from the shells. If desired, remove and discard the small rubber-like bands around the mussels.

4. Add the mussels to the sauce. Heat briefly and serve with the spaghetti.

YIELD: 4 servings.

Note: A dark, heavy olive oil is recommended for this dish.

A great personal favorite among oddments from the sea is conch, which Italians call scungilli. Living in the Hamptons, I have access to scungilli already prepared—in a tomato sauce with linguine, or in a zesty, piquant salad. The chef of these good things is Eduardo Giurici of the Casa Albona restaurant in Amagansett. He came into my kitchen to demonstrate the simple (if time consuming) method for cooking scungilli.

Scungilli (Conch) with Diavolo Sauce and Linguine

- 2 cans, 2 pounds, 3 ounces each, imported Italian peeled tomatoes
- ¼ cup olive oil
- 4 tablespoons finely chopped garlic
- ½ cup dry white wine
- 1½ teaspoons dried oregano
- Salt to taste
- 1 teaspoon freshly ground black pepper
- 3 tablespoons butter
- 3 cups cooked, cleaned, sliced conch (see Note and following recipe)
- ¼ to 1 teaspoon hot red pepper flakes, according to strength desired
- 1½ pounds linguine, cooked to the desired degree of doneness

1. Empty the tomatoes into a large bowl and crush well with the hands.

2. Heat the oil in a wide, not too deep casserole and add 3 tablespoons of the garlic. Cook, stirring, until the garlic is lightly browned. Do not burn. Add half the wine and cook until the wine has almost evaporated. Add the tomatoes.

3. Bring to the boil. Add 1 teaspoon of oregano, salt to taste and the pepper. Cook over high heat, stirring often with a wooden spoon so that the tomatoes do not stick. Cook for 20 minutes. This sauce should not be dark, but thick and reddish. When ready, there should be about 7 cups.

4. Melt the butter in a saucepan or small casserole and add the remaining tablespoon of garlic. Cook, stirring, until the garlic is lightly browned. Do not allow it to burn.

5. Add the conch and remaining wine. Cook down briefly and add the remaining oregano, salt, pepper and hot red pepper flakes. Continue cooking until the wine is reduced by half. Add the tomato sauce and heat through. Put the drained linguine in a large serving bowl and toss with the sauce.

YIELD: 6 servings.

Note: Canned scungilli, or conch, is available at many stores that specialize in Italian foods. It is an excellent product and can be substituted for the fresh. It is, however, fairly expensive. Drain well before using.

COOKED CONCH

16 large conch, each about ¾ pound (total weight is 10 to 11 pounds)

1. The conch may be sandy so wash them before cooking. Put them in a basin with warm water and rub them carefully to remove surface sand. Drain.

2. Put the conch in one or two large kettles. Add hot water from the tap to barely cover. Do not add salt. Bring to the boil and cook for 1 hour. Drain well.

3. Remove the conch from the shell, using a two-pronged fork. Holding the body in one hand, remove and discard the soft, flabby portions that hang and cling to the body at the bottom and inside. Split open the body sac with the fingers and pull out the inside organ. Discard it. Hold the conch under cold running water and scrub off as much of the black coating as possible. Feel all over for traces of sand.

4. Return the conch meat to a clean kettle and add water to cover about 5 inches above the surface of the conch. Do not add salt. Put on the stove and bring to the boil. Cook 4 hours, or until tender. If conch are quite large, it may be necessary to cook them for up to 5 hours.

5. At this point you may freeze the conch meat. You may cover closely and freeze the entire batch, or divide into portions, wrap tightly and freeze.

6. When ready to serve, place the conch pieces, one at a time, on a flat surface and cut into ¼-inch-thick slices.

YIELD: About 6 cups.

Within the past two decades, Americans have become admirably aware of one of the most elegant of all French creations, a delicate specialty called quenelles, primarily quenelles of pike or other fish. There are many things that can be turned into these tiny French dumplings but, aside from fish, one of the finest and most delicate is chicken.

There was a time when these dumplings were particularly tricky to make in the home because of the labor involved in grinding the fish, chicken or whatever, chilling it all the while as cream and eggs were added. Today, this is no trick at all with the help of a food processor, and the dumpling mixture can be made in a minute or less. When cooked and drained, they are a great companion for pasta, such as fettuccine with cream.

Pasta with Chicken Quenelles

- 60 chicken quenelles (see following recipe)
- 2 pounds asparagus spears, trimmed, scraped and cut into ½-inch lengths
- Salt
- 1 pound fettuccine or other pasta, such as spaghetti or spaghettini
- 1½ cups heavy cream
- Freshly ground black pepper to taste
- ⅛ teaspoon grated nutmeg
- ½ teaspoon finely minced garlic
- 4 tablespoons butter at room temperature
- ½ cup freshly grated Parmesan cheese plus additional cheese on the side
- ¾ cup toasted pine nuts, optional

1. Prepare the quenelles and, the moment they are done, turn off the heat but let the quenelles rest in the hot water until the pasta is ready to be tossed with the other ingredients.

2. Drop the asparagus into a little boiling, salted water. Simmer for about 1 minute and drain well.

3. Cook the pasta to the desired degree of doneness.

4. As the pasta cooks, select a casserole and add the cream, salt and pepper to taste, nutmeg and garlic. Bring barely to the simmer.

5. Drain the pasta and add it to the casserole. Add the asparagus and butter and sprinkle with ½ cup grated cheese and the pine nuts. Toss well.

6. Drain the quenelles and toss with the pasta. Add a generous grinding of black pepper. Serve with additional grated Parmesan cheese on the side.

YIELD: 4 to 6 servings.

QUENELLES DE VOLAILLE

Chicken Quenelles

- 1 whole, boneless chicken breast, about ½ pound
- Salt and freshly ground black pepper to taste
- 1 tablespoon freshly grated Parmesan cheese
- Grated nutmeg to taste
- 1 egg
- ½ cup heavy cream

1. Cut the chicken meat into 1-inch cubes and chill thoroughly.

2. Put the chicken, salt and pepper to taste, cheese, nutmeg and egg into the container of a food processor. Blend thoroughly.

3. Gradually add the cream, pouring it through the funnel of the processor.

4. Bring about 3 quarts of water to the boil in a casserole.

5. Outfit a pastry bag with a round No. 7 pastry tube. Fill the bag with the chicken mixture.

6. Hold the tube over the simmering water. Squeeze out a little of the chicken mixture. As the mixture emerges from the tube, cut it off at 1-inch intervals, letting the pieces fall into the simmering water.

7. Cook the pieces in gently simmering water for about 2½ minutes. The quenelles should be cooked through but not overcooked, or they will taste dry. Turn off the heat. At this point the quenelles may remain in the water for a few minutes. Drain well in a sieve.

YIELD: About 60 pieces.

Fettuccine with Prosciutto and Peas

- 1¼ cups freshly shelled peas, or 1 10-ounce package frozen peas
- ½ cup heavy cream
- ¼ cup finely shredded prosciutto
- 1 pound fettuccine
- 8 tablespoons butter, cut into small pieces
- ¾ cup freshly grated Parmesan cheese
- ⅛ teaspoon grated nutmeg
- Salt and freshly ground black pepper to taste

1. Drop the peas into boiling water. If fresh, they should cook in 1 or 2 minutes. If frozen, they should cook 10 seconds, or just until the peas are no longer sticking together. Drain and run briefly under cold water. Drain again and return to a saucepan. Add the cream and prosciutto and set aside.

2. Cook the pasta to the desired degree of doneness. Drain quickly.

3. Put the butter in a hot serving dish for tossing the pasta. Add the hot pasta.

4. Heat the cream briefly. Add the peas and prosciutto in the cream to the pasta. Add the cheese, nutmeg, salt and pepper to taste. Toss well and serve hot.

YIELD: 4 servings.

Broccoli, Tuna and Rigatoni Salad

- ½ pound rigatoni or ziti
- Salt to taste
- 2 cups broccoli cut into flowerets
- 2 cups tomatoes cut into ½-inch cubes
- 1 8-ounce can tuna fish packed in olive oil, preferably imported
- Freshly ground black pepper to taste
- 3 to 4 tablespoons red wine vinegar
- ½ cup olive oil
- ¼ teaspoon hot red pepper flakes
- ½ cup finely chopped parsley
- ½ cup thinly sliced red onion

1. Drop the rigatoni into a kettle of boiling salted water. When the water returns to the boil, cook for about 10 minutes, or until just tender. Drain and run briefly under cold running water. Drain well.

2. Put the rigatoni in a mixing bowl.

3. Drop the broccoli into a saucepan of boiling salted water and cook until tender, about 5 minutes. Do not overcook. Drain well.

4. Add the broccoli, the remaining ingredients and salt to taste to the rigatoni. Toss well. Serve at room temperature.

YIELD: 8 or more servings.

Shrimp and Peas with Pasta Salad

- 48 cooked, peeled and deveined shrimp
- 1 pound tubular pasta, such as ziti or, preferably, penne
- 2¼ cups spicy mayonnaise (see recipe page 417)
- 2 cups cooked fresh or frozen peas (see Note)
- ½ cup finely chopped herbs, such as basil, dill and parsley, either separate or blended
- ¾ cup finely chopped scallions
- 2 to 4 tablespoons tarragon wine vinegar, according to taste
- ¼ cup drained capers
- Salt to taste, if desired
- Freshly ground black pepper to taste
- Finely chopped parsley for garnish

1. Cut the shrimp in half crosswise.

2. Cook the pasta to the desired degree of doneness. Drain and let cool.

3. Combine the shrimp and pasta in a mixing bowl and add the remaining ingredients except the chopped parsley. Blend well. Serve sprinkled with chopped parsley.

YIELD: 10 to 12 servings.

Note: If frozen peas are to be used, empty them frozen into a sieve and pour boiling hot water over them. Let drain. Further cooking is not necessary.

Volumes could be written on recipes that at first sight seem foreign but are, in fact, distinctly American. One such recipe, remembered from a Southern childhood, is for an unusual pasta dish. Although it is made with pasta of Italian origin and marinated in French dressing, it is dubbed New Orleans style and was a specialty of a Memphis golf club.

Cold Pasta, New Orleans Style

- ½ pound pasta, preferably vermicelli or spaghettini
- Salt
- 1 cup mustard vinaigrette (see recipe page 413)
- 1 3-pound poached chicken
- 1 cup spicy mayonnaise (see recipe page 417)
- Mushrooms à la grecque (see following recipe)
- 12 small whole cooked beets
- 1 9-ounce package frozen artichoke hearts, cooked according to package directions
- 1 avocado, seeded, peeled and cut into 16 wedges
- 12 cherry tomatoes or an equal number of tomato wedges
- Chopped scallions for garnish, optional
- Chopped parsley for garnish, optional

1. Drop the pasta into boiling salted water and cook to the desired degree of doneness. Do not overcook or the pasta will become mushy. Drain well.

2. Put the drained pasta into a mixing bowl while still warm and pour one third of the salad dressing over it. Toss well. Let it cool. Cover with plastic wrap and refrigerate several hours or overnight.

3. Remove the chicken meat from the bones. Discard the bones and skin. Cut the meat into bite-sized pieces.

4. Add the chicken to the pasta. Add the mayonnaise and gently toss to blend the ingredients.

5. Serve the pasta in a mound on a round plate. Garnish as follows: Arrange the mushrooms around the pasta or serve separately. Put the beets, artichoke hearts and avocado wedges in separate bowls. Add equal parts of the remaining salad dressing to each bowl. Stir each to coat. Arrange these, and the tomatoes, around the pasta. Sprinkle with chopped scallions and parsley if desired.

YIELD: 6 to 8 servings.

MUSHROOMS À LA GRECQUE

- ½ pound small mushrooms, preferably button mushrooms
- 1½ tablespoons lemon juice
- 4½ tablespoons olive oil
- ½ teaspoon coriander seeds
- 1 small clove garlic, crushed and peeled
- Salt and freshly ground black pepper to taste
- 2 tablespoons chicken broth

1. If the mushrooms are small, leave them whole. Otherwise, cut into quarters. Put them in a saucepan with lemon juice and stir to coat. Add the remaining ingredients.

2. Cover and cook for 7 to 8 minutes, stirring occasionally. Uncover and cook over high heat for about 5 minutes, shaking the pan occasionally. Remove from the heat and let cool. Remove the garlic clove before serving.

YIELD: About 2 cups.

Cold Spaghetti Primavera

- 4 asparagus spears
- 1 or 2 zucchini, about ½ pound
- ½ cup fresh green peas
- 1 cup broccoli cut into small flowerets
- Salt to taste
- ½ pound spaghetti
- ¼ pound sliced mushrooms, about 1½ cups
- 2 cups tomatoes cut into ½-inch cubes
- 3 tablespoons chopped fresh basil leaves
- ¼ cup chopped fresh parsley
- 1½ cups mayonnaise (see recipe page 415)
- 2 teaspoons finely minced garlic
- 2 tablespoons white vinegar
- Freshly ground black pepper to taste
- ½ cup toasted pine nuts

1. Trim and scrape the asparagus. Cut each spear on the bias into 1-inch lengths.

2. Trim off the ends of the zucchini. Slice it lengthwise into quarters. Cut each quarter crosswise into ½-inch-thick pieces. There should be about 2 cups.

3. Use separate saucepans to cook the asparagus, zucchini, peas and broccoli. Add enough water to each saucepan to cover the vegetables when added. Add salt to taste.

4. Add the vegetables to the saucepans and bring to the boil. Cook each vegetable until crisp-tender. Cook the peas and asparagus for 1 minute or longer, depending on age. Cook the broccoli and zucchini for 5 minutes or less. As the vegetables are cooked drain them. Set aside.

5. Break the spaghetti strands in half. Cook the spaghetti in boiling salted water until tender, about 7 minutes. Drain and run briefly under cold running water. Drain thoroughly.

6. Put the spaghetti in a mixing bowl and add the cooked vegetables, mushrooms, tomatoes, fresh basil and parsley. Blend the mayonnaise, garlic and vinegar in a small bowl. Add this to the spaghetti and vegetable mixture. Add salt and pepper to taste. Toss to blend.

7. Sprinkle with pine nuts and serve at room temperature.

YIELD: 8 servings.

Cold Spaghetti with Garlic and Anchovies

- ⅓ cup plus 1 tablespoon olive oil
- 2 teaspoons finely chopped garlic
- 1 cup thinly sliced mushrooms
- ⅓ cup chopped anchovy fillets
- Juice of 1 lemon
- Freshly ground black pepper to taste
- ½ cup imported black olives, pitted
- ¼ teaspoon crushed hot red pepper flakes
- 1 pound spaghetti

1. Heat ⅓ cup olive oil in a small skillet. Add the garlic and cook, stirring, without browning.

2. Add the mushrooms and cook until mushrooms wilt. Add the chopped anchovy fillets. Stir and remove from the heat.

3. Add the lemon juice, black pepper, olives and pepper flakes and stir. Set aside.

4. Cook the spaghetti to the desired degree of doneness. Drain and toss with the remaining 1 tablespoon of olive oil. Add the anchovy sauce and toss. Let stand until lukewarm.

YIELD: About 6 servings.

Lasagne is a first-rate solution to the dilemma of what to serve a party of 10 or more that is festive enough to be special yet can be made and served in one dish—thus minimizing the clean-up process. The problem, however, is that in America most people's lasagne is apt to taste very much like that of their neighbors: a standard compendium of lasagne noodles, meat sauce, mozzarella and ricotta cheeses.

The fact is that with a little imagination the flavors and textures of baked lasagne can achieve a far greater latitude than most home cooks believe—

from a blend of seafood in a light tomato and cream sauce to a fine, lusty blend of chicken with sausage and beef. And these lasagne dishes may be prepared in advance, to be popped into the oven on signal. Here, two recipes of decidedly different flavors.

Lasagne Frutta di Mare

SEAFOOD IN A CREAM TOMATO SAUCE WITH LASAGNE

- 1 tablespoon butter
- 1 tablespoon finely chopped shallots
- ¾ pound raw shrimp, peeled
- 1 pint scallops
- Salt and freshly ground black pepper to taste
- ½ cup dry white wine
- 2 cups thinly sliced mushrooms
- 2 cups béchamel sauce (see recipe page 402)
- 1 cup crushed canned tomatoes
- ½ cup heavy cream
- ¼ teaspoon crushed hot red pepper flakes
- 3 tablespoons finely chopped parsley
- 9 lasagne strips
- 4 small skinless, boneless flounder fillets, about 1 pound total weight
- 1 cup grated Gruyère or Swiss cheese

1. Melt the butter in a large skillet and add the shallots. Cook for about 30 seconds and add the shrimp and scallops. (If the scallops are bay scallops and small, leave them whole. Otherwise, cut them into small, bite-sized pieces.) Sprinkle with salt and pepper.

2. When the shrimp start to turn pink, add the wine. Cook, stirring briefly, just until the wine comes to the boil.

3. The moment the wine boils, turn off the heat. Using a slotted spoon, transfer the seafood to a mixing bowl.

4. Bring the cooking liquid to the simmer and add the mushrooms. Cook for about 5 minutes and add the béchamel sauce, stirring.

5. Add the tomatoes and simmer for about 5 minutes. Add the cream, pepper flakes and salt and pepper. Add the parsley. Add any liquid that may have accumulated around the shrimp and scallops to the sauce.

6. Preheat the oven to 375 degrees.

7. Cook the lasagne according to taste.

8. Butter the bottom and sides of a lasagne pan (a pan measuring 9½ by 13½ by 2 inches is suitable).

9. Spoon a layer of the sauce over the bottom. Add half the shrimp and scallops.

10. Spoon some of the sauce over the shrimp and scallops.

11. Cover with 3 strips of lasagne.

12. Add a layer of flounder. Add salt and pepper and a thin layer of sauce.

13. Cover with 3 strips of lasagne.

14. Scatter the remaining shrimp and scallops over and spoon a light layer of sauce over this, leaving enough sauce for a final layer.

15. Cover with 3 strips of lasagne. Spoon a final layer of sauce over this. Sprinkle with cheese.

16. Place in the oven and bake for 30 minutes.

YIELD: About 10 servings.

Chicken, Sausage and Beef Lasagne

- 2 cups tomatoes
- 5 tablespoons butter
- 4 tablespoons flour
- 2 cups rich chicken broth (see recipe page 418)
- 1 cup heavy cream
- Salt and freshly ground black pepper to taste
- ⅛ teaspoon grated nutmeg
- ½ pound hot or sweet Italian sausages
- 1 cup finely chopped green pepper
- 1 cup finely chopped celery
- 1 cup finely chopped onion
- 1 to 2 tablespoons finely chopped garlic
- ½ pound ground sirloin
- 2 cups thinly sliced mushrooms
- Tabasco sauce to taste
- 1 teaspoon Worcestershire sauce
- 1 cup frozen or very fresh, freshly shelled green peas
- 9 lasagne strips
- 2 cups shredded, skinless, boneless cooked chicken
- 2 cups grated Cheddar cheese
- ¾ cup freshly grated Parmesan cheese

1. Put the tomatoes in a saucepan and cook down for 30 minutes to about 1½ cups.

2. Melt 3 tablespoons of the butter in a saucepan and add the flour, stirring with a wire whisk. When blended, add the broth, stirring rapidly with the whisk. Cook for about 10 minutes, stirring occasionally. Add the cream, salt and pepper and nutmeg.

3. Remove and discard the skin of the sausages. Add the flesh to a skillet and cook, stirring with the side of a heavy, metal kitchen spoon to break up

any lumps. Cook until the meat loses its raw color. Drain off and discard the fat. Set the meat aside.

4. Melt the remaining 2 tablespoons of butter in a skillet and add the green pepper, celery, onion and garlic. Cook, stirring briefly, until crisp-tender.

5. Add the beef and cook, cutting down with the sides of a heavy metal kitchen spoon to break up any lumps. Add the sausage meat and mushrooms and cook briefly. Add salt and pepper to taste.

6. Add the tomatoes to the cream sauce. Pour this combined sauce over the meat mixture and stir to blend. Add the Tabasco and Worcestershire sauce and salt and pepper to taste. Add the peas and bring to the boil.

7. Preheat the oven to 375 degrees.

8. Cook the lasagne according to taste. Drain.

9. Butter a lasagne baking dish (a dish measuring about 9½ by 13½ by 2 inches is suitable).

10. Arrange 3 lasagne strips over the dish. Add a layer of chicken and spoon some of the meat sauce over. Add about a third of the grated Cheddar cheese.

11. Cover with 3 lasagne strips.

12. Add a layer of chicken and another layer of meat sauce and grated cheese.

13. Add a third layer of lasagne. Add the remaining chicken and spoon the remaining meat sauce over all. Sprinkle with the remaining grated Cheddar cheese.

14. Bake for 30 minutes. Serve with grated Parmesan cheese on the side.

YIELD: 10 or more servings.

Barbara Tropp's Tangy Noodles

- 1 pound fresh long, thin Chinese egg noodles, available in Oriental supermarkets and grocery stores
- 3½ tablespoons Chinese or Japanese sesame oil
- 3½ tablespoons black (dark) soy sauce
- 1½ tablespoons vinegar, preferably Chinese black vinegar, or use red wine vinegar
- 2 tablespoons sugar
- 2 teaspoons kosher salt
- ½ to 1 tablespoon hot chili oil
- 5 or 6 tablespoons thinly cut scallion rings, white and green parts

1. Toss and separate the fresh uncooked noodles by hand to release any tangles. Do not break them.

2. Bring a generous quantity of water to the boil. Add the noodles, stirring with chopsticks or wooden spoons to separate. Cook, stirring occasionally, for 3 or 4 minutes. Do not overcook or they will become soggy and sticky. Drain immediately in a colander. Run under cold water until chilled. Shake off excess water.

3. Put the noodles in a clean bowl or dry pot.

4. Combine the sesame oil, soy sauce, vinegar, sugar, salt and hot oil in a mixing bowl. Blend well.

5. Pour the sauce over the noodles and mix well, preferably with the hands. Add the scallions and toss again.

6. Cover and set aside for several hours at room temperature. Or store overnight in the refrigerator. Serve in individuals bowls with more chopped scallions, if desired. The noodles can be refrigerated several days, but they are best on the second day. Serve at room temperature.

YIELD: 6 to 8 servings.

Crown of Noodles with Mushrooms

THE NOODLE RING

- ½ pound medium noodles
- Salt
- 2½ tablespoons butter
- 2 tablespoons flour
- ½ cup milk
- ⅓ cup heavy cream
- Freshly ground black pepper to taste
- Pinch of cayenne pepper
- ⅛ teaspoon grated nutmeg
- 1 egg, lightly beaten
- ⅓ cup freshly grated Parmesan cheese

THE MUSHROOM FILLING

- 2 tablespoons butter
- 8 cups thinly sliced mushrooms
- Juice of ½ lemon
- 2 tablespoons finely chopped shallots
- ⅓ cup dry sherry
- Salt and freshly ground black pepper to taste
- 1 cup heavy cream
- 1 teaspoon arrowroot
- Chopped parsley for garnish

1. Preheat the oven to 375 degrees.

2. Cook the noodles in boiling water to cover with salt to taste. Let cook 5 minutes until almost but not quite tender. Drain and run briefly under cold running water. Drain well.

3. Meanwhile, rub the inside of a 4-cup ring mold with 1 tablespoon of butter.

4. Melt the remaining 1½ tablespoons of butter in a saucepan and add the flour, stirring with a wire whisk. Add the milk, stirring rapidly with the whisk. Add the ⅓ cup of heavy cream, stirring. Add salt and pepper to taste, cayenne and nutmeg.

5. Beat in the egg and stir in the cheese. Pour the mixture into a bowl. Add the noodles and stir. Pour the noodle mixture into the mold and smooth the top.

6. Place the mold in the oven and bake for 30 to 35 minutes, or until set.

7. Meanwhile, prepare the filling. Melt the 2 tablespoons of the butter in a skillet and add the mushrooms and lemon juice. Cook until mushrooms give up their liquid and the liquid is almost evaporated.

8. Add the shallots and stir. Add all but 1 tablespoon of the wine. Bring to the boil. Add salt and pepper to taste and the cup of heavy cream. Bring to the boil.

9. Combine the reserved tablespoon of wine and the arrowroot and stir it into the sauce. Cook briefly.

10. Unmold the noodle ring onto a round plate and spoon the mushrooms into the center. Sprinkle the filling with chopped parsley.

YIELD: 4 to 6 servings.

Salmon and Noodle Casserole

- 2 cups freshly cooked or canned skinless, boneless salmon
- ¼ pound (about 3 cups) broad noodles
- Salt
- 2 tablespoons butter plus butter for greasing the pan
- ½ cup finely chopped onion
- ½ cup diced sweet red or green pepper
- 2 tablespoons flour
- 2 cups milk
- ¼ teaspoon grated nutmeg
- Freshly ground black pepper to taste
- ¼ pound grated Cheddar cheese, about ½ cup
- 2 tablespoons finely chopped parsley
- 2 tablespoons freshly grated Parmesan cheese

1. Preheat the oven to 400 degrees.

2. Pick over the salmon to remove all traces of skin and bones. Set aside.

3. Bring enough water to the boil to cover the noodles when they are added. Add salt to taste. Add the noodles and bring to the boil again. Let simmer for about 5 minutes until almost but not quite tender. Drain and run briefly under cold water. Drain. There should be about 3 cups.

4. Meanwhile, melt the butter in a saucepan and add the onion and diced pepper. Cook briefly, stirring, until the onion is wilted. Add the flour, stirring with a wire whisk until the mixture is blended and smooth. Add the milk, stirring rapidly with the whisk, then add the nutmeg and salt and pepper to taste.

5. Remove from the heat and add the Cheddar cheese. Stir until melted. Add the salmon, noodles and parsley. Stir gently to blend.

6. Lightly grease a 1½-quart baking dish and pour in the creamed mixture. Sprinkle with the Parmesan cheese. Place the dish in the oven and bake for 15 minutes. If desired, run the dish briefly under the broiler to brown the top.

YIELD: 4 to 6 servings.

Chicken Livers and Mushrooms with Spinach Noodles

1 pound chicken livers
2 tablespoons butter
½ pound thinly sliced mushrooms
Salt and freshly ground black pepper to taste
1 cup thinly sliced onion
1 teaspoon finely minced garlic
½ cup flour
⅓ cup peanut, vegetable or corn oil
⅛ teaspoon grated nutmeg
1 tablespoon chopped fresh rosemary, or half the amount dried
¾ cup heavy cream
½ pound green spinach noodles, cooked according to taste
Freshly grated Parmesan cheese

1. Cut the livers in half, pick over and discard all tough connecting membranes and set the livers aside.

2. Melt the butter in a skillet and add the mushrooms. Add the salt and pepper and cook until the mushrooms are wilted. Continue cooking, stirring often, until lightly browned. Add the onion and garlic. Cook, stirring often, until the onion is wilted. Transfer the mushroom-onion mixture to a small casserole and set aside.

3. Put the flour in a flat dish and add salt and pepper to taste. Add the livers and stir to thoroughly coat them.

4. Heat the oil in a large, heavy skillet and, when it is hot and almost smoking, add the livers, a handful at a time. Cook over high heat, turning the livers as necessary so that they brown evenly. Cook until well browned, about 3 minutes. Transfer the livers with a slotted spoon to the small casserole containing the mushroom mixture. Sprinkle with nutmeg and rosemary.

5. Add the cream to the casserole and bring to the boil.

6. Meanwhile, cook and drain the noodles. Add the noodles to the livers and toss. Serve with Parmesan cheese on the side.

YIELD: 4 to 6 servings.

❧

Noodles with Hot Meat Sauce for a Crowd

- 1 cup corn, peanut or vegetable oil
- 4 pounds ground pork, preferably not too lean and not too finely ground
- 1⅓ cups brown bean sauce (see Note)
- 2 tablespoons bottled chili paste with garlic (see Note)
- 4 tablespoons sugar
- 4 tablespoons dry sherry
- 2 pounds fresh Chinese egg noodles (see Note)
- 1 cup minced scallions, green and white parts combined

GARNISHES

- 4 cups picked-over bean sprouts
- 3 cups peeled, seeded and shredded cucumbers
- ¾ cup hot chili oil (see Note)

1. Heat a wok and add half the oil. Add half the pork and cook quickly over high heat, stirring and chopping down to break up any lumps. Cook only until the pork loses its raw look.

2. Add ⅔ cup of the brown bean sauce and half the chili paste with garlic. Cook, stirring rapidly, for 1 or 2 minutes. Add half the sugar and half the sherry and cook for 1 minute longer over high heat.

3. Turn the mixture into a 4-quart casserole.

4. Rinse and wipe out the wok, and repeat the procedure using the remaining half of the corn oil, pork, brown bean sauce, chili paste with garlic, sugar and wine. Add the second batch to the first. Let stand to room

temperature. Refrigerate for up to 3 days (or the mixture may be frozen in small batches up to a month or longer).

5. When ready to serve, bring to room temperature. Reheat the sauce gently. Twenty minutes before serving, bring a large kettle of water to the boil. Add the noodles and cook for 4 minutes.

6. Drain the noodles and cut them into shreds of manageable length. Pour the noodles into a heated, heatproof serving dish.

7. Add the scallions to the simmering sauce and stir. Pour the sauce over the hot noodles and toss to blend. Serve with the three garnishes, letting guests help themselves.

YIELD: 25 to 30 servings.

Note: These ingredients are available in Oriental groceries and supermarkets.

Weinlokshen

WINE NOODLES

- 2 cups uncooked thin noodles
- Salt
- 1 cup white wine, preferably a Rhine or Alsatian wine
- 6 tablespoons sugar
- 3 tablespoons butter plus butter for greasing the pan
- 3 eggs, separated
- 1 tablespoon grated lemon rind
- Juice of ½ lemon

1. Preheat the oven to 350 degrees.

2. Drop the noodles into boiling water to cover, with salt added to taste. Let cook for about 5 minutes until almost but not quite tender. Drain and run briefly under cold water. Drain well.

3. Combine the wine and 3 tablespoons of the sugar in a saucepan. Bring to the boil, stirring just until the sugar dissolves. Pour the mixture into a mixing bowl. Add the noodles and stir. Set aside.

4. Cream together in a bowl the butter, the remaining 3 tablespoons sugar, egg yolks, lemon rind and lemon juice.

5. Add the lemon mixture to the noodles.

6. Beat the egg whites until stiff and fold them into the noodle mixture.

7. Pour the mixture into a buttered 8- or 9-inch quiche pan and bake for 15 to 20 minutes.

YIELD: 4 to 6 servings.

❧

Rice with Zucchini à la Grecque

- 1½ pounds zucchini
- ¼ cup olive oil
- 3 cups coarsely chopped onion
- 3 sprigs fresh thyme, or ½ teaspoon dried
- 1 bay leaf
- Salt and freshly ground black pepper to taste
- 1 cup rice
- 1 cup fresh or canned chicken broth

1. Preheat the oven to 400 degrees.

2. Trim off and discard the ends of the zucchini. Do not peel the vegetable. Cut the zucchini into 1½-inch cubes. Set aside.

3. In a large heavy casserole, heat the oil and add the onion, thyme, bay leaf and salt and pepper. Cover tightly. Cook until the onion is tender but not brown.

4. Add the zucchini, rice and chicken broth. Bring to the boil on top of the stove. Cover and bake in the oven for 20 minutes—no longer. Remove the bay leaf and serve.

YIELD: 6 to 8 servings.

❧

Rice for a Crowd

- 12 tablespoons butter
- 1 cup finely chopped onion
- 8 cups long-grain rice
- 12 cups fresh or canned chicken broth
- 6 sprigs fresh parsley
- 2 bay leaves
- 4 sprigs fresh thyme, or 1 teaspoon dried
- Salt
- Tabasco sauce

1. Melt 8 tablespoons of the butter in a large kettle with a tight-fitting lid.

2. Add the onion and cook until wilted. Add the rice and stir. Add the broth. Tie the parsley, bay leaves and thyme into a bundle and add the bundle to the rice. Add salt and Tabasco sauce to taste.

3. Bring the broth to the boil. Cover tightly and cook over low heat for exactly 17 minutes. Uncover and remove the bundle of spices. Dot with the remaining 4 tablespoons of butter and fluff the rice with a fork until the butter is incorporated.

YIELD: 30 servings.

Saffron Rice

- 3 tablespoons butter
- 2 tablespoons finely chopped onion
- 1½ cups long-grain rice
- 2¼ cups fresh or canned chicken broth
- ¼ cup currants
- 1 strip of lemon peel
- 1 bay leaf
- ½ teaspoon saffron threads
- Salt, if desired

1. Preheat the oven to 425 degrees.

2. Use a heavy saucepan with a tight-fitting lid. Melt 1 tablespoon of the butter in the saucepan and add the onion. Cook, stirring, until the onion is wilted. Add the rice and cook, stirring, for about 30 seconds. Add all of the remaining ingredients except the remaining butter and bring to the boil.

3. Cover and place the saucepan in the oven. Cook for exactly 20 minutes. Uncover and stir. Keep covered until ready to serve. When ready to serve, discard the bay leaf. Fluff the rice with a fork and stir in the remaining butter.

YIELD: 8 servings.

Riz Sauvage au Beurre

BUTTERED WILD RICE

- 1 cup wild rice
- 5 cups cold water
- Salt to taste
- 4 tablespoons butter
- 2 tablespoons finely chopped shallots
- ½ cup finely diced celery
- Freshly ground black pepper to taste

1. Run cold water over the rice and drain until the water runs clear.

2. Put the rice in a saucepan and add the water and salt to taste.

3. Bring to the boil and simmer for 1 hour. At this point the rice grains should be puffed open. If not, remove from the heat and let the rice stand in the hot cooking water until puffed.

4. When ready, drain the water off and cover tightly.

5. Melt half the butter in a small skillet and add the shallots and celery. Cook, stirring often, for about 5 minutes. The celery should retain some of its crispy texture.

6. Add the celery, shallots, salt and pepper to taste to the rice and stir.

7. Just before serving, add the remaining butter and reheat, stirring from the bottom.

YIELD: 6 servings.

❧

Riz Sauvage Derby

WILD RICE WITH LIVER AND MUSHROOMS

- ¾ cup wild rice
- 2¼ cups cold water
- Salt, if desired
- 1 duck liver
- ¼ pound mushrooms
- 2 tablespoons butter
- 2 tablespoons finely chopped white onion
- Freshly ground black pepper to taste

1. Run cold water over the rice and drain until the water runs clear.

2. Put the rice in a saucepan and add the water and salt to taste.

3. Bring to the boil and simmer for 1 hour. At this point the rice grains should be puffed open. If not, remove from the heat and let the rice stand in the hot cooking water until puffed. Drain well.

4. Put the liver on a flat surface and chop it finely.

5. Cut the mushrooms into ½-inch cubes. There should be about 1 cup.

6. Melt the butter in a small skillet and add the mushrooms. Cook, stirring, for about 30 seconds. Add the liver and cook, stirring, for about 30 seconds longer. Add the onion and cook, stirring, for about 15 seconds. Sprinkle with salt and pepper to taste.

7. Add the rice and stir to blend. Heat thoroughly and serve.

YIELD: 4 servings.

Dirty Rice

- 1 pound chicken livers
- 1 pound chicken gizzards
- 10 tablespoons peanut, vegetable or corn oil
- 6 cups peeled eggplant cut into 1-inch cubes
- 1 pound ground pork
- 1½ cups finely chopped green pepper
- 1 cup finely chopped celery
- 1 cup finely chopped onion
- 1 teaspoon cayenne pepper
- Salt to taste
- 1 teaspoon freshly ground white pepper
- 1½ teaspoons freshly ground black pepper
- 6½ cups rich chicken broth (see recipe page 418)
- 1 cup rice
- 1 cup chopped scallions

1. Put the livers and gizzards in separate piles on a flat surface and chop until fine, or use a food processor but do not blend to a purée. The gizzards and livers must retain their character.

2. Heat the oil in a skillet until it is almost smoking. Add the eggplant and cook, stirring, for about 5 minutes.

3. Add the pork and stir with a heavy metal spoon, chopping down with the sides of the spoon to break up lumps. Add the gizzards. Cover closely and cook for about 10 minutes.

4. With the spoon, mash down on the eggplant pieces. Add the green pepper, celery and onion. Continue cooking, covered, over high heat for about 10 minutes. Cook, stirring from the bottom to scrape up the brown particles. Add the cayenne pepper, salt, white pepper and black pepper. Cook, stirring always from the bottom to incorporate the dark brown matter that sticks to the bottom of the skillet, for about 10 minutes.

5. Add the broth and stir to clean the bottom. Cover and cook for about 20 minutes. Uncover and stir in the livers. Cook for about 5 minutes and add the rice and cover. Cook for 15 to 20 minutes, or until the rice is tender. Stir in the scallions and serve.

YIELD: 10 to 12 servings.

Red Beans with Rice

- 1 pound dried red kidney beans
- 20 or more cups water
- 1 pound lean salt pork, cut into 1½-inch cubes
- ¾ pound smoked ham, cut into ½-inch cubes
- 2½ cups finely chopped onion
- 2½ cups finely chopped green pepper
- 1½ cups finely chopped celery
- 2 bay leaves
- 2½ teaspoons finely minced garlic
- ½ teaspoon dried thyme
- ¼ teaspoon dried basil
- ¼ teaspoon cayenne pepper
- ¼ teaspoon freshly ground white pepper
- Salt to taste
- 1 teaspoon paprika
- 2 cups rice
- ¼ cup chopped parsley

1. Rinse the beans and drain well. Put them in a kettle with 6 cups of the water and cover. Bring to the boil and cook for about 30 minutes, or until the beans are almost mealy.

2. Meanwhile, put the pork cubes in a skillet and cook until the pork is rendered of much of its fat. Cover closely and cook over high heat, stirring occasionally, until it is browned and crisp. Add the ham, onion, green pepper, celery, bay leaves, 1½ teaspoons garlic, thyme, basil, cayenne pepper, white pepper, salt and paprika. Cook, stirring often, for about 30 minutes.

3. Add the pork and vegetables to the beans. Add 4 cups of water to the skillet in which the pork and vegetables cooked and stir to dissolve brown particles that cling to the bottom and sides of the skillet. Bring to the boil and add to the beans. Cook for about 20 minutes and add 4 more cups of water. Cover and continue cooking for about 30 minutes and add 2 more cups of water. Cover and continue cooking for about 1½ hours. It is imperative that you stir the bean mixture from the bottom often or it will stick.

4. Meanwhile, combine the rice and remaining 4 cups of water in a saucepan or kettle and bring to the boil. Add salt to taste. Cover and cook for 10 minutes. Turn off the heat and let the rice stand for about 15 minutes.

5. Chop the parsley and remaining teaspoon of chopped garlic together and stir it into the beans.

6. Spoon rice into individual serving plates and add beans as desired.

YIELD: 12 servings.

There are three foods of consummate goodness that may be served as either a main course or a side dish in the Italian kitchen. These are pasta, rice in the form of risotto and polenta. Of the three, polenta, which is a form of cornmeal mush, is relatively little known and appreciated in this country. A pity, too, for polenta has scores of delectable uses. It can be served piping hot the moment it is taken from the stove, or it can be chilled, cut into various shapes, sprinkled with butter and cheese and baked for a sumptuous side dish. It is also delectable when topped with Gorgonzola cheese and baked. Although cornmeal that is produced commercially in this country can be used to prepare polenta, it is far better to use cornmeal (sold as raw polenta) imported from Italy.

❧

Polenta

- 2 cups coarse cornmeal, preferably imported from Italy (see Note)
- 8½ cups water
- Salt, if desired
- 1 tablespoon olive oil

1. Measure the cornmeal and set aside.

2. Put the water in a heavy casserole and bring to a full rolling boil over high heat. Add salt to taste.

3. Start stirring vigorously with a wire whisk. Gradually add the cornmeal in a thin, steady stream. One must stir rapidly as the meal is added to prevent lumping. Stir constantly for at least 5 minutes, covering the inside of the casserole, bottom and sides, to blend well and prevent lumping.

4. At the end of 5 minutes, turn the heat to moderately low and continue cooking, stirring quite often with a heavy wooden spoon all around the bottom and sides.

5. At the end of 15 or 20 minutes, a light crust will start to form on the bottom of the casserole. Add the olive oil and continue stirring with the spoon. For this quantity of cornmeal, the total cooking time should be about 20 minutes.

6. To unmold quickly, invert the casserole on top of a clean, flat surface. Traditionally, Italian cooks use a string to cut the polenta into serving portions. Hold a string taut at both ends and slip it carefully under the bed of polenta, holding the string close against the flat surface. Slide the string under the polenta to a distance of from 1 to 2 inches. Bring it up quickly to make a long slice. Repeat, pushing the string farther away from you and

bringing it up to make a second long slice. Repeat. Now, turn the string and repeat slicing in the other direction.

7. Serve hot with any of various savory stews. Or chill the polenta and bake it later with cheese on top.

YIELD: 6 to 10 servings.

Note: Imported cornmeal (referred to as raw polenta) is widely available in specialty shops that offer imported foods and in grocery stores that specialize in Italian foods.

Polenta with Gorgonzola Cheese

- 2 to 3 cups cooked polenta
- ¼ pound Gorgonzola cheese
- 4 tablespoons butter
- 10 or 12 sage leaves, preferably fresh
- Freshly grated Parmesan cheese

1. Preheat the oven to 450 degrees.

2. Cut off enough freshly made polenta to cover the bottom of an oval baking dish measuring 10 by 7 by 1½ inches. Press it down to make a solid layer. Cover with half of the Gorgonzola cheese, crumbled. Add the remaining polenta and press down.

3. Melt the butter and add the sage leaves. Let simmer over very low heat for about 1 minute without browning.

4. Cut the remaining cheese into 4 or 5 small triangles and press them into the top of the top layer of polenta. Pour the butter over the top and arrange the sage leaves around the polenta. Press the leaves down in the butter or they will burn. Sprinkle with Parmesan cheese.

5. Place in the oven and bake for about 5 minutes. Run under the broiler for about 2 minutes, or until bubbling and piping hot.

YIELD: 4 servings.

Egi Maccioni's Gorgonzola-Mascarpone Cheese with Polenta

- 4 cups water
- Salt to taste, if desired
- 1 cup fine or coarse ground cornmeal, preferably imported
- 4 tablespoons butter
- 6 ¼-inch-thick slices Gorgonzola-Mascarpone cheese (see Note)

1. Bring the water to the boil with salt to taste. Add the cornmeal while stirring vigorously with a wire whisk.

2. Continue cooking, stirring often and rapidly with the whisk, taking care to stir well over the bottom and sides so that the mixture cooks evenly and does not lump. Stir in the butter.

3. Very hot plates are essential for the success of this dish. Heat six plates and place one slice of the cheese on each. Spoon an equal portion of the cornmeal mixture over each serving and serve immediately.

YIELD: 6 servings.

Note: Gorgonzola-Mascarpone is a very rich, pungent-mild cheese from Italy. It is widely available in the finest cheese and specialty food shops in metropolitan areas.

Despite the fact that America is supposed to be in the midst of a regional cooking renaissance, we are still a nation of strangers where many native dishes are concerned. One Southern specialty that I would love to convince Northerners to eat is hominy. It is delectable and teams notably well with grated cheese. Another specialty dear to Southerners is hush puppies, those deep-fried cornmeal patties that were said to come about during the Civil War when a group of Southerners were cooking over an open fire. When a platoon of Yankee soldiers came nearby, the Southerners would fry up a few patties and toss them to their yelping dogs with the admonition, "Hush, puppies."

Hominy and Cheese Casserole

- 1 can whole white or yellow hominy
- 1 cup grated Cheddar cheese
- 1 4-ounce can chopped green chilies
- ½ cup sour cream
- Salt to taste if desired
- Freshly ground black pepper to taste
- ¼ cup heavy cream

1. Preheat the oven to 350 degrees.

2. Drain the hominy. There should be about 3 cups. Set aside ¼ cup of the cheese for topping.

3. Using a 4-cup casserole, put a layer of hominy on the bottom. Start forming layers of the chilies, sour cream, remaining ¾ cup of cheese, salt and pepper to taste. Pour on the heavy cream.

4. Sprinkle the reserved ¼ cup of cheese on top and place in the oven. Bake for 25 minutes.

YIELD: 4 servings.

Hush Puppies

- 1½ cups white cornmeal
- 4 teaspoons flour
- 2 teaspoons baking powder
- Salt to taste, if desired
- 1 tablespoon sugar
- ¼ cup grated onion
- 1 egg, lightly beaten
- 1 cup rapidly boiling water
- Fresh corn oil to cover

1. Combine the cornmeal, flour, baking powder, salt, sugar, grated onion and egg and blend well. Add the water rapidly while stirring. The water must be boiling when added.

2. Heat the oil to 370 degrees. Drop the mixture by rounded spoonfuls into the oil. Cook until golden brown. Drain on paper toweling.

YIELD: About 36.

BREADS, BISCUITS AND CRACKERS

A SPONGE is a starter for bread making, and the one that impresses us most is from a 75-year-old bread-making manual published by a flour manufacturer. This sponge is made by kneading a small quantity of flour with a blend of yeast and water. It is shaped into a ball, submerged in a small amount of lukewarm water and, within 15 minutes or less, the ball rises to the top as a sponge-like round mass. It is then ready to be used as the basis for long, crusty loaves of French or Italian bread, or it may be shaped and baked in an old-fashioned loaf pan.

Bread Dough

- 2¼ cups lukewarm water
- 4 teaspoons granular yeast
- 6½ cups unbleached flour, approximately
- 1 teaspoon salt, if desired

1. Put ¼ cup of lukewarm water in a small, warmed mixing bowl and add the yeast. Stir to dissolve.

2. Add ¾ cup of the flour and the salt and mix thoroughly until the dough can be shaped into a ball. Turn the ball out onto a lightly floured board and knead until smooth and elastic.

3. Put the remaining 2 cups of lukewarm water into a 1-quart glass measuring cup.

4. Cut a cross in the top of the ball of dough. Put the ball, cross side up, in the water. Let stand for 15 minutes. The dough will rise to the top as a light puffy ball. This is known as a sponge.

5. It is easy to make the remainder of the bread dough in a food processor, although it may be done by hand. If the processor is used, add the remaining 5¾ cups of flour to the container of the processor outfitted with

a metal blade. If the container of the food processor is not large enough, make the dough in two steps, using half of the flour, half of the sponge and half of the water in which it soaked at a time. Repeat. If the processor is not used, put the flour onto a flat surface and make a well in the center.

6. Add the sponge and water in which it sets to the processor or to the well in the center of the flour. Process until it is a fairly stiff dough and turn out onto a lightly floured surface. Or knead the dough by hand on the lightly floured surface for 15 to 20 minutes, or until it is quite elastic. Shape the dough into a ball.

7. Lightly sprinkle the inside of a mixing bowl with flour and add the ball of dough. Cover closely with a cloth. Set aside in a warm place and let stand for 45 minutes to 1 hour, or until doubled in bulk.

YIELD: Enough dough for 6 French loaves or 2 standard loaves.

French Bread

- 1 recipe for bread dough (see preceding recipe)
- Butter or other fat for greasing molds or baking sheet
- Cornmeal for the baking sheet, if used
- 1 egg white
- 1 tablespoon cold water

1. Prepare the dough and let it rise until doubled in bulk as indicated in the recipe.

2. The most convenient pans for shaping and baking long loaves are French bread molds. If they are used, brush the inside bottom lightly with butter. Or use a baking sheet and brush it lightly with oil or melted lard. Sprinkle the sheet lightly with cornmeal and shake off any excess.

3. Punch the dough down and divide it into 6 equal portions. Place the portions of dough, one at a time, onto a lightly floured board. Roll the dough beneath the palms of the hands, stretching as necessary to produce 6 sausage shapes, each measuring 17 or 18 inches in length. As each roll of dough is prepared, arrange it in one of the bread molds or on the prepared baking sheet. If the baking sheet is used, arrange the rolls parallel and about 3 inches apart. When the dough is ready, cover closely with a clean cloth and let stand in a warm place until doubled in bulk. An unlighted gas-fired oven with the door partly ajar can be a comfortably warm place to let dough rise. If the oven is used as a warming place, remove the dough before preheating the oven.

4. Preheat the oven to 500 degrees. Have ready a hand spray such as that used for spraying household plants. Fill it with water.

5. You may gash the tops or not. If you desire, use a very sharp razor blade and cut the long loaves diagonally on top with 3 parallel and not-too-deep gashes. Before putting the loaves in the oven, remember that the total baking time is 25 minutes or slightly less.

6. Immediately place the molds or baking sheet in the oven and quickly spray inside the oven generously. Quickly close the oven door and let bake for 3 minutes. Quickly give the oven a second spray. Close the door and bake for 3 minutes longer. Give a third and final spray inside the oven. At this point the loaves have baked about 6 minutes. Reduce the oven temperature to 400 degrees.

7. Continue baking for 14 minutes longer, or until done.

8. Beat together the egg white and water and brush the top of each loaf with the mixture. It may be wise to reverse the pans in the oven to ensure even baking and browning. Continue baking for 5 minutes longer, or until nicely browned all over.

9. Remove the loaves and arrange them on a rack to cool.

YIELD: 6 loaves.

Spiral Herb Bread

- 1 recipe for bread dough (see recipe page 388)
- 2 tablespoons butter plus butter to grease the pans
- 2 teaspoons finely minced garlic
- 2 cups finely chopped parsley
- 2 cups finely chopped scallions
- 1 cup finely chopped fresh dill
- Salt to taste, if desired
- Freshly ground black pepper to taste
- 2 eggs, lightly beaten
- 1 teaspoon corn, peanut or vegetable oil

1. Prepare the dough and let it rise until doubled in bulk as indicated in the recipe.

2. Melt the 2 tablespoons of butter in a saucepan and add the garlic. Cook briefly and add the parsley, scallions, dill, salt and pepper. Add all but 2 tablespoons of the beaten eggs to the herb mixture. Set aside and let cool.

3. Lightly grease 2 loaf pans that are 9¾ by 5½ by 3 inches in dimension.

4. Divide the dough in half and roll out one-half at a time into a rectangle about ¼ inch thick, 9 inches wide and 12 inches long.

5. Brush the top lightly with the reserved beaten egg. Spoon half of the filling on top and spread it over, leaving a margin of about 1 inch all around. Roll jelly roll fashion and pinch the edges to seal. Place the filled dough in one of the pans, seam side down.

6. Roll out the second half of the dough into a rectangle of the same size, spread with the remaining filling, roll and seal as before. Place it in the second pan.

7. Brush the top of each loaf with a little oil. Cover the loaves and let stand in a warm place for 50 to 60 minutes, or until slightly higher in the middle than around the edges.

8. Preheat the oven to 400 degrees.

9. Cut gashes in the top of the loaves with a very sharp razor blade, if desired. Place in the oven and bake for 1 hour. Turn onto a rack and let cool.

YIELD: 2 loaves.

Tjasa Sprague's Whole Wheat Bread

- 1 ¾-ounce cube of fresh yeast, or 1 envelope granular yeast
- 1 cup lukewarm water
- 2 tablespoons honey
- 2 tablespoons salt
- 3 cups milk
- 4 cups whole wheat flour
- 4 cups white all-purpose flour, approximately
- Butter for greasing the bowl and pan

1. Place the yeast in a large mixing bowl and add the water. Stir to dissolve. Add the honey and salt. Add the milk and stir to blend well.

2. Add the whole wheat flour and beat with a wire whisk (or use an electric mixer) for 5 minutes.

3. Add the all-purpose flour and beat with a wooden spoon 50 times. If necessary, add more flour, but the dough should remain a little sticky. Scrape the dough out onto a floured surface and turn to coat lightly with flour. Shape the dough into a ball.

4. Grease a large mixing bowl and add the ball of dough. Cover with a clean towel and let stand at room temperature overnight.

5. Turn the dough out onto a floured board and knead briefly. Shape it into a ball. Grease a deep skillet (preferably an 8-inch skillet with a 14-cup capacity) or use a casserole of the same size. Add the ball of dough.

6. Let the dough rise until doubled in bulk, an hour or longer.

7. Preheat the oven to 425 degrees. When the dough has risen, place it in the oven and bake for 1 hour, or until nicely browned.

YIELD: 1 large loaf.

Italian Rye Bread

- 2 packages granular yeast
- 1¾ cups lukewarm water
- 1 teaspoon sugar
- 2 tablespoons plus 1 teaspoon olive oil
- 1 cup rye flour
- 4 cups unbleached flour
- Salt
- 1 teaspoon fennel seeds
- 1 tablespoon cornmeal
- 1 egg
- 2 teaspoons water

1. Combine in the container of a food processor the yeast, ¼ cup lukewarm water, sugar and 2 tablespoons of the olive oil. Process for about 5 seconds.

2. Add the rye flour, unbleached flour, salt to taste, fennel seeds and the remaining 1½ cups of lukewarm water. Blend thoroughly.

3. Lightly flour a flat surface and turn the dough out onto it. Knead briefly and shape into a smooth ball. Lightly flour the inside of a bowl and add the ball of dough. Cover with a clean cloth and place in a warm but not too hot place. Let rise until doubled in bulk, about 1½ hours.

4. Turn the dough out onto a lightly floured surface and knead briefly. Shape it into a ball and return it to the bowl. Cover and let rise a second time, about 1 hour.

5. Divide the dough in half. Roll out each half into a rectangle measuring about 15 inches long and 12 inches wide. Roll each half of dough like a long jelly roll, pressing lightly to seal the bottom seam. Tuck in and press the ends to make them smooth.

6. Lightly oil a baking sheet with a little of the remaining 1 teaspoon of oil and sprinkle with the cornmeal. Arrange the loaves on this. Brush the dough with the remaining oil. Cover with a clean cloth and let stand for about 30 minutes, or until doubled in bulk.

7. Preheat the oven to 425 degrees.

8. Beat the egg with the 2 teaspoons of water and brush the surface of the dough all over with a little of the mixture. Using a very sharp knife or razor, slash the top of the bread. Place in the oven and bake for 25 to 30 minutes.

YIELD: 2 loaves.

Beer Rye Bread

- 3 cups beer
- ⅓ cup lard or bacon fat
- ½ cup firmly packed light brown sugar
- ½ cup light molasses
- 1½ tablespoons salt
- 2 tablespoons grated orange rind
- 2 tablespoons caraway seeds
- 2 packages active dry yeast
- ½ cup warm water
- 5 cups unsifted rye flour
- 5 to 6 cups unsifted white flour

1. Heat the beer in a saucepan until it just bubbles. Add the lard, brown sugar, molasses, salt, orange rind and caraway seeds. Cool to lukewarm.

2. In a large mixing bowl, dissolve the yeast in the warm water. Add the lukewarm beer mixture. Beat in the rye flour and enough white flour to make a soft dough.

3. Turn the dough out on a heavily floured board and knead it until it is smooth and elastic. Place the dough in a greased bowl, turning it until it is greased all over. Cover and let rise in a warm place until doubled in bulk.

4. Punch down the dough and knead again. Divide the dough in half and shape into 2 round or long oval shapes on a greased baking sheet. Slash the top of the loaves with a sharp knife. Let rise until doubled in bulk.

5. Preheat the oven to 350 degrees.

6. Place the loaves in the oven and bake for 40 to 45 minutes, or until done.

YIELD: 2 loaves.

Panettone

ITALIAN FEAST-DAY BREAD

- 3 envelopes granular yeast
- ⅓ cup warm water
- ¼ cup sugar
- ½ cup dark raisins
- ½ cup diced citron
- 1 tablespoon dark rum
- 8 egg yolks
- 1 teaspoon pure vanilla extract
- Grated rind of 1 lemon
- Salt
- ¼ pound sweet butter at room temperature
- 1½ cups flour
- 4 tablespoons melted butter

1. Put the yeast and water in a small mixing bowl. Add 1 teaspoon of the sugar and stir to dissolve the yeast. Set aside in a warm place until it foams.

2. Combine the raisins, citron and rum in a mixing bowl. Set aside until ready to use.

3. Rinse out a large mixing bowl with hot water. Drain and dry thoroughly. Add the egg yolks and the remaining sugar. Beat with a wire whisk until pale yellow. Beat in the vanilla, lemon rind and salt to taste.

4. Add the yeast mixture and beat, adding the ¼ pound butter about a tablespoon at a time. Beat well.

5. Add the flour and beat briskly for 5 to 10 minutes.

6. Scrape the sides of the bowl, letting the dough rest in the center. Cover and let stand in a warm place for about 1 hour, or until doubled in bulk.

7. Preheat the oven to 400 degrees. Butter the inside of a 6- or 7-cup fluted mold.

8. Punch the dough down. Drain the raisins and citron and knead them briefly into the dough.

9. Turn the dough into the prepared mold. Brush the top with melted butter and place the mold in the oven. Bake for 10 minutes, then reduce the oven temperature to 325 degrees. Continue baking for about 40 minutes longer, basting often with more melted butter.

YIELD: 1 loaf.

Pao Doce

PORTUGUESE SWEET BREAD

- 2 packages active dry yeast
- ¼ cup lukewarm water
- 5 to 6 cups flour
- 1 teaspoon salt
- 5 eggs
- 1 cup lukewarm milk
- 6 tablespoons melted butter
- 1¼ cups sugar
- Butter for greasing the bowl and pans
- 1 teaspoon cold water

1. Combine the yeast and lukewarm water and stir until the yeast is dissolved. Set aside.

2. Sift together the flour and salt into a large bowl and set aside.

3. Beat 4 of the eggs lightly in a small bowl.

4. Combine the milk and the melted butter in a mixing bowl. Beat in the sugar. Add the yeast mixture and the beaten eggs and stir until well blended.

5. Add about 4 cups of flour, 1 cup at a time, incorporating it with your fingers and kneading as you add it. Add enough flour to make a soft dough.

6. Turn the dough out onto a floured board and knead until smooth and elastic. Add only enough flour to make a dough that is not sticky.

7. Butter a large bowl and add the dough. Turn the dough upside down so that it is lightly covered with butter. Cover and let stand in a warm place until doubled in bulk.

8. Punch the dough down and knead it briefly on the floured board.

9. Divide the dough in half, on a lightly floured board, and shape each half into a flattened round shape.

10. Butter 2 8-inch cake pans and add one round of dough to each.

11. Cover with a cloth and let stand until doubled in bulk, about 1½ hours.

12. Beat the remaining egg with the teaspoon of cold water. Brush the top of each bread lightly with a little of the mixture.

13. Fifteen minutes before the rising time is up, preheat the oven to 350 degrees.

14. Place the breads in the oven and bake for 30 to 40 minutes. Turn out onto racks to cool.

YIELD: 2 loaves.

Jalapeño Corn Bread

1 8½-ounce can cream-style corn
1 cup yellow cornmeal
3 eggs
1 teaspoon salt
½ teaspoon baking soda
¾ cup milk
⅓ cup corn oil
1 cup grated sharp Cheddar cheese
¼ cup chopped jalapeño peppers
2 tablespoons butter

1. Preheat the oven to 400 degrees.

2. In a mixing bowl, combine the corn, cornmeal, eggs, salt, baking soda, milk, oil, half of the cheese and the peppers. Blend well.

3. Meanwhile, put the 2 tablespoons of butter in a 1½-quart casserole (preferably a glazed Mexican earthenware casserole) or a 9-inch skillet. Place the casserole in the oven until the butter is hot but not brown. Immediately pour in the corn bread mixture. Sprinkle with the remaining cheese and bake for 40 minutes.

YIELD: 8 servings.

On a visit to Mississippi, the land of my birth, I was fascinated to sample a sausage dish that was totally new to my palate. It was a kind of biscuit, but with ground sausage meat and grated cheese added before it was shaped into balls and baked in a fairly hot oven.

The result was something as insidious to the taste and appetite as peanuts. The flavor grew on you, and one couldn't stop eating them. It seemed an excellent breakfast dish, to go with fried eggs and the like. Without toast.

When we were browsing through regional Southern cookbooks, we found several recipes for it, and they all recommended a staple, supermarket biscuit mix. We preferred to make our own—from scratch, as the saying goes. Also in that browsing, however, we discovered another fascinating recipe for something called sausage rolls. We saw this in one of the best regional Southern cookbooks, *The Cotton Country Collection,* printed by the Junior Charity League of Monroe, Louisiana. The recipe is credited to Mrs. Paul Lansing of New Orleans.

Sausage–Cheese Biscuits

- 1½ cups sifted flour
- 1 teaspoon baking powder
- ½ teaspoon baking soda
- ½ teaspoon salt
- 2 tablespoons solid white shortening
- 2 tablespoons cultured buttermilk powder, available in many supermarkets and most health food stores
- ½ pound sharp Cheddar cheese, grated
- 1 pound homemade spiced sausage (see following recipe), or 1 pound purchased in bulk

1. Preheat the oven to 425 degrees.

2. Set aside 1 tablespoon of the flour for kneading the dough.

3. Combine the remaining flour, baking powder, baking soda and salt in a mixing bowl. Blend well. Add the shortening and cut it in with a pastry cutter. Add the buttermilk powder and blend well with fingers.

4. Add the cheese and uncooked sausage and blend thoroughly. Shape the mixture into balls about 1 inch in diameter, rolling between the palms of the hands. As the balls are shaped, arrange them on a baking sheet.

5. Place in the oven and bake for 15 to 20 minutes.

YIELD: About 5 dozen.

SPICED SAUSAGE

- 1 pound ground pork
- ¼ teaspoon freshly ground black pepper
- ¼ teaspoon hot red pepper flakes
- ⅛ teaspoon ground allspice
- Pinch of ground cloves
- Pinch of ground cinnamon
- 2 tablespoons cold water
- Salt to taste, if desired

1. Combine the pork, black pepper, pepper flakes, allspice, cloves, cinnamon, water and salt to taste in a mixing bowl. Blend thoroughly. If desired, you may substitute ½ tablespoon crumbled sage for the allspice, cloves and cinnamon.

2. To test the mixture for seasoning, shape a small patty with the fingers. Heat a small skillet and cook the patty on both sides until thoroughly cooked. Taste and add more seasoning as desired.

YIELD: About 1 pound.

❧

Mrs. Paul Lansing's Southern Sausage Rolls

- 2 cups flour
- Salt to taste, if desired
- 1 tablespoon baking powder
- 5 tablespoons solid white shortening
- ⅔ cup milk
- 1 pound spiced sausage (see preceding recipe)

1. Combine the flour, salt to taste and baking powder in a mixing bowl. Add the shortening and milk. Blend well.

2. Divide the dough in half. Roll each half into a rectangle about ½ inch thick. Top each half with half of the uncooked sausage. Using a spatula, smooth the sausage over the dough. Roll each half as for a jelly roll.

3. Wrap closely in clear plastic wrap or in foil. Freeze.

4. When ready to cook, preheat the oven to 400 degrees.

5. Place a rack in a baking dish. Cut each roll into rounds about ½ inch thick. Each roll should yield about 16 slices. Arrange the slices on the rack in the baking dish and bake for 30 to 35 minutes.

YIELD: About 32 rolls.

Curiously, one of the few foods for which we have never printed a recipe is any variety of cracker, including a basic soda cracker and its variations. When we mentioned this in writing, we received scores of letters from readers offering us recipes for crackers.

In addition to the basic soda cracker recipe, we received a fine one for a cornmeal cracker that is crisp and reminiscent of a good tortilla. We also received a recipe for an arrowroot biscuit, referred to as a cracker. It is crisp and excellent and, while crackers are often defined as unsweetened biscuits, this one does contain a bit of sugar.

Terrence Janericco's Soda Crackers

- 3 cups flour
- ½ teaspoon baking soda
- 1 tablespoon butter
- ¾ cup buttermilk
- Coarse salt

1. Preheat the oven to 350 degrees.

2. Put the flour, baking soda and butter into the container of a food processor.

3. Start processing and gradually add the milk, incorporating only enough milk to make a very stiff dough that can be gathered into a ball. Knead the dough briefly on a lightly floured board. Wrap the dough in plastic wrap and let it rest for 15 minutes.

4. Divide the dough in half and roll out each half to ⅛-inch thickness. (Ideally, you should use a pasta machine for this; otherwise it may be difficult to roll the dough thin enough.) Cut the dough into cracker-sized squares and prick the squares with a fork. Sprinkle lightly with salt.

5. Arrange the squares on a lightly greased baking sheet. Bake for 10 minutes, or until crisp and lightly browned.

YIELD: About 36 crackers.

Joan Bayles's Cornmeal Crackers

- 1 cup cornmeal
- ½ cup flour
- ¾ teaspoon salt
- ¼ teaspoon baking soda
- ½ cup milk
- 3 tablespoons peanut, vegetable or corn oil
- ¼ teaspoon Worcestershire sauce

1. Preheat the oven to 350 degrees.

2. Combine the cornmeal, flour, salt and baking soda in the container of a food processor.

3. Combine the milk, oil and Worcestershire sauce. Gradually add the milk mixture to the cornmeal mixture while processing.

4. Knead the dough on a lightly floured board for 5 minutes.

5. Divide the dough in half. Roll out each half into a 12-inch square. Cut into 2-inch squares. Place on a lightly greased baking sheet. Bake for 15 minutes, or until the edges are golden brown. Let cool before removing from the baking sheet.

YIELD: About 6 dozen.

Arrowroot Crackers

- ½ cup plus 3 tablespoons arrowroot
- ½ cup plus 3 tablespoons flour
- 4 tablespoons butter
- ¼ teaspoon salt
- ½ teaspoon baking powder
- ¼ cup sugar
- 2 to 3 tablespoons milk

1. Preheat the oven to 350 degrees.

2. Put the arrowroot, flour, butter, salt, baking powder and sugar into the container of a food processor.

3. Start processing while gradually adding the milk. Add only enough milk to make a dough that will hold together and can be rolled out. Knead the dough briefly on a lightly floured board.

4. Roll out the dough to a ⅛-inch thickness. Using a 2-inch biscuit cutter, cut the dough into rounds.

5. Prick each round with a fork and place on a lightly floured baking sheet. Bake for 15 to 20 minutes, or until they are lightly browned.

YIELD: About 25 crackers.

SAUCES

Beurre Blanc

WHITE BUTTER SAUCE

- 6 tablespoons finely chopped shallots
- 1½ cups dry white wine
- 12 tablespoons cold butter
- Salt and freshly ground black pepper to taste

1. Combine the shallots and wine in a saucepan and bring to a vigorous boil.

2. Let the wine cook down to about ⅓ cup. Continue cooking over moderate heat, stirring rapidly with a wire whisk. Add the butter, about 2 tablespoons at a time, stirring vigorously and constantly.

3. Add the salt and pepper and remove from the heat.

YIELD: About 1¼ cups.

Beurre Blanc au Cari

WHITE BUTTER SAUCE WITH CURRY

Prepare the recipe for beurre blanc but add 1 tablespoon of curry powder to the raw shallots in the very beginning of the recipe.

Beurre Rouge

RED WINE BUTTER SAUCE

- 6 tablespoons finely chopped shallots
- 1½ cups red Burgundy wine
- 12 tablespoons butter
- Salt and freshly ground black pepper to taste

1. Combine the shallots and wine in a saucepan and bring to a vigorous boil.

2. Let the wine cook down to about ⅓ cup. Continue cooking over moderate heat, stirring rapidly with a wire whisk. Add the butter, about 2 tablespoons at a time, stirring vigorously and constantly. Add the salt and pepper and remove from the heat.

YIELD: About 1¼ cups.

Sauce Béarnaise

- ½ pound butter
- 2 tablespoons finely chopped shallots
- 2 tablespoons tarragon vinegar
- 1 teaspoon crushed black peppercorns
- 1 teaspoon dried tarragon
- 2 egg yolks
- 1 tablespoon cold water

1. Put the butter in a small heavy saucepan and let it melt slowly. Skim off the foam that rises to the top.

2. Heat the shallots, vinegar, peppercorns and tarragon in another small, heavy saucepan and cook until all the liquid evaporates. Remove from the heat and let the saucepan cool slightly.

3. Add the egg yolks and water to the shallots.

4. Return the saucepan to the stove and stir the yolk mixture vigorously over very low heat. Do not overheat or the eggs will curdle. Remove the saucepan from the heat and place it on a cold surface. Add the melted butter, ladle by ladle, stirring vigorously after each addition. Do not add the butter too rapidly and do not add the milky substance at the bottom.

YIELD: About 1 cup.

Mustard Hollandaise

THE MUSTARD

- 3 tablespoons powdered mustard
- ¼ teaspoon salt
- ½ teaspoon sugar
- 2 tablespoons water

THE HOLLANDAISE

- ½ pound butter
- 2 egg yolks
- 1 tablespoon water
- 1 tablespoon lemon juice

1. Put the mustard in a small bowl and add the salt, sugar and water. Mix and let stand for at least 10 minutes to develop flavor.

2. Preheat the oven to 200 degrees.

3. Put the butter in a 1-quart heatproof glass measuring cup (this will facilitate pouring the butter after it is melted) and set it carefully in the oven to melt.

4. When the butter has melted, carefully skim the foam and scum off the top of the butter. Carefully pour off the clear golden liquid. Discard the milky substance on the bottom. There should be about ¾ cup of clear, liquid butter.

5. In a heavy saucepan, combine the egg yolks with the water. Place the saucepan on a Flame-tamer and start whisking the yolks rapidly with the water. Whisk thoroughly until the mixture becomes thick and foamy like a custard, 5 to 10 minutes. Do not let the mixture become too hot or it will break down and curdle. Remove the saucepan from the heat and, beating vigorously, gradually add the melted butter. Add the lemon juice. Stir in the mustard according to taste.

YIELD: 1¼ cups.

Béchamel Sauce

4 tablespoons butter
4 tablespoons flour
2 cups milk
Salt and freshly ground black pepper to taste

1. Melt the butter in a saucepan and add the flour, stirring with a wire whisk. When blended, add the milk, stirring rapidly with the whisk. Add the salt and pepper.

2. When thickened and smooth, reduce the heat and cook, stirring occasionally, for about 5 minutes.

YIELD: 2 cups.

Sauce Suprême

CHICKEN AND CREAM SAUCE

6 tablespoons butter
⅓ cup flour
4 cups chicken broth
1⅓ cups heavy cream
Salt to taste, if desired
Freshly ground black pepper to taste

1. Melt the butter in a 1½- to 3-quart saucepan and add the flour, stirring with a wire whisk. When blended and smooth, add the broth, stirring rapidly with the whisk. When thickened, simmer for about 5 minutes, stirring often.

2. Add the cream, salt and pepper. Simmer for 5 minutes longer.

YIELD: About 5 cups.

Sauce Bonne Femme

MUSHROOM AND WHITE WINE SAUCE

- 2 tablespoons butter
- 2 tablespoons finely chopped shallots
- ½ pound mushrooms, thinly sliced, about 3 cups
- ½ cup dry white wine
- ½ cup fish stock or chicken broth
- ¾ cup heavy cream
- 1 tablespoon flour
- 2 tablespoons finely chopped parsley

1. Melt 1 tablespoon of the butter in a skillet and add the shallots. Cook briefly, stirring, and add the mushrooms. Cook, stirring, until the mushrooms are wilted.

2. Add the wine and continue cooking until the liquid is almost, but not totally, evaporated.

3. Add the stock and cook over high heat for about 1 minute. Add the cream and cook for about 30 seconds.

4. Meanwhile, blend the remaining tablespoon of butter and the flour and stir it into the sauce. Stir in the parsley and serve.

YIELD: About 3 cups.

Sauce Verte

GREEN SAUCE

- 1 egg yolk
- 2 teaspoons prepared mustard, preferably imported Dijon
- 1 teaspoon red wine vinegar
- Salt and freshly ground black pepper to taste
- ½ cup olive oil
- 2 tablespoons lemon juice
- 2 cups loosely packed spinach leaves
- ⅓ cup coarsely chopped celery
- ½ cup loosely packed watercress
- ½ cup loosely packed chopped parsley

1. Put the egg yolk, mustard, vinegar and salt and pepper into a mixing bowl. Start beating with a wire whisk. When blended and smooth, gradually add the oil, beating until smooth and thickened. Beat in the lemon juice. Set aside.

2. Drop the spinach into boiling water to cover. Cook for about 30 seconds, or until the spinach is wilted. Drain well. Squeeze to extract most of the water from the spinach. There should be about ¼ cup spinach.

3. Put the spinach, celery, watercress and parsley into the container of a food processor. Process until smooth.

4. Line a small bowl with a square of cheesecloth. Spoon and scrape the mixture into it. Bring up the ends of the cheesecloth to make a small bag. Squeeze the juice from the spinach mixture into the bowl. Add 2 tablespoons of this to the lemon and egg sauce. Stir. Discard the remaining vegetable liquid and spinach mixture.

YIELD: About ¾ cup.

Sauce Bordelaise

A RED WINE SAUCE

- 3 tablespoons thinly sliced shallots
- 1 cup dry red wine, preferably a Bordeaux
- 2 cups demi-glace (see following recipe)

1. Combine the shallots and wine in a saucepan and bring to the boil. Cook over high heat until all the wine has evaporated.

2. Add the meat glaze and simmer for about 2 minutes.

3. Strain the sauce through a fine-meshed sieve, pushing the solids through.

YIELD: 2 cups.

Demi-glace

A BASIC MEAT GLAZE

- 4 pounds veal bones, cracked
- 1½ cups coarsely chopped carrot
- 1½ cups coarsely chopped celery
- 1½ cups coarsely chopped onion
- 2 cloves garlic, peeled
- 1 medium-sized tomato, coarsely chopped
- 12 cups water
- 6 sprigs fresh parsley
- 2 bay leaves
- ½ teaspoon dried thyme
- Salt to taste
- 6 whole black peppercorns, crushed

1. Preheat the broiler.

2. Put the veal bones in one layer in a roasting pan. Place them under the broiler and broil until browned, about 5 minutes. Turn the pieces and continue broiling for about 5 minutes longer.

3. Scatter the carrot, celery, onion, garlic and tomato over the bones. Broil for about 10 minutes.

4. Transfer the ingredients to a kettle and add the water, parsley sprigs, bay leaves, thyme, salt and peppercorns. Bring to the boil and simmer over low heat for 7 hours. Skim the surface frequently during the first 2 hours.

5. Strain the liquid and discard the solids. There should be 4½ to 5 cups. At this point the stock can be frozen, if desired.

6. For the glaze, return the stock to a saucepan and continue cooking down for about 2 hours, or until it is reduced to 2 cups.

YIELD: 2 cups.

Sauce au Raifort

HORSERADISH SAUCE

- 2 tablespoons butter
- 2 tablespoons flour
- 1 cup clear beef broth
- ¼ cup heavy cream
- Salt to taste, if desired
- Freshly ground black pepper to taste
- ½ cup grated fresh horseradish, or bottled horseradish to taste

1. Melt the butter in a saucepan and add the flour, stirring with a wire whisk.

2. Add the broth, stirring rapidly with a whisk. When thickened and smooth, add the cream. Add the salt, pepper and horseradish.

YIELD: About 1½ cups.

Sauce Périgourdine

BLACK TRUFFLE SAUCE

- 2 large truffles
- 1 tablespoon butter
- 3 tablespoons Madeira wine
- Salt and freshly ground black pepper to taste
- 6 tablespoons demi-glace (see recipe page 404)

1. Pare away the outside skin of the truffles and chop the outside skin. There should be about 2 tablespoons. If the truffles are canned, save the liquid for another use.

2. Cut the peeled truffles into very thin slices.

3. Melt the butter in a small casserole and add the chopped truffle peelings and the truffle slices. Add the Madeira and salt and pepper. Cook briefly, for about 30 seconds, and add the demi-glace. Simmer for about 1 minute.

YIELD: About ½ cup.

Sauce Diable

- 1 tablespoon butter
- 2 tablespoons finely chopped shallots
- ¼ cup dry white wine
- 1 teaspoon Worcestershire sauce
- ½ cup chicken broth
- 1 tablespoon tomato paste
- ½ cup heavy cream
- 1 tablespoon extra-strong, imported prepared mustard
- Salt and freshly ground black pepper to taste

1. Melt the butter in a saucepan and add the shallots. Cook briefly, stirring. Add the wine and cook down to about 2 tablespoons.

2. Add the Worcestershire sauce and chicken broth. Stir in the tomato paste and cook down by almost half. Add the cream and stir. Add the mustard, salt to taste and a generous grinding of black pepper. Stir well to combine and serve hot.

YIELD: About ¾ cup.

Yogurt and Chili Sauce

- 1 cup plain yogurt
- 1 small hot green pepper, preferably a jalapeño pepper, trimmed and seeded
- 8 tender sprigs fresh coriander leaves, optional
- 1 clove garlic, finely minced
- Juice of ½ lime
- 1 teaspoon toasted cumin seeds, crushed
- 1 tablespoon coarsely chopped fresh mint leaves
- 2 scallions, trimmed and chopped
- ¼ cup coarsely chopped fresh arugula leaves, optional

1. Put the yogurt in a mixing bowl. Do not blend it or it will become too thin.

2. Blend the pepper, coriander, garlic, lime juice, cumin and mint in a food processor or electric blender.

3. Spoon the mixture into the yogurt and stir in the scallions and arugula. Stir until well blended. Serve with broiled fish, grilled meat or chicken, on salads and as a dip for raw vegetables.

YIELD: About 2¼ cups.

Crème Fraîche

A THICKENED FRESH CREAM

- 2 cups heavy cream
- 2 teaspoons buttermilk

Pour the cream into a jar or mixing bowl. Add the buttermilk and stir. Cover tightly with plastic wrap and let stand in a slightly warm place for 12 hours, or until the cream is about twice as thick as ordinary heavy cream. Transfer to a jar with a tight-fitting lid and refrigerate. Use as desired.

YIELD: 2 cups.

Fresh Tomato Sauce

- 2 tablespoons butter
- ¼ cup finely chopped onion
- ½ teaspoon finely minced garlic
- ⅓ cup dry white wine
- 2 cups tomatoes, cored, seeded and cut into 1-inch cubes
- 3 fresh basil leaves, or 1 teaspoon dried basil
- Salt and freshly ground black pepper to taste

1. Melt the butter in a saucepan and add the onion and garlic. Cook briefly, stirring. Add the wine and cook to reduce the liquid by about half. Add the tomatoes, basil and salt and pepper. Cook for about 5 minutes.

2. Pour the mixture into the container of a blender or food processor and blend to a purée. Return the sauce to the saucepan. Reheat and serve.

YIELD: About 2½ cups.

Sauce Tomate à la Française

TOMATO SAUCE, FRENCH STYLE

- 4 tablespoons butter
- ½ cup finely chopped onion
- ½ cup finely chopped carrot
- 1 clove garlic, finely minced
- 1 bay leaf
- ¼ teaspoon dried thyme
- ¼ cup flour
- 4½ cups imported canned tomatoes
- Salt and freshly ground black pepper to taste
- ½ cup chicken broth

1. Melt 2 tablespoons of the butter in a saucepan and add the onion, carrot, garlic, bay leaf and thyme. Cook, stirring, until the onion is wilted.

2. Add the flour and stir to coat the vegetables.

3. Add the tomatoes and salt and pepper and stir. Add the broth. Bring to the boil and cook, stirring often, for about 20 minutes.

4. Put the sauce through a food mill or purée it in a food processor.

5. Return the sauce to the saucepan and swirl in the remaining butter until it melts.

YIELD: 3½ to 4 cups.

Tomato Sauce with Mushrooms

- 3 tablespoons butter
- 1 tablespoon finely chopped shallots
- 1 tablespoon finely chopped onion
- ½ teaspoon finely minced garlic
- ¼ pound mushrooms, thinly sliced, about 2 cups
- Salt and freshly ground black pepper to taste
- 1 tablespoon flour
- 2 cups crushed tomatoes
- ½ bay leaf
- ¼ teaspoon dried thyme
- Tabasco sauce

1. Melt 1 tablespoon of the butter in a saucepan and add the shallots, onion and garlic. Cook, stirring, for about 5 minutes. Add the mushrooms and salt and pepper. Cook, stirring, for about 3 minutes and sprinkle with flour. Stir to blend well.

2. Blend in the tomatoes. Add the bay leaf and thyme and simmer over low heat for about 45 minutes. Stir in the remaining butter and salt and pepper to taste. Add a few drops of Tabasco and serve hot.

YIELD: About 3 cups.

Tomato Sauce with Peppers

- 3 fresh ripe tomatoes, about 1¾ pounds, or use 4 cups canned tomatoes
- 2 tablespoons olive oil
- ¾ cup finely chopped onion
- 1 tablespoon finely chopped garlic
- ¾ cup finely chopped green pepper
- ¾ cup finely chopped celery
- ¼ teaspoon hot red pepper flakes
- 1 bay leaf
- ¼ teaspoon dried thyme
- Salt and freshly ground black pepper to taste
- 1 tablespoon chopped fresh basil, or 1 teaspoon dried, optional
- 1 tablespoon butter, optional

1. Remove the cores from the tomatoes. Cut the tomatoes into 1-inch cubes. There should be about 4 cups. Set aside.

2. Heat the oil in a saucepan and add the onion, garlic, green pepper, celery and pepper flakes. Cook, stirring often, for about 5 minutes.

3. Add the tomatoes, bay leaf, thyme, salt to taste and a generous grinding of black pepper. Bring to the boil and simmer for 20 minutes.

4. Spoon and scrape the mixture into the container of a food processor. Blend to a fine purée. Add the basil. Reheat. If desired, swirl in the butter.

YIELD: 3 cups.

Sauce Portugaise

A CREAM AND TOMATO SAUCE

- 2 cups fish stock (see recipe page 419)
- ½ cup dry white wine
- ½ pound tomatoes
- 2 tablespoons finely chopped parsley
- ¼ cup finely chopped onion
- 2 tablespoons butter
- Salt and freshly ground black pepper to taste
- 1 cup heavy cream

1. Pour the fish stock and wine into a saucepan and bring to the boil. Cook down over high heat until about ¼ cup of the mixture remains. Set aside.

2. Peel and core the tomatoes. Cut each tomato in half and squeeze to extract most of the seeds. Chop the tomatoes. There should be about 1¼ cups. Chop the parsley and onion.

3. Melt half the butter in a saucepan and add the onion. Cook until the onion wilts.

4. Add the tomatoes and salt and pepper. Cook for about 10 minutes, or until most of the liquid has disappeared. Set aside.

5. Add the cream to the cooked-down fish stock. Cook over high heat for about 5 minutes and then add the cooked tomato mixture. Cook down for about 1 minute.

6. Swirl in the remaining butter and stir in the chopped parsley.

YIELD: About 3 cups.

Sauce Suédoise

TOMATO SAUCE WITH DILL

- ¼ pound mushrooms
- 2 tablespoons butter
- 2 tablespoons finely minced shallots
- ½ pound ripe tomatoes, peeled, seeded and diced, about 1 cup
- ½ cup fish stock (see recipe page 419)
- Salt and freshly ground black pepper to taste
- ½ cup heavy cream
- 2 tablespoons finely chopped dill

1. Cut the mushrooms into very thin slices.

2. Melt 1 tablespoon of the butter in a saucepan and add the shallots. Cook briefly and add the mushrooms. Cook until the mushrooms give up their liquid.

3. Add the tomatoes, fish stock and salt and pepper. Bring to the boil and simmer for about 5 minutes. Add the cream and bring to the boil.

4. Swirl in the remaining tablespoon of butter. Add the dill.

YIELD: About 2 cups.

Marinara Sauce

- 4 cups imported canned tomatoes
- 6 tablespoons olive oil
- 2 teaspoons finely minced garlic
- ¼ cup dry white wine
- 1 teaspoon crushed dried oregano
- Salt to taste, if desired
- Freshly ground black pepper to taste

1. Crush the tomatoes with the hands, or put them in a food processor.

2. Heat the oil in a skillet and add the garlic. Cook, stirring, until lightly browned.

3. Add the wine and cook until it has evaporated. Add the tomatoes, oregano, salt and pepper. Cook for about 15 minutes.

YIELD: About 4 cups.

Marinara Sauce for Pizza

- 2½ cups imported canned tomatoes
- 2 tablespoons olive oil
- 1 tablespoon finely minced garlic
- ¼ cup tomato paste
- 1 teaspoon dried oregano
- Salt, if desired
- Freshly ground black pepper to taste
- ¼ cup finely chopped parsley

1. Put the tomatoes through a sieve or purée them in the container of a food processor or blender.

2. Heat the oil in a saucepan and add the garlic. Cook briefly without browning. Add the tomatoes, tomato paste, oregano, salt and pepper. Bring to the boil and simmer for 20 minutes. Stir in the parsley.

YIELD: About 2¾ cups.

Soy Sauce Marinade for Barbecues

FOR CHICKEN, PORK AND FISH

- ½ cup soy sauce
- ¼ cup dry sherry
- 1 tablespoon finely chopped fresh ginger
- 2 teaspoons finely minced garlic
- 2 teaspoons sugar
- ¼ teaspoon hot red pepper flakes

Combine all the ingredients in a mixing bowl. Stir until the sugar dissolves. Use to baste charcoal-grilled chicken, pork and fish when they are almost done.

YIELD: About ¾ cup.

Ketchup Sauce for Barbecues

FOR CHICKEN, PORK AND BEEF

- 1 cup tomato ketchup
- 3 tablespoons lemon juice
- 2 tablespoons honey
- 1 tablespoon finely minced garlic
- 1 tablespoon Worcestershire sauce
- Tabasco sauce to taste
- 4 tablespoons butter
- Salt and freshly ground black pepper to taste
- 4 thin, seeded lemon slices

Combine all the ingredients in a saucepan and bring to the boil, stirring. Use to baste charcoal-grilled meats when they are almost done.

YIELD: About 1½ cups.

Texas Barbecue Sauce

- 1¾ cups tomato ketchup
- 1⅓ cups (the contents of one large bottle) Worcestershire sauce
- 1⅓ cups cider vinegar
- 2 large lemons
- 2 cups coarsely chopped onion
- 3 tablespoons unsulfured molasses
- 2 large cloves garlic, peeled and cut into slivers
- 1 bay leaf
- ½ teaspoon dried oregano
- 1 tablespoon chopped fresh basil, or half the amount dried
- 2 tablespoons powdered mustard
- ½ teaspoon freshly ground black pepper
- 4 drops Tabasco sauce

1. Pour the ketchup, Worcestershire and cider vinegar into a saucepan.

2. Cut the lemons in half. Squeeze the juice. Add the juice and rind halves to the sauce. Add the remaining ingredients and cook, stirring often, for about 30 minutes. Use as a sauce for baking or charcoal-grilling 8 pounds of spareribs or 6 pounds of chicken cut into serving pieces. Marinate the ribs or chicken parts in the sauce for 6 hours.

YIELD: About 5 cups.

Note: Leftover sauce may be bottled, sealed tightly and refrigerated. It will keep indefinitely.

Lemon Marinade for Barbecues

FOR CHICKEN, FISH, LAMB AND VEAL

- ⅓ cup fresh lemon juice
- ½ cup olive oil
- 1 teaspoon finely minced garlic
- Salt and freshly ground black pepper to taste
- 1 teaspoon dried oregano
- 6 very thin, seeded lemon slices

Put the lemon juice in a small mixing bowl. Add the oil while stirring vigorously with a whisk. Add the remaining ingredients and blend well. Use to baste charcoal-grilled chicken, fish, lamb and veal.

YIELD: About 1 cup.

Tarragon Marinade for Barbecues

FOR CHICKEN, FISH, LAMB AND VEAL

- ¼ cup red wine vinegar
- ½ cup peanut, vegetable or corn oil
- 2 teaspoons chopped fresh tarragon
- Salt and freshly ground black pepper to taste

Put the vinegar in a small mixing bowl and add the oil, beating with a wire whisk. Add the tarragon and salt and pepper. Blend well. Use to baste charcoal-grilled chicken, lamb, fish and veal.

YIELD: About ¾ cup.

Mustard Vinaigrette

- 2 teaspoons prepared mustard, preferably imported Dijon or Düsseldorf
- 1 tablespoon wine vinegar
- Salt and freshly ground black pepper to taste
- ¾ cup olive oil
- 1 teaspoon finely minced garlic

1. Put the mustard in a bowl and add the vinegar and salt and pepper.
2. Start blending with a wire whisk, gradually adding the oil. Stir vigorously as the oil is added. Stir in the garlic.

YIELD: About 1 cup.

Sauce Salade aux Fines Herbes

SALAD DRESSING WITH FRESH HERBS

- 1 tablespoon prepared mustard, preferably imported Dijon or Düsseldorf
- 2 teaspoons red wine vinegar
- Salt and freshly ground black pepper to taste
- ½ cup olive oil, or a combination of olive oil and peanut, vegetable or corn oils
- 1 teaspoon chopped fresh tarragon
- 1 teaspoon chopped fresh chives
- 1 teaspoon chopped fresh chervil, optional
- ½ teaspoon finely minced garlic, optional

1. Put the mustard and vinegar in a mixing bowl.

2. Add the salt and pepper. Start stirring with a wire whisk.

3. When thoroughly blended, stir vigorously with the whisk and gradually add the oil.

4. Stir in the herbs.

YIELD: About ⅔ cup.

Sauce Vinaigrette au Vermouth

VERMOUTH VINAIGRETTE FOR SALADS

- 1½ tablespoons prepared mustard, preferably imported Dijon
- 1 tablespoon red wine or malt vinegar
- ¼ cup dry white vermouth
- ½ cup olive oil
- 2 tablespoons finely chopped shallots
- Salt, if desired
- Freshly ground black pepper to taste

1. Put the mustard and vinegar in a mixing bowl and add the vermouth while beating with a wire whisk.

2. Add the oil gradually, beating vigorously with the whisk. Add the shallots, salt and pepper.

YIELD: About 1 cup.

Mayonnaise

- 1 egg yolk
- Salt and freshly ground black pepper to taste
- 1 teaspoon prepared mustard, preferably imported Dijon or Düsseldorf
- 1 teaspoon vinegar or lemon juice
- 1 cup peanut, vegetable or corn oil

1. Put the egg yolk in a mixing bowl and add the salt and pepper. Add the mustard and vinegar and beat vigorously for a second or two with a wire whisk or electric beater.

2. Add the oil gradually, beating continuously with the whisk or beater. Continue beating and adding oil until all of it is used. If the mayonnaise is not to be used immediately, beat in a tablespoon of water, which will stabilize it.

YIELD: 1 cup.

Herb Mayonnaise

- 1 egg yolk
- 1 teaspoon prepared mustard, preferably imported Dijon or Düsseldorf
- 1 tablespoon white wine vinegar
- 1 tablespoon finely chopped parsley
- 1 tablespoon finely chopped fresh tarragon
- 2 tablespoons finely chopped cornichons (small sour gherkins)
- 2 tablespoons finely chopped drained capers
- 1 tablespoon finely chopped shallots
- 1 cup olive oil
- Salt to taste, if desired
- Freshly ground black pepper to taste

1. Put the egg yolk, mustard, white wine vinegar, parsley, tarragon, cornichons, capers and shallots in a mixing bowl.

2. Start beating with a wire whisk while gradually adding the oil. Beat until thickened. Add the salt and pepper.

YIELD: 1¼ cups.

Yogurt and Watercress Mayonnaise

- 1 egg yolk
- 2 teaspoons prepared mustard, preferably imported Dijon
- 2½ tablespoons malt vinegar
- Salt to taste, if desired
- Freshly ground black pepper to taste
- ¾ cup corn, peanut or vegetable oil
- ½ cup plain yogurt
- 1 bunch watercress
- ½ cup finely chopped scallions
- ¾ cup finely diced, seeded cucumber

1. Put the egg yolk, mustard, 1 tablespoon of the vinegar, salt and pepper in a mixing bowl and start beating with a wire whisk. Gradually add the oil, beating vigorously with the whisk. Beat in the yogurt and remaining vinegar.

2. Trim off and discard the tough stem ends of the watercress. Rinse and drain well. There should be about 2 cups fairly firmly packed.

3. Use a food processor or electric blender to purée the watercress.

4. Scrape the watercress into a length of cheesecloth or a clean kitchen towel. Squeeze to extract most of the liquid. There should be about ¾ cup of watercress solids. Add this to the mayonnaise. Add the scallions and cucumber and blend. Serve with fish or seafood, fish or seafood salads, vegetable salads and so on.

YIELD: About 2 cups.

Anchovy Mayonnaise

- 1 egg yolk
- 2 teaspoons prepared mustard, preferably imported Dijon
- Salt and freshly ground black pepper
- 1½ tablespoons white wine vinegar
- 1 cup olive oil
- A few drops Tabasco sauce
- ¼ teaspoon Worcestershire sauce
- 6 flat anchovy fillets, finely chopped

1. Put the yolk, mustard, very little salt, pepper to taste and the vinegar in a small mixing bowl. Start stirring with a wire whisk.

2. Gradually add the oil, stirring constantly with the whisk. Beat until thickened and smooth. Beat in the Tabasco sauce, Worcestershire sauce and anchovies.

YIELD: About 1 cup.

Spicy Mayonnaise

- 2 egg yolks
- 2 tablespoons red wine vinegar
- 4 teaspoons imported strong prepared mustard
- ¼ teaspoon Tabasco sauce
- ½ teaspoon Worcestershire sauce
- Salt to taste, if desired
- Freshly ground black pepper to taste
- 2 cups corn, peanut or vegetable oil

1. Put the yolks in a mixing bowl and add the vinegar, mustard, Tabasco, Worcestershire, salt and pepper.

2. Start beating with a wire whisk and, when blended, gradually add the oil. Continue beating until all the oil is added and the mixture has thickened.

YIELD: About 2¼ cups.

Curried Yogurt Mayonnaise

- 1 egg yolk
- 2 teaspoons prepared mustard, preferably imported Dijon
- 1 tablespoon malt vinegar
- Salt to taste, if desired
- Freshly ground black pepper to taste
- ¾ cup corn, peanut or vegetable oil
- ½ cup plain yogurt
- ¼ cup bottled chutney, chopped as finely as possible
- 2 tablespoons curry paste (see following recipe)

1. Put the egg yolk, mustard, vinegar, salt and pepper in a mixing bowl and start beating with a wire whisk. Gradually add the oil, beating vigorously with the whisk.

2. Beat in the yogurt, chutney and curry paste. Serve with seafood, fruit salads and so on.

YIELD: About 1⅔ cups.

CURRY PASTE

- 2 tablespoons corn, peanut or vegetable oil
- 2 tablespoons curry powder
- 2 teaspoons flour
- ½ cup chicken or meat broth

1. Heat the oil in a small saucepan and add the curry powder and flour, stirring with a wire whisk.

2. When the mixture is blended and smooth, add the broth, stirring rapidly with the whisk. When the mixture has thickened, remove it from the heat. Let cool.

YIELD: About ½ cup.

Note: This paste will keep indefinitely under refrigeration.

Rich Chicken Broth

- 5 pounds meaty chicken bones
- 2 cups coarsely chopped onion
- ½ pound carrots, coarsely chopped, about 2 cups
- 1 cup coarsely chopped celery
- 1 clove garlic, peeled
- 10 sprigs fresh parsley
- 1 bay leaf
- ½ teaspoon dried thyme
- 10 whole black peppercorns
- 16 cups water

1. Put the chicken bones in a large stockpot and cover with water. Bring to the boil and drain, discarding the water. Rinse the bones thoroughly and return to the stockpot.

2. Add the remaining ingredients and bring to the boil. Reduce the heat so the broth simmers slowly. Cook for 2 hours, skimming fat and scum from the surface every 15 or 20 minutes.

3. Strain the broth through a fine sieve into a large bowl. Let cool and then cover and refrigerate.

4. Remove the fat from the top of the broth with a slotted spoon. Use the clear broth as needed. It can be frozen in convenient-sized containers.

YIELD: 10 cups.

Velouté de Poisson

A BASIC FISH SAUCE

- 2 tablespoons butter
- 3 tablespoons flour
- 1 cup fish stock (see following recipe)

1. Melt the butter in a saucepan and add the flour, stirring with a wire whisk. When blended, add the stock, stirring rapidly with the whisk. When thickened and smooth, simmer for about 30 minutes, stirring often with the whisk.

2. As the sauce cooks, globules or rivulets of butter will probably rise to the top. Skim off and discard this butter.

YIELD: About ¾ cup.

Fumet de Poisson

FISH STOCK

- 3 pounds meaty fish bones, preferably with head and tail on but gills removed
- 8 cups water
- 1 cup dry white wine
- 2 cups coarsely chopped onion
- 4 sprigs fresh parsley
- 1 cup coarsely chopped celery
- 1 bay leaf
- ½ teaspoon dried thyme
- 6 whole black peppercorns
- Salt to taste
- ½ cup chopped green part of leeks, optional

1. Combine all the ingredients in a kettle or large saucepan.

2. Bring to the boil and simmer for 20 minutes. Strain and discard the solids.

YIELD: About 10 cups.

Note: Leftover stock can be frozen.

Coconut Milk and Coconut Cream

To crack one or more coconuts, pierce the "eyes" of each coconut with an ice pick. Drain and discard the liquid. Preheat the oven to 275 degrees.

Using a hammer, crack the shell of each coconut in half. Arrange the coconut halves, cracked side up, on a baking sheet. Place in the oven and bake for 15 or 20 minutes.

Remove the coconut halves. Pry the meat from the shells. Peel away the brown skin from the meat. Cut the meat into ½-inch cubes. Two coconuts should yield about 5 cups of cubed meat.

Put the coconut meat into the container of a food processor and add 4 cups of warm water. Purée thoroughly.

Line a colander with cheesecloth. Pour in the coconut mixture. Bring up the ends of the cheesecloth and squeeze to extract as much liquid as possible. There should be about 4½ cups. The white cream-like substance that rises to the top of the liquid on standing is coconut cream. The bottom layer is coconut milk.

DESSERTS

THE one dessert that best distinguishes the differences between the cuisines of France and America is apple pie. The most obvious difference has to do with the presentation. An American apple pie is almost invariably a two-crust affair, one on top and one on the bottom. A French apple tart is just as invariably an open, single-crust creation. And, whereas the American dough for a pastry crust may be made with white shortening or lard or butter—and often a combination of two—a French pastry crust is almost always made with butter.

When we dined with Genevieve Riordan of St. Louis, she told us that the recipe she uses for her two-crust apple pie is one used by her mother for fifty or more years. She states that her mother was quite specific about what an apple pie should be. In the first place, there should be a "goodly mountain" of apples in the filling. "And my father," she added, "hated pale-faced pies, so she kept the pie in the oven until the top was pretty brown."

The French apple tart is one that you might encounter anywhere in France.

Genevieve Riordan's Apple Pie

Pastry for a 2-crust pie (see following recipe)
5 or 6 firm, tart-sweet, unblemished cooking apples, such as Granny Smith, Rhode Island Greenings, or McIntosh, about 1¾ pounds
½ to ⅔ cup plus 1½ tablespoons sugar
1 teaspoon ground cinnamon
1 teaspoon grated nutmeg
1½ tablespoons flour
2 tablespoons butter
Juice of ½ lemon
1 tablespoon milk, cream or beaten egg

1. Cut the pastry in half. Roll out one half of it on a lightly floured surface and line a 9-inch pie plate with the dough. Set the other half of the dough aside.

2. Preheat the oven to 450 degrees.

3. Peel the apples and cut them into quarters. Cut away the core. Cut the quarters lengthwise into pieces about ⅛ inch thick. There should be 6 or 7 cups.

4. Put the slices into a mixing bowl. Add ½ to ⅔ cup of sugar and the cinnamon and nutmeg. Blend well with the hands.

5. Blend the flour with the 1½ tablespoons sugar. Sprinkle this over the bottom pastry in the pie plate.

6. Pour the apples into the prepared pie plate. There should be a "goodly mountain" of apple slices. Dot with butter and sprinkle lemon juice over all.

7. Roll out the second half of the dough.

8. Moisten the rim of the bottom pie crust with a little water. Cover the apple slices with the second crust. Press the rim of the second crust down onto the first. Cut around the pie plate to trim off any excess dough. Press around the edges to seal.

9. Cut small slits in the top of the pie to allow steam to escape. Brush the top with milk, cream or beaten egg.

10. Place the pie in the oven and bake for 10 minutes. Reduce the oven temperature to 400 degrees. Continue baking for 35 to 40 minutes longer. Let cool on a rack or serve hot.

YIELD: 6 to 8 servings.

PASTRY FOR A TWO-CRUST PIE

2 cups flour
½ teaspoon salt
⅔ cup solid white shortening
1½ to 3 tablespoons ice water

1. Put the flour into the container of a food processor and add the salt.

2. Add the shortening in small spoonfuls.

3. Start processing, adding the water gradually. Add only enough water so that the dough can be gathered into a ball and rolled out. One and one-half tablespoons of water should be sufficient.

4. Gather the dough, wrap it in wax paper and refrigerate it for at least ½ hour before rolling.

YIELD: Pastry for a 2-crust pie.

Tarte aux Pommes

FRENCH APPLE TART

French pastry for a 1-crust pie (see following recipe)
5 firm, tart-sweet, unblemished cooking apples, such as McIntosh or Granny Smith
½ cup sugar
2 tablespoons butter
⅓ cup clear apple jelly

1. Preheat the oven to 400 degrees.
2. Roll out the pastry and line an 11-inch pie tin, preferably a quiche pan with removable bottom.
3. Peel the apples and cut them into quarters. Cut away and discard the cores. Trim off and reserve the ends of the apple quarters. Chop these pieces. There should be about ½ cup.
4. Cut the quarters lengthwise into slices. There should be 5 cups of sliced apples.
5. Scatter the chopped apple ends over the pie shell.
6. Arrange the apple slices overlapping in concentric circles starting with the outer layer and working to the center.
7. Sprinkle the apples with the sugar and dot with the butter.
8. Place the pie in the oven and bake for 15 minutes. Reduce the oven temperature to 375 degrees and continue baking for 25 minutes longer.
9. Heat the apple jelly over low heat, stirring, until melted. Brush the top of the hot apple tart with the jelly. Serve hot or cold.

YIELD: 6 to 8 servings.

FRENCH PASTRY FOR A ONE-CRUST PIE

12 tablespoons cold butter
1½ cups flour
2 tablespoons sugar
2 to 3 tablespoons ice water

1. Cut the butter into small cubes and put them in the container of a food processor. Add the flour and sugar.
2. Start processing while gradually adding the water. Add only enough water so that the dough holds together and can be shaped into a ball.
3. Gather the dough into a ball. Wrap it in wax paper and refrigerate for 30 minutes or longer before rolling.

YIELD: Pastry for a 1-crust pie.

In the world of food, one of the most quoted of writers is an English clergyman named Sydney Smith, who lived from 1771 to 1845. He wrote about tea and how to make salads and how he managed to pursue his gourmet concerns in spite of difficulties such as isolation: "My living in Yorkshire was so far out of the way," he wrote, "that it was actually 12 miles from a lemon."

A dozen miles from the nearest lemon would be a sorry plight indeed, for without the lemon there would not be such great dishes as the Greek soup avgolemono, the French maquereau au vin blanc and the very American lemon meringue pie. Best of all is a French lemon tart. Those who try this tart may never again hunger for lemon meringue pie.

Tarte au Citron

FRENCH LEMON TART

French pastry for a 1-crust pie (see preceding recipe)
5 egg yolks
½ cup sugar
½ cup heavy cream
6 tablespoons fresh lemon juice
1 tablespoon grated lemon rind
½ cup finely chopped peeled apple

1. Preheat the oven to 400 degrees.

2. Roll the dough out on a lightly floured board to a thickness of ⅛ inch. Fit it into a 10-inch metal quiche or flan pan with removable bottom. Trim off the edges.

3. Line the pastry with wax paper and add dried beans to cover the bottom.

4. Place the pastry in the oven and bake for 10 minutes.

5. Remove the beans and wax paper. Reduce the oven temperature to 350 degrees.

6. Combine the yolks and sugar in a mixing bowl. Beat vigorously with a wire whisk until the mixture is thick and light lemon in color.

7. Beat in the cream, lemon juice, lemon rind and chopped apple.

8. Pour the mixture into the prepared pastry and place the pie on the bottom rack of the oven. Bake for 30 minutes. Let cool before serving.

YIELD: 4 servings.

Key Lime Pie

THE GRAHAM CRACKER CRUST

1½ cups graham cracker crumbs
¼ cup sugar
¼ cup finely chopped almonds
4 tablespoons melted butter

THE PIE FILLING

6 egg yolks
1 14-ounce can sweetened condensed milk, about 1¼ cups
¾ cup fresh lime juice, preferably Key limes
2 teaspoons grated lime rind

THE MERINGUE (SEE NOTE)

6 egg whites
1 cup sugar
½ teaspoon cream of tartar

1. Preheat the oven to 375 degrees.

2. Combine the crumbs, sugar, almonds and butter in a bowl. Blend well.

3. Use the mixture to line the bottom and sides of a 10-inch pie plate. Bake for 8 to 10 minutes. Remove the crust to a rack and let cool.

4. Reduce the oven temperature to 350 degrees.

5. Beat the yolks in a mixing bowl. Pour in the condensed milk, stirring constantly. Add the lime juice and rind.

6. Pour the mixture into the crumb crust. Place the pie in the oven and bake for 15 minutes. Transfer to a rack and let cool.

7. In a mixing bowl beat the egg whites until frothy.

8. Gradually add the sugar and cream of tartar, beating constantly until peaks form. Continue beating until stiff.

9. Spread the meringue over the pie, being sure to cover all the way to the edge of the crust. Bake for 5 to 6 minutes, or until the meringue is nicely browned. Remove to a rack to cool. Serve chilled.

YIELD: 6 to 8 servings.

Note: If you prefer, you may ignore the meringue and spread the pie, once baked and cooled, with a layer of sweetened whipped cream.

Rhubarb and Strawberry Tart

- Pastry for a 1-crust pie (see following recipe)
- 2 cups fresh young rhubarb cut into ½-inch cubes (do not use the leaves)
- 2 cups fresh strawberries, halved if small, quartered if large
- 1 cup sugar
- ½ teaspoon ground cardamom
- 3 tablespoons flour
- 2 eggs, lightly beaten
- ½ cup orange marmalade
- 1 tablespoon water

1. Preheat the oven to 400 degrees.

2. Prepare the pastry and use it to line a 9- or 10-inch pie plate, preferably a quiche pan with a removable bottom.

3. Put the rhubarb and strawberries in a mixing bowl and add the sugar and cardamom blended with the flour. Toss. Add the eggs and blend thoroughly. Pour this mixture into the prepared pie shell and place on a baking sheet. Bake for 40 minutes, or until set. Remove and let cool.

4. Heat the marmalade with the water, stirring, until melted. Spoon this over the pie and smooth it over. Remove the pie from the quiche pan, if used, or cut it directly into wedges from the pie plate.

YIELD: 8 or more servings.

PASTRY FOR A ONE-CRUST PIE

- 1½ cups flour
- 2 egg yolks
- 2 tablespoons confectioners' sugar
- Salt
- 8 tablespoons cold butter
- 3 tablespoons water, approximately

1. Combine the flour, yolks, sugar and salt to taste in the container of a food processor. Cut the butter into fine pieces and add it. Process, adding just enough water to make the pastry hold together.

2. Remove the dough and shape it into a ball or rectangle. Wrap in wax paper and chill for 30 minutes or longer.

3. Roll the dough out on a floured board, turning as necessary and using a little more flour as necessary to prevent sticking as it is rolled.

4. Line a pie plate with the pastry and trim off the excess around the edge.

YIELD: Pastry for a 1-crust pie.

Nectarine Pie

- Pastry for a 1-crust pie (see preceding recipe)
- 7 to 8 cups sliced nectarines, about 2½ pounds (see Note)
- ⅔ cup sugar
- ⅓ cup flour
- ¼ teaspoon ground mace or grated nutmeg
- ⅛ teaspoon ground ginger, or ½ teaspoon grated fresh ginger
- Salt to taste
- 1 teaspoon lemon juice
- ¼ teaspoon grated lemon rind

1. Line a 10-inch pie plate with the pastry. Chill.
2. Preheat the oven to 425 degrees.
3. In a mixing bowl, combine the nectarines, sugar, flour, mace, ginger, salt, lemon juice and lemon rind. Spoon the mixture into the prepared shell. Decorate the top, if desired, with pastry cutouts or lattice work.
4. Place in the oven and bake for 25 to 35 minutes. Remove from the oven. Dip a pastry brush in the syrup surrounding the fruit slices and glaze the top.

YIELD: 6 to 10 servings.

Note: The nectarines should be quite ripe without being mushy.

Fudge Pie

- 11 tablespoons butter
- 3 ounces unsweetened chocolate squares (see Note)
- 1½ cups sugar
- ⅓ cup flour
- 2 eggs
- 1½ teaspoons pure vanilla extract
- Salt to taste
- 1 cup pecans, coarsely chopped

1. Preheat the oven to 475 degrees.
2. Butter the bottom and sides of an 8-inch pie plate. Sprinkle with flour and shake to coat the bottom. Shake out any excess flour.
3. Combine the 11 tablespoons butter and chocolate in a saucepan and place over low heat until the butter melts and bubbles slightly. Blend well. Remove from the heat.

4. Spoon the sugar and flour into a mixing bowl and add the eggs. Beat well. Add the vanilla, salt and pecans. Pour in the chocolate mixture. Beat with a whisk until glossy.

5. Pour the mixture into the prepared pie plate and place in the oven. Bake for 15 to 20 minutes, or until the pie is dark but not burned at the edges. Make certain the center is set. Remove from the oven and let stand until thoroughly cool. Chill until the pie can be sliced, about 1 hour.

YIELD: 8 to 12 servings.

Note: Semisweet chocolate squares may be substituted for the bittersweet chocolate; if they are, reduce the quantity of sugar to 1 cup.

Deborah Davis Rabinowitz's Chess Pie

Pastry for a 1-crust pie (see recipe page 426)
8 tablespoons butter
1 tablespoon apple cider vinegar
3 eggs
1½ cups sugar
1 teaspoon pure vanilla extract

1. Line a 9-inch pie plate with the pastry. Chill.

2. Preheat the oven to 350 degrees.

3. Melt the butter in a saucepan and add the vinegar. Remove from the heat.

4. Beat the eggs in a mixing bowl and add the sugar. Continue beating until pale and lemon colored. Gradually beat in the butter and vinegar mixture. Add the vanilla extract.

5. Pour the filling into the unbaked pie shell. Place in the oven and bake for 30 to 40 minutes, or until a knife inserted into the center comes out clean. Serve warm or cold.

YIELD: 4 servings.

We have long enjoyed beets as a vegetable, and we recently conceived the notion of a beet pie, which has been well received by neighbors and friends. We combined the puréed beets with a little corn syrup, eggs, raisins and nuts, and the result was admirable. Curiously enough, the flavor of the pie filling is such that there was a good deal of guessing about the major ingredient of the filling. Few could determine that it was the humble beet.

Tarte au Betterave

BEET PIE

Pastry for a 1-crust pie (see recipe page 426)
1 pound beets, cooked until tender
½ cup golden or dark raisins
3 eggs, lightly beaten
1 cup golden or light corn syrup
½ cup broken walnut meats
2 tablespoons melted butter
Sweetened whipped cream for garnish, optional

1. Prepare the pastry and refrigerate.

2. As the beets cook, put the raisins in a mixing bowl and cover them with warm water. Let stand until ready to use.

3. When the beets are tender, drain and peel them. Slice them into the container of a food processor or an electric blender and blend until fine. There should be about 2 cups. Put the beets into a mixing bowl.

4. Preheat the oven to 350 degrees.

5. Drain the raisins and add them to the beets. Add the eggs, corn syrup, walnuts and butter. Stir to blend.

6. Roll out the pastry and use it to line an 8- or 9-inch pie plate. Pour in the beet filling. Place in the oven and bake for 1 hour. Serve sliced in wedges with a dollop of sweetened whipped cream on each serving, if desired.

YIELD: 6 servings.

When we were asked if there were such a thing as a mud pie, we offered a vague definition from a book that spoke of a creation from Mississippi: a chocolate-cookie crust filled with chocolate or coffee-brandy ice cream. To our enormous surprise, the printed question and answer elicited scores of recipes from all over the nation, not only for Mississippi mud pies but for mud cakes as well. Both of them, as readers warned us, are sinfully rich.

The Mississippi pie, with its dominant, emphatic chocolate flavor, may be served lukewarm with a scoop of vanilla ice cream on top. If allowed to cool, the filling becomes almost like a fine chocolate candy. The mud pie recipe printed here is that of Dorothy Ann Webb, a native Mississippian.

Our version of the Mississippi cake, a cocoa-and-nut creation with a baked marshmallow topping and a cocoa and pecan icing, is the result of blending many recipes received from readers.

Mississippi Mud Pie

Pastry for a 1-crust pie (see recipe page 426, but omit egg yolks)
8 tablespoons butter
3 ounces (squares) unsweetened chocolate
3 eggs
3 tablespoons light corn syrup
1½ cups sugar
1 teaspoon pure vanilla extract
Vanilla ice cream, optional

1. Preheat the oven to 350 degrees.

2. Line a 9-inch pie plate with the pastry.

3. Combine the butter and chocolate in a saucepan. Heat gently, stirring often, until melted and blended.

4. Beat the eggs until light and frothy. Stir in the syrup, sugar and vanilla. Pour in the chocolate mixture, stirring.

5. Pour the filling into the prepared pie shell.

6. Place in the oven and bake for 35 to 40 minutes, or until the top is slightly crunchy and the filling is set. Do not overcook. The filling should remain soft inside. This is best served warm with a spoonful of vanilla ice cream on top, but it is excellent served at room temperature or cold.

YIELD: 6 to 8 servings.

Mississippi Mud Cake

THE CAKE

½ pound butter
2 cups sugar
4 eggs
1½ cups flour
⅓ cup cocoa powder
1 cup coarsely chopped pecans
1 teaspoon pure vanilla extract
3 cups miniature marshmallows or large marshmallows cut into ½-inch pieces

THE ICING

½ pound butter
1 pound confectioners' sugar
⅓ cup cocoa powder
1 cup coarsely chopped pecans
½ cup evaporated milk

1. Preheat the oven to 350 degrees.

2. To make the cake, combine the butter and sugar in a mixing bowl. Beat well until creamy. Add the eggs, one at a time, beating thoroughly after each addition.

3. Sift together the flour and cocoa. Fold this into the creamed mixture. Add the 1 cup of chopped nuts and the vanilla. Beat well.

4. Butter the bottom and sides of a 9- by 13-inch baking pan. Add a little flour and shake it around to coat the bottom and sides of the pan. Shake out any excess.

5. Spoon the cake mixture into the pan and smooth it over. Place in the oven and bake for 30 to 35 minutes. Remove from the oven and sprinkle the top with the marshmallows. Return to the oven and bake for about 10 minutes longer, or until the marshmallows are melted and starting to brown. Remove from the oven and cool in the pan for 30 minutes.

6. For the icing, melt the butter in a saucepan.

7. Sift together the confectioners' sugar and cocoa. Stir this into the butter along with the nuts and milk. Spread this over the cake and let stand until thoroughly cool. Cut into slices and serve.

YIELD: 12 or more servings.

The single most complicated pastry, the one most difficult to describe with mere words, is puff pastry. It requires tedious hours of folding and chilling, and otherwise getting things together.

We have come up with what we consider a fine and far less elaborate version of puff pastry that could be referred to as à la minute.

The most common use for puff pastry in the French kitchen is in the preparation of mille-feuille, or thousand-leaf pastry. That is because when the pastry is rolled out and baked, it puffs into an inestimable number of flaky, thin layers, a thousand or more according to some pastry cooks.

Our hasty version of puff pastry does not shape up into that degree of puffiness, but it is rich, light and delicate.

Chaussons aux Pommes

APPLE TURNOVERS

- Fast puff pastry (see following recipe)
- 4 apples, such as McIntosh or Delicious, about 1½ pounds
- 2 tablespoons butter
- ½ cup sugar
- ¼ teaspoon pure vanilla extract
- 1 egg, lightly beaten

1. Prepare the pastry and chill as indicated in the recipe.

2. Peel the apples and quarter them. Cut away and discard the stems and cores. Cut each quarter into thin slices.

3. Melt the butter in a saucepan and add the apples and sugar. Add the vanilla, cover and cook for about 5 minutes.

4. Roll out the chilled, folded dough on a flat, cold, floured surface. Roll it into a rectangle. Fold it like a letter.

5. Roll it out again into a thin rectangle. Using a sharp, heavy knife, cut the rectangle neatly into 8 or 10 squares of approximately the same size.

6. Spoon an equal portion of the apple mixture into the center of each. Brush the edges of each square with beaten egg. Fold over one half of each square to make a triangle-shaped turnover.

7. Using the tines of a fork, press the folded-over edges to seal. As the turnovers are sealed, arrange them on a baking sheet.

8. Brush the top of each turnover with beaten egg. Make a slight slit in the top of each turnover to allow steam to escape. Refrigerate for at least 15 minutes.

9. When ready to bake, preheat the oven to 375 degrees.

10. Place the turnovers in the oven and bake for 30 to 40 minutes. Use a pancake turner or spatula and run it under the turnovers to loosen them. Serve hot or cold.

YIELD: 8 to 10 turnovers.

FAST PUFF PASTRY

½ pound very cold butter
1¾ cups flour
Salt, if desired
¼ teaspoon cream of tartar
½ cup ice water

1. Cut the butter into very small cubes. Put the cubes on a plate and put the plate in the freezer. The dough may be made by hand or in the container of a food processor. It is best to chill the rolling pin before rolling out the dough.

2. If the food processor is used, put the cold butter, flour, salt to taste and cream of tartar into the container of the processor. Work quickly. Start processing and hastily add enough water so that the dough will hold together. There will be bits of butter that are apparent in the dough.

3. If you do this by hand, combine the flour, salt to taste and cream of tartar on a cold, flat, smooth surface, preferably marble. Make a well in the center and add the cold butter and water. Bring the flour up to enclose and

coat the butter, and start working the dough with the hands, kneading. Work rapidly to the point where the dough can be gathered together in a ball. There will be bits of butter apparent in the dough.

4. Whatever the technique used, shape the dough into a ball. Shape the ball of dough into a flat patty about 5 inches in diameter. Wrap it closely in plastic wrap and refrigerate for 15 minutes.

5. When ready to roll out the dough, sprinkle a flat cold surface with flour and lay the dough on it. Roll out the dough into a rectangle measuring roughly 18 by 12 inches. It is important that you keep the surface lightly floured as you work. Turn the pastry over once or twice as you roll it out. If the butter sticks to the surface, scrape under it with a knife, flour the surface and continue rolling.

6. Fold one third of the rectangle toward and over the center. Brush the top and bottom of the dough with a clean, dry pastry brush to remove any excess flour. Fold down the upper third just as you would normally fold a letter before inserting it in an envelope. Brush off any excess flour top and bottom.

7. Roll the dough out into another rectangle of about the same size. Fold it a second time just as you did the first, letter-fashion. Arrange the folded dough on a lightly floured baking sheet. Cover with a clean cloth and chill for 15 to 20 minutes.

YIELD: About 1 pound of pastry, or enough for 8 to 10 turnovers.

Dessert fritters offer a nice change from pies, ice creams and other expected fare at the end of the meal. They benefit from a quickly made sauce, and we offer an excellent one made with apricot preserves.

Beignets d'Ananas Sauce Abricot

PINEAPPLE FRITTERS WITH APRICOT SAUCE

- 8 pineapple rings
- Corn, peanut or vegetable oil for deep-fat frying
- 3½ cups fritter batter (see following recipe)
- ¼ cup confectioners' sugar
- 1¼ cups apricot sauce (see following recipe)

1. Cut the pineapple rings into quarters.

2. Heat the oil to 350 degrees. Dip one piece of pineapple at a time in the batter and add it to the hot fat. Cook, turning once or twice until the fritters are puffed and browned.

3. As the fritters are cooked, drain well on paper toweling. Continue cooking until all the pineapple pieces are fried. If the batter becomes thin, it is due to the liquid given up by the fruit. You may thicken it by stirring in a little more flour.

4. Before serving, sprinkle the fritters with confectioners' sugar, using a small sieve. Serve with apricot sauce spooned over.

YIELD: 8 or more servings.

FRITTER BATTER FOR FRUIT

- 1¾ cups flour
- 1 egg
- 1 tablespoon sugar
- Salt to taste, if desired
- 1 tablespoon corn, peanut or vegetable oil
- 1 cup beer at room temperature
- ¼ cup water
- ½ cup egg whites (about 4)

1. Combine the flour, egg, sugar, salt and oil in a mixing bowl. Start blending with a wire whisk. Add the beer and water and continue beating until smooth.

2. Beat the whites until stiff and fold them in.

YIELD: About 3½ cups.

APRICOT SAUCE

- 1 cup apricot preserves
- ¼ cup water
- 2 tablespoons kirschwasser, optional

1. Put the apricot preserves in a saucepan and add the water. Stir, over medium heat, until blended.

2. Put the sauce through a sieve. Return the sauce to the saucepan and reheat. Add the kirschwasser and serve.

YIELD: About 1¼ cups.

Beignets Soufflé Sauce Abricot

DEEP-FRIED CREAM PUFFS WITH APRICOT SAUCE

- 1 cup cold water
- 8 tablespoons butter
- Salt to taste, if desired
- 1 tablespoon sugar
- 1 cup flour
- 4 large eggs
- 2 teaspoons grated orange rind
- Corn, peanut or vegetable oil for deep-fat frying
- ¼ cup confectioners' sugar
- Apricot sauce (see preceding recipe)

1. Put the water in a saucepan and add the butter, salt and sugar. Bring to the boil.

2. Add the flour all at once, stirring vigorously and thoroughly in a circular motion with a wooden spoon until a ball is formed and the mixture cleans the side of the saucepan. Remove from the heat. Do not let cool.

3. Add the eggs, one at a time, beating vigorously and rapidly with the spoon until the egg is well blended with the mixture. Add another egg, beat and so on, until all 4 eggs are beaten in. Beat in the orange rind.

4. Heat about 1 inch of oil in a skillet or fryer to a temperature of 360 degrees.

5. Using a teaspoon, drop the batter by heaping spoonfuls into the oil. Cook, stirring occasionally so that the fritters cook evenly, for 4 or 5 minutes, or until they are crisp and golden brown. Remove the cooked fritters and drain them on paper toweling. Sprinkle the confectioners' sugar over the fritters, using a small sieve, and toss them in the sugar. Serve the fritters with hot apricot sauce spooned over.

YIELD: 4 to 5 dozen fritters.

Coconut Layer Cake

- 2 cups sifted all-purpose unbleached flour
- 1 tablespoon baking powder
- ¼ teaspoon salt
- 8 tablespoons butter
- 1¼ cups superfine sugar
- 2 egg yolks, beaten
- 2 teaspoons pure vanilla extract
- 2 teaspoons freshly squeezed lemon juice
- 1 cup milk at room temperature
- 3 egg whites
- Boiled frosting (see following recipe)
- Grated coconut, fresh (see instructions) or canned

1. Preheat the oven to 375 degrees.

2. Butter the inside bottom and sides of 2 9-inch cake pans. Sprinkle with flour and shake to coat the insides. Shake out any excess flour.

3. Combine the 2 cups flour, baking powder and salt in a flour sifter. Sift the ingredients into a mixing bowl and set aside.

4. Put the butter in another bowl and stir briskly with a wooden spoon until it is soft. Continue beating until it becomes glossy in appearance. Add the sugar, ¼ cup at a time, beating well after each addition. Beat until pale and most of the granulated feel of the sugar dissolves. Beat in the egg yolks.

5. Beat in the vanilla and lemon juice.

6. Add ½ cup of the sifted flour mixture and ¼ cup of the milk, stirring rapidly until blended. Continue adding flour and milk in these proportions until all is used. The last addition should be the flour.

7. Beat the whites until they stand in soft peaks and fold them into the batter, using a rubber or plastic spatula.

8. Pour and scrape equal amounts of the batter into each prepared cake pan.

9. Place the pans on the middle rack of the oven and bake for 30 minutes, or until the cakes have shrunk from the sides of the pan.

10. Remove the cakes from the oven and turn them out onto wire cake racks. Let cool for 10 minutes. Cover with a light, clean cloth and let stand until ready to frost.

11. When ready to frost, dust off any crumbs from the layers. Place one layer on a serving dish and spread over it a generous amount of frosting. Spread frosting over the top and sides. Place the second layer on top, making sure it is flush with the bottom. Frost the second layer. Pour the remaining frosting over the top and spread it over the top and around the sides. Sprinkle the grated coconut over the top and sides. A frosted coconut cake is better when served the next day.

YIELD: 12 or more servings.

BOILED FROSTING

1 cup plus 2 tablespoons sugar
¼ cup cold water
3 large egg whites
1 teaspoon fresh lemon juice

1. Combine the sugar and cold water in a small saucepan. Let stand at room temperature for about 15 minutes.

2. Place the saucepan on the stove. Bring the mixture to the boil and cook over medium-high heat. Watch carefully as the syrup cooks. It must

not discolor around the edges of the pan. Cook until the syrup spins a thread when dropped from a spoon.

3. Meanwhile, beat the egg whites until stiff and pour the hot syrup slowly into the whites, beating briskly. Continue adding and beating until the frosting holds its shape. Beat in the lemon juice. Let cool for a few minutes, but use before the icing becomes firm.

YIELD: Frosting for a 2-layer cake.

GRATED FRESH COCONUT

Use one or two coconuts. It is best to use two in case one isn't sweet enough. Select large coconuts that are heavy and contain a lot of liquid. You can determine the amount of liquid when you shake the coconut.

Pierce the "eyes" of the coconut with an ice pick. Crack the shell of the coconut in several places, using a hammer or hatchet.

Pry out the flesh with a blunt knife. Pare away the dark skin. Grate the coconut using the coarse blade of a grater.

One of the grandest desserts we know is a luxurious chocolate cake that is made wholly without flour. It consists of a single preparation, which is basically a chocolate mousse. Take a portion of that mousse and bake it in a springform pan. You set the remainder aside. After the baked mousse is firm, you simply frost it with the remainder.

❧

Gâteau de Mousse au Chocolat

A FRENCH CHOCOLATE MOUSSE CAKE

- ½ pound (8 squares) unsweetened chocolate
- ½ pound sweet butter, cut into cubes, plus butter for greasing the pan
- 8 egg yolks
- 1¼ cups sugar
- 5 egg whites
- 1 tablespoon cocoa powder
- 1 teaspoon confectioners' sugar

1. Preheat the oven to 350 degrees.

2. Put the chocolate squares and butter in a saucepan. Set the saucepan in a skillet of boiling water. Keep the water at the simmer. Stir the chocolate and butter until the chocolate has melted.

3. Combine the egg yolks and sugar in the bowl of an electric mixer. Beat until the mixture is light and lemon-colored.

4. Add the chocolate sauce to the egg mixture, stirring to blend thoroughly.

5. Beat the whites until stiff but not brittle. If the whites are too stiffly beaten, they will not fold in properly.

6. Add half the egg whites to the chocolate mixture and beat. Fold in the remaining whites.

7. Butter the bottom and sides of an 8-inch springform pan. Pour three quarters of the mixture into the pan.

8. Set the remaining chocolate mixture aside. This will be used as a filling and frosting.

9. Place the pan in the oven and bake for 1 hour and 15 minutes.

10. When the cake is done, transfer it to a rack. Let stand for about 10 minutes. Remove the rim from the springform pan. Let the cake stand until thoroughly cool.

11. Spoon a portion of the reserved, uncooked chocolate mixture around the sides of the cake, smoothing it over like an icing. Build it up slightly around the top of the cake. Spoon the remainder of the mixture on top of the cake and smooth it over.

12. Hold a small sieve over the cake and spoon the cocoa into it. Sprinkle it evenly over the top of cake. Chill briefly.

13. Add the confectioners' sugar to the sieve and sprinkle it over the top of the cake.

YIELD: 8 to 10 servings.

Not so many years ago, there was a small, almost legendary pastry shop in the Hamptons on the eastern tip of Long Island. It was a family-type place where the owner made wonderful things to tempt the eye and palate, but nothing was equal to her walnut cake with chocolate topping. It wasn't a European cake—no French gâteau, no German torte—just a simple, honest and unforgettable American creation. Over the years we tried to persuade the owner and cook to divulge her recipe for the fabulous cake. Alas, she declared that her secrets were not to be revealed. Well, when the shop closed and the owner-cook retired, we once more pleaded for her recipe. No dice, she said. She did, however, offer us a clue. She said the basic cake recipe could be found on the back of a box of cake flour and that the frosting was a simple chocolate butter cream. This walnut cake is a result of our experiments. It may not quite measure up to the manna that came out of our friend's oven, but it is a reasonable—and delicious—facsimile.

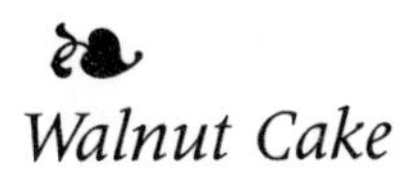

Walnut Cake

- ½ pound butter
- 2 cups sugar
- 3 cups sifted cake flour plus 1 tablespoon unsifted
- 1 tablespoon baking powder
- ¼ teaspoon salt
- 2 cups broken walnut meats
- 4 large eggs
- 1 cup milk
- 1 teaspoon pure vanilla extract
- ½ teaspoon almond extract
- Chocolate walnut butter cream (see following recipe)
- 12 whole, large walnut meats for garnish

1. Preheat the oven to 350 degrees.

2. Cut the butter into cubes and put it in the bowl of an electric mixer.

3. Gradually add the sugar and beat on medium speed for at least 10 minutes.

4. Sift together the 3 cups of flour, baking powder and salt.

5. Toss the broken walnut meats with the remaining tablespoon unsifted flour and set aside.

6. Add the eggs to the creamed mixture, one at a time, beating well after each addition.

7. Combine the milk with the vanilla and almond extracts.

8. Alternately, add the flour mixture and milk to the creamed mixture. Beat well after each addition.

9. Add the floured walnut meats and continue beating on low speed until well blended.

10. Lightly butter 2 loaf pans measuring 9 by 5 by 3 inches.

11. Spoon and scrape equal portions of the cake batter into the prepared pans.

12. Put the pans in the oven and bake for 50 minutes, or until a needle inserted in the center of the cakes comes out clean.

13. Let the pans cool on a rack for 10 minutes. Turn the cakes out onto the rack and cool completely.

14. Spread the top of each cake with equal portions of butter cream. Garnish the top of each cake with whole walnut meats.

YIELD: About 24 servings.

CHOCOLATE–WALNUT BUTTER CREAM

- ¼ pound (4 squares) unsweetened chocolate
- 2 tablespoons very strong coffee
- 4 egg yolks
- ¼ teaspoon salt
- ½ cup sugar
- ½ pound butter
- 1 cup broken walnut meats

1. Set a mixing bowl in a basin of simmering water. Add the chocolate and coffee and heat, stirring often, until the chocolate is melted and blended.

2. Combine the yolks, salt and sugar in another bowl. Set the bowl in a basin of simmering water and beat the yolk mixture rapidly with a wire whisk or a portable electric mixer. Beat until the mixture is thickened and falls in a ribbon when the beater is held up.

3. Spoon and scrape the chocolate into the yolk mixture. Return the bowl to the simmering water and continue beating. Gradually beat in the butter, bit by bit.

4. Remove the bowl from the heat. Continue beating in a cool place until the mixture thickens slightly and becomes spreadable. Beat in the walnuts. Continue beating with a wooden spoon until the chocolate cream becomes somewhat lighter. Let cool until spreadable.

5. Spread the butter cream over the cakes.

YIELD: Enough icing for 2 loaf cakes.

One of the most interesting and curiously named pastries bears the name Mary Ann. Mary Ann cakes, as they are sometimes called, come in two sizes: large and small, or miniature. Basically, a Mary Ann is spongecake that is round like a standard cake, but has a shallow, uniform depression in the center. (Mary Ann pans, essential for creating this shape, can be purchased in fine kitchenware shops across the country.) The reason for the depression is to receive an assortment of garnishes—such as sweetened cut fruits or berries, custard or whipped cream and, quite often, a combination of such good things.

The design of Mary Anns, the small versions in particular, makes them ideal for such desserts as strawberry and other shortcakes as well as for baked Alaskas.

Mary Ann Spongecakes

- 1 cup sifted confectioners' sugar
- ⅔ cup sifted cornstarch
- 3 eggs, separated
- ⅛ teaspoon cream of tartar
- 2 tablespoons water
- ½ teaspoon pure vanilla extract

1. Preheat the oven to 350 degrees.

2. Sift together ½ cup of the sugar and the cornstarch three times. Set aside.

3. Beat the egg whites, cream of tartar and water in a large bowl with a rotary beater or electric mixer until the mixture stands in soft peaks. Gradually beat in the remaining ½ cup of sugar, a little at a time, continuing to beat until stiff peaks form when the beater is raised. Add the egg yolks and vanilla, beating only until well blended.

4. Fold in the sugar-cornstarch mixture, a little at a time, until it is all added and well blended.

5. Pour the batter into 9 lightly buttered, individual Mary Ann tins (the capacity of each tin is about ¾ cup). Or pour the batter into 2 ungreased 8-inch cake pans. Bake until the cake rebounds to the touch when pressed lightly in the center. For the Mary Ann pans, the baking time is about 15 minutes; for the cake pans, about 30 minutes. Place on wire racks and cool. Cut around the edges of the cakes before removing them from the pans.

YIELD: 9 Mary Ann cakes or 2 8-inch layers.

Note: Leftover Mary Ann cakes freeze very well. You can make these in batches and use them anytime.

Baked Alaska Mary Anns

- 6 individual Mary Ann cakes (see preceding recipe)
- 6 large scoops ice cream of any flavor
- 6 egg whites
- 1 cup superfine sugar
- ½ teaspoon cream of tartar

1. Place the Mary Ann cakes on a baking sheet and place in the freezer.

2. Scoop one round portion of ice cream into the depression of each cake. Place in the freezer until the ice cream is thoroughly hardened.

3. In a mixing bowl, beat the egg whites until frothy. Gradually add the sugar and cream of tartar, beating constantly until peaks form. Continue beating until stiff.

4. Use a pastry bag fitted with a round, flat-tipped No. 7 pastry tube. Spoon the meringue into the pastry bag. Pipe out the meringue from bottom to top, completely covering each cake and ice cream.

5. You may bake the Alaskas now. Or they may be placed in the freezer for a few hours or even days. When ready to bake, preheat the oven to 500 degrees. If frozen, bake them directly from the freezer.

6. Bake for 5 minutes. Serve immediately.

YIELD: 6 servings.

Strawberry Shortcakes Mary Ann

- 1 pint ripe, unblemished strawberries
- ⅓ cup sugar
- 6 individual Mary Ann cakes (see recipe page 441)
- 6 large scoops strawberry ice cream
- 2 cups heavy cream, whipped and sweetened to taste

1. Rinse and drain the strawberries. Remove and discard the stems. Set aside 6 perfect berries.

2. Cut the remaining strawberries in half. There should be about 2 cups. Put the cut strawberries into a bowl and add the sugar. Blend and set aside.

3. Put one Mary Ann cake on each of six plates. Put equal portions of the sweetened strawberries into the depression of each cake. Add 1 scoop of ice cream for each serving. Using a pastry bag, decorate each serving, top to bottom, with the whipped cream. Garnish with 1 whole strawberry on top. Serve immediately.

YIELD: 6 servings.

One of the most celebrated meringue desserts in the world hails, oddly enough, from Australia and New Zealand and, for some inexplicable reason, it is named for Anna Pavlova, the celebrated Russian ballerina. A Pavlova consists of a thick meringue layer served with tropical fruits (including kiwi) or berries and sweetened whipped cream.

Pavlova

- Butter
- Flour
- 3 egg whites
- ¾ cup plus 2 tablespoons sugar
- ¼ teaspoon salt
- 1 teaspoon white vinegar
- ½ teaspoon pure vanilla extract
- 1 teaspoon cornstarch
- 4 kiwis or peaches, or 1 pint berries or other fruit
- 1 cup heavy cream

1. Preheat the oven to 250 degrees.

2. Butter the bottom and sides of an 8- or 9-inch springform pan. Sprinkle with flour and shake to coat the bottom and sides. Shake out any excess flour.

3. Line the pan with a round of wax paper and butter the top of the paper.

4. Beat the egg whites until frothy. Continue beating while gradually adding the ¾ cup sugar and the salt. Add the vinegar and vanilla and continue beating until the meringue is stiff.

5. Sift the cornstarch over the meringue and fold it in with a rubber spatula.

6. Scrape the meringue into the prepared pan and smooth it over. Make a slight indentation extending from the center of the meringue out to about 1 inch from the sides of the pan. Build up the sides of the meringue slightly. The indentation will hold when the meringue is baked.

7. Place the pan in the oven and bake for 30 minutes. Turn off the oven heat and let the meringue rest in the oven for 1 hour longer. Remove and let stand until thoroughly cool. Unmold the meringue.

8. Peel the kiwis or peaches. Cut one of them into 10 round slices. Garnish the upper outside rim of the meringue with the slices.

9. Cut the remaining kiwis or peaches lengthwise into quarters. Cut the quarters crosswise into 1-inch pieces. Use the berries whole or sliced. Put the fruit in a bowl and add 1 tablespoon sugar. Stir until the sugar dissolves. Spoon this into the center of the meringue surrounded by the sliced fruit.

10. Whip the cream until frothy and add the remaining tablespoon of sugar. Continue beating until stiff. Use a pastry tube and pipe the whipped cream over the fruit. Or you may use a spatula to cover the fruit-filled meringue with the cream.

YIELD: 6 to 8 servings.

Ginger Cheesecake

- Butter
- ½ cup crushed gingersnaps
- ½ cup crushed chocolate wafers
- ⅓ cup melted butter
- 2 pounds cream cheese at room temperature
- ½ cup heavy cream
- 4 eggs
- 1½ cups sugar
- 1 teaspoon pure vanilla extract
- 2 tablespoons freshly grated ginger
- 1 cup finely chopped candied ginger

1. Preheat the oven to 300 degrees.

2. Butter the inside of a metal cheesecake pan 8 inches wide and 3 inches deep. Combine the crushed gingersnaps and chocolate wafers and mix with the melted butter. Press the crumbs into the bottom and halfway up the sides of the pan.

3. Place the cream cheese, heavy cream, eggs, sugar, vanilla and grated ginger in the bowl of an electric mixer. Beat the ingredients until thoroughly blended and quite smooth. Mix in the chopped ginger.

4. Pour the batter into the prepared pan and shake gently to level it.

5. Set the pan into a slightly larger pan and pour boiling water into the larger pan to a depth of 2 inches. Do not let the edges of the pans touch. Bake for 1 hour and 40 minutes. At the end of that time, turn off the oven heat and let the cake sit in the oven for 1 hour longer.

6. Lift the cake out of its water bath and place it on a rack to cool for at least 2 hours before unmolding.

7. To unmold, place a round cake plate over the cake and carefully turn both upside down.

YIELD: 12 to 14 servings.

Poires des Îles

SPICED PEARS

- 6 ripe, firm, unblemished pears, preferably Anjou, about 1½ pounds
- 4 cups dry red wine, preferably Burgundy
- ¾ cup honey
- 1 bay leaf
- ½ teaspoon whole black peppercorns
- 2 whole cloves
- 1 2-inch piece cinnamon stick

1. Remove the core from each of the pears, but leave the stem intact. Peel the pears.

2. Combine the wine, honey, bay leaf, peppercorns, cloves and cinnamon in a saucepan. Bring to the boil.

3. Add the pears and cook, uncovered, for 45 minutes, or until the pears are tender. Remove from the heat. Let the pears cool in their cooking liquid. Cover and chill for several hours.

YIELD: 6 servings.

New Year's Eve Fruit Compote

- 4 pounds mixed dried fruit, including, preferably, equal amounts of prunes, pears, peaches and apples
- 3 17-ounce jars Kadota figs in syrup
- 2 pounds (drained weight) fresh or canned dark sweet pitted cherries, about 4 cups
- Sugar to taste
- 1 cup or more Armagnac or Cognac
- 4 to 6 bananas, peeled and sliced
- 2 cups fresh berries, such as blueberries, strawberries or raspberries

1. If the dried fruit has pits, cut away and remove them. Cut all the fruit in half and add to a kettle or casserole. Add water to cover and bring to the boil. Simmer for 20 minutes. Let cool.

2. Pour the fruit and the cooking liquid into a mixing bowl. Cut the figs in half and add them along with their syrup to the fruit in the bowl. Add the cherries and sugar to taste. Add the Armagnac to taste.

3. Cover closely and refrigerate for at least 24 hours to ripen. When ready to serve, add the sliced bananas and berries. Add more sugar and Armagnac, if desired.

YIELD: 30 servings.

Bananes au Gingembre

BANANAS IN GINGER SYRUP

- 3 or 4 bananas, about 1½ pounds
- ½ teaspoon ground ginger
- ¼ cup sugar
- ⅓ cup water
- 2 tablespoons lemon juice

1. Peel the bananas and cut them into ¼-inch-thick rounds. There should be about 3½ cups. Arrange half of the rounds close together on a flat plate. Sprinkle lightly with half of the ginger. Cover with the remaining slices and sprinkle with the remaining ginger.

2. Combine the sugar and water in a small saucepan and bring to the boil, stirring constantly until the sugar is dissolved. Add the lemon juice. Cook for 15 minutes and pour the syrup over the bananas. Let stand until cool. Chill.

YIELD: 4 to 6 servings.

Chocolate Fudge Cookies

- ¼ pound butter
- 5 ounces (5 squares) unsweetened chocolate, grated
- ¼ cup dark corn syrup
- ⅓ cup sugar
- 1 teaspoon pure vanilla extract
- 1 extra large egg
- 1 cup sifted flour
- ½ teaspoon baking soda
- ⅛ teaspoon salt, if desired

1. Preheat the oven to 350 degrees.

2. Put the butter in a saucepan with a heavy bottom. Place the saucepan over very low heat and let stand until the butter melts. Add the grated chocolate, corn syrup, sugar and vanilla. Stir occasionally with a wire whisk until the chocolate melts.

3. Remove from the heat and let stand for 10 minutes. Add the egg and blend well.

4. Sift together the flour, baking soda and salt. Add it to the chocolate mixture and blend well. Scrape the mixture into a mixing bowl.

5. Line a baking sheet with a length of wax paper. Cover this with a sheet of aluminum foil.

6. Spoon 1 tablespoon of the mixture at 2-inch intervals over the foil.

7. Place in the oven and bake for 10 to 15 minutes, watching carefully that the cookies do not burn on the bottom. It may be necessary to turn the baking sheet and to shift it to a higher position in the oven to prevent burning.

8. Turn off the oven heat and open the oven door. Let the cookies rest in the oven for 5 minutes. Remove and transfer the cookies to a rack to cool.

YIELD: About 2 dozen cookies.

Polvorones Sevillanos

SAND COOKIES SEVILLE STYLE

- ½ pound butter at room temperature
- 1 egg yolk
- 1 tablespoon confectioners' sugar
- 1 tablespoon Cognac
- 2 cups sifted flour
- ½ teaspoon ground cinnamon
- 2 cups, approximately, confectioners' sugar for coating

1. Preheat the oven to 300 degrees.

2. Cream the butter until it is light-colored and fluffy, using an electric beater or food processor.

3. Beat together the egg yolk and the 1 tablespoon of confectioners' sugar. Add the Cognac and beat once more. Add this to the butter while beating. Scrape this mixture into a bowl.

4. Sift together the flour and cinnamon.

5. Fold the flour mixture into the egg mixture, using a rubber spatula. The dough will be a little sticky.

6. Using floured hands, shape the dough into ovals measuring about 2 inches long and ½ inch high. Arrange the ovals on an ungreased baking sheet. The dough should be enough to make about 20 cookies.

7. Place the cookies in the oven and bake for about 30 minutes. The cookies should not brown. Let cool for 2 or 3 minutes.

8. Sift 1 cup of the confectioners' sugar onto a sheet of wax paper. Reserve the remainder. Roll the warm cookies in the sugar to coat them thoroughly. Let the cookies stand until thoroughly cool. Arrange them on a dessert dish and sift the remaining confectioners' sugar over them.

YIELD: About 20 cookies.

Florentines with Ginger

- ¾ cup heavy cream
- 4 tablespoons butter
- ¾ cup sugar
- 1¾ cups coarsely grated or chopped almonds
- ½ cup flour
- 6 tablespoons finely chopped candied ginger
- 3 ounces (squares) semisweet chocolate

1. Preheat the oven to 350 degrees.

2. Combine the cream, butter and sugar in a heavy saucepan. Bring to the boil, stirring until the sugar is dissolved and all ingredients are well blended.

3. Fold in the almonds, flour and candied ginger.

4. Rub 1 or 2 baking sheets with a light coating of peanut or corn oil. Drop the batter, about a tablespoon at a time, onto the baking sheet, keeping the mounds 3 inches apart. Bake for 10 to 12 minutes.

5. Remove from the oven and let cool briefly. If they become too cool, they will stick to the pan. Remove the cookies with a spatula and transfer to a rack. Let cool.

6. Place a small saucepan inside a small skillet of boiling water and add the chocolate squares. Place the skillet on the stove and let the water simmer until the chocolate melts. Stir the chocolate occasionally.

7. When the cookies are thoroughly cold, smear a little chocolate over the bottom of each cookie, using a spatula.

YIELD: 2 dozen or more cookies.

Centimes

MERINGUE AND ALMOND COOKIES

- 5⅓ tablespoons butter
- 3 egg whites
- ¾ cup confectioners' sugar
- ½ cup flour
- ⅓ cup blanched, grated almonds
- ½ teaspoon pure vanilla extract
- ¼ cup granulated sugar

1. Preheat the oven to 350 degrees.

2. Melt the butter over gentle heat. Let it cool.

3. Put the egg whites in the bowl of an electric mixer and beat until frothy but not stiff.

4. Gradually add the confectioners' sugar to the egg whites, beating on high speed.

5. Blend the flour and almonds. Fold them into the meringue, using a rubber or plastic spatula. Fold in the melted butter and vanilla.

6. Butter 1 or 2 baking sheets. Outfit a pastry bag with a round No. 4 tube. Fill the pastry bag with the meringue mix and push small mounds onto the baking sheet, about 1 teaspoon at a time. The mounds should be about 2 inches apart. Tap the baking sheet against a flat surface so that the mounds flatten somewhat. Sprinkle the tops lightly with granulated sugar.

7. Place the baking sheets in the oven and bake for 10 minutes, or until the mounds are not sticky throughout.

YIELD: About 36 cookies.

Sara Burke's Banana and Date Squares

- 1 cup dark brown sugar
- 1⅓ cups Scottish oats
- 1½ cups plus 1 tablespoon flour
- Salt to taste
- 1 teaspoon baking soda
- 12 tablespoons butter at room temperature
- 10 ounces pitted dates
- ½ cup granulated sugar
- 1 cup boiling water
- 3 bananas

1. Preheat the oven to 350 degrees.

2. Put the brown sugar, oats and 1½ cups of the flour into a mixing bowl. Add the salt, baking soda and butter. Blend well with the fingers.

3. Lightly grease a pan measuring 8 or 9 inches square. Add half the oats mixture to the pan and press down until the bottom is covered. Set aside.

4. Using scissors, cut the dates into small pieces. Put them in a bowl and mix in the granulated sugar and the tablespoon of flour. Pour the boiling water over the mixture. Let stand for 5 minutes.

5. Mash the bananas with a fork. Add them to the date mixture and blend well.

6. Pour the banana mixture into the pan. Flatten the remaining oats mixture between the hands. Arrange this over the top of the banana filling until the filling is completely covered.

7. Place the pan in the oven and bake for about 40 minutes, or until nicely browned. Let cool. Cut into squares and serve.

YIELD: 10 to 12 servings.

Peanut Cookies

- 2 cups sifted flour
- ½ teaspoon salt
- 1½ teaspoons baking powder
- 12 tablespoons butter at room temperature
- 1 cup light or dark brown sugar
- ½ cup creamy peanut butter
- 2 tablespoons milk
- 2 eggs, lightly beaten
- 1 cup toasted, unsalted peanuts

1. Preheat the oven to 350 degrees.

2. Sift together the flour, salt and baking powder. Set aside.

3. Put the butter and sugar into the bowl of an electric mixer. Beat until light and fluffy. Add the peanut butter and continue beating. Beat in the milk, eggs and sifted flour mixture. Fold in the nuts.

4. Drop about 2 tablespoons of the mixture at a time about 2 inches apart onto a buttered baking sheet.

5. Bake for 15 to 20 minutes.

YIELD: About 24 cookies.

Oatmeal–Raisin Cookies

- 1 cup sifted flour
- ¼ teaspoon baking soda
- 1 teaspoon baking powder
- ¼ teaspoon salt
- ¼ teaspoon ground cloves
- ¼ teaspoon ground allspice
- 12 tablespoons butter at room temperature
- 1 cup dark brown sugar
- 1 egg, lightly beaten
- ⅓ cup buttermilk
- ¾ cup rolled (quick-cooking) oats
- ½ cup dark raisins
- ¾ cup coarsely chopped pecans

1. Preheat the oven to 350 degrees.

2. Sift together the flour, baking soda, baking powder, salt, cloves and allspice. Set aside.

3. Cream together the butter and brown sugar in a mixing bowl until light and fluffy. Add the egg and beat well.

4. Fold in the flour mixture and buttermilk, adding each alternately.

5. Fold in the oats, raisins and pecans.

6. Drop about 2 tablespoons at a time about 2 inches apart onto a lightly buttered baking sheet. Flatten each cookie.

7. Place in the oven and bake for 10 to 15 minutes, or until nicely browned and cooked through.

YIELD: About 24 large cookies.

There are subtle but delectable fashions in many of the world's foods. Twenty years ago, for example, one of the favorite pastries in every fine pastry shop in America was the éclair. Although that finger-shaped delicacy is still to be found, the demand for it seems to have diminished over the years. That is a pity because, to our minds at least, it is still one of the most interesting, delectable desserts in the pâtissier's repertory.

Éclairs are made with a cream puff dough and actually they are quite simple to prepare. Traditionally they are filled with a pastry cream, although they can be, of course, stuffed with ice cream and frozen. In any event, they should be masked with an easily made chocolate and/or mocha frosting.

Éclairs

- 8 tablespoons butter plus additional butter for greasing a pan
- 1 cup flour plus additional flour for flouring a pan
- 1 cup water
- Salt
- ½ teaspoon sugar
- 4 large eggs

1. Preheat the oven to 425 degrees.

2. Lightly but thoroughly butter a jelly roll pan. Sprinkle the pan with flour and shake it around until well coated. Shake and tap out any excess flour.

3. Put the water in a saucepan and add the 8 tablespoons of butter, salt to taste and the sugar. Bring to the boil and add 1 cup of flour, all at once, stirring vigorously and thoroughly in a circular motion until a ball is formed and the mixture cleans the sides of the saucepan.

4. Add the eggs, one at a time, beating thoroughly and rapidly with a spoon until each egg is well blended with the mixture. When all the eggs are added, outfit a pastry bag with a No. 8 pastry tube.

5. Spoon the mixture into the bag. Hold the pastry bag at a slight angle to the buttered and floured jelly roll pan. Pipe out the mixture in a straight line about 5 inches long, drawing the bag toward you as you pipe. There should be about 12 éclairs.

6. Place the pan in the oven and bake for 15 minutes, or until golden brown and cooked through.

YIELD: About 12 éclairs.

❧

Éclairs with Two Flavors

- 12 éclairs (see preceding recipe)
- 2½ cups pastry cream (see following recipe)
- 2 ounces semisweet chocolate, grated
- 1 tablespoon instant coffee powder
- Chocolate frosting (see following recipe)
- Mocha frosting (see following recipe)

1. Prepare the éclairs and the pastry cream.

2. Divide the hot pastry cream into two batches.

3. Add the grated chocolate to one batch and stir until the chocolate is melted and smooth. Set aside.

4. Add the instant coffee powder to the second batch of pastry cream. Beat well to blend. Set aside.

5. Outfit 2 pastry bags with 2 No. 6 pastry tubes.

6. Using a sharp knife, make a slit down one side of each éclair.

7. Fill one pastry bag with the chocolate pastry cream. Pipe the pastry cream to fill the center of 6 of the éclairs.

8. Fill the other pastry bag with mocha pastry cream. Pipe the pastry cream to fill the center of the remaining éclairs.

9. Arrange the filled éclairs on a rack or racks.

10. Spoon the chocolate frosting over the tops of the chocolate-filled éclairs. Let some of the frosting run down the sides. Chill.

11. Spoon the mocha frosting over the remaining éclairs, letting the frosting run down the sides. Chill.

YIELD: 12 éclairs.

CRÈME PÂTISSIÈRE

Pastry Cream

- 2 cups milk
- ½ vanilla bean, or 1 teaspoon pure vanilla extract
- ⅔ cup sugar
- 6 egg yolks
- 4 tablespoons cornstarch
- 1 tablespoon soft butter, optional

1. Put the milk and split vanilla bean, if used, in a saucepan and bring to the boil. Cover and keep hot.

2. Put the sugar and egg yolks into a mixing bowl and beat with a wire whisk (this may be done with a mixer) until the mixture is golden yellow and forms a ribbon. Using the whisk, stir in the cornstarch.

3. Strain the hot milk into the egg and sugar mixture, beating constantly with the whisk. The vanilla bean may be rinsed off and stored in sugar.

4. Pour the mixture back into the saucepan and bring to the boil, stirring constantly with the whisk. Cook for 1 minute, stirring vigorously. Add the vanilla extract, if used. If the pastry cream is not to be used immediately, rub the surface with butter to prevent a skin from forming as it cools.

YIELD: About 2½ cups.

MOCHA FROSTING

- 2 tablespoons butter
- 1 teaspoon instant coffee powder
- ½ cup confectioners' sugar
- 1 tablespoon heavy cream

1. Melt the butter in a small saucepan and stir in the instant coffee powder and confectioners' sugar.

2. Stir briskly with a wire whisk. Add the cream and beat to blend. Let cool slightly to thicken before using.

YIELD: About ⅓ cup.

CHOCOLATE FROSTING

- 2 tablespoons butter
- 1½ ounces semisweet chocolate
- 2 tablespoons milk
- ½ cup confectioners' sugar

1. Combine the butter and chocolate in a small saucepan. Heat, stirring, until the chocolate melts.

2. Remove the saucepan from the heat and stir to blend while gradually adding the milk.

3. Add the sugar and stir briskly to blend.

YIELD: About ⅓ cup.

One of the most delicate, elegant and yet easily made of French pastries is something known in the pastry chef's kitchen as tulipes. They are fragile, brittle, wafer-thin cups into which a multitude of good things go. The fillings may consist of one or more scoops of sherbet or ice cream, either a single flavor or several; a fine layer of irresistible pastry cream topped with fresh fruits or berries and perhaps a dusting of confectioners' sugar, and so on.

Tulipes

FREE-FORM DESSERT CUPS

- 6 tablespoons butter plus butter for brushing the baking sheet
- ¼ cup sugar
- ½ cup sifted flour
- ½ teaspoon pure vanilla extract
- 2 egg whites

1. Preheat the oven to 425 degrees.
2. Put the 6 tablespoons of butter and the sugar into a mixing bowl and beat with a wire whisk or an electric mixer until light and creamy.
3. Beat in the flour and vanilla.
4. Beat the egg whites until they stand in soft peaks. Fold the whites into the creamed mixture.
5. Select a baking sheet large enough to fit neatly in the oven. Brush the top surface with butter.
6. Using a mixing or other round bowl that is 5 inches in diameter, invert it onto the baking sheet and trace a circle in the light butter coating. Make as many separately traced circles as possible; you may be able to get only 2 or 3 to a sheet.
7. Spoon 1 or 2 tablespoons of the batter into the center of each circle. Carefully smooth the batter into one very thin layer, less than ⅛ inch thick, to cover the circle. Continue filling the circles.
8. Place the baking sheet in the oven and bake for 3 to 3½ minutes, watching carefully that the pastries do not burn. Remove the sheet from the oven and immediately lift up the circles one at a time, carefully shaping them while hot (place the brown bottom side up) in the center of a cup (a regular-shape rounded coffee cup or Chinese soup or rice bowl is suitable). When pushed into the center, the edges should be neatly fluted or ruffled. Let cool and remove from the mold. Continue until all the cups are baked and shaped.

YIELD: 10 to 12 free-form dessert cups.

Tulipes aux Fraises

DESSERT PASTRIES WITH STRAWBERRIES

- 10 to 12 free-form dessert cups (see preceding recipe)
- 2½ cups pastry cream (see following recipe)
- 30 to 36 ripe strawberries, stems removed (see Note)
- Confectioners' sugar for garnish

1. Arrange 1 dessert cup on each of 10 or 12 plates.

2. Spoon an equal portion of the pastry cream in the center of each cup. Garnish the top of the pastry cream decoratively with 3 strawberries.

3. Hold a small sieve over the top of each serving and add a little confectioners' sugar. Sprinkle the tops with sugar.

YIELD: 10 to 12 servings.

Note: One may substitute almost any fresh fruit or berry in season as a garnish for the tops of these desserts. Use raspberries, peaches, seedless grapes and so on, according to choice.

CRÈME PÂTISSIÈRE

Pastry Cream

- 1 cup milk
- ¼ vanilla bean, or ½ teaspoon pure vanilla extract
- ⅓ cup granulated sugar
- 3 egg yolks
- 2 tablespoons cornstarch
- 1 cup heavy cream, whipped
- 3 tablespoons Grand Marnier

1. Put the milk and split vanilla bean, if used, in a saucepan and bring to the boil. Cover and keep hot.

2. Put the sugar and egg yolks in a mixing bowl (this may be done in a mixer) and beat with a wire whisk until the mixture is golden yellow and forms a ribbon. Using the whisk, stir in the cornstarch.

3. Strain the hot milk into the egg and sugar mixture, beating constantly with the whisk. The vanilla bean may be rinsed off and stored in sugar.

4. Pour the mixture back into the saucepan and bring to the boil, stirring constantly with the whisk. Cook for 1 minute, stirring vigorously. Remove from the heat. Add the vanilla extract, if used. Cover and let cool. Fold in the whipped cream and Grand Marnier.

YIELD: About 2½ cups.

❧

Buckwheat Crêpes with Glazed Fruits

1½ cups buckwheat crêpe batter (see following recipe)
12 to 16 tablespoons glazed fruit butter (see following recipe)
2 cups drained, seedless orange sections, preferably made from blood oranges (see Note) or tangerines
½ cup liquid from glazed fruits (see following recipe)

1. Preheat the oven to 350 degrees.

2. Lightly butter the bottom of a 7-inch crêpe pan. When quite hot, add 2 or 3 tablespoons of crêpe batter. Swirl the pan around to coat the bottom of the pan evenly. Let cook until lightly browned on the bottom, about 20 seconds. Turn and cook about 15 seconds on the second side and turn out onto a platter. Continue until 12 to 16 crêpes are made.

3. Lay out 1 crêpe at a time on a flat surface. Spread each crêpe with an equal portion of glazed fruit butter. Reserve a small portion of butter for the top of the crêpes when they are all filled and arranged on the dish. Make a row of about 2 tablespoons of the orange sections down each crêpe, but reserve ½ cup of orange sections for a top garnish. Roll each crêpe as it is prepared and arrange them uniformly and close together on a heatproof baking dish. Scatter the remaining orange sections on top.

4. Dot the top of the crêpes with the reserved fruit butter. Pour the ½ cup of drained liquid from the glazed fruit over the filled crêpes.

5. Place the baking dish in the oven and bake for 10 minutes, or until the crêpes are bubbling and piping hot.

YIELD: 4 to 8 servings.

Note: Blood oranges, which are occasionally but rarely found in markets, are small oranges with a blood-red interior. They are sweeter than most oranges.

BUCKWHEAT CRÊPE BATTER

4 tablespoons butter
1 cup milk
¼ cup buckwheat flour
¾ cup all-purpose flour
Salt, if desired
¾ teaspoon sugar
2 eggs
1 teaspoon peanut, vegetable or corn oil
½ cup beer

1. Heat the butter and milk in a saucepan until the butter is melted. Stir and let cool.

2. Sift together the buckwheat flour and all-purpose flour into a mixing bowl. Add the salt, sugar and eggs. Add the oil.

3. Stir the mixture with a wire whisk or wooden spoon. Add the milk and butter mixture gradually, stirring constantly. Stir in the beer.

4. If the mixture is lumpy, strain it through a sieve. Chill until ready to use. Leftover batter may be covered and refrigerated for later use.

YIELD: About 2½ cups, or enough for 40 or more crêpes.

GLAZED FRUIT BUTTER

3 to 4 glazed fruits such as clementines or kumquats packed in syrup (see Note)
8 tablespoons butter
2 teaspoons sugar

1. Remove the fruits from their packing liquid. Squeeze each fruit to remove any excess interior liquid. Put the fruits on a flat surface and chop finely. There should be ⅓ cup or slightly more. Reserve the liquid for another recipe.

2. Cut the butter into pieces and blend with the chopped fruits. Add the sugar and blend well.

YIELD: About ¾ cup, or enough for 12 to 16 crêpes.

Note: Although almost any fruit packed in syrup is suitable for this recipe, Alice Waters of Chez Panisse prefers imported clementines packed in "eau de Provence." These are sold in specialty shops where fine imported produce is available.

❧

Soufflé de Pain d'Épices au Sabayon à la Bière Brune

GINGERBREAD PUDDING WITH DARK BEER SABAYON

- 4 tablespoons butter
- 1 teaspoon granulated sugar plus sugar to coat the ramekins
- 1½ cups coarsely crumbled gingersnaps
- ¼ cup milk
- 4 eggs, separated
- ⅓ ounce sweet chocolate
- ½ cup broken walnuts
- ¼ teaspoon grated lemon rind
- Dark beer sabayon sauce (see following recipe)
- Strawberry slices for garnish, optional

1. Preheat the oven to 375 degrees.

2. Use 1 tablespoon of the butter to butter 8 small soufflé ramekins. Sprinkle equal amounts of sugar into each ramekin and shake to coat the sides.

3. Put the remaining 3 tablespoons of butter in a mixing bowl and add the teaspoon of sugar. Beat until well creamed.

4. Combine the gingersnaps and milk and stir briefly. Set aside.

5. Add the egg yolks to the creamed butter mixture.

6. Melt the chocolate over boiling water until completely soft.

7. Scrape the chocolate into the creamed mixture and stir to blend.

8. Squeeze the gingersnaps to extract any excess liquid. Add the gingersnaps, walnuts and lemon rind to the yolk batter. Blend well.

9. Beat the egg whites until stiff. Add about one third of the egg whites to the gingersnap batter. Beat them in with a wire whisk. Add the remaining whites and fold them in with a spatula.

10. Fill each ramekin almost to the top with the soufflé mixture.

11. Place a double sheet of wax paper in a shallow roasting pan large enough to hold the ramekins. Arrange them in the pan. Add boiling water to cover the bottom of the ramekins by half an inch. Place the pan in the oven and bake for 25 to 35 minutes, or until well puffed. The puddings can stand in the oven with the heat turned off for an additional 10 minutes. Or they may be served immediately.

12. Unmold the puddings onto individual serving plates. Spoon the sabayon sauce over. Garnish, if desired, with strawberry slices.

YIELD: 8 servings.

SABAYON À LA BIÈRE BRUNE

Dark Beer Sabayon

- 4 egg yolks
- 2 tablespoons sugar
- ¾ teaspoon lemon juice
- ¼ cup dark beer
- ¼ cup whipped cream (measured after whipping)

1. It is best to make this in an unlined, round-bottom copper basin, but another metal bowl or saucepan will do.

2. Put the yolks, sugar and lemon juice in the basin and beat rapidly with a wire whisk. Place the basin over gentle heat (you may set it in a water bath). Beat rapidly while adding the beer. Beat vigorously with a heavy whisk until the sauce is about four or five times its original volume.

3. Set the basin on a bed of ice cubes and continue beating until cold.

4. Fold in the whipped cream.

YIELD: 8 servings.

Bread-and-Butter Pudding

- ¾ cup mixed candied fruit or dried currants
- 2 tablespoons Cognac
- 20 slices untrimmed French bread, each slice about ⅓ inch thick
- 3 egg yolks
- 3 whole eggs
- 1 cup granulated sugar
- 2 cups milk
- 1 cup heavy cream
- 4 tablespoons melted butter
- Confectioners' sugar

1. Preheat the oven to 350 degrees.

2. Mix the candied fruit with the Cognac in a bowl and set aside for 30 minutes.

3. Select a heatproof baking dish. (An oval dish that measures 14 by 18 by 2 inches is ideal.)

4. Slice the bread. Preferably, the diameter of the bread should not exceed 3 inches. If much larger, cut the pieces in half.

5. Combine the egg yolks, whole eggs and sugar in a mixing bowl. Beat with a whisk until blended. Stir in the milk and cream. Drain the Cognac from the fruit and add the Cognac to the cream mixture.

6. Scatter the fruit over the bottom of the baking dish.

7. Brush one side of each bread slice with butter. Arrange the bread slices neatly and symmetrically overlapping to cover the bottom of the dish.

8. Strain the custard over the bread slices.

9. Set the baking dish in a larger heatproof baking dish. Pour about 1 inch of water around the baking dish. Bring the water to the boil on top of the stove. Place in the oven and bake for 40 minutes to 1 hour, or until the custard is set.

10. Remove the dish to a rack and let cool. Serve sprinkled with confectioners' sugar

YIELD: 8 to 12 servings.

Chocolate Bread Pudding

- 3 tablespoons melted butter
- 15 slices French bread, approximately, each about ½ inch thick (there should be enough slices to cover the bottom of an oval baking dish with the slices slightly overlapping)
- ¼ pound (4 squares) sweet chocolate
- 3 cups milk
- 3 eggs
- 3 egg yolks
- ½ cup granulated sugar
- 1 tablespoon confectioners' sugar

1. Preheat the oven to 375 degrees.

2. Butter the bread on both sides. Arrange the slices in one layer on a baking sheet. Bake until lightly golden on one side. Turn the slices and continue baking for about 2 minutes longer, or until totally golden on both sides.

3. Put the chocolate in a saucepan and set the saucepan in a basin of simmering water. Stir until melted.

4. Meanwhile, heat the milk almost but not quite to the boiling point. Add the chocolate, stirring.

5. Beat the whole eggs, egg yolks and sugar until well blended. Pour in the chocolate mixture, stirring.

6. Add the milk, stirring.

7. Arrange the toast pieces slightly overlapping on the bottom of an oval dish measuring about 14 by 8 by 2 inches. Carefully ladle the chocolate mixture over all.

8. Select a baking dish large enough to hold the oval dish. Pour boiling water into the baking dish. Set the oval dish in the water and place it in the oven.

9. Bake for 30 minutes. Before serving, sprinkle the top with confectioners' sugar. Serve, if desired, with whipped cream.

YIELD: 8 or more servings.

Mousse au Chocolat Amer

BITTER CHOCOLATE MOUSSE

- 4½ ounces unsweetened chocolate
- 3 tablespoons extra strong coffee, preferably espresso
- 1 tablespoon cocoa powder
- 6 tablespoons heavy cream, optional
- 8 egg whites
- 4 tablespoons sugar

1. Combine the chocolate, coffee and cocoa in a mixing bowl. Put the bowl in a skillet and add water to a depth of about 1 inch. Bring the water to the boil and heat, stirring the chocolate mixture occasionally, until the ingredients are blended and smooth.

2. Beat the mixture with a whisk. If the mixture does not become liquid, beat in the cream.

3. Beat the whites until stiff while gradually adding the sugar. Add half the whites to the chocolate mixture. Beat them in. Fold in the remaining whites.

4. Pour and scrape the mixture into an appropriate dish and chill thoroughly.

YIELD: 4 servings.

Parfait à la Vanille

VANILLA PARFAIT

- ⅔ cup plus 2 tablespoons sugar
- ⅔ cup water
- ½ teaspoon pure vanilla extract
- 1 cup heavy cream
- 8 egg yolks
- Raspberry sauce (see following recipe)

1. Combine the sugar and water in a saucepan. Bring to the boil and add the vanilla. Let simmer briefly.

2. Put the cream in a chilled bowl and beat until stiff. Chill until ready to use.

3. Meanwhile, put the yolks in a heavy saucepan and start beating with a wire whisk. Continue beating vigorously while gradually adding the simmering syrup.

4. Put the saucepan on a heatproof pad and continue beating until the volume increases four or five times the original. Do not let the mixture get too hot or it will scramble. It will resemble a light yellow, frothy but well-thickened custard or a sabayon. This should require 4 or 5 minutes of vigorous beating.

5. Pour and scrape the mixture into the bowl of an electric mixer. Beat on high speed until the custard is cooled to room temperature, 7 minutes or longer.

6. Scrape the whipped cream onto the yolk mixture. Carefully fold it in until well blended. Pour and scrape the mixture into a decorative crystal or other bowl or serving dish.

7. Place the dish in the freezer and let stand several hours or, preferably, overnight until frozen. Serve with raspberry sauce.

YIELD: 8 servings.

SAUCE AUX FRAMBOISE

Raspberry Sauce

- 2 packages, 10 ounces, frozen raspberries in syrup
- ½ cup sugar

1. Let the raspberries thaw partly. Put them through a sieve, pressing to extract as much liquid as possible. Discard the seeds. There should be about 1⅔ cups of purée.

2. To the sauce add the sugar and stir to dissolve. Chill until ready to serve.

YIELD: About 1⅔ cups.

Pots de Crème

- 3 egg yolks
- 3 eggs
- ¾ cup sugar
- 2 cups milk
- 1 cup heavy cream
- 5 teaspoons instant espresso powder

1. Preheat the oven to 350 degrees.

2. Put the yolks, eggs and sugar into a mixing bowl and beat well.

3. Combine the milk, cream and instant espresso powder in a saucepan and blend well. Bring barely to the boil.

4. Pour the milk mixture into the egg mixture, beating continuously until well blended.

5. Pour the mixture into 6 to 8 individual pots de crème or soufflé dishes. The number will depend on the capacity of each dish, which should hold 5 to 7 ounces. Fill the dishes almost to the top.

6. Arrange the dishes in a heatproof baking dish and pour water around them. Bring the water to the boil on top of the stove. Place the baking dish with the individual dishes in the oven and bake for 30 minutes, or until set.

YIELD: 6 to 8 servings.

Marlborough Pudding

- 3 apples, about 1¼ pounds, or use 1⅓ cups applesauce
- ¼ cup water
- 2 tablespoons plus 1 teaspoon butter
- 2 large eggs
- ½ cup sugar
- ½ cup heavy cream
- ¼ teaspoon ground mace or grated nutmeg
- 1 teaspoon grated lemon rind
- Juice of ½ lemon

1. Preheat the oven to 350 degrees.

2. Peel the apples and cut them into quarters. Carve away the core and stems. Cut the quartered apples into thin slices. Put the apples in a heavy saucepan and add the water. Cover and cook for about 5 minutes, or until the apples are tender.

3. Put the mixture into the container of a food processor or blender and blend to a purée. There should be about 1⅓ cups.

4. Pour and scrape the mixture into a saucepan and add 2 tablespoons of the butter, the eggs, sugar, heavy cream, mace, lemon rind and lemon juice. Blend.

5. Butter a small baking dish (one measuring 10 by 7 by 1½ inches is ideal) with the remaining 1 teaspoon of butter. Pour in the apple mixture. Set the dish inside a larger heatproof dish and pour boiling water around it. Bring the water to the boil again. Place in the oven and bake for about 45 minutes, or until the custard is set in the center.

YIELD: 6 servings.

The spirit called applejack or Calvados is—to turn a phrase of Clifton Fadiman's to our own purposes—apples' leap into immortality. Although applejack or Calvados is delectable as a simple beverage and as a basis for many old-fashioned cocktails, it is also an excellent ingredient for cooking. It goes superbly with almost any roast made with apples. It is almost an essential for many tripe dishes, and it reaches what might be called its zenith in that butter-rich dessert called apple charlotte.

Apple Charlotte with Calvados

- ½ cup golden raisins
- 1 cup warm water
- 5 or 6 firm, ripe, slightly tart cooking apples, about 2 pounds
- 16 tablespoons butter
- ⅓ cup sugar
- 1 teaspoon grated lemon rind
- 4 tablespoons Calvados or applejack
- 7 slices white bread, trimmed of crusts
- Crème anglaise (see following recipe) flavored with 1 tablespoon Calvados or applejack

1. Put the raisins in a mixing bowl and add the warm water to cover. Let soak for about 20 minutes. Drain.

2. Meanwhile, preheat the oven to 400 degrees.

3. Peel and core the applies. Cut them into quarters, then cut each quarter into ¼-inch-thick slices.

4. Heat 8 tablespoons of the butter in a large, heavy skillet and, when it is melted, add the apple slices and sprinkle with sugar and lemon rind. Cook, stirring often without breaking up the slices, for about 10 minutes. Add half of the Calvados.

5. Cut 1 slice of bread into ½-inch cubes. Melt about 4 tablespoons of the

butter and toss the bread cubes in it without browning. Add this and the raisins to the apples. Stir.

6. Meanwhile, rub the inside of a 4-cup charlotte mold with 1 tablespoon of butter. Trim 1 slice of bread to fit the inside bottom of the mold. Butter it generously on top. Cut about 4 slices of bread into rectangles sufficient to line the inside bottom of the mold. Butter them generously on top. Cut about 4 slices of bread into rectangles sufficient to line the inside of the mold, each rectangle standing up close together but not overlapping. Butter the rectangles generously.

7. Spoon and scrape the apple mixture into the bread-lined mold.

8. Cut the remaining slice of bread into a round shape to fit inside the lined mold to neatly cover the apple filling. Butter this on both sides with the remaining butter. Fit the round of bread on top.

9. Place the mold in the oven and bake for 15 minutes.

10. Reduce the oven temperature to 350 degrees and bake for 15 minutes longer.

11. Remove from the oven and let stand for 15 minutes. Unmold the charlotte onto a round serving dish. Pour the remaining 2 tablespoons of Calvados over the mold. Serve with crème anglaise flavored with Calvados.

YIELD: 8 servings.

CRÈME ANGLAISE

English Custard

5 egg yolks
⅔ cup sugar
2 cups milk
⅛ teaspoon salt

1. Put the yolks in a saucepan and add the sugar. Beat with a wire whisk until thick and lemon-colored.

2. Meanwhile, bring the milk almost but not quite to the boil.

3. Gradually add the milk to the yolk mixture, beating constantly, this way and that, making certain that the spoon touches all over the bottom of the saucepan. Cook, stirring, and add the salt. Cook until the mixture has a custard-like consistency and coats the sides of the spoon. Do not let the sauce boil, or it will curdle.

4. Immediately remove the sauce from the stove, but continue stirring. Set the saucepan in a basin of cold water to reduce the temperature. Let the sauce cool to room temperature. Chill for an hour or longer.

YIELD: 8 to 12 servings.

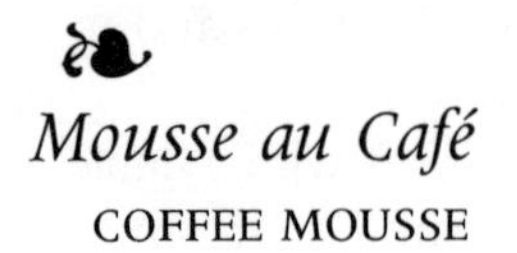

Mousse au Café

COFFEE MOUSSE

- 1 teaspoon peanut, vegetable or corn oil
- 4 cups plus 2 tablespoons cold water
- 2 envelopes unflavored gelatin
- 1 cup sugar
- 3 to 4 tablespoons freeze-dried or instant espresso coffee powder
- ¼ cup cornstarch
- 4 eggs, separated
- 6 tablespoons coffee liqueur, such as Kahlua or Bahia
- 1 cup heavy cream

1. Lightly grease the inside of an 8-cup mold with the oil, wiping off the excess.

2. Combine 4 cups of water, the gelatin and ½ cup of the sugar in a saucepan. Bring to the boil and simmer for about 5 minutes, stirring constantly. Remove from the heat and add the coffee, stirring.

3. Blend the cornstarch and 2 tablespoons of water and add it to the syrup. Cook, stirring, until the mixture thickens.

4. Beat the yolks and add them to the syrup, stirring rapidly with a whisk. Remove from the heat. Add the coffee liqueur. Spoon and scrape the mixture into a mixing bowl. Let cool.

5. Beat the egg whites and, when almost stiff, add ¼ cup sugar, beating constantly until stiff. Fold this into the mixture.

6. Whip the cream until it is almost stiff and gradually add the remaining ¼ cup sugar, beating constantly. Fold this into the mousse mixture.

7. Pour the mousse mixture into the oiled mold and refrigerate for several hours, preferably overnight, or until set. Unmold. To unmold, wipe around the outside of the mold with a hot, damp, squeezed-out sponge until the mousse loosens within.

YIELD: 8 or more servings.

Soufflé au Citron

LEMON SOUFFLÉ

- 2 large lemons
- 2 cups sugar
- Juice of 1 lemon
- 2 cups milk
- ½ cup flour
- 8 eggs, separated
- 1 tablespoon cornstarch

1. Peel the lemons with a swivel-bladed peeler, removing all the yellow but as little of the white of the skin as possible.

2. Place the rind on a board and cut it into the thinnest possible strips. Cut these strips into bits and chop them as small as possible. Put them into a mixing bowl and add 1 cup of sugar. Mix well with the fingers. Cover and let stand for 24 hours.

3. Spoon the lemon rind and sugar mixture into a small saucepan. Add the lemon juice and bring to the boil. Simmer over low heat, stirring frequently, for about 10 minutes. Let cool, then chill well.

4. Generously butter a 9- or 10-cup soufflé dish and chill it in the freezer.

5. In a saucepan, combine the milk, flour, egg yolks, ½ cup of sugar and cornstarch. Cook over low heat, stirring constantly, until thickened. Add the lemon mixture and bring just to the boil, stirring. Spoon this into a large mixing bowl and let it cool.

6. Preheat the oven to 400 degrees.

7. Beat the whites and, when they start to form peaks, gradually beat in the remaining ½ cup of sugar. Continue beating to make a stiff meringue.

8. Add one third of the whites to the lemon mixture and beat in with a whisk. Fold in the remaining whites with a plastic spatula. Pour the mixture into the prepared soufflé dish and place in the oven. Bake for 10 minutes and reduce the oven temperature to 375 degrees. Bake for 15 minutes longer. If you want the soufflé to be less moist in the center, bake 10 minutes longer.

YIELD: 6 to 8 servings.

In recent years pear sherbet has become one of the most popular desserts in Europe. It is often served with a glass of iced vodka poured over it. An even better idea may be a sweetened sauce made with fresh or frozen strawberries and pear liqueur. Although the clear eau de vie de poire is widely available in this country, it is rather obscure on most American wine and spirit shelves. It is delectable in fruit sauces and is especially compatible in sauces for pear desserts.

Sorbet aux Poires

PEAR SHERBET

- 4 ripe, not too firm, unblemished pears, preferably Bosc pears, about 2½ pounds
- 2½ cups sugar
- 2¼ cups water
- 1 tablespoon fresh lemon juice
- Sauce aux fraises, optional (see following recipe)

1. Remove the core and stem from each of the pears. Peel the pears. Cut the pears in half lengthwise. Using a melon ball cutter, remove the center core. Cut away the bottom center line leading from the core to the stem end.

2. Combine the sugar and water in a saucepan. Bring to the boil and simmer for 5 minutes. Add the pears and simmer, uncovered, until the pears are tender, about 15 minutes.

3. Remove from the heat and let the pears cool in the syrup. Refrigerate until thoroughly chilled.

4. Drain the pears, but save the liquid. There should be about 1⅓ cups of liquid. Put the pears into the container of a food processor and process as finely as possible. There should be about 3 cups of purée.

5. Combine the purée, cooking liquid and lemon juice in the container of an electric or hand-cranked ice cream freezer. Freeze according to manufacturer's instructions. Serve with sauce aux fraises, if desired.

YIELD: 8 to 12 servings.

SAUCE AUX FRAISES

Cold Strawberry Sauce

- 2 ½-pint containers of fresh strawberries, or 2 10-ounce packages of frozen strawberries
- ½ cup sugar, approximately
- ¼ cup white pear liqueur (eau de vie de poire) or kirschwasser

1. Place the strawberries in the container of a food processor or electric blender.

2. If fresh strawberries are used, add the sugar, or even more to taste. If frozen berries are used, remember that they are already sweetened. Purée as finely as possible.

3. Place a fine sieve inside a mixing bowl. Pour in the strawberry purée.

4. Strain the pulp through the sieve, pressing the sides with a rubber or plastic spatula. Discard the seeds.

5. Add the pear liqueur or kirschwasser. Chill thoroughly.

6. Serve over frozen desserts, such as sherbets, ices or ice cream.

YIELD: 1½ to 2 cups.

❧

Granité de Fruits

FRUIT OR BERRY ICE

- 3 pounds berries or fruits, such as strawberries. raspberries or soft-flesh fruits, such as peaches or nectarines
- 1½ cups superfine sugar, approximately

1. If berries such as strawberries are used, remove the stems. Wash and drain well. If fruits such as peaches are used, peel them and remove the pits. Weigh the flesh. There should be 3 pounds. Cut the flesh into sections.

2. Add the berries or prepared fruit to the container of a food processor. Blend to a fine purée. There should be slightly more than 6 cups.

3. Transfer the purée to a large mixing bowl. Add the sugar, starting with 1 cup. The amount of sugar to be added will depend on the sweetness of the berries and individual taste. Add, if desired, ½ cup or more sugar. Blend well.

4. Put the mixture into the container of an electric or hand-cranked ice cream freezer and freeze according to the manufacturer's instructions.

YIELD: 12 or more servings.

Sorbet au Melon

CANTALOUPE SHERBET

2 ripe, unblemished cantaloupes, about 2 pounds each
1 cup water
1 cup sugar
2 tablespoons lemon juice

1. Cut the cantaloupe in half and scrape out the seeds. Cut the cantaloupe halves into wedges. Using a sharp knife, cut away the skin from the flesh of each wedge. Cut the flesh into cubes. Discard the skins.

2. Put the cantaloupe flesh into the container of a food processor. Process to a fine purée. There should be 4½ to 5 cups. Chill.

3. Combine the water and sugar in a saucepan. Bring to the boil and cook for about 5 minutes. Let cool. Chill.

4. Combine the melon purée, syrup and lemon juice.

5. Pour the mixture into the container of an electric or hand-cranked ice cream freezer. Freeze according to the manufacturer's instructions.

YIELD: About 6 servings.

Grapefruit and Lemon Ice

2 cups sugar
2 cups water
Grated rind of 1 grapefruit
4 cups fresh, unsweetened grapefruit juice (4 or 5 grapefruits)
⅓ cup lemon juice

1. Combine the sugar and water in a saucepan and bring to the boil, stirring until the sugar is dissolved. Boil for 5 minutes and add the grated rind. Remove from the heat and let cool.

2. Combine the syrup, grapefruit juice and lemon juice in the container of an electric or hand-cranked ice cream freezer. Freeze according to the manufacturer's instructions. Scoop out the grapefruit ice into a mixing bowl, packing it down. Cover with plastic wrap and place in the freezer until ready to use.

YIELD: 2 quarts, or 12 to 14 servings.

Note: This ice is delectable when served with sweetened grapefruit sections steeped in a little vodka as a garnish.

Granité au Citron et à la Menthe

LEMON AND MINT ICE

- 14 fresh lemons, approximately
- 2 cups sugar
- 4 cups water
- 4 sprigs fresh mint
- 3 tablespoons finely chopped fresh mint leaves
- Sprigs of fresh mint for garnish

1. Grate the rind of 2 lemons and set the gratings aside. Cut these lemons in half and squeeze the juice. Set the juice aside.

2. Cut off a thin slice from the bottom of each remaining lemon so that they will stand upright when later filled with lemon ice.

3. Cut off a thin slice of the top of each lemon about ½ inch from the top. Leave enough of the center part of the lemon exposed so that you can scoop out the pulp, using a sturdy coffee spoon. Reserve the cut-off tops of each lemon. Press the pulp of these lemons through a sieve and add this juice to the other lemon juice. You will need 2 cups of lemon juice in all.

4. Arrange the hollowed-out lemon shells on a platter and put them in the freezer.

5. Combine the sugar, water and the 4 fresh mint sprigs in a saucepan. Bring to the boil and boil for 5 minutes. Add the lemon rind and lemon juice and cool. Chill thoroughly. Add the chopped mint leaves.

6. Pour the mixture into the container of an electric or hand-cranked ice cream freezer and freeze according to the manufacturer's instructions.

7. Spoon enough of the ice into each of the frozen lemons to fill them. Return the lemons to the freezer until ready to serve. Garnish the top of each filled lemon with a sprig of mint. Put the lemon tops on the side of each serving as decoration. The remaining ice can be served on another occasion.

YIELD: 12 servings.

Leche Merengada

SPICED LEMON ICE

- 3 cups milk
- 1 cup heavy cream
- ¾ cup plus 2 tablespoons sugar
- 2 2-inch pieces cinnamon stick
- Peel of 1 lemon
- 4 egg whites
- ½ teaspoon lemon juice
- Ground cinnamon for garnish

1. Combine the milk, cream, ¾ cup sugar, cinnamon sticks and lemon peel in a saucepan. Bring to the boil and simmer for 30 minutes.

2. Remove the mixture from the heat and set aside. Let cool. Refrigerate until cold. Remove and discard the lemon peel and cinnamon sticks.

3. Beat the egg whites and lemon juice until soft peaks form. Gradually beat in the remaining 2 tablespoons of sugar. Continue beating until stiff.

4. Beat in the chilled cream mixture.

5. Pour the mixture into the canister of an ice cream machine. Follow the manufacturer's instructions for freezing.

6. Sprinkle each portion with a little ground cinnamon before serving.

YIELD: 6 to 8 servings.

Young people in this country accept yogurt as a run-of-the-mill staple, but they do not realize that until the 1960s, yogurt was a relative curiosity, something to be consumed by eccentrics and food faddists. I personally prefer yogurt when it is converted into cheese, which is easily if not hastily done. Simply line a sieve or colander with cheesecloth that has been wrung out in cold water. Empty the yogurt into it and bring up the corners of the cloth and tie with string. Then suspend the cheesecloth bag over a bowl and let it hang overnight in a cool place, preferably the refrigerator. The yogurt takes on the texture of a tender cottage cheese. If you sweeten the yogurt before letting it drain, it makes a fine filling for a pie with berries. The yogurt cheese also produces a better yogurt ice cream than does plain yogurt.

Strawberry–Yogurt Ice Cream

1 quart plain yogurt
1 pint strawberries, hulled and cut in half
1 cup sugar
6 egg yolks
1 quart milk
¼ cup heavy cream

1. Line a colander with cheesecloth and spoon and scrape the yogurt into it. Bring up the edges of the cheesecloth and tie the ends with string. Hang the cheesecloth bag in the refrigerator, letting the yogurt drip into a bowl. Let stand overnight.

2. Put the strawberries into a saucepan and add ¼ cup of the sugar. Cook over low heat, stirring often, until the sugar is dissolved. Do not cook until the berries soften.

3. Beat the egg yolks and remaining sugar in a large mixing bowl until light and lemon-colored.

4. Combine the milk and cream in a saucepan and bring to the boil. Add this gradually to the yolk mixture, beating rapidly with a wire whisk. Pour this into the saucepan and return to the boil. Cook, stirring, until the mixture coats a wooden spoon. On a thermometer, cook to 180 degrees. Do not boil or it will curdle.

5. Open the cheesecloth bag and remove the yogurt. There should be about 1½ cups. Add this to the hot custard, beating it in. Let the custard cool.

6. Partly freeze the custard in an electric or hand-cranked ice cream freezer. Add the strawberry mixture. Continue freezing until frozen.

YIELD: 8 TO 10 SERVINGS.

Strawberry Ice Cream

- 10 cups ripe, firm, unblemished strawberries
- 1¾ cups sugar
- 4 cups milk
- 1 cup heavy cream
- 10 egg yolks
- 1 teaspoon pure vanilla extract, or 1 split 3-inch length of vanilla bean

1. Hull, rinse and drain the strawberries.

2. Place 2 cups of the whole berries in a skillet and add 1 cup of the sugar. Cook, stirring gently and shaking the skillet, for about 5 minutes. Drain the juice and reserve both juice and berries.

3. Place the remaining berries, a few at a time, into the container of a food processor or blender. Blend to a fine purée. Continue until all the berries are puréed. There should be about 1 quart of berry purée. Add the strained liquid from the cooked berries. Set aside.

4. Combine the milk and cream in a saucepan and bring just to the boil.

5. Place the remaining sugar and the yolks in a mixing bowl and beat with a wire whisk to the ribbon stage: i.e., until the mixture is thick and pale yellow in color and, when the beater is lifted, it falls back on itself like a ribbon.

6. Pour a cup or so of the hot milk and cream mixture into the egg mixture, beating rapidly with the whisk. Return this mixture to the hot milk mixture in the saucepan, scraping the bowl clean. Add the vanilla bean, if used.

7. Using a wooden spoon, cook the sauce over low heat, stirring this way and that all over the bottom of the saucepan, taking care that the sauce does not stick. Do not at any point boil the sauce or it will curdle. Cook only until the mixture coats the back of the spoon like very thick cream. Add the vanilla extract at this time.

8. Immediately strain the sauce into a mixing bowl. Let stand until cool. Add the puréed berries and the whole cooked berries. Chill.

9. Pour the custard into the canister of a hand-cranked or electric ice cream machine and freeze according to the manufacturer's instructions.

YIELD: About 3 quarts.

Pernod and Ricard are a form of anise, better known in the region around Marseilles as pastis. Originally pastis was developed as a substitute for absinthe, which was banned by law many years ago because it contained wormwood, an ingredient that was, in the words of one book on herbs and spices, "guilty of putting off an evil day to a yet more evil one." Interestingly enough, the word "vermouth" derives from the German word *Wermut,* which means wormwood. Needless to say, the vermouths, Pernod and Ricard, on the market today do not contain a trace of wormwood.

Pastis has a concentrated flavor like that of star anise. The drink becomes milky—actually, opalescent—when water is added to it. It has long been our opinion that a dash of pastis can add a congenial flavor to many dishes, particularly fish soups of the sort for which Marseilles is famous. On a recent occasion we produced an admirable ice cream containing a small quantity of pastis as a flavoring.

Glace au Pernod

PERNOD ICE CREAM

- 2 cups heavy cream
- 2 cups milk
- 4 egg yolks
- ¾ cups sugar
- 3 tablespoons Pernod or Ricard
- 1 or 2 drops green food coloring
- ½ cup unsalted, hulled pistachios or coarsely chopped toasted hazelnuts, optional

1. In a saucepan with a heavy bottom combine the cream, milk, egg yolks and sugar. Cook over low heat or in a double boiler, stirring constantly all over the bottom with a wooden spoon to make sure the custard does not stick at any point.

2. Continue cooking and stirring until the custard is as thick as very heavy cream. Pour the custard immediately into a metal bowl and stir a minute or so. Let cool. Chill.

3. Pour the custard into the container of a hand-cranked or electric ice cream machine. Add the Pernod or Ricard and food coloring. Start freezing according to the manufacturer's instructions. When the ice cream is almost but not quite frozen, add the nuts. Continue freezing until properly frozen.

YIELD: About 8 servings.

Caramel–Pecan Ice Cream

- 6 egg yolks
- 1¼ cups sugar
- 4 cups milk
- 1 cup heavy cream
- 1 vanilla bean, or 2 teaspoons pure vanilla extract
- 2 tablespoons water
- 1½ cups pecans, coarsely broken

1. Preheat the oven to 350 degrees.

2. Put the egg yolks and ¾ cup of the sugar in a heavy casserole. Beat with a wire whisk until pale yellow.

3. In a saucepan, combine the milk and cream. Bring just to the boil.

4. Add about ½ cup of the hot mixture to the egg yolk mixture and beat rapidly. Add the remaining hot mixture, stirring rapidly. Scrape the tiny black seeds from the center of the vanilla bean into the custard. (If the extract is used, it will be added later.) Heat slowly, stirring and scraping all around the bottom of the pan with a wooden spoon. Bring the mixture almost but not quite to the boil. The correct temperature is 180 degrees. This cooking will rid the custard of the raw taste of the yolks.

5. As the custard heats, combine the remaining ½ cup sugar with the water. Heat slowly. Cook gently, stirring, until the sugar becomes golden brown. Continue cooking until the sugar is a dark amber. Take extreme care that the sugar does not burn; if it burns, it will be bitter.

6. Add a cup or so of the custard to the caramel, stirring. Return this caramel mixture to the custard, stirring.

7. Pour the mixture into a cold mixing bowl. This will prevent the mixture from cooking further. Let stand until cool or at room temperature. If the vanilla bean is not used, add the vanilla extract at this point.

8. Meanwhile, put the pecans in a pan and place in the oven. Bake for 10 minutes or until crisp and nicely toasted. Let cool.

9. Pour the custard mixture into the container of an electric or hand-cranked ice cream maker. Partly freeze according to the manufacturer's instructions.

10. Add the pecans and continue freezing until the ice cream is ready.

YIELD: 8 to 12 servings.

If pistachio is not the most lyrical word in the cook's vocabulary, it is one of the nicest ingredients in the cook's cupboard. For those who wonder about such things, the origin of the word is Persian. It derives from pistah, which means simply nut, and was dubbed "pistachio" by the Italians.

Pistachio Ice Cream

- 1 cup shelled pistachios, preferably unsalted natural
- 4 cups milk
- 1 cup heavy cream
- 1½ cups sugar
- 10 egg yolks
- 1 tablespoon almond extract
- 5 drops pure vegetable green food coloring

1. Unless they are blanched, drop the pistachios into boiling water and simmer for about 2 minutes, or until outer coating can be removed easily with the fingers. Drain and remove the outer coating. Put the pistachios in a small skillet and cook over low heat, shaking the skillet continuously, until the nuts are lightly toasted. Set aside.

2. Combine the milk and cream in a saucepan and bring just to the boil.

3. Put the sugar and egg yolks in a mixing bowl and beat with a wire whisk to the ribbon stage—that is, until thick and pale yellow in color and, when the beater is lifted, the mixture falls back on itself ribbon-like.

4. Pour a cup or so of the combined hot milk and cream into the egg mixture, beating rapidly with the whisk. Scrape the entire contents of the bowl into the saucepan containing the hot milk mixture.

5. Using a wooden spoon, cook the sauce over low heat, stirring this way and that all over the bottom of the saucepan, taking care that the sauce does not stick. Cook only until the mixture coats the back of the spoon like

very thick cream. Do not at any point boil the sauce, or it will curdle. Add the almond extract and food coloring.

6. Immediately strain the sauce into a mixing bowl. Let stand until cool. Chill thoroughly in the refrigerator or freezer without freezing.

7. Pour the custard into the canister of a hand-cranked or electric ice cream machine and freeze according to the manufacturer's instructions. When the ice cream is partly frozen, add the pistachios and continue freezing.

YIELD: 1½ to 2 quarts.

Glace à la Menthe

PEPPERMINT STICK ICE CREAM

- 4 egg yolks
- ¾ cup sugar
- 3 cups milk
- 1 cup heavy cream
- ½ teaspoon peppermint spirit, available in pharmacies
- 3 or more drops red food coloring
- ¼ pound (about 18 pieces) peppermint or mint candy kisses

1. Combine the yolks and sugar in a mixing bowl and beat until pale yellow.

2. Combine the milk and cream in a saucepan and bring just to the simmer. Add the yolk mixture and cook over low heat, stirring with a wooden spoon, until the mixture thickens slightly and coats the back of the spoon. (When you run your finger over the spoon, it will leave a channel.) The proper temperature is 180 degrees on a thermometer. Do not let it overcook or the sauce will curdle. Let cool.

3. Add the peppermint spirit and food coloring. Pour the mixture into the container of a hand-cranked or electric ice cream freezer and start freezing according to the manufacturer's instructions.

4. When the mixture is almost frozen, chop the candy kisses finely or coarsely, depending on the desired texture. Add the chopped candies to the ice cream and continue freezing until frozen.

YIELD: 6 servings.

ACKNOWLEDGMENTS

MANY professional chefs and amateur cooks have been generous with their time and in sharing techniques and recipes that are included in this book. To all we are grateful.

Marty Allen
Steak Marty
Spinach pancakes

Sybil Arant
Catfish baked with cheese

Lee Barnes
Chaurice sausages

Joan Bayles
Cornmeal crackers

Sheridan Blackman and Steve Busby
Spinach and clam soup

Alison Boteler
Tarte aux épinards

Gerard Boyer of Chez Boyer in Reims
Bar rayé aux courgettes
Poulet Zaza
Parfait à la vanille

Lora Brody
Smoked salmon and onion cheesecake
Blue cheese cheesecake
Ginger cheesecake

Ruth Adams Bronz
- Julia Harrison Adams's pimiento cheese spread
- Texas barbecue sauce
- Fudge pie

Sara Burke
- Nectarine pie
- Banana and date nut squares

Penelope Casas
- Mejillones rellenos gayango
- Gazpacho extremeño
- Leche merengada
- Polvorones sevillanos

Maurice Cazalis of Henri IV restaurant in Chartres
- Pot au feu de fruits de mer

Nancy and Robert Charles
- Asparagus salad with Thai dressing
- Stuffed squid soup, Thai style
- Gai yang
- Kay Ahuja's Indian okra and onions

Charles Chevillot of La Petite Ferme and Les Tournebroches in Manhattan
- Poached striped bass with sauce Chevillot
- Brochettes de fruits de mer
- Moules vinaigrette
- Brochette de rognons de veau
- Brochette de boeuf

Pier Angelo Cornaro of Dell'Angelo Antico in Bergamo
- Pollo pastacciata
- Vitello all'uccelletto
- Fegato di vitello alla crema di cipolle
- Polenta with Gorgonzola cheese

Serge Coulon of Serge Restaurant in La Rochelle
- Blanquette de homard

Marcel Dragon of the Stanford Court in San Francisco
Caviar and potatoes

Daniel Fuchs of Maxwell's Plum in Manhattan
Duck and string bean salad

Nico Girolla
Orechiette al Gorgonzola

Eduardo Giurici of the Casa Albona in Amagansett, New York
Scungilli with diavolo sauce and linguine
Scungilli salad
Brodetto alla triestina
Pollo cacciatore

Montse Guillen of Montse Guillen in Barcelona
Lamb chops with four garlic sauces
Escalibada

Terrence Janericco
Soda crackers

Suzy Larochette of Maison Arabe in Marrakesh
Poisson aux épices
Poulet aux gingembre et herbes
Courgettes farcies marocaine
Salade Arabe traditionelle
Salade de laitue sucrée marocaine
Bananes au gingembre

Virginia Lee
Chicken with mushrooms and tiger lily stems
Stir-fried fish with tree ears
Summer oyster mushrooms with tree ears and corn
Shrimp balls with tree ears and snow peas

Edna Lewis
Liver pudding
Sautéed fresh roe
Lentil and scallion salad
Coconut layer cake

Aphrodite and Leon Lianides
Avgolemono soup with orzo
Seafood and orzo salad
Roast leg of lamb with orzo

Marianne Lipsky
Chesa Grischuna shrimp
Mustard herring

Egi Maccioni
Gorgonzola-Mascarpone cheese with polenta

Sara Mann
Chicken paprikash

Luigi Nanni of Nanni's and Il Valetto in Manhattan
Pasta alla funghi prataioli
Pasta alla militare

Amnuay Nethongkome of Bangkok Cuisine in Miami
Cucumber salad
Thai shrimp soup
Masman beef curry
Poo chah

Leslie Newman
Lotos salad for a crowd
Braised Chinese mushrooms
Red-cooked duck
Many flavor duck salad
Bean curd in spicy meat sauce
Noodles with hot meat sauce
Chinese roast pork
New Year's Eve fruit compote

Paul Prudhomme of K. Paul's Louisiana Kitchen in New Orleans
Blackened redfish
Seafood gumbo
Seafood jambalaya
Chicken gumbo
Red beans with rice
Dirty rice

Deborah Davis Rabinowitz
  Chess pie

Genevieve Riordan
  Apple pie

Jane Ryan
  Margretha's zucchini soup

Julie Sahni
  Sookha keema

Alain Senderens of L'Archestrate in Paris
  Pigeon aux endives confites
  Huîtres chaudes aux blancs de poireaux
  Homards rôtis à la sauce vanille

Margaret Sichel
  Herring salad

Tjasa Sprague
  Whole wheat bread

Ruth Stefanycia
  Stuffed cabbage in a mold

Paul Steindler
  Caviar parfait
  Eggs with caviar

Barbara Tropp
  Strange flavor eggplant
  Ma-la cold chicken with two sauces
  Tangy noodles

Roger Vergé of Moulin de Mougins above Cannes
  Les huîtres chaudes au beurre d'orange
  Carré d'agneau rôti aux poivres verts
  Tian de courgettes et tomates
  Mousse au chocolat amer

Alice Waters of Chez Panisse in Berkeley, California
Grilled salmon and tuna with anchovy butter
Baked goat cheese with lettuce salad
Buckwheat crêpes with glazed fruits in syrup
Calzoni

Dorothy Ann Webb
Mississippi mud pie

Eckart Witzigmann of the Aubergine in Munich
Fricassée de flétan au coulis de tomates
Pigeon aux pommes fruits et truffes
Crème de petits pois parfumé à la menthe
Soufflé de pain d'éspices au sabayon à la bière brune

Shirley Estabrook Wood
Zucchini bread

INDEX

C

D

E

F

G

H

M

N

O

P

Q

R

S

T

V

W

Y

Z